China's Long March to Freedom

China's Long March to Freedom

March to

Freedom

Grassroots Modernization

Kate Zhou

Transaction Publishers
New Brunswick (U.S.A.) and London (U.K.)

Library of Congress Catalog Number: 2009007967
ISBN: 978-1-4128-1029-6
Printed in the United States of America

Library of Congress Cataloging-in-Publication Data

Zhou, Kate Xiao, 1956-
China's long march to freedom : grassroots modernization movements / Kate Zhou.
p. cm.
Includes bibliographical references and index.
ISBN 978-1-4128-1029-6 (acid-free paper)
1. China--Social conditions--1976-2000. 2. China--Social conditions--2000- 3. Social change--China. 4. Social movements--China. 5. China--Economic conditions--1976-2000. 6. China--Economic conditions--2000- I. Title.

HN733.5.Z537 2009
303.48'4095109045--dc22

2009007967

To my beloved professor—(The late) Marion J. Levy. Marion was known as a hard, tough maverick. Behind his tough exterior there was a tender, caring heart.

Contents

Foreword

Powerful glaciers can flatten mountains, but they begin as the cumulation of light, quiet snowflakes. Some revolutions, too, do not require loud headlines. Serious political science can take account of progressive and massive changes that shape regimes without spectacular violence. This book proves that individuals from many walks of life—not just intellectuals and not just politicians—have created crucial reforms in contemporary China.

Even before Mao Zedong's death, farmers began to found rural factories. They have now flooded into cities, despite the government's attempt to control residence registrations. Local leaders in both country and city have found ways to exploit cheap labor and make money. Wanting to communicate with each other while facing the hidebound Ministry of Telecommunications, many have jumped for new technologies including cell phones and the worldwide web. Wanting to transport goods, local leaders have developed better road and water routes whenever the arthritic Ministry of Railroads could not meet their demand. Tired of Party patriarchy, they have experimented with a wide array of new sexual mores. They sometimes register civil societies when required to do so, but their NGOs are more independent than heretofore. This book is their story.

It greatly expands and updates Kate Xiao Zhou's earlier study that showed *How the Farmers Changed China*. Many other kinds of people are now also busy changing China, with or without government help. Some officials cooperate with non-state citizen-reformers, either because they personally want to do so or because they are bribed to do so. *China's Long March to Freedom* explores changes that happened after de-collectivization, and not just to farmers. This takes Zhou's analysis into varied kinds of habits and institutions:

- into China's fastest-growing economic sector, the small and medium enterprises;
- into popular culture, including movies, TV, and sexual norms;
- into China's burgeoning religious institutions, including churches and lineage temples;
- into legal and quasi-legal institutions such as property rights (whose fuzziness in China allows some Schumpeterian efficiencies and mobilization incentives);
- into new ways in which Chinese citizens now find housing, schooling, and jobs;

ix

- into the ways in which women, partly because of their traditional abilities in horizontal networks that can generate power (e.g., markets) rather than vertical networks that generate power (e.g., governments) affect political change distinctively.

Writing powerful English, Zhou uses extensive new Chinese data to reveal both the links and separations between local networks and the more central state. The result is evidence that cohorts of people who act singly but cumulatively in their own interests are powerful. The changes that Zhou describes are revolutionary, but the structures of action that realize these are not formally organized. Some rational-actionist theories suggest that change occurs mainly when sets of individuals who have enough information about each other put themselves under a leader to overcome their "free-rider problem," thus obtaining more coordinated power. That doctrine suggests small groups should be able to do this more easily than large groups. Yet that is not what is happening in China. Zhou shows that huge numbers of separated Chinese individuals who do not know much about each other, have no leader, believe no common ideology, and are wildly diverse (journalists, houseowners, smugglers, churchgoers, gays, entrepreneurs) nonetheless have a combined effect on the regime's effective structure. The vectors along which they push the polity's form are more parallel than random. This insight has seldom been made for the politics of any country and never before so boldly for China.[1]

In the West, there has long been a notion that everything liberal or liberalizing happens openly in public spaces. But actually, this is nowhere true. So the question becomes: What makes polities more transparent? Secrecy within the Chinese Communist Party (CCP) is a Leninist rule, but others can keep secrets too. People's Republic of China (PRC) government impulses to control all aspects of life do not succeed. The immense size of the Chinese polity makes for considerable lankiness between places. Political bosses heading the central government in Beijing are sometimes less arbitrary than are the heads (official or not) of many medium-sized networks. Local leaders and individual citizens can find liberties to do what they want, especially if they do not advertise what they are doing.

This freedom seeking, against restraints at many sizes of collectivity in China, is the political simile to economic market haggling. Such bargaining can be fun. The party-state includes cadres who also participate in these exchanges along with other individual citizens. Links between local officials and entrepreneurs, for example, were informally institutionalized early during reforms. Private business people wore "red hats" to facilitate profits. Their firms were often "dependent houses" (*guahu*), "hanging" from legitimated state or collective companies that in practice contributed nothing to their operations except an occasional red chop on a document.

Zhou explores the "communist bourgeoisie" or "intrapreneurs," who both manage state firms and maximize their earnings from private companies in which they own shares. Some of these, such as Zhang Ruimin who heads the Haier group, have become major global capitalists. Zhou discovers that the most common way for entrepreneurs to bribe officials in China is to lose deliberately while gambling at *majiang*. This method has both legal and interpersonal advantages. She also sensitively shows both the advantages and downsides faced by entrepreneurs when they join the Party. What many writers have called the "local state" is a concept that, in effect, Zhou uses her copious data to redefine. When power is local, there is usually not much state in it.

Schumpeter described capitalism's crucial feat as "creative destruction." Zhou applies that idea to the effect of free markets on the CCP. A contribution of this book is that it goes beyond descriptions of just one specific social sector in China's reforms; it deals with many modern changes together. Zhou shows, for example, that China's recent and surprisingly extensive sexual revolution has political relevance. Some "creative decadence" might even prove to be constitutionally healthy.

Sexual reform is not an official CCP keynote. Such a change is all about increased liberty—including its libertine facets—although freedom is not the theme of that Party. Zhou reveals new activities (not usually activisms) among transsexuals, lesbians, and gays, as well as in unmarried straight couples. The scope of this change is far greater than has been previously reported. It is a clear sign of reform freedom, although puritan Communists and neo-traditionalists alike are aghast at it. Homosexuals enjoy far more social license than heretofore. Gay bars flourish in Shanghai, Beijing, Wuhan, Shenzhen, and elsewhere. The one-child policy may inadvertently have created more gays and lesbians. The much larger group of heterosexuals also now acts with fewer restraints than in the era when most Chinese urban people hid their bodies under standard-issue blue "Mao suits." Some newly rich men take "second wives" (*erna*) and have multiple families. Although high Chinese traditions scarcely support gay or promiscuous sex, China lacks Levitican injunctions against it. In the Confucian legacy at least, discourtesy or disloyalty are more pre-eminent faults than fleshly sin. Western ideas about sex do not all travel to China. But patriotic CCP intellectuals tend to blame China's sexual changes on Hollywood movies and imported Western music. In any case, there is a behavioral link between sociopolitical tolerance for lewdness and allowances of liberty. Zhou's is the first account to treat that connection systematically in China.

PRC officials have long seen that state control of people depends partly on control of public knowledge. News was rationed in pre-reform China, as was food, or houses, or jobs. Public consciousness was planned. The media that fashioned it were all owned by the party-state, and they were structured hierarchically. Newspapers, for example, ranged from high-circulation dailies (especially some evening papers carrying scant political information) to more stately Party organs, and then also to limited-circulation journals that contained more sensitive political news. These last were available, in tiers, only to higher cadres. Wired broadcast networks of loudspeakers brought the official truth to very extensive groups of rural and urban settlements. During reforms, however, both print and broadcast media became more beholden to advertisers, less dependent on CCP propaganda departments, less hierarchically structured, and more entertaining.

Appointment powers remain the strongest Leninist levers of political control. Yet China is centralized only in a one-level-up sense. That is the level from which a Party organization chooses all-important official leaders for just one administrative level down. But there are so many layers in China's immense administrative system, this merely scalar Leninism allows for sharp differences between regions, whose cadres do not have coherent policies because they are not responsible to the appointing officials in other regions. Zhou gives an example in which Shenzhen journalists tried to report that a local hospital had infected 120 people with HIV/AIDS by using unclean hypodermic needles. The reports of this scandal could not be published in Shenzhen. But when data about the tragedy reached Guangzhou, they could be printed because the editors there are appointed by different hierarchs. Chinese readers want the truth, and slowly journalists may find sufficient incentives to deliver it.

The CCP system mandates officials (and reporters, hospital heads, professors, bishops, prosecutors, judges, or anybody else who is deemed important) to follow their appointers rather than perform their natural functions—but just within an administrative or geographical jurisdiction. The state in 2006 tried to squelch the possibility that journalists could at a distance report truths that they find. But China's size and increasing diversity means that appointers cannot monitor appointees far below them in the bureaucracy.[2] The CCP's own need for centralization only to a point militates against total control. Modern diversity, as Zhou shows, gives ordinary Chinese many ways to achieve their goals despite the apparent beauty of the Leninist organization chart.

The Nielsen Agency, importing its "peoplemeter" that rates media audiences, came to China in 2005. It threatens old-style propaganda, whose unpopularity it shows. The advent of the Internet also spreads many more kinds of information widely. In this book, you can read about the popularity of hymns by Xiaomin, a young woman composer whom the state jailed for a while because her Christian music was so widespread. Anyone can "google" her name on the worldwide web and find her Canaan Songs on YouTube. Networks of cell phone users also have, in effect, become a major new collective medium of millions that allows individuals to disperse their own ideas. So state monitors now realize that they would, in a situation of political crisis, have somewhat more difficulty controlling what people say and know.

Rule of law is a theme that many writers have stressed as an aspect of China's reforms, but Zhou points out that legal rationalization is not always the bringer of progress. When filmmakers of the stature of Zhang Yimou and Chen Kaige have some of their works banned in China, as has occurred, they become less concerned about intellectual property rights. PRC pirates sell their movies to a market from which the state excludes them anyway.

Nuisances of this and other kinds are common in reform China. The state is responsible for many of them. Zhou describes not just popular anger at diurnal repressions, e.g., among women who want to have babies, street vendors whose carts are smashed by police thugs, or urban residents evicted from their homes. It also describes their revenges against officials who abuse them. These people would be ineffective if there were not so many of them—and their number is a reason for their power, even when they remain unorganized.

Zhou raises due doubts about much that has been written of "civil society" in China from the viewpoints of various "-isms," including capitalism, socialism, and some kinds of feminism. She always looks at politics from the viewpoint of individuals' life situations. Many political research agenda, both right and left, turn out to be vapid in comparison with this perspective. They say little about the specific mechanisms by which national and local politics affect people. Citizens affect the regime type in "long marches" over extended periods of time. Zhou gets beyond many fads of recent politics and social science, writing about China's people instead.

Many authors treat China as if it were a small polity, not quite like Liechtenstein, but rather like the Vatican, where a central leader is legitimated to decide everything. Chinese change has long been attributed to the "thoughts" of one or a few wise gurus in Beijing. Intellectuals who want jobs in the state, and who are themselves thought-jugglers, like this causal discourse. The ideas of a Mao or a Deng—and now of less radical but also less prepossessing figures such as Jiang or Hu—are said to rule everything. Jiang Zemin's "three represents" and Hu Jintao's "scientific development" are supposed to be the main keys to national progress.

Kate Zhou, however, writes as if China were a big country. Chinese people have many diverse thoughts and desires. She admits effective causes of China's reforms in both unintended situations and intentional ideas. Her acknowledged debt to Friedrich Hayek's individualism includes an understanding that actors, working for their own ends but cumulating their effects, can be powerful. She gives evidence that in China ideals of freedom are now held broadly by many, not just by a few leaders.

Usual discourse implies that reforms always require guidance, organization, ideology, high leadership, and political clout. But Zhou shows they can be "spontaneous, unorganized, non-ideological, leaderless, and apolitical." A perennial problem is that common terms of language, either Chinese or English, suggest that power is always exercised from an official administrative center. Words implying verticality, such as "level," "high," "top," "bottom," "policy," or even "institution" can be behaviorally inaccurate if they imply presumptions about the location of power. Potent citizenship is not always planned or articulate. It can be ad lib. It is sometimes organized but sometimes unarranged. It is practically always based on some kind of goal—but often on vague notions that the actor could not articulate even while actually helping to achieve it. (What "account of democracy" would a philosopher have heard, for example, interviewing minutemen at Concord Bridge or *sans-culottes* storming the Bastille? Yet, these actors knew very roughly what they were doing, and the distant, eventual result of their actions was indeed somewhat more fairness.) Usually there are hopes, but they are often more visceral than cerebral. Usually there are leaders, but they can be in groups as small as villages or families.

Always there is politics, but some thinkers do not perceive it as political because it is not open in public. It is often in private networks, and it is sometimes the more powerful for being secret. For better or for worse, not all politics takes the supposed Athenian form. As Zhou shows, most of the Chinese change that started slowly and now races ahead began in rural and suburban areas, below the effective radar vision of the government. The power of the state is attested in part by all the evidence of new non-state powers that have challenged it. But the weaknesses of pretentious planning, rational systematization, formalistic ideas, high leaders, and public politics become clear when they face freedoms that they have failed to stop. This book should cause many writers to re-conceptualize most of what is happening in China. By the same token, it should cause thinkers also to expand the range of traits that they can rightly apply to power and to politics.

The CCP already has had to tolerate disobedience to its publicized ideals of economic planning, residential registration, information censorship, sexual puritanism, and bias against anything with foreign characteristics. All this does not, however, ensure that China will shortly become a democracy. If mass national elections were held soon, the winner would probably be an anti-liberal patriotic populist in the mold of Hitler, Marcos, or Thaksin after those three were elected. But micro-separations of power have emerged in China, despite state wishes. *If* these later erode the Leninist appointment structure that is the CCP's only remaining major resource, *if* judges and legislators become more independent of executives, and *if* the economic and moral chaos of the present time does not lead to an electorally legitimated demagogue, there is at least some chance that China could have a smooth path to democracy in the sense of a more liberal polity.[3]

Transitions to democracy, according to many comparativists, require decisions by state leaders.[4] Increasing social divisions of labor, however, make such leaders various. Politicians begin to conflict not just as faction leaders, but also as leaders espousing different policies or "tendencies of articulation."[5] This creates policy choices that may become political feuds. The CCP still has a habit of trying to hide its divisions from the public. Party gurus in Beijing nonetheless try to decide for the whole country on modern issues, e.g., whether to favor capital or labor in development.[6] Kate Zhou, following Hayek, puts this discourse into radically new perspective by going far beyond these few top leaders and by stressing the concurrent roles of millions of private individuals.[7]

Ordinary Chinese citizens—unorganized but acting in similar ways—can be leaders whether they have public intentions or not. They increasingly determine effective "policy" because they have their own policies. The PRC state in general can endure only by accommodating them somewhat. Decisions of increasingly diverse official leaders are influenced by the onslaught of complexity among private and semi-private power networks. Eventually, decisions between relatively authoritarian or relatively liberal regime types will respond one way or another to mass pressures. That has just begun to occur in China, and (as Zhou recognizes) there are major dangers of illiberal backsliding if a chauvinistic populist were to replace the current uncharismatic technocrats. But she shows that, even as elites at high sizes of collectivity in China remain important, they operate in a context of many citizens who have their own ideas and increasingly have resources to implement these.

Anyone who wants to understand what is happening in the world's most populous nation, as seen from the viewpoint of most of its people, will learn a very great deal from this book.

—Lynn T. White III
Princeton, New Jersey

Notes

1. There are distant echoes of Zhou's approach in work by the Americanists Frances Fox Piven and Richard Cloward, *Poor People's Movements: Why They Succeed, How They Fail,* (New York: Vintage, 1979). But the originality of the book in your hands, especially among researches about China, cannot be overstated.
2. Combine Pierre Landry, *Decentralized Authoritarianism in China,* (New York: Cambridge University Press, 2008) with Susan L. Shirk, *The Political Logic of Economic Reform in China,* (Berkeley: University of California Press, 1993), ch. 7.
3. This issue is explored in many other publications including Bruce Gilley, *China's Democratic Future: How it will Happen and Where it will Lead,* (New York: Columbia University Press, 2004). For the crucial insight that no regime's movement toward greater inclusiveness is nearly complete, see E.E. Schattschneider, *The Semi-Sovereign People: A Realist's View of Democracy in America,* (Hinsdale, IL: Dreyden Press, 1975).
4. A classic article is by Dankwart Rustow, "Transitions to Democracy," *Comparative Politics* 2:3, (1970), pp. 337-63. Many Latin Americanists have similarly suggested that mutual "*garantismo*" among elites is a necessary precursor of democratic openings in which some of them risk power. A source for further reading, cited here partly because it refers to earlier works of equal interest, is Carles Boix and Susan Stokes, "Endogenous Democratization," *World Politics* 55:4 (2003), pp. 517-49.
5. The phrase "tendencies of articulation" comes from study of the late great USSR before its demise, especially by H. Gordon Skilling, in *Interest Groups in Soviet*

Politics, Skilling and Franklyn Griffiths, eds., (Princeton, NJ: Princeton University Press, 1971).

6.   Theory behind this finding that modern politicians of capital tense against modern politicians of labor may be found in many sources, famously Karl Polanyi, *The Great Transformation: The Social and Economic Origins of our Time,* (New York: Rinehart, 1944). Evidence of such divisions among Beijing leaders is in sources such as Li Cheng, *China's Leaders,* (Lanham, MD: Rowman and Littlefield, 2001).

7.   See Friedrich Hayek, *The Road to Serfdom,* (London: Routledge, 1944).

Acknowledgements

This book about China's social transformation would not be possible without the hard work and brave action of the millions of people who spend their daily lives changing China. I am grateful and indebted to these men and women. Many people spoke with me during the past ten years of researching and assembling this book. While it would be impossible to cite all the Chinese who helped me in my research field trips, the list should begin with the millions of rural migrants who blocked the entrances of so many train and bus stations, contributing to what became China's relatively free labor market.

The list should also include the dozens of Chinese entrepreneurs in different regions. I should specifically mention Simon Wong, a Taiwanese businessman resident in Shanghai, Sun Dawu in Hebei, Zhou Yasheng in Hunan, Wang Yingchun in Yunnan, Chen Xiaowu in Liaoning, Zhang Changle in Shandong, Chen Chaorao, and Lei Tao in Shenzhen, Wu Zhengzhang in Beijing, and Wu Litang and Liu Chuner in Wuhan, all of whom spent many days assisting me in understanding the complex situation of entrepreneurs.

I am also more than grateful for the help of a number of Chinese who guided me through Chinese sources, introduced me to government officials, and provided their own interpretation of a changing China. First among them are Gao Binzhong and Wang Hansheng of Beijing University—pioneers in civil society research—as well as Zhou Weiwen at the Hebei Sociology Research Institute, Hu Jingbei of Tongji University (a leading labor economist), Gao Song of Financial Times (China), Shen Dinlin, Li Hongtu, and Zhou Dunren of Fudan University, Xiao Yuan (an environmental activist) in Beijing, Yuan Yawen (of the Shenzhen Opera House), and Liu Haibo and Fa Yafeng of Law Institute in Beijing, all of whom dedicated themselves to this project with enthusiasm.

I am also indebted to the Internet blogs and online media and websites such as Sina.com, CHINAPOL, Sohu.com, easy.com, Chinese News Digest, and China Digital Times, which became invaluable resources for my understanding of this new China. I am indebted, too, to the work of F. Heykey and James Scott of Yale University that helped me to understand unorganized and leaderless movements in China.

My mentors at Princeton University, the late Marion J. Levy, Perry Link, and Lynn White, offered valuable suggestions on the theory of modernization.

Lynn White and Perry Link provided academic help and moral encouragement. My colleagues at the Center for Chinese Studies at the University of Hawai'i have been supportive and cordial.

Friends and colleagues in the United States offered their criticism and help: Cheng Li, Diqing Jiang, David Zweig, Richar Baum, Guoguang Wu, David Boaz, Roger Ames, Anna Nadgrodkiewicz, Tom Palmer, Paul Gregory, Reginald Kwok, Elisabeth Davis, Sun Yan, Cheng Xiaonong, and Rosita Chang.

David Menser edited four chapters of the first draft in 2005 and deserves much credit for his valuable work. My colleagues Manfred Henningsen, Jonathan Goldberg-Hiller, and Kathy Ferguson at the University of Hawai'i at Maona Political Science Department read one chapter and provided suggestions for its improvement. My graduate students, Qinghong Wang, John Sullivan, Yoshi Amae, Tim Conkling, Peter Hsu, Zeng Qi, Ian Donahue, Aaron Hunger, You Jeong Lee, Li Yao, and Eun Kyong Choi have stimulated many interesting discussions.

I am grateful to colleagues Dr. Sally Blair, Louisa Coan Greve, Minyang Jiang, Dr. Marc F. Plattner, Dr. Anna Brettell, Zerxes Spencer, and Michelle Engamann at the National Endowment for Democracy (NED) in Washington, D.C., who provided financial and staff support for my residence at the Endowment as a Reagan-Fascell Democracy Fellow in spring 2008. Michelle Engamann kindly edited the latest draft of the manuscript while I was there.

I owe a special debt to the Cato Institute and the Atlas Foundation, which provided financial assistance for two field trips, and to the University of Hawai'i, which provided funding for two further research trips. My editor at Transaction Press, Jennifer Nippins, has been excellent.

This book is particularly indebted to my friend Dr. Charles Bahmueller of the Center for Civic Education in Los Angeles. Calling upon his knowledge of political science and of the English language, he meticulously read the entire manuscript and offered innumerable suggestions for improvement. Our many conversations allowed me to clarify my ideas and their expression. The project would not have reached its current state without his assistance.

Others deserve a different kind of thanks. My father, Mingsheng Zhou, helped to shape concept of the book. My sister, Bonita, offered her practical help during the writing of the book. My friend, Dr. Hongying Jiang, and her son, Telon Yan, provided hospitality and a comforting living environment for me and my son during our stay in the Washington, DC, area during my NED residence.

My husband, Thomas David Burns, provided editorial, emotional, and household support throughout the writing of the book. I am very grateful to him.

Introduction

*Revolutions, genuine revolutions, not those which
simply change the political forms and members of
the government but those which transform institutions and alter property relations, advance unseen
for a long time before bursting into the sunlight
impelled by some circumstance.*
—*Albert Matheiz, The French Revolution*

How Do We Qualify the Reform Era?

In the summer of 2005, while visiting in Shenzhen, I took a morning walk
with friends to Lotus Hill Park, where a statue of Deng Xiaoping stands atop
the pinnacle of a small overlook. He is not exactly standing but rather caught
in the midst of a confident stride, as if marching towards the future of what
China could become, as represented by Shenzhen. Caught up in the moment,
in the place where Deng's 1981 speech officially kicked off the reform era, I
began to question how the transformation began that has been taking place in
China over the last three decades and what has kept it going. Why did not events
such as Tiananmen Square, widespread corruption within the party-state, and
a backwards technology base prevent the economic and social transformation
from succeeding?

These questions again came to mind on May 12, 2008, when an earthquake
shook both Sichuan and all of China both physically and morally. U.S. Secretary of State Condoleezza Rice praised the Chinese government for its relief
work, degree of openness and transparency, and for seeking assistance from
the international community. For quite a few weeks, the Chinese press successfully fought against government censorship and gained a certain amount of
freedom, while millions of Chinese went online to express their opinions about
the government's relief work, track down the disposition of private donations
and expose local government corruption. Chinese society responded with an
outpouring of private charitable giving, an indication of the growing momentum
of the philanthropic impulse in the country. Where volunteers across China
rushed to assist victims directly or sent cash, food, and clothing, informal and
non-government organizations boomed overnight. Many blogs were created for
collecting donations and supervising relief efforts. Within two weeks, more than
$6.3 billion in relief donations from at home and abroad had been collected.

Hundreds of informal groups and tens of thousands of volunteers rushed to the quake area to lend assistance. Premier Wen Jiabao went to the disaster region immediately after the quake, as if he was running for election. With the nation watching, the government competed with unofficial sources of data on the number of dead. When victims of the earthquake organized a protest march to Sichuan provincial government headquarters, the local party boss knelt down, begging residents not to proceed to the provincial capital, Chengdu.

One-and-a-half months later, on June 28, in Wengan county, Guizhou, one of China's poorest areas, more than thirty thousand residents clashed with local police and the party machine over the death of a teenage girl. The Beijing government had to restore order by firing local officials while sending troops to arrest rioters. The government held a press conference to inform the Chinese public, especially more than 200 million Chinese online netizens and 600 million cell phone holders, that the death was a suicide and not a police cover-up.

In May 2007, residents of Xiamen (Fujian province) sent more than 1 million text messages warning of possible pollution from paraxylene production, forcing the government to halt construction of a $1.4 billion facility and move the site. Encouraged by the Xiamen success, Shanghai residents, in June 2007, started a "*sanbu*" (group walk) the very day when the government announced a revised maglev route connecting the city's Pudong and Hongqiao airports. Text messages in Shanghai coordinated several hundred walkers, forcing the government to extend the time for the expression of public opinion on the matter.

The same year brought the world a new image of Chinese represented by a Chongqi nail house (Dingzihu, 钉子户) owner, Wu Ping, who refused to vacate her home to make way for a 800 million dollar government approved real estate development project despite having water and electricity shut down and a 30ft deep man-made pit in her yard. Instead of holding up military tanks, the Wu family became the heros by fighting for their property rights against the strong state and rich developers. Wu finally won a huge compensation in court in 2007.

On May 4, 2008, two hundred Chengdu residents held a *sanbu* to express their concerns over the environmental impact of proposed ethylene plants. This protest was organized by blogs, chat rooms, and cell phones. The May Chengdu walk took the local government by surprise, leading it to send plainclothes officers to videotape the walk and afterwards punish the six leaders.

The most important political news that emerged from China in 2008 was the constitutional reform petition drive signed initially by more than three hundred prominent Chinese individuals (mostly highly respected intellectuals). First released on December 10, 2008 (anniversary of the United Nations' 1948 Universal Declaration of Human Rights), *lingba xianzhang* (零八宪章 Charter 08 hereafter) was much like Czechoslovakia's Charter 77, released in January 1977, when "more than two hundred Czech and Slovak intellectuals formed a loose, informal, and open association of people...united by the will to strive individually and collectively for respect for human and civil rights...."[1]

This is the first time in the fifty-nine year history of the Peoples Republic of China that so many Chinese openly called for the end of one-party rule and advocated human rights and democracy. The Chinese government's response was the old tactic of "killing a few chickens to scare the monkeys" by arresting two prominent signers of the Charter 08, Zhang Zuhua and Liu Xiaobo. But this time the tactic was unavailing. With so many "chickens" coming into the open, the "monkeys" had become emboldened. Within a week of its publication on the Internet, five thousand more Chinese signed their names to Charter 08.

None of above-mentioned events were organized or led by state-approved organizations.

How should we characterize such a grassroots democratic movement arising in an authoritarian state like China that bans any form of independent organization liable to challenge its power? Is Charter 08 simply an incident of public discontent? Why has the government changed how they govern by appearing to be more transparent? Is the Chinese state leading the rapid social and political transformation that has swept and continues to sweep the nation? What pressures led the party-state to cede space for public expression? What are the root causes of conflicts between state and society? What is a new balance between the power of the people and the power of the one party-state?

Before delving into the substance of this discussion, we must first determine where and to what ends this transformation is happening and what the principal characteristics and main actors of this vast drama are. Only then could we ensure that we were even asking the right questions.

This book provides a new perspective on China that differs from two common, sharply contrasting views of China that exist in the world today. On the one hand, China is often seen as a rising superpower predicted to have the world's largest economy by the middle of the twenty-first century. In this view, a modernizing China will bring liberalization and democratization, what James Mann terms "the Soothing Scenario" in his *The China Fantasy* (2007). Conversely, and rather less soothing, China is regarded as a brutal, repressive regime whose power, often growing surreptitiously, increasingly threatens the stability of the industrial world. The Chinese military's 2007 destruction of one of its aging weather satellites is given as a case in point, spurring incoming French President Sarkozy to warn the world of China's "insatiable search for raw materials as a strategy of control, particularly in Africa."[2]

The focus of these two views is on China's government and its machinations. This book, however, focuses on the nation from the perspective of ordinary Chinese. It explores China's social, economic, political, and cultural systems and, most controversially, the pursuit by common men and women of civil, political, and personal rights in the context of a communist regime. This book also critically evaluates the benefits of globalization and liberalization as well as normative democratic values in contrast with the obsession of many in the West with elections and an openly organized opposition.

The central premise of this book argues that grassroots social revolution through entrepreneurship, migration of millions from countryside to cities, the explosion of information available to ordinary people (especially via the Internet), deepening international engagement, and a multifaceted sexual revolution has fundamentally altered key elements of the moral and material content of the party-state regime and society at large. This social revolution is moving China towards a more liberal society, even while the government continues its illiberal and grasping mode of control. An important finding of this book is that the Chinese government in this transformative process has been one of response and not of leadership.

This argument is at odds with the conclusions of major Sinologists and with conventional understanding of China in general. When such a radical social transformation is taking place, it is quite understandable that scholars trace the remarks of powerful leaders and the acts of members of existing organizations. The conventional and seemingly obvious answer is that, at its core, China's reform has been an economically driven transformation led by a succession of reform-minded leaders. These men chipped away at the once immobile foundations of the state-planned economy by providing increasingly larger degrees of economic freedom, resulting in the "socialist market economy." From Deng Xiaoping to Hu Jintao, battles have been fought resulting in narrow but consistent victories for the economically reform-minded. This process officially passed the point of no return after Deng's 1992 southern tour, when the government officially acknowledged the existence of a market system.[3] Society has been profoundly influenced by the widespread and transformative power of this market system. This argument is in line with Ronald Inglehart, who argues that economic development, political change, and cultural change go together in coherent, and to some extent even predictable patterns.[4]

Regardless of which specific aspect of the reform era is being addressed, many scholars at least implicitly accept the process described in the previous paragraph as an underlying premise. Variations of this focus on the leadership also include analyses that give credit for the reform to provincial leaders rather than those at the top.[5] These theories exemplify what we label as top-down methodology. By this, we mean that they emphasize the power of leaders, who set a course to which the people respond. Scholars using this approach often look to pinpoint key decisions or policy actions, analyze what occurred afterwards, and then attribute the resultant state of society to these decisions. These actions can then be linked together to create a history of the process (reform) and a linkage to the present situation. We call it top-down, as only leaders have the ability to make decisions with such far-reaching consequences, absent some sort of revolution.

This type of analysis is useful when analyzing the changing policies of China's reform period: it, however, does not adequately address the question of *why* the tremendous social change has occurred. In other words, China's economic and social transformation is driven from above. The argument of this book, however, is that China's transformation has been driven very largely, if not entirely, from below.

An increasing number of studies have focused on the effects of globalization and economic liberalization in China. Even the fortieth edition of Milton Friedman's classic *Capitalism and Freedom* now includes a line in the preface; "The limited increase in economic freedom has changed the face of China, strikingly confirming our faith in the power of free markets."[6] Of the many other books that have been written touting economic liberalization and market transformation, we must cite Deborah S. Davis, Richard Kraus, Barry Naughton, and Elizabeth Perry's (editors) *Urban Spaces in Contemporary China: The Potential for Autonomy and Community in Post-Mao China*, Deborah S. Davis's (editor) *The Consumer Revolution in Urban China*, William H. Overholt's *The Rise of China*, and Jonathan Story's *China: the Race to Market*. The authors of these books accurately assess the role of economic liberalization and markets on helping to provide more freedom to the Chinese people. We also agree with their assertion that opening new spaces for consumption and communication has transformed China to the point that millions of ordinary people can now explore new identities and experience increased individual autonomy.

We support the contention that economic liberalization has played a powerful role in China's transformation. In fact, we consider economic liberalization to be the primary facilitator, not simply the anchor. This thought leads to the reason for this book. We believe that at the core of China's transformation has been a rights acquisition movement undertaken by individual citizens who were fed up with the government controlling every aspect of their lives. Thus, in addressing where to look for an engine for social change, we contend that one must look to the actions of ordinary Chinese themselves. For the last three decades, their actions have made it clear what their objectives are: more non-governmental space and more individual rights. As such, much of China's reform has proceeded from the bottom-up, with government at the top reacting to the demands and extra-legal behaviors of tens of millions of ordinary Chinese. This is true even in the economic arena, since it was farmers, not government policy, who created the first markets of the post-Mao era.[7] From our perspective, although some members of state and provincial governments were indeed pro-market, they were not the driving force behind the fundamental change that defines China's reform era. People's desire for change was fundamentally a drive for improvement in their situation, not only economic but also social, cultural, and spiritual improvement.

Examining Rights

In examining the last three decades as a rights acquisition movement, we contend that citizens who were unhappy with their immediate socio-political-economic situation decided to change that situation as much as they could on the individual level. Before we continue, it is important to define the term "movement," as it is used in varying contexts throughout the book. Although movement is typically defined as a series of organized activities working toward an objective, we remove the word, "organized." Thus, although many people may have been simultaneously working to gain access to more rights, for the most part, they did so as individuals, not as groups. The reason that this requires additional emphasis is that we strongly believe that the lack of cohesion and organization involved in the different movements has been critical to their success.

The social explanation for why such a large number of people acted along similar lines in their pursuit of rights without any unified direction can best be explained by the theories of Anthony Giddens and Max Weber. Giddens' reference to a "cluster of class situations with common mobility"[8] works well to describe the rural populace, which had similar lifestyles (income, education, culture, etc.) and chances for mobility, both within the career of individuals and across generations. Weber describes a similar situation in terms of "life chances."[9] Because this equally desperate existence was endured by such a large percentage of the population for so long, the stage was set for like-minded individuals to pursue common objectives without the need for leadership or ideology.

Another theory useful in explaining the evolution of the Chinese experience is Freidrich August von Hayek's theory of "spontaneous order."[10] In *The Road to Serfdom* and other writings, F. A. Hayek pointed out the close relationship between a state-controlled economy and the strong probability of totalitarianism, as total domination would override individual preferences in economic and social life.[11] His theory of information through pricing mechanisms also supports our contentions of individual empowerment through informal markets. When ordinary people, through a principle of self-organization, share and synchronize local and personal knowledge, they reduce the formal structural power of the communist state.[12]

We must also point out that although we call the overarching pursuit of rights "the rights acquisition movement," it has meant different things to different people. Some will regard them as economic interests in the area of land rights and private businesses; others will regard migration as the effect of industrialization; still others consider it a social habit of following the trend. Accepting this, we still contend that the underlying themes have been consistent: a push for greater self-sufficiency and less government intrusion into citizens' lives. These desires have manifested themselves in the pursuit of the following rights, which are described in this book: property rights, free speech, freedom of religion, better access to information (including the elimination of censorship), privacy, sexual liberty, the right to choose one's work, and the right to move freely throughout the country.

Civil Society

Defining the reform era in such terms as rights, liberties, and non-governmental spaces invariably leads to a discussion of the development of civil society. The debate over civil society in China has garnered much attention during the course of the reform era, as has the definition of the phrase itself.[13] We define civil society as a set of voluntary, non-governmental-based, non-familial-based interactions, which include commercial activities. Our definition follows that of Adam Ferguson, an early Scottish enlightenment thinker, who defined civil society as a means to end corrupt feudalism and bring about individual freedom.[14] The process of building Chinese civil society is both a means and an end in the decline of Chinese communist feudalism and despotism, and the empowerment of individuals.

Of the books that tackle this particular aspect of the reform era, we highlight: Gordon White, Jude Howell, and Shang Xiaoyuan's *In Search of Civil Society: Market Reform and Social Change in Contemporary China*; Timothy Brook and B. Michael Frolic's (editors) *Civil Society in China*; He Baogang's *The Democratic Implication of Civil Society in China*; and Wang Mingmin and Wang Shifu's *Xiangtu Shehui de Chixu, Gongzheng yu Chenwei*. These books offer important contributions in their analysis of the previously defined associations. Another book that looks more at the role of individuals in the context of liberalizing networks is Randy Kluver and John H. Powers' (editors) *Civic Discourse, Civil Society, and Chinese Communities*. This book examines the pursuit of individual liberty in terms of enablers, such as technology, which allow certain kinds of public spheres to come into being.

This book reports how progress has actually taken place in China. In areas of endeavor, ranging from decollectivization to gay awareness, from Internet dissent to individual rights pursuit, from the movement of millions (both physical and social) to the information explosion, the book shows how and why an unorganized and leaderless movement—rather than one that conforms to a single central vision—has been the key to the improvement of citizens' rights in China.

The reason why civil society is important to our discussion is that it is a sphere created by individuals, not by the state. Consequently, its existence (or development thereof) lends credence to both our contention that the movement has been primarily bottom-up and grassroots in origin, and that rights and the pursuit of non-governmental spaces have been crucial components of the reform era transformation.

Liberalization and Globalization

The Chinese case will shed light on theories of globalization and liberalization. The Chinese people's desire for liberalization demonstrates an essential precondition: may global forces (capital, trade, media, technology, and professional networks) provide the material that enables conditions for social revolution. The material self-interest of Chinese officials and consumers allowed the emergence of a cosmopolitan culture that has mounted a frontal assault on the regime's puritanical ideology.

The Chinese case confirms Thomas Friedman's theory of a global pursuit for liberty. The Chinese, like any other people, also demand "the basic human desire for a better life: a life with more choices as to what to eat, what to wear, where to live, where to travel, how to work, what to read, what to write, and what to learn."[15] What is interesting about the Chinese globalization is that Friedman's choices have become possible for 1.3 billion people, one-fifth of the world's total population. This will have great impact on the world as a whole. It contradicts Benjamin Barber's new global world, where "globalization enriches the consumer in us, but it can also shrink the citizen and the space for individual cultural and political expression."[16] Conversely, global linkage in China in fact creates the rise of citizenship and cultural expression, a destructive process in which the old communist ideology, together with some elements of tradition, is undermined.

Social Movement Literature

The discussion of Chinese social movements in this book differs from traditional ones. In existing social movement literature, to be a social movement, a phenomenon needs, first, to be *public*. But such a movement is impossible given that the state cracks down on any social manifestation in the realm of "advocacy politics." Advocacy politics involves direct, open activities to support, criticize, or oppose the regime's policies, programs, and resource distributions. The existing literature on social movement excludes the secret social phenomena involving millions of people such as the decollectivization movements migration of millions, and the house church movement in China.

Also, in existing social movement literature, a social movement, must involves *contentious* issues: contentious politics expresses unhappiness, discontent with the status quo—it involves ordinary people, often in league with more influential persons, confronting elites, opponents, and authorities.[17] Some writers argue that contentious politics must involve government as a claimant or as the object of claims.

Another key feature of conventional social movements is that they must involve collective action, organized activity performed as members of a group, not as isolated individuals (Piven and Cloward, 1979, p. 4).[18]

Moreover, social movements involve "*sustained interaction* with opponents," Sidney Tarrow, the leading scholar on social movements, argues that *sustained interaction* means sequences of contentious politics based on underlying social networks and collective action that develop the capacity to maintain challenges against powerful opponents.[19]

In short, a social movement has *four* "empirical properties": *collective challenge* to opponents [through disruptive direction action against elites, authorities, other groups, or cultural codes], *common purpose, social solidarity, and sustained interaction* (Tarrow, *Power in Movement*, p. 2).

For a movement to sustain collective contentious politics, it also requires organization and leadership. Otherwise, activity dies out or is repressed, etc., perhaps to reemerge—becoming episodic contentiousness but not a *movement*.

The Chinese social phenomena we wish to examine lack the above mentioned elements of movements. Although sit-ins, strikes, and protests have taken place recently in China, open confrontation is rare because the elite have the capacity to strike swiftly and hard at any infraction of public order. When ten thousand Falun Gong practitioners surrounded the Zhongnanhai (the national elite's compound [near the Forbidden City] in Beijing), the state launched a national crackdown, sending thousands to labor camps. By the conventional definition, all Chinese social movements are failures.

Although certain violent and other open forms of resistance are everyday events in China, the most successful and effective modes of resistance are everyday forms, such as bribing officials to gain liberty to read, to buy and sell, to worship as one pleases and other form of simple law breaking, such as illegal migration and defiance of the "One Child" policy. All of this has the effect of eroding state power or, in other words, expanding liberty and individual social space on a massive scale.[20]

Although organized protests like the 2007 farmers' land demands and the 2008 Wanan incidents involved *collective* action, most resistance is non-organized. What is more, many successful social movements in China like migration, entrepreneurship, and house churches take the form of individual action and small informal networks or cells. But those movements, despite of the lack of key features identified in social movement literature, have sustained themselves and had structural impact on Chinese society.

SULNAM: Theory of a Critical Mass Formation in Communist Regime

Most social movements described here are *essentially spontaneous*, with no identifiable spokespersons or leaders. Yet, the desire to reduce state control over all aspects of life is so prevalent that *almost simultaneously, virtually millions of individuals chose to act in directions that would benefit their families and themselves, often at the cost of state control.*

This book shows that the main driving forces which have created the new social revolution are not the government officials or state policies, but professionals, consumers, migrant workers, gay rights activists, entrepreneurs, high technology (especially the Internet), and global linkages. The Chinese people acted, and the state—under pressure from local forces and a vigilant international community—reacted. But how can a critical mass of resistance to party-state domination form in a communist regime when the state bans any form of non-state collective action? How could such a massive movement escape the notice of the government? Some scholars suggest that the lack of state intervention in the grassroots pursuit for liberty came from a benign neglect: Deng and his followers chose to look the other way. However, this view is contradicted by their constant but increasingly ineffective resistance to rural-urban migration, government censorship over press and association, the lack of rule of law, and the state's control over a mother's rights to give birth to children. I argue that a critical mass is formed through SULNAM (a spontaneous, unorganized, leaderless, non-ideological, and apolitical movement) and the government's focus on urban areas.[21]

In his classic 1965 work, *The Logic of Collective Action*, Mancur Olson argued that people generally will not contribute to public goods because they believe that others will not contribute their fair share, or they can gain the benefits of others' contributions without paying the price themselves.[22] The latter circumstance is the classic "free rider problem." According to this argument, only small groups can induce members to make the sacrifices necessary to obtain public goods. They can do so because individual responsibility is visible to all members and internal pressures can produce conformity. According to public choice theory, the free rider problem would have inhibited the Chinese people from participating in the social revolution. Any individual who attempted to defy the state to achieve personal liberty should be crushed by the state's powerful apparatus of oppression. Clearly, however, this is not case with regards to the Chinese social revolution. Private provision of services, the rise of cosmopolitan society, global linkage, migration of millions, modern technology (the Internet and cell phones) and the declined of the party-state ideology confirm that the free rider problem can be overcome if people can individually but simultaneously benefit from the "public good" in question.

Calamities and Public Defiance

In China, a critical mass for the appearance of an anti-state counter-culture was reached when, tired of the state's oppressive control, many Chinese sought to seek choices and liberty in their lives. The grassroots resistance was the result of the regime's total control of basic elements of human life. For example, the term "birth certificate" has a different meaning in China than elsewhere. In the United States, a birth certificate is a document that shows that someone has been born. But in China it is a "permission slip" to become pregnant before the fact. Without such permission, a child cannot be born in the hospital. After the birth, he or she cannot go to the state school without a heavy fine nor can she or he receive any state welfare. Throughout the book, we describe how this kind of dominance became a fuel driving liberal movements in all walks of life.

The historical memory of the time of collective madness, starvation, and total control is the "fuel" driving the leaderless mass movements for liberty. All Chinese over fifty experienced catastrophic famine (GL1959-1961) brought about by Mao's so-called Great Leap, followed closely by the devastating Cultural Revolution (CR1966-1976). While GL led to the death of at least 30 million rural people, perhaps as many as 45 million (most of them women and children), the CR violently destroyed the lives of urbanites through regime-induced collective madness.[23] The Great Leap Famine, according to Dali Yang, created "incentives for decollectivization, which became a reality when the Chinese leadership jockeyed for power following Mao's death."[24] This was not an accident, as the grassroots decollectivization (*baochao daohu*) movement spread most quickly in the provinces whose mortality rates were the highest and which were far from Beijing. This movement was the first example of massive spontaneous, unorganized, leaderless, non-ideological, and apolitical movement.[25] It was ostensibly apolitical, but it had profound political consequences as it was a de facto rejection of the state's control.

By the party's own admission at the Eleventh Party Congress in 1978, the Cultural Revolution destroyed the lives of more than 100 million persons.[26] Thus, there is a strong correlation between popular revulsion at sufferings caused by the CR and, however unorganized, a consciously collective sentiment for change. The source of the suffering was clear to all: the government's overarching control. Liberty—freedom from the state's control of every aspect of their life—now became overwhelmingly attractive as hundreds of millions of Chinese sought any means possible to stop the horrific calamities associated with the despotic government. This revulsion and instinctive search for the means to prevent its recurrence led to the emergence of liberal practices that formed bases for future demands for freedom. The revulsion at the horrors of the recent past effectively fulfilled the function of mass "coordination." It was at this time (1977-1982) that farmers acted upon their revulsion with the government-controlled commune system, under which they had lived as de facto slaves of the government, by embarking on a massive exodus from the collective farms. Intellectuals at the same time had their own eruption: a five-year torrent of art and literature, a literature of suffering, *shanghen wenxue*, a literary period remembered by intellectuals in China.[27] In these circumstances, liberty became attractive to the Chinese like a force of nature.

These leaderless movements constituted a kind of 'big bang," setting in motion a series of unorganized and leaderless movements seeking release from state control, such as mass rural-urban migration in defiance of the state resident's *hukou* policy; circulation of non-government news and banned books, films, journals, and articles; the home church movement in defiance of state regulations; rebellion against the state's ban on homosexuality and wide spread use of *guahu* to erect private enterprises under the guise of collectives. This list is by no means exhaustive. For example, the Internet has provided Chinese new opportunities: sex, network/association, critical commentaries on the government, and a spontaneous generation of civil society groups or cyber groups—autonomous groups outside the state control, which are officially banned.

The arrival of cell phones facilitated wide spread dissemination of anti-government jokes and commentary through text messages, which circulate with lightning speed. For example, in 2005 in Heilongjia, a rich woman hit and seriously injured a pedestrian, and her family members tried to use their government connections to avoid consequences. Subsequently, a mobile phone campaign triggered a national outcry such that the local court was ordered to arrest the driver. This social resistance is what James Scott terms "every day forms of resistance" and what Václav Havel has called "living in truth."[28] Like Havel's grocer, who decided no longer to co-operate with Communist authorities in spreading propaganda by stepping "outside the lie" to live a truthful life, millions of Chinese have also begun living in truth. Living in truth, Havel says, is like a contagion that spreads from individual to individual, making it possible for large number of people to change their lives.

One way to understand China's dramatic transformation is to apply Malcolm Gladwell's "tipping point" theory. In *The Tipping Point: How Little Things Can Make a Big Difference*, Gladwell links tipping points to epidemics: "Ideas and products and messages and behaviors spread just like viruses do."[29] As Chinese increasingly become involved in everyday resistance to the party-state, they are powerfully affected by the anti-state counterculture around them, pushing them to participate in recalcitrant activities (establishing home churches, reading and disseminating banned books, consuming alternative media), actions formerly considered criminal. Gladwell labels this process as "the power of context,"[30] because people are powerfully affected by proximate circumstances in making their decisions. In China, there is saying that a ubiquitous "crime" is no crime at all (*zuibu fanzong* 罪不犯纵). People are emboldened to act in a similar manner. This is how the explanation of the process of leaderless movements exists. Global linkages (trade, media, international NGOs, foreign visitors to China, Chinese foreign travel, and global media) provide an enabling mechanism, or a connector, linking individuals with diversified interests, so that even self-regarding and prudent individuals fearful of state reprisal, may in aggregate defy authority and move in liberal directions by combating the state's norms.

The ripple effect of such action is important here. When a few farmers became wealthy by taking on long-distance trade, others heard, saw, and followed the same path. Chinese rural people imprisoned in the commune system had a strong desire for a better life and became pioneers of Chinese reform, from politics to economics. The snowball effect of workers migration allowed spontaneous coordination without the benefit of formal organization or leadership.

What is more important to know, the elements of SULNAM help to sustain wide spread common action enough to constitute a social movement despite the apparent absence of a formal hierarchical organization.

Corruption as Means to Gain Liberty

The new social environment created by new social norms has also altered party-state political culture. The state bureaucracy has undergone a metamorphosis of opportunistic adaptation, exchanging political control for economic extortion, as huge segments of the bureaucracy become rent seekers. Entrepreneurs and ordinary people attempt to buy their way out of constrictive regulation. In this process, moral norms are jettisoned wholesale, as financial gain colonizes the moral high ground as the new social norm. The authority of the party apparatus has become progressively delegitimized as people realize that all is for sale, even as its power (measured by the rapid increase of military and police spending) swells. In this process, millions of Chinese seek opportunities to escape the party-state's enmity toward civil liberty—buying ISBN numbers to evade censorship, opening gay bars and massage parlors (sex clubs), buying birth permits, purchasing residents' permits (*hukou*), and so on. As a result of this complex process, the Chinese have found a way to a new comparative autonomy and independence. Some may even argue that corruption leads to crises of political legitimacy and, thus, pushes for political change, as testified by the Tiananmen incident.[31]

The Chinese communist regime has been unintentionally transformed. Had government bureaucracy been incorruptible, most private enterprise would have been stopped in its tracks. This reform and development process had its root in the late 1970s while Mao's body was still warm, when rural markets and industrial development began. Chinese migrants, entrepreneurs, and unemployed people used bribery to get away from the state's restrictions on businesses. Without bribery, it was impossible to obtain various permits that were essential for any business transactions. In China, a bribe is a "freedom tax": you get a little piece of freedom for your money. For many Chinese, this kind of corruption is much better than honest officials denying the freedom! This explains the saying in the 1980s, *"meiyou buzhengzhifeng jiu meiyou xiangzhen qiye"* (no winds of corruption, no rural enterprises).[32] This saying challenges the fallacious view that changes occurred through government directives and reforms. Corruption weakened party discipline, greatly reducing the central government's capacity for social control despite its continuing monopoly on military and armed police power.

It is Impossible to Shoot Down a Leaderless Movement

The theme of corruption runs as a unifying thread through the course of this book. The farmers' *baochan daohu* movement (turning production to household or decollectivization) could never have worked if government cadres had been incorruptible. In this period of social revolutionary change, corruption was a primary means of shifting resources from relatively unproductive uses to spectacularly more productive employment, and, in the process, delegitimizing the Communist regime in the eyes of hundreds of millions of Chinese. As Havel points out, in the Czechoslovakian context, "Anything which leads people to overstep their predetermined rules is regarded by the system as an attack upon itself. And in this respect it is correct; every instance of such transgression is a genuine denial of the system."[33]

In the beginning, corruption was a liberating factor, but as time progresses, in the long run, corruption appears as a malignancy choking off the development of rule of law, respect for private property, protection of human rights, and environmental security. Because corruption helps the middle class to attain liberal rights through bribery, the interest for pushing for democracy is exchanged for political stability.

Grassroots as a Dominating Force for Social Change: A New Methodology

It is difficult to write the kind of grassroots analysis offered in this book. An established anthropological method is as a participatory observer. Returning regularly to China for more than thirteen years allows one to observe change more clearly than may be possible during continuous residency. Such analysis, which depends heavily on a multitude of in-depth interviews with a wide sample of Chinese society (from prostitutes to prima donna intellectuals), provides readers with a sense of what many Chinese are actually doing, thinking, and feeling.

In the Chinese case, it is ordinary individuals who have made history. They, not their leaders, are the principal architects of the great drama of social transformation in China. The analysis of the book reveals that most grassroots movements were spontaneous, unorganized, leaderless, non-ideological, and apolitical, yet cumulatively have revolutionized Chinese society. Most studies of social movements tend to emphasize organization, leadership, and ideology. But such movements are impossible in China with the Communist regime's tight control of all non-governmental organizations. Had these "movements" been formally organized with defined leadership structures, they would have been targeted and suppressed by a regime intensely protective of its powers. Thus, only leaderless movements had any chance of success.

Compared with overt protests, such as the 1989 student movements, the grassroots movements of today, though unorganized and leaderless, have pushed China in a liberal direction. Had the rural migrant movement of the 1980s and 1990s formally organized and called openly for the end of the *hukou* system, it would surely have been crushed, as occured in Tiananmen in 1989 and Falungong's Zhongnanhai demonstration in 2001. While the regime is focused on organizations such as Falungong, students movements, Christian associations and activities, independent movements in East Turkistan, and Dalai Lama Buddhist networks, grassroots social movements like migration, the sexual revolution, and a wide variety of social clubs slip through their fingers. In this way, organizational weakness becomes a strength. Using ingenious methods and taking advantage of historical circumstances (such as globalization), tens of millions of Chinese have successfully challenged the Chinese party-state and decisively transformed its social system. As a few raindrops initiate a torrent, unorganized Chinese quietly initiated a storm of social change.

The preoccupation of the Chinese leadership with organized collective action played an important role in the success of less-organized, new grassroots movements. The watchful structure of the People's Republic was poised to strike hard at organized opposition of any kind. It had no mercy toward Falungong and the 1989 student movements.[34] More recently, the state has paid attention to a large number of protests and riots like the 1999 Falun Gong protests, the 2006 rural protests over land rights in Panyu, protests in Guangzhou, and the 2008 Tibet protests (mainly religious in motivation). Sometimes organized, sometimes spontaneous and unorganized, these protests reached thousands each year and have overwhelmed the state.

In short, the spontaneous, unorganized, leaderless, non-ideological, apolitical grassroots movements seeking a comprehensive range of basic liberties avoided all direct challenge to the regime. When bribery failed, members of these movements avoided contact with authority as much as possible, seeking only to achieve their purposes with as little fuss, ruffled feathers, and injured party-state's pride as possible. Their engagement involves no overt seizure of power, but nevertheless leaches power away from the government, assisted by China's gradual opening to the world at large through globalization. In essence, millions of Chinese have gained limited liberty, not because the government was flexible and benign, still less because it condoned increased freedom, but rather because the state is overwhelmed by the magnitude of sheer numbers: 120 million to 200 million migrants, millions of industries providing sexual services, roughly 35 to 50 million gays, several millions of prostitutes/sex workers, 120 million Christians, thousands of online and face-to-face forums.[35] The regime lacks the organizational capacity and resources to deal with illegality on such a scale.

Limitations

The theory presented here has certain limitations, the first of which is the fact that there is no way of predicting social revolutions or recognizing them when they transpire. Only when it has passed and the change has occurred we can see where the critical point was reached. The theory is weak in explaining changes that are linked to the elite learning curve, such as the creation of the stock market, the cutting of tariffs due to WTO regulations, the special economic zones and recent increases of massive organized collective protests and riots in

China. What is more, SULNAM may not lead China towards democracy and rule of law because it encourages the habit of circumventing the official rules. The passage of laws covering property rights and privacy may not lead to rule of law, which requires popular acceptance of those laws.

The Chapters

The following seven chapters attempt to present the extent of these grassroots liberty-seeking, rights acquisition movements. We choose to focus on rural decollectiviation, mobility, entrepreneurship, global linkage, freedom of expression including speech, the sexual revolution, intellectual liberal trends, and the rise of civil society, without going into extensive detail on other factors that have affected social transformation in ways we view as less influential than the pursuit of rights. These other issues can be further examined in many of the books cited throughout our discussion. We will now provide a brief overview of the breakdown of our argument.

Chapter 1: The Right to Be Let Alone: The Grassroots Decollectivization Movement and *Baochan Daohu*

This chapter introduces the root cause of the civil liberty movements in China: the farmers' decollectivization movement, *baochan daohu* (contracting production to the household), in the late 1970s. Without this grassroots institutional transformation, all forms of movements such as land rights, mobility, entrepreneurship, markets, and religious movements would have been impossible. Farmers used bribery to gain limited control over their harvest by circumventing the collective commune system, which tied them to their land. Here, corruption is the price of liberty for 80 percent of Chinese people. This idea was vividly expressed by the late farmer, Chu Shu, in Tongxin village in Hubei: "Please let me farm alone. I will give you the state quota and collective quota and some good rice to you, too."[36] The Chinese writer Mo Yan uses the words of a despairing farmer, Lian, to express this desire to be left alone: "I have nothing against the Communist Party and I definitely have nothing against Chairman Mao. I'm not opposed to the People's Commune or to collectivization. I just want to be left alone to work for myself."[37]

Farmers' desire to be left alone, and their courage to act on that desire, helped to destroy the commune system. This chapter links the farmers' grassroots decollectivization movement to the Great Leap Famine (1961 to 1969). Because this devastating famine was endured by such a large percentage of the population for so long, the stage was set for like-minded individuals to pursue common objectives without the need for leadership or ideology. The deaths of so many rural people during this famine formed the backdrop for the success of the rural decollectivization movement. Those involved are not leaders, and most are unknown in the West because they do not engage in face-to-face confrontation with the state. Wishing to be let alone, they vote with their feet against the socialist planned economic system. By 1982, more than 90 percent of rural people were engaged in the household production system, which has major social, economic, and political significance for China. The most visible impact of *baochan daohu's* success is the growth of free markets in China.

Chapter 2: Struggling to Move Freely

Powerless and impoverished, rural migrants have become a significant social and political force in bringing freedom to China. They are successful precisely because they have made the connection between self-interest and the mistakes of the regime. They vote with their feet and practice a variety of democratic values in the course of daily resistance to the regime and its rules. Despite the mobility-restricting Hukou system, over 150 million people have made the decision to leave their homes and pursue a better life. This huge migration of rural people constitutes the largest civil disobedience movement in the world against the Hukou system (household registration system).

These individuals endure everything from social discrimination and a harsh work environment to government round-ups and imprisonment. There have been several detailed studies of the plight of migrants, including Dorothy J. Solinger's *Contesting Citizenship in Urban China: Peasant Migrants, the State, and the Logic of Market*. We recognize the importance of the issues of migrant abuse and their ramifications on the state-society relationship in China; however, we also focus on migrants' influence on the liberalization of Chinese society and the development of a civil society. Seizing, by force, the right to move is truly demonstrative of the will of the people to have more control over their destiny. As a result, many of the people who have continued to move in violation of government regulations over the last three decades are in search of something more than simple economic prosperity. An important part of our discussion in this chapter is an examination of the impact of migration on Chinese women. As an integral subsection of the migrant group, they have broken out of their traditional and more contemporary roles, gaining status both socially and economically.

Both women and men, as individuals, have felt the liberating effect of choosing where to live and where to work. They understand that through their actions they have become an inalterable part of China's global economy. In doing so, they have advanced not only their own interests, but also those of society as a whole, by creating an environment of decreased reliance on the government.

Chapter 3: The Chinese Entrepreneur: Challenging the Status Quo

This chapter details the role of entrepreneurs in transforming the socio-economic and political landscape of China. The entrepreneurs were some of the first Chinese to test this water, as each market they attempted to create was either for a product or service that did not exist or one whose existence was previously restricted—or exclusively managed—by the government. As such, these individuals were not only working without the protection of the law, but were often in violation of existing regulations. Thus, we reemphasize the fact that the initial entrepreneurs were not beneficiaries of economic liberalism, but rather they helped facilitate its development.

In addition to their role in creating markets, the businesses created by entrepreneurs, along with those newly established by global firms, helped set the conditions for the freedom of mobility movement, competitive printing, and freelance journalists. Had the government still been the only employer, those who left their villages in violation of established law would have had even less opportunity for success, and writers and journalists would have remained mouths of the party-state or continued to practice self-censorship. The majority of Chinese do not work for the government; this circumstance in itself emboldens critical voices.

Chapter 4: Capitalism with Chinese Characteristics and the Basis of Civil Society

As part of this process, we note the entrepreneurs' importance in the development of civil society. As stated previously, some definitions of civil society exclude the private business sector. As just one example of this view, Larry Diamond states, "civil society in general is commonly employed to refer to a 'third system' of agents, namely, privately organized citizens as distinguished from government or profit-seeking actors."[38] In our view, because the initiative of entrepreneurs produced a synergism crucial not only to the success of the economic reform, but also to a greater self-reliance and a subsequent diminution of the role of government, the entrepreneurs themselves must be included in the civil society discussion. By helping to create markets, rather than waiting for the government to initiate change, they have facilitated the development of private space in which this "third system" of agents can exist.

Although entrepreneurs with varying degrees of government dependence exist across the economic landscape, the majority have succeeded in spite of, not because of, the government. The unique Chinese formula of entrepreneurship entails not only risk-taking, but also cultivated *guanxi* (personal connections) to reduce the limitations of and restrictions on private enterprises.[39] We do not disagree with Dickson's assertion that this segment of entrepreneurs are not necessarily reformers, as they would like to see a continuation of the status quo; we simply focus on the larger percentage of entrepreneurs, those who do not receive government backing and who have continually challenged the status quo. Kellee Tsai's *Back-Alley Banking: Private Entrepreneurs in China* provides information on government funding of private enterprises that supports this contention. In addition, the emphasis of James McGregor's *One Billion Customers: Lessons from the Front Lines of Doing Business in China* on the power of informal deals in business today further reinforces how much is going on outside of the government-established economic framework.

Chinese economic success is also about people seeking liberty on a daily basis, the result of which has been phenomenal growth despite single party rule. So much has been said about the rise of the Chinese economy, but the state-led development model does not fit the reality. China has a long way to go before Chinese have the right to engage in any business, occupation, or enterprise without government interference. Entrepreneurs still do not have the right to decide what to do with profits they make. But the story is simple: when people have liberty, limited though it may be, development occurs. Friedrich von Hayek's theory of "spontaneous order" explains the destructive power of entrepreneurship. When ordinary people, through a principle of self-organization, share and synchronize local and personal knowledge, they reduce the formal structural power of the communist state.

Chapter 5: Information Wants to Be Free

This chapter may be one of our more contentious arguments, because as we examine the production and dissemination of what we dub "TIA" (technology, information, and artistic creation), we contend that pirating, and other forms of intellectual property rights infringement, have been a necessary part of the evolution of Chinese society. Controlling access to information has been a cornerstone of the Communist Party's control since its inception. However, this dominance is being challenged as technology and the will of the people strengthen and force a change. By explaining the history of information control from its early years to the present day, this chapter lays the groundwork for understanding the complexity of the current state of China with regard to issues such as TIA and the media.

With the government as the sole producer and distributor of information and artistic expression, the people had no choice but to create their own unsanctioned materials and distribution channels. This fits into the rights acquisition movement under the broad context of the fight for more control and access to TIA. As part of this quest, a parallel society was created, existing out of the government's sight. Here, people were able to "create" on their own, and new ideas flourished. Because of its influence on the people, this parallel society has affected the government-controlled society and subsequently government policy. The two cannot be kept apart indefinitely, and their emergence is defining the new China.

Chinese enjoy relative freedom, much of it enabled by technology, with more than 230 million Internet users and 650 million cell phones, as well as by piracy. Piracy was not and is not an end state, but was an opportunistic first step in a complex process of achieving a critical mass of independent (non-state) information in the hands of ordinary Chinese. Pirated entertainment, including Hollywood movies, has provided widespread knowledge and awareness of alternative values, ways of life, and social arrangements.

Chapter 6: Sexual Revolution in China

Combined with the *baochan dahou* movement, growing wealth in the industrial revolution, the migration of millions from villages to cities, the global financial revolution, the information explosion to ordinary people, and vast and far reaching international influences, the new sexual revolution, a potent indicator of personal liberty, has fundamentally altered key elements of the moral content of the party-state regime, even if it has not changed its name. Puritanism, so fundamental a component of the new revolutionary regime installed in 1949, is now in the process of being swept away.[40]

Chinese women and gays have played a key role in this sexual revolution. The new sexual revolution is both anti-traditional and anti-communist. The Chinese people's preference to have control over their own sex life is another indicator of social rights awakenings in China. Market development in housing, non-state jobs, global media and trade have provided the material foundation for China's sexual revolution with its cultural diversity, tolerance, openness, and (limited) freedom of expression.

Without elements of capitalism, there will be no progress in individual liberty. Adam Smith's description of a free market system as a "system of natural liberty" is verified by the rise of personal liberty in China. The sexual revolution illustrates the Chinese people's natural desire for liberty. Liberty has come because they had seized it despite the state's continuing authoritarianism. Sexual liberty is the most important measure for personal liberty in any country.

The government's inability to deal with so many issues resulted in grassroots disobediences of so many kinds (gay culture, millions of taboo websites, tens of millions of migrants, several millions prostitutes/sex workers, tens of millions of text messages and chat rooms) that it was forced to tolerate a certain type of action despite the fact that the people initiated it; consequently, the issue became how far to push the limits.

Chapter 7: Global Trade, Foreign Influence, and the Effects of Globalization

We must introduce this chapter with a statement that we understand the Chinese government plays an integral role in the discussion of globalization in China. Accepting this, we provide limited detail of the government's role in our own discussion of globalization and foreign influence. We do this primarily for two reasons: first, because the focus of this book is on ordinary Chinese citizens, foreign influence is analyzed in the context of further empowering the individual; and second, because the government tried to limit the non-monetary aspects of global trade. We contend that aside from "opening the door," the government did not facilitate those effects which we view as most beneficial to the growth of society. Thus, the discussion of government's role is limited, without any implication that its role was trivial.

A great deal of scholarship has attempted to explain the actions of those who worked within the government trade structure, and we hope to add insight to the discussion by providing accounts of those who worked around or even counter to government regulations, yet still contributed to the growth of China. For this reason, we begin this chapter with an examination of smuggling. Its impact cannot always be measured in dollar value or other statistics, but is very much present in the way China conducts business today. When looking at society, it becomes clear in many cases that people act the way they do more because of these counter influences than as a result of governmental action.[41]

The focus of the remainder of the chapter is that, through trade, in addition to goods, comes the exchange of culture and ideas. This is not a new revelation and is discussed in many globalization books including Martin Wolf's *Why Globalization Works*, and Thomas Friedman's *The World is Flat*. This argument is important as it exhibits an additional non-governmental source that is helping the liberalization process. As we have already stated, we do not contend that trade initiated the liberalization, but merely that it facilitated its continuance outside of the government purview. Finally, China's entry in the world economy has also brought more visibility to its domestic situation, further enhancing the individual's ability to confront the government.

Final Thoughts

We wrote this book to challenge many of the prevailing assumptions regarding the impetus for reform. The central premise of this book argues that a grassroots social revolution through entrepreneurship, migration of millions from the countryside to cities, the explosion of information available to ordinary people (especially via the Internet), vast, far-reaching international influences, and a multifaceted sexual revolution has fundamentally altered key elements of the moral and material content of China's party-state regime and society at large, even if it has not changed its name. This social revolution is pushing China towards a more liberal society, even if the government remains in its current illiberal and grasping mode. An important finding of this book is that the Chinese government reacts, rather than leads, in this transformative process.

We articulate this argument by examining the actions of individuals in the context of existing government policy. If the government supports free enterprise, why did entrepreneurs face harassment and imprisonment? If the government supported the growth of global firms, why were the majority of workers at these firms illegal migrants who had broken the law to move towards their opportunities? Why have over 150 million people migrated without the consent of the government, despite the conditions they often face at their destination? How does one explain the failure of government restrictions on speech and publication to prevent growth of artistic expression, exchange of information, and alternative media? In addressing these questions, we contend that the contradictions arise out of the reality of China's state-society relationship in which the people are pursuing rights, while government continues to focus overwhelmingly on regime stability.

When one looks at the history of China's reforms, while telling the story of the entrepreneurs, migrants, and others who have taken their future into their own hands, the actions of the government seem less reform-minded than is often portrayed. There has been a daily struggle between the government and individuals for the past three decades. As a result, there has been a forcible acquisition of limited civil liberties and the non-state sector has grown tremendously despite, not because of the government, thus affecting permanent change in the structure of China far beyond how the economy operates. The reform has not been a government-initiated policy program, but more the result of the will and desire of the Chinese people to attain basic rights and place some distance between themselves and the government. To truly grasp the role of the individual is to have a more comprehensive understanding of the complexity of how and why China is transforming. The pursuit of rights has translated into economic prosperity and increased social liberalism, as opposed to the common perception that economic liberalism has been the driving force. We hope this book helps to provide a new methodology for understanding China.

If we have to describe the Chinese transformation in one sentence, it is a short one: liberty prevailed over despotism and communism.

> *It cannot be repeated too often: nothing is more fertile in marvels than the art of being free, but nothing is harder than freedom's apprenticeship. The same is not true of despotism. Despotism often presents itself as the repairer of all the ills suffered, the support of just rights, defender of the oppressed, and founder of order. People are lulled to sleep by the temporary prosperity it engenders, and when they do wake up, they are wretched. But liberty is generally born in stormy weather, growing with difficulty amid civil discords, and only when it is already old does one see the blessings it has brought.*
>
> —*Alexis de Tocqueville,* Democracy in America

Notes

1. Charter 08, Translated from the Chinese by Perry Link, *New York Review of Books:* http://www.nybooks.com/articles/2a2210.
2. The *Wall Street Journal*, "Sarko Steps Up: The French President's Un-Chirac foreign policy," August 29, 2007, http://www.opinionjournal.com/editorial/feature.html?id=110010535.
3. Li, Cheng, *China's Leaders: The New Generation*, (New York: Rowman & Littlefield Publishing, 2001).
4. Ronald Inglehart, *Modernization and Postmodernization*, (Princeton, NJ: Princeton University Press, 1997).

5. For discussions on provincial leadership see: Peter T.Y. Cheung, Jae Ho Chung, and Zhimin Lin's (editors), *Provincial Strategies of Economic Reform in Post-Mao China: Leadership, Politics, and Implementation.*

6. Milton Friedman, *Capitalism and Freedom* (Fortieth Anniversary Edition), (Chicago: University of Chicago Press, 2002). pp. viii-ix.

7. Kate Zhou, *How The Peasants Changed China, Power of the People*, (Boulder,CO: Westview Press).

8. Anthony Giddens and David Held, *Classes, Power, and Conflict: Classical and Contemporary Debates*, (Berkeley: University of California Press, 1982).

9. Hans Heinrich Gerth and C. Wright Mills, *From Max Weber: Essays in Sociology*, (New York: Oxford University Press, 1958).

10. F. A. Hayek, *The Fatal Conceit: The Errors of Socialism* (The Collected Works of F. A. Hayek), (Chicago: University Of Chicago Press, Reprint edition, 1991); "The Use of Knowledge in Society," *The American Economic Review*, XXXV, No. 4, (September 1945), pp. 519-30.

11. F. A. Hayek, *The Road to Serfdom,* (Chicago: University Of Chicago Press, 50th Anniversary edition, 1994); *Law, Legislation and Liberty, Volume 1: Rules and Order*, (Chicago, University of Chicago Press, 1978); *The Constitution of Liberty*, (Chicago, University of Chicago Press, 1978).

12. F. A. Hayek, *The Use of Knowledge in Society*, 1945.

13. For a thorough discussion on the relevance of the Civil Society debate, see Charles Bahmueller, Chapter 5, "Civil Society and Democracy Reconsidered." Charles F. Bahmueller, "Civil Society Reconsidered," in Charles F. Bahmueller and John F. Patrick, eds., *Principles and Practices of Education for Democratic Citizenship: International Perspectives and Practices,* (Bloomington, IN: ERIC Clearinghouse for Social Studies/Social Science Education, 1999), pp. 101-121.

14. Adam Ferguson, "An Essay on the History of Civil Society," 5th ed. (London: T. Cadell, 1782). http://oll.libertyfund.org/Home3/Book.php?recordID=1229.

15. Thomas Friedman, *The Lexus and the Olive Tree*, (Anchor Books, 2000).

16. Benjamin Barber, *Jihad Vs. McWorld*, (Times Books, 1995).

17. Tarrow, Sidney. 1998. *Power in Movement: Social Movements and Cotentious Politics*, 2nd ed., (Cambridge, England: Cambridge University Press), p. 2.

18. Piven, Frances Fox and Richard Cloward, *Poor People's Movements: Why they Succeed, How they Fail,* (New York: Vintage Books, 1979).

19. Tarrow, Sidney, *Power in Movement: Social Movements and Cotentious Politics*, 2nd ed. (Cambridge: Cambridge University Press, 1998).

20. See a different view on rural resistance in China in Lucien Bianco, "Peasant Revolts from Pre-1949 Days to the Present," *China Perspectives*, No. 24, (July-August 1999), pp. 56-65. Editor's note:

    To commemorate the ninth anniversary of the April 25 Appeal, Clearwisdom presents this as one of a series of republished articles from years past. The April 25th Appeal was notable not only for its size, but also because it was remarkably peaceful and orderly. Some 10,000 practitioners gathered in central Beijing that day, peacefully protesting for their civil rights. The CCP propaganda machine, however, in its quest to crush Falun Gong at the bidding of then Party Chairman Jiang Zemin, twisted the facts to serve its own motives. To this day, CCP propaganda accuses Falun Gong of "laying seige to the Zhongnanhai Central Government Compound" on April 25, 1999, falsely alleging that the 10,000 gathered posed a violent threat to the nation and its leaders. Nothing could be further from the truth, of course, as this series of articles documents from various angles (Falun Gong Website).

21. Elsewhere I have defined SULNAM as spontaneous, unorganized, leaderless, non-ideological, and apolitical movement. (Zhou, 1996).
22. Mancur Olson, The Logic of Collective Action, (Cambridge, MA: Harvard University Press, 1965).
23. Dali Yang, *Calamity and Reform in China: State, Rural Society, and Institutional Change Since the Great Leap Famine*, (Stanford, CA: Stanford University Press, 1996); and Lynn White, *Policies of Chaos: The Organizational Causes of Violence in China's Cultural Revolution*, (Princeton, NJ: Princeton University Press, 1990). For more on The Chinese Holocaust Memorial page http://www.chinese-memorial.org.htm.
24. Dali Yang, *Calamity and Reform in China: State, Rural Society, and Institutional Change since the Great Leap Famine*, (Stanford, CA: Stanford University Press, 1996), p. 252.
25. Zhou, 1996.
26. The party document.
27. The writers of this genre were many including Liu Binyan, Yu Luojing. Geremie Barme, "Chaotou Wenxue—China's New Literature," *The Australian Journal of Chinese Affairs*, No. 2 (Jul., 1979), pp. 137-148. *Chaotou* or *shanghen wenxue* is an expression of this situation. Respect for the experienced and aged is a theme highlighted by stories. Form of *shanghen wenxue* (literature of wounded), *feixu wenxue* (literature of the ruins), *menglong shi* (anti-socialist and political art, it is reactive to socialism realism. obscure poetry), and so forth, see the intellectual chapter.
28. Václav Havel, "Politics and Conscience," in *Open Letters: Selected Writings*, selected and ed. Paul Wilson, (New York: Random House, 1985), pp. 249-71. James C. Scott, *Weapons of the Weak: Everyday Forms of Peasant Resistance*, (New Haven, CT: Yale University Press, 1985).
29. Malcolm Gladwell, *The Tipping Point: How Little Things Can Make a Big Difference*, (Abacus, New Ed edition, 2002).
30. Malcolm Gladwell, *The Tipping Point: How Little Things Can Make a Big Difference*, (Abacus, New Ed edition, 2002).
31. Yan Sun, "Reform, State and Corruption: Is Corruption Less Destructive in China than in Russia?" *Comparative Politics,* 32, 1, (1999), pp. 1-20. p.16
32. Zhou, 1996.
33. Vaclav Havel, *The Power of the Powerless: Citizens Against the State in Central-Eastern Europe,* (Armonk, NY: M. E. Sharpe, 1985), p. 30.
34. See my discussion adapted here, in Zhou, 1996.
35. There is argument that some do this for a living while some forced prostitution is modern day slavery.
36. Personal interview with Chu, in February 8th, 1986 in Tongxin, Jingshan, Hubei.
37. Mo Yan. *Life and Death Are Wearing Me Out*. Translated by Howard Goldblatt, (Arcade Publishing, 2008).
38. Richard Price, "Transnational Civil Society and Advocacy in World Politics," *World Politics 55*, (2003), p. 580.
39. For a detailed account of those who have prospered through the government, see Bruce Dickson's *Red Capitalists in China: The Party, Private Entrepreneurs, and Prospects for Political Change*, (Cambridge: Cambridge University Press, 2003).
40. The first law government passed was the 1950 marriage law, which banned prostitution and polygamy.
41. More insight into the scope of smuggling can be found in James McGregor's *One Billion Customers: Lessons from the Front Lines of Doing Business*.

1

The Right to Be Let Alone: The Grassroots Decollectivization Movement and *Baochan Daohu*

*The natural progress of things is for liberty to yield
and government to gain ground.*
—*Thomas Jefferson*

*I had nothing against the state. I just wanted to be
left alone to farm for my family.*
—*Lao Chu, a farmer in Tongxin Village, Hubei*

China's grassroots civil disobedience movements are the result of thirty years of Chinese communist total control over society. This control reached so thoroughly into individual life that in some instances children went to sleep fearing that they might unknowingly cry out forbidden thoughts, such as a dislike for Mao-style clothes. One young girl used to ask her sister to awaken her if she started violating such taboos in her sleep. The state dictated how much to eat, where to eat, what to wear, whom to marry, where to live and work, and what children to have. But the most oppressive control mechanism under Mao was the commune system.

Social Transformation: Becoming Communist "Peasants"

The Chinese Communist leaders won military victories largely because of rural support. But those same rural people became the victims, rather than victors, of Mao's revolution. Through the party's overreaching organization, collectivization, and the *hukou*'s (household registration through grain rationing) systematic control over mobility, the Chinese state transformed traditional Chinese farmers from legally mobile independent proprietors into commune peasants who were "bound legally and substantively to the land."[1] They no longer owned land, could not move from the land, and had no escape from the social class in which they were born. They were subject to direct and comprehensive control by the Communist state.

1

Collectivization was the most important means of transformation of Chinese farmers. The Communist leaders implemented collectivization in China by the use of two effective methods that consolidated their control in the countryside: class labeling and land reform.

The state used class labeling to divide the rural population which had formerly organized itself along clan, family, and village lines. The Communists assigned each family to a class, based on the family's economic circumstances at the time of land reform (1947-52). Mao defined six classes: landlords, rich peasants, upper-middle peasants, middle peasants, lower-middle peasants, and poor peasants. Landlord and rich peasant classes were considered wicked, while the lower-middle and poor peasants were considered virtuous classes. Through the struggle against former local elites, the state recruited new local leaders who were loyal to the party.

In the beginning, the state used the image of a helpless and impoverished peasantry to mobilize the majority against rural elites. During land reform (1950-53), class struggle offered many poor farmers tangible rewards in the form of land. By promising "land to the tiller," the state mobilized the poor against the rich, destroying the power base of the traditional elites.

However, land reform did not give land entitlement to the poor. It confiscated land from all classes. The state allocated land for the farmers' use, *but denied them both ownership and control.* Although before communism, many farmers had lived a life of landless *rentier* subsistence, at least 60 percent of the rural population consisted of small, relatively independent landowners. Many peasants both owned and cultivated rented land; some rented and others rented out, including middle peasants and even some who were rather poor. This varied regionally, with a high tenancy rate in the South and central areas and a low tenancy rate (but a higher rate of hired labor) in the North. Under Mao, land reform transferred the land from independent proprietors, most of whom were poor, to the collective (i.e., a local state organization).[2]

Even before land reform started, the communist leadership had already committed to a collective future modeled on the Soviet collective experience. From a political perspective, Mao used land reform as a stepping-stone to collectivization. Immediately after the land reform, the government launched a campaign to attack the anti-revolutionaries (mostly landlords, other wealthy people, and people who had connections with the former nationalist government). Between 1950 and 1951, 712,000 were executed, 1,290,000 were imprisoned and 1,200,000 were sent to labor camps.[3] The repression of the campaign set a precedent, establishing the state as a source of coercing and silencing any political oponents.

Very often, both Chinese and international scholars and the Beijing elites have regarded the Great Leap Forward and the People's Commune policy as the work of Mao only and maintained that Mao's associates such as Deng Xiaoping, Chen Yun and Liu Shaoqi opposed these policies. However, this is not true. Influenced by the communist view of socialism, most Chinese leaders of the 1950s, like their Soviet counterparts, pushed massive collectivization. Socialism was to incorporate collective ownership, as Bo Yibo recalled in "Our Advanced Cooperatives Copied the Soviet Collective Farms" (1991).[4] Such ideological attachment to an accelerated industrialization process was the root cause of conflicts between nearly the whole of the party elite and the majority of rural people who hungered for land. In common with many underdeveloped countries in Asia and Africa where elites attempted to rush industrialization at the expense of rural populations, China adopted an industrialization policy designed to squeeze resources from rural areas to feed workers in a newly industrializing planned economy. This ideological attachment pushed all top CCP leaders to support the Great Leap Forward, the People's Commune policy, and the Socialist General Principles. Justifying their actions with alleged social justice, they ruthlessly used all available means to push their idea of a utopian society.

Abolition of Private Property and the Procurement System

In 1953, four years after the new Communist government took power, it began a strict policy of curtailing the rights of farmers that reached fruition in 1958 and remained in force until 1978. It began by abolishing private property and proceeded to restrict the rights of the new peasant class to buy, sell, or rent land. Key rural properties such as housing, land, grain, labor, animal husbandry, farm tools, farm animals, and even kitchen utensils (during the Great Leap Forward period) became collective goods.

Figure 1.1
China's First Generation of Communist Leaders Shared
Mao's Socialist Vision in 1950s

Note: (from left to right) Zhu De, Zhou Enlai, Chen Yun, Liu Shaoqi, Mao Zedong, Deng Xiaoping
Source: http://en.wikipedia.org/wiki/History_of_the_People's_Republic_of_China_ (1949-1976)

The introduction of *tonggou tongxiao* (the procurement system) in 1953 was the first mechanism to control rural people. On November 23, 1953, the state issued a directive to ban all private grain sales.[5] During its entire previous history the Chinese state had never been able to control the national grain market. Before 1949, the government (both local and national) collected taxes, sometimes years in advance, but never laid claim to the entire harvest. However, the procurement system overcame the farmers' resistance to taxation by nationalizing the grain market so that the state became the only buyer of grain. Further, the government set the selling price, which was low. Rural people were forced to sell fixed quotas of grain to the government at official prices. Only after farmers reached the state's procurement quotas, were they allowed to sell at state-supervised grain markets. In 1954 the state also took control over the trading of vegetable oil and raw cotton, bringing a several thousand-year-old commercial system of private grain merchants and grain mills to an end. According to a document from the Shaoxin government, state procurement workers banned market activities for grain, cotton, oil, and raw materials in 1952 in order to ensure that the state procurement target was met, as American anthropologist Helen Siu found in her examination of old government commerce documents.[6]

From time to time, the compulsory grain purchases generated fear and confusion. As described in retrospect by a Chinese study, the government was ill prepared to set up a realistic system for the unified procurement of grain based on estimates of individual production. It set guideline quotas subject to negotiation, but peasants were unsure how much grain the government actually intended to procure. Many feared that the more they produced, the more they would be duty-bound to sell. In 1954, when natural disasters caused crop failures, the government took 7 billion catties beyond what would have been realistic adjustments, thus, drastically shrinking peasant reserves. The study acknowledges that anxiety over grain procurement stirred unrest in the rural areas.[7] However, with the establishment of the procurement system, the state was able to force rural people to foot its industrial bills.

The state-planned grain procurement system was economically devastating for those rural peasants who traditionally were not grain farmers. Helen Siu's research in the Pearl River delta confirmed our research in Hunan, Hubei, Hebei, Shandong, and Fujian provinces that the grain command quota hurt farmers who had historically relied on grain imports because of highly valued local production of cash crops. Farmers called them *yidaoqie zhengci* (policies of one knife cutting all). Fruit farmers in Shandong, Guangdong, and Fujian provinces had to cut down fruit trees that yielded higher returns in order to meet the state grain quota. Despite rural resistance at many local levels, both the central and the provincial governments continued the rigid and inflexible policies. For example, Tao Zhu, the party secretary in charge of Guangdong province, continued to demand that Guangzhou not only be self-sufficient in grain but that it must also reserve a portion of its grain for national allocation, as described by Helen Siu:

> In the meeting of the People's Political Consultative Committee held in November 1956, a speaker pointed out that collectives had overstressed grain production at the expense of other activities. Meijiang's citrus crop was estimated to have dropped 10 percent. Grain yields did rise, but peasant income did not. Moreover, cadres restricted the subsidiary activities for fear that work on grain would suffer. For example, in the neighboring district of Shuangshui, the 348 households of a collective raised only 137 pigs in 1954; the number dropped further to 126 in 1955, and 74 in 1956. Private plots where peasants grew vegetables for their own consumption were also abolished. The speaker expressed his worries that if all peasant households had to buy their vegetables, they would not be able to make ends meet; indeed 270 households in the collective had to borrow from the village credit cooperative. As it was, the problems were many. Members of the collectives were punished if they did not fulfill their quotas. Cadres who organized the work would not allow any time for rest and expected their orders to be followed exactly. Women complained that they lacked the time even to do washing and cooking. The men protested that the collectives were equivalent to forced labor [camps].[8]

Worse, the state banned farmers from engaging in animal husbandry, such as raising pigs, chickens, ducks, and cows for commercial purposes. In the early 1980s, G. B. Talovich interviewed a Fujian tea farmer, Mr. Wei, who recounts the blind command of local officials:

> We were told that tea is decadent and capitalistic. We were ordered to tear out all the tea trees and plant grain. Our family has farmed those hills for generation after generation. We know the soil, we know the climate, and we know that grain cannot grow there. We were ordered to build a dam. We didn't know how, so we asked the cadres. They said, "Ask an old farmer." We had no choice, so a couple old farmers got together and planned a dam, even though they had never seen one, either. We toiled and toiled. Since we were producing no crops, we had little to eat. Finally, our dam was finished. As soon as we let the water flow, it washed away the dam. We asked the cadres what to do. They said, "Grow tea." But we couldn't harvest tea for several years. For three years, we had nothing to eat. Many of my relatives starved.[9]

The state's control of farmers was not limited to agricultural production. In its effort to eliminate small and private businesses, the state reduced employment in rural industry (mostly family handicrafts), sidelines, and services (such as private shops and medical practices), leading to a rapid decline of market towns in the countryside.[10] The state's ownership of all resources and control over the market subjected farmers to the mercy of the state planning system. Through the *jiandaocha* (scissors pricing: high prices for industrial goods and low prices for agricultural goods) the state extorted surplus agricultural value from farmers for industrial development. Through the procurement system and scissors pricing, the state extracted 800 billion Yuan from farmers between 1953 and 1978.[11] According to the State Statistics Bureau (which tends to underreport state extortion), during the commune period of 1958 to 1978, the average annual contribution to urban industrialization reached 21 billion Yuan.[12] The state forced farmers to pay their taxes in grain, rather than cash. Farmers with insufficient grain had to buy grain at a premium (non-subsidized) price to meet the government's demand. This hidden side effect of the grain tax contributed to the already rampant rural poverty.[13] In addition, rural people were conscripted to work on government projects like mines, roads, water conservation, forest work, and other public projects with no compensation. Farmers had to work through the winter. Before Mao, farmers regarded the winter season as *xianji* (slack seasons). Mao forced them to "donate" their labor to public work activities such as military projects, roads, and reservoirs. Throughout the country (both in the countryside and the cities), millions of farmers and their families dug countless *fangkongdong* (massive military cave sites) by hand, without benefit of machines, in the 1970s. Farmers living close to military bases in the mountains suffered most because the state wanted to store military equipment deep in the mountains. All of this free labor saved the state up to 500,000 million Yuan. [14]

We may readily assume that no previous Chinese regime had ever been so successful in extracting goods and materials from the farmers or in undermining such a huge amount of potential labor production in rural areas.

Collectivization and State Industrialization

While land reform and class labeling consolidated political control in rural China, the procurement system gave the state complete control over grain marketing. All three policies together paved the way for collectivization. Chen Yun, a Communist economist in the early 1950s, clearly stated the relationship between collectivization and the state-planned economy: "There were three ways to increase rural production: cultivate waste land, water conservation facilities, and collectivization....According to past experience, collectivization could increase average production 15% to 30%."[15] Mao shared Chen's view and linked rural collectivization to China's socialist planned industrial development.[16] In his speech on rural collectivization, Mao discussed his reason for believing that China's socialist industrialization could not develop independently of rural collectivization:

> In order to accumulate large capital for state industrialization and rural technological innovation, a major part of such accumulation must come from rural accumulation. Apart from agricultural taxes, it is important to develop light industrial products to meet the demand of farmers. Light industrial products can be used to exchange grain and raw materials for light industries. This development provides capital for the state while at the same time developing light industry. Large scale light industrial development depends not only on the development of heavy industry but also agricultural development. But large scale light industrial development cannot depend on a base of small farmers but on large scale agricultural development. In our country, such large scale development is socialist collectivization of agriculture.[17]

This passage shows that Mao consciously planned the collectivization to meet his socialist industrial plan.

Collectivization also helped the state to overcome its organization problems. As Chen Yun stated, "facing so many individual rural households, we met with difficulties in grain procurement and marketing....It is difficult to assess productivity and to detail surplus and debt. Thus it is important to positively develop rural production cooperatives so that 110 million rural households can become rural cooperatives. At that moment, our procurement work will be easy and rational."[18] Wu Li, a China scholar, argued that one of the most important reasons for the state to establish both rural cooperatives and people's communes was to increase government control over farmers.[19] By cutting the ties of private economic interests and silencing the voices of intellectuals through repeated political campaigns, the state killed "the flexibility of local structures; at the same time the villages witnessed the creation of a stratum of activists whose function was to assist the party-state in managing rural society according to its priorities."[20]

State Control Magnets: *Hukou* and *Liangpiao*

Facing such state exploitation, many rural people tried to leave their land. But through *hukou* (household registration certificates) and *liangpiao* (ration coupons) control magnets, fully 80 percent of the Chinese population became virtual slaves.[21] Imprisoned by the inability to leave their place of birth and change their designated status as commune members; by the state's scissor pricing procurement system, which forced farmers to sell their products below-market prices and buy manufactured products at artificially elevated prices; by the state's anti-rural policies, under which, for example, the state provided next to no social welfare, such as health care and education; by banning rural-urban migration; and by the state's outlawing of markets, once poor but independent Chinese farmers were transformed into destitute communist slaves.[22]

To illustrate the paucity of social welfare under this system, education counted for less than 2 percent of the government's total budget: of this 2 percent, more than 90 percent went to the cities.[23] Thus, just 0.2 percent of the government's budget was channeled to rural areas, where at that time more than 80 percent of the population lived. This was the substance of the party-state's much vaunted egalitarianism as it affected the education of the children of more than 80 percent of the population.

The consequences of this strict control are vividly described in Daniel Kelliher's *Peasant Power in China*. China's collective system locked rural people into an identity as peasants, and this became the first and last fact of their social existence. They lived a life of enforced separateness. Rural people were effectively tied to the land, with the army (mainly for men) and marriage (mainly for women) offering the only possible opportunities for escape. They were barred by law from residing in the cities by a system of household registration (*hukou*) that severely restricted internal migration (and continued to do so through the 1980s). In effect, state socialism in China created a structure in which ascribed status was personal destiny, under the guise of a "modern" social system. People were born into peasant status and most were bound to die with it.[24]

Structurally, the commune system tied rural people to the land but prevented them from owning it, thus binding them to local commune leaders but depriving them of the power to make production decisions. In many poor regions, rural people lost even the right to beg or had to gain permission to beg.

This kind of backward feudal arrangement hurt both the economy and personal liberty. As one articulate rural resident informed Helen Siu in 1982:

> Collective ownership means that the collective "owns" us peasants as well as the resources we work with. The cadres who control the collective often do whatever they please with our lives. They behave no differently than the local bullies we heard so much about in the "recall bitterness" accounts of our fathers. However, the strong men of the 1930s and 1940s had no legitimate claim on the [farmers] peasants, who regarded them as excesses of traditional society. The cadres, on the other hand, enjoy total authority given by the socialist system. Chairman Mao once said that the scriptures were good, except that from time to time they had been recited by monks with crooked mouths. I wonder about these scriptures; it seems that they have distorted the mouths instead.[25]

The commune system of control retarded economic development by denying free movement of labor and deprivation of private property rights, leading to de-urbanization. For example, in North Zhejiang province, the rural population dropped from 80-95 percent to 40-50 percent of the total population between 1860 and 1920 due to rapid commercial and industrial development in nearby Shanghai. This free flow of labor was one of the main factors that allowed Shanghai to become a commercial and industrial city of 4 million by 1949. The commune system, however, halted this natural rural/urban flow for almost thirty years (1953-80), using the *hukou* system to ban rural to urban migration. As a result, Chinese farmers became the state peasants, "bound legally and substantively to the land,"[26]

Political Campaigns

To ensure that there was no opposition to these anti-rural policies, the government launched several political campaigns to make people toe the party line.[27] The 1950s repressing counter-revolutionaries movement, the Anti-Rightist Campaign, the Great Leap Forward, the people's communes, the Socialist Education campaign, and the Cultural Revolution eliminated any open dissent and opposition.

In the countryside, the political campaigns were linked to mass movements to eliminate rats, mosquitoes, flies, and sparrows. Under the leadership of Mao, the state set up agricultural development guidelines that included the elimination of these four harmful pests. Those mass movements created an environment of fear, making noncompliance difficult or impossible. Mr. Wang Wenhua, a farmer in Tongxin village in Jingshan, Hubei, recalled the campaign: "If not even the mosquitoes could have peace, how could we ordinary people do anything to resist the government's harmful policies?"[28] This life was described well by R.J. Rummel:

> The peasant was now the property of the commune, to labor like factory workers in teams and brigades at whatever was commanded, to eat in common mess halls, and often to sleep together in barracks. Family life and traditions, personal property and privacy, personal initiative and individual freedom, were destroyed or lost in an instant for around one-seventh of all mankind.[29]

Daniel Kelliher explained the relationship between the regime's total control of rural people and their resulting opposition to the state:

> In China, the structure of state socialism itself gave peasants cohesion. This was never the state's intention, of course. The collective structure had the primary effect of giving the People's Republic the ability to reach directly and immediately into the lowest level of society anywhere in the vast countryside—*an intrusive power possessed by no other state in Chinese history.* Yet the quiet, almost unnoticed, consequence of this structure was to lock peasants into a sameness of circumstances that could produce *unconsciously* uniform peasant action on an enormous scale.[30]

When the government started collectivization in 1956, rural people lost their autonomy and, with it, their incentive to work hard. Most rural resistance came in the form of these newly-created peasants dragging their feet while at work. Such resistance further lowered the rural standard of living (*per capita* food consumption declined below the 1957 level) in addition to the blow it had already taken in the name of industrialization. According to data collected by the State Council's Development Research Center, *per capita* productivity in the countryside in 1978 was below the 1957 level, the year before the Great Leap Forward. The same data shows that in 1978 some 20 percent of the rural Chinese population (100 million) suffered from hunger.[31] Government control became even more unbearable when the state failed to provide relief to rural peasants during the famine in which at least 30 million citizens died of starvation. Even former vice premier Tian Jiyun later acknowledged (in 2004) that under the commune system, the peasants were in fact slaves.[32] Common peasants' feeling of disgust for their status led to a unified response in the "leave me alone" movement known as *Baochan daohu* (contracting production to the household). Rural people had a spontaneously expressed a common interest in getting the government "off their backs." Formal leadership was not required.

The Great Leap Forward Famine:
The Straw that Broke the Communes' Back

In order to build a communist society, Mao and his associates, including Liu Shaoqi and Deng Xiaoping, launched the Great Leap Forward movement in 1958 in which private plots and farm animals were eliminated. To ensure that all rural women were involved in this great communist revolution, commune nurseries, great mess halls (*gonggong shitang*), and tailor shops were set up in August 1958. A month after the commune experiment in Xushui, Hebei, in September 1958, the commune system became a social reality in China, as 70 percent to 90 percent of China's rural population dined at 265,000 great mess halls.[33]

The commune system facilitated the state's extraction of grain and raw materials from rural territories and shipping of them to urban areas with little reinvestment in the rural areas, leading to the massive famine across China that soon followed. With one vast and awesome gust, the winds of communist change confiscated all private property, including land, houses, grain, labor, farm animals, and farm tools, as well as household items such as cooking utensils. Some farmers in Fengyuan were so afraid of such drastic change that they wore one set of clothes on top of another, fearing that spare clothing would be com-munized.[34] In Xushui, Hebei Province, everything except a pair of chopsticks and a rice bowl were labeled as public property.[35]

All major decisions were dictated from the central government in Beijing. Local officials were promoted based on their loyalty to Beijing rather than on responsible actions reflecting the interests of the local people. Cadres boasted of their production targets, causing the state to take taxes based on inflated figures, leaving the rural people little with which to survive.

This was especially true in Sichuan province, where on September 1, 1960, the provincial government suddenly cancelled existing grain coupons and printed a new grain coupon, depriving millions of people of their savings overnight. According to Ding Shu, Dong Fu, and Tian Jiaying, the Party Secretary Li Jingquan used this inhuman means to squeeze grain savings from the peasants, making Sichuan one of the provinces hit worst by the famine.[36] Ms. Cao Nan (pseudonym) in Chongqing recalled:

> The government did not issue any notice before the new *liangpiao* (grain coupon) was issued. I saved 50 *jin* (25 kilograms) in *liangpiao* in order to help my mother who lived in the countryside. My entire year of savings was gone overnight. I dared not complain, but my family cried for days. Many people in my mother's village died in the 1960 famine. We Sichuan people hated Li very much. This is why during the early part of the Cultural Revolution (CR) Li and members of his family were physically attacked and hurt. No one felt any sympathy for him. When I later learned that most of his family died during the CR, I hoped that he had experienced the same pain as millions of Sichuan people who lost their loved ones.[37]

Interviews with five Chengdu people revealed their still-vivid memories of days during the famine. Some were angry with Mr. Li and with Deng Xiaoping for protecting him. All spoke pitilessly of Li's family tragedy (Li's son was murdered and his wife committed suicide), using words like *shangdi you yan* ("the Gods must have eyes") suggesting that he deserved what befell him.[38]

In 1989, using then newly-released secret party documents (under Zhao Ziyang's leadership), Feng Xianzhi discovered that in the spring of 1959, the central government sent Tian Jiaying (then Mao's secretary) to investigate rural Sichuan. Tian had a heated argument with the leading provincial leader, Li Jingquan, who exaggerated rural productivity achieved by "deep planting" methods. Wherever Tian went, the county and commune officials insisted on Mao's idea of "deep planting" rather than trying household production.[39] To prove their claims, these provincial leaders submitted exaggerated figures by eliminating the *liaopiao*, canceling grain rationing, and forcing people in some cities to use pig feed in urban people's food rations, deepening the already huge crippling effect of the Great Leap Forward. Li's promotion to the political bureau was tainted by the vast suffering caused by his grain rationing system: the hunger of twelve million Sichuan people, millions suffering illnesses brought on by malnutrition, and the death of several hundred thousand people.[40] In response, Li stated, "China is so huge. Every dynasty has had famines resulting in the death of people,"[41] proving Li, like Mao, cared little for human life.[42]

Instead of punishing leaders like him, the central government promoted Li Jingquan to the political bureau, one of the only two appointed provincial leaders. This promotion informed party officials that promotion depended on loyalty to Mao and to centrally planned socialism rather than the livelihood of their people. Critics of this practice expressing concern for such neglect, such as Peng Dehuai, Tien Jiaying, and Li Rui, were labeled as rightists and silenced during the 1959 Lushan Conference. The attack against dissent and the protection of subordinates like Li signaled to the officials that it was critical to send reports reflecting what Mao wanted to hear, regardless of the reality on the ground. In doing so, Mao fostered a system of intimidation for government officials along with that of the rural peasants.

In a 2008 book, *Tombstone*, a thirty-year veteran journalist, Jisheng Yang, put the Great Leap Famine death figure at 36 million, after spending more than a decade conducting meticulous research and extensive interviews with more than one hundred surviving witnesses and academics across China. Yang stated that the more a region carried out the People's Commune and the Great Leap policies, the greater the death toll. In Xingyang, Henan province, the model of the People's Commune, for example, one million persons died of starvation. Yang was able to gain government archival materials due to his status as a Xinhua journalist. Famine deaths could have been reduced if the government had faced the truth and imported grain. Despite the enormous death rate, during the four famine years (1958-61), the Chinese state exported grain in order to buy machines. The state exported 6,800,000 tons of grain between 1959 and 1960 and bought large gold reserves, resulting in a death toll of more than 35 million throughout the country.[43] The government refused to use the grain reserve to save life because to do so would undermine the Great Leap's purposes.

Yang's investigation showed that people resorted to cannibalism (human flesh from corpses on the street or even relatives) when hunger drove them to eat anything they could get their hands on: Guangying mud, tree bark, roots, wildflowers, and bird droppings.[44] As farmers witnessed corpses everywhere—in ditches, by roads, in farmlands—their trust in the commune system evaporated. Thus, the famine later played a key role in decollectivization. In Xiaogang village (population four hundred), Anhui province, the Great Leap Famine led to the deaths of sixty-seven villagers, including six entire families between 1960 and 1962.[45] During this period, when the country was devastated by protracted famine and international isolation, many Xiaogang villagers were forced to beg to survive.

According to one estimate, 40 percent of rural Anhui practiced some form of *baochan daohu* during the famine. One Anhui local official summarized rural residents' grassroots reform as, "It doesn't matter if a cat is black or white, as long as it catches mice it is a good cat."[46] When Deng quoted this saying at a closed top party meeting in 1962, he was attacked for "taking the capitalist road." Later on, this pithy idiom became famous as a Deng *bon mot*.[47]

The state imposed a national steel production quota, forcing more than 90 million peasants to participate, leaving their crops to rot in the fields due to lack of labor. According to a new report from Chinese scholars, 36 million died of starvation, 40 million babies were not born due to famine (women could not conceive and starved people did not make love). This was the twice number of Chinese being killed during the World War II. In Sichuan alone, 8 million died of starvation. When one million people in Xingyang died of starvation, there was a 2.5 billion grain reservation in Henan province (where Xingyang was located) and a 1.3 billion grain reservation in neighboring Hubei.[48] If the grain reserve had been used, none in Xingyang should have died. In 1959, China exported 4 million catties of grain overseas, enough to feed 20 million people for one year.[49]

When Liu Xiaoqi and Deng Xiaoping tried to relieve the famine by encouraging more liberal market practices in rural areas, Mao and his associates launched the Socialist Education Campaign, the Campaign of Agricultural Learning From Dazhai, the Four Clean-ups Movement, and finally the Cultural Revolution.

Peasants lacked the strength to work, and some collapsed in the fields and died. City government organizations and schools sent people to the villages by night to buy food, bartering clothes and furniture for it. In Shenyang the newspaper reported cannibalism. Desperate mothers strangled children who cried for food. Many reported that villagers were flocking into the cities in search of food; many villages were left empty, only the old people who were not strong enough to go into the cities being left behind. It was also said that peasants were digging underground pits to hide their food.[50]

In his book *Hungry Ghosts: Mao's Secret Famine*, Jasper Becker described how the famine led to cannibalism:

> All the time, the peasants were in fact starving—in the millions. In their dreadful state, the peasants sank to the lowest form of human survival—they resorted to cannibalism. They dug up the bodies of the recently dead. They hid the fact that family members had died: first, to continue to obtain an extra food ration from the party distributors; and second, to hide the fact that the deceased had been eaten. Then, finally, at the lowest level of an instinct for survival, adults began to kill and eat their own children, usually trading their living child for that of a neighbor's, so they would not have to literally murder and eat their own son or daughter. Children would beg their parents not to let them be eaten.[51]

The Chinese Communist power reached its peak during the Great Leap Forward period, when the state was in total control of labor allocation, wealth and welfare redistribution, production decisions, and all other key decisions in rural society. It was at this time that the Chinese state forced rural people to join in "non-compensation water infrastructure building" without providing machine equipment. Mao's slogan, "*ren di shengtian* (Man will conquer nature)" was the spirit that drove the nation to deforest mountains and build dams across China. By January 1958, more than 100,000 rural people had worked on those project sites, while by mid-1958, 60 million Chinese rural people were forced to participate in the backyard furnace industrial development.[52] Our investigation in rural Hubei (Jingshang county) and Hunan (Yueyang county and Jishou region) suggests that nearly half of the able labor force (age twenty to forty-five) was allocated to work unrelated to agricultural production.[53]

Elimination of private property was another feature of the commune movement imposed from above. The Chinese commune system demanded a process of *yida ergong* (large-scale first and public ownership second). Between 1955 and 1956, the state transferred farmers' land,[54] cattle, cash, and tools to the collectives so that the government could have total access to this limited wealth. In 1958, the Chinese Central Committee under Mao's leadership issued a directive to "Establish the People's Communes in the Countryside." Within less than a year, more than 90 percent of Chinese villages were transformed into communes. Between late August to early October, 16,824 agricultural co-ops became 1054 communes, involving 772,000,000 rural households, 99.85 percent of rural people.[55] The average size of the commune was about 6,746, but the largest one reached 40,000. The people's communes system confiscated all items of private property, private plots, and family sidelines, requiring everyone to join the great mess halls and abandoning family cooking. All such policies suggested that Mao and most of his associates were more interested in carrying out socialist plans, according to Stalin and Marx, than they were in the lives of Chinese people.

Old farmers complained about the forced confiscation of such private goods as cooking pots, spoons, and rice bowls—even houses. One local cadre told rural people in Fengyang county, Anhui province: "What is yours? Only the teeth in your mouth."[56] In 1971, Grandma Pan in Tongxi village, Jingshang Country, Hubei told a group of young urban people in a political study session that she had to dig a hole in her bedroom to hide two cakes of soap, which she saved to give to her future daughter-in-law when her son got married.[57]

The Great Leap Famine was the bitter fruit of the Chinese Communist Party's attempt to eliminate the small-scale household production unit. Mao and his associates shared Lenin's the belief that "Petty production will inevitably lead to capitalism and capitalists."[58] Like Lenin, Mao regarded private ownership as the basis of feudalism, leading to capitalism. He remarked, "In the rural frontier, if socialism does not occupy, capitalism will occupy."[59] In another article published on October 11, 1955, Mao stated that China must "eliminate capitalism and also the petty production unit," illustrating Mao's planned adherence to radical communism prior to the Great Leap Forward.[60]

Farmers' Spontaneous and Leaderless Movements: *Baochan Daohu*

Since farmers could not openly organize as an opposition group under the communist regime, their actions were necessarily SULNAM (a spontaneous, unorganized, leaderless, non-ideological, and apolitical movement).[61] Throughout this book, we will shift to a shortened version of this idea that we will call "spontaneous and leaderless" or "unorganized and leaderless."

Like the situation of Hegel's slave, who can achieve his freedom through rebellion only after he realizes the full horror of his total dependence on the master, it is the horror of the totalitarian commune system and its consequences (the Great Leap Famine) that led peasants to rebel against the system by practicing *baochan daohu* (contracting production to the household). Once they achieved *baochan daohu*, its success spread to other areas of life officially banned by the state (freedom of movement, religion, occupational choice, free exchange, private enterprises).

The farmers' actions followed Jefferson's description of the background of the American Revolution. As he wrote in the Declaration of Independence:

Prudence, indeed will dictate that Governments long established should not be changed for light and transient causes; and accordingly all experience hath shewn that mankind are more disposed to suffer, while evils are sufferable than to right themselves by abolishing the forms to which they are accustomed. But when a long train of abuses and usurpations, pursuing invariably the same Object evinces a design to reduce them under absolute Despotism, it is their right, it is their duty, to throw off such Government, and to provide new Guards for their future security.—Such has been the patient sufferance of these Colonies; and such is now the necessity which constrains them to alter their former Systems of Government.[62]

Thus, Chinese farmers tolerated the abuse (confiscation of their land, depriving them market access, and migration) only for so long. The Great Leap Forward was the last straw, eliminating any remaining attachment they had to the regime. Unlike the American people in 1776, however, the Chinese rural people from the 1950s onward, due to the all-encompassing hand of the government, were unable to organize and had no way to arm themselves. There were, however, pockets of spontaneous, even massive, resistance in certain areas throughout the 1950s and early 1960s and even during the Cultural Revolution.

There was no single event propelling the people to rebellion against the commune system. Instead, there was a gradual process of decollectivization, beginning with the 1960 post-famine recovery, the death of Mao, and the arrest of the Gang of Four in 1976—and, by the next year, the power vacuum that had risen on account of the power struggle between the Deng Xiaoping and the Hua Guofeng factions. The natural inclination of rural people was to make use of any opportunity to escape from the commune system that oppressed them.

Given this situation, we also recognize the validity of the theories of scholars, such as Dali Yang, who contend that the Great Leap Forward famine, in which at least 30 million rural people died of starvation and malnourishment, created the mass dissatisfaction that bred the seeds of the grassroots rural reform of the late 1970s:

> By using multiple case studies and statistical tests, I suggest that the reforms may best be regarded as the outcome of interaction or struggle between state and peasants, mediated by local and regional leaders and fundamentally conditioned by the Great Leap Famine, which delegitimated collective institutions in rural China. In short, the reintroduction of household farming will be interpreted as the outcome of a historically grounded political struggle between the state and the peasant.[63]

During the last decade, several leading government officials and their children began writing about the Great Leap period. In *One of History's Whirlpools: Recollections of Xiao, Li and Liao Case,* Liao Bokang estimates the number of deaths to be between 30 and 40 million throughout the country. He cites data that show 10 million deaths in Sichuan province alone, nick-named "the heaven of rice,",which had rarely experienced famine before then.[64]

Former vice premier Tian Jiyun arrived at similar conclusions in 1988 after his investigations in rural China:

> Let us recall the "Three Difficult Years," when people died of starvation and suffered from famine related diseases. The total death toll reached dozens of millions, higher than the democratic revolution period, World War II, and the Chinese Civil War of 1945-1949. What caused this? Liu Shaoqi said it was "30% natural causes but 70% man made error." We know that it was basically a man-made disaster, composted of blind leadership, utopian socialism, and leftist opportunism.[65]

This view is consistent with our analytic thesis which links rural grassroots anti-commune reform to the famine and the commune system. Our historical basis explains why China's first-ever civil disobedience on a mass scale appeared in the countryside.

The primary issue of the leaderless mass decollectivization movement was control over harvests and labor allocation, as was the case with *baochan daohu*. The reason why we begin with *baochan daohu* is its SULNAM nature and its resulting success; it not only served as a catalyst for immediate developments, but also set the tone for how large numbers of Chinese people would proceed for the next three decades.

We do not contend that the advent of *baochan daohu* marked the beginning of one continuous, cohesive movement, but rather that it was the first of what would become many uncoordinated rights acquisition efforts occurring on a large enough scale to be considered a movement. As such, one of its lasting effects was that it reaffirmed the mindset in many people that they could make certain decisions regarding their existence better than the government. This would invariably be a sentiment that originated in rural rather than urban areas, because the rural citizens were systematically excluded from the benefits of the Chinese welfare state. As such, only they themselves could make decisions that were truly in their best interests, since the government was far more of an impediment than a facilitator in their quest to attain a better life.

Now that we have identified the importance of *baochan daohu*, we will provide a brief history of its development.

Resistance Before 1977

China's economic miracle of the reform era would have been impossible without the farmers' *baochan daohu* movement. This movement was a precursor of the market development and industrial takeoff that touched even the poorest regions of China.

It is important to point out that the leadership's support for the farmers' actions played a crucial role in institutionalizing the farmers' grassroots movement. Wan Li, Zhao Ziyang and later Deng Xiaoping supported the farmer-initiated *baochan daohu* movement in rural China, first through non-interference and later through open support. Realizing that farmers' independent control over their labor and production led to increased productivity and more grain for the state, those leaders came to support the farmers' initiative. Wan Li was the most crucial supporter of the movement, while Zhao was the second leader to stand on the side of people.

Baochan daohu, in fact, was a struggle between the state and farmers over the ownership of their labor and production.[66] They sought autonomy or, in essence, the end of their enslavement on collective land. They wanted to put an end to government directives telling them what to do with their lives.

The grassroots farmers' leaderless and unorganized movement for this autonomy began in 1957 when most rural areas in China suffered under the imposed collectives and the state procurement system brought about mainly by government policies.[67] Once farmers gained some production control, some refused to sell to the state at below-market prices. The demonstration effect was so beneficial to rural people that few wanted to remain in the collectives.

But the government under Mao then launched the political movements of the Great Leap Forward and the General Socialist Road and the People's Communes, smothering the farmers' initiatives. At the Party's Seven Thousand People's Meeting in 1962, Liu openly admitted that state policies shared 70 percent of the responsibility for the 1959 to 1961 famine, while natural disaster accounted for the other 30 percent.[68] Economists Wei Li and Dennis Tao Yang attributed 61 percent of the decline in output in 1960 to the policies of resource diversion and excessive procurement from the center.[69] We will never be sure how widespread the rural resistance was against the Chinese regime between 1961 to 1977. However, we can see the low productivity of the period, despite the increased use of fertilizer. A rural proverb circulated during that time in the rich planting regions of Hunan, Hubei, Sichuan, Anhui, Jiangxi, and Guangdong, it said: "*Chugong yitiao nong, ganghuo yitiao cong, shougong da congfeng,*" ([Commune members] line up to go to work like the body of a dragon, but work as slow as worms, charge off work like soldiers [so that they could work on their private plots]).[70] The slowing down of work revealed the farmers' resistance, though they also paid a price for the low productivity.

Faced with this threat to their survival, some farmers quietly began to resist, taking the initial form of *baochan daohu*. In 1960, farmers in the Fenghuang brigade of Zhongxin Commune, Qingyuan county in Guangdong began to divide the commune land among their households in order to avoid famine. Realizing that the farmers' innovation helped to reduce the famine, Zhao Ziyang, then the party secretary of Guangdong, allowed the farmers to practice "*lianchan chengbao*" (allocating production to household) to avoid the more provocative words of *baochan daohu* (contracting production to the household).[71] When he went to Zijing County and discovered that farmers refused to cultivate when private initiative was not allowed, Zhao said, "private work is work and it is better than doing nothing." [72] Thus, in early 1962, Zhao used his political non-action to support the farmers' private system of contracting. Under such pressure, the central government revised the radical commune plan and reduced the scale of the Great Leap Forward, allowing rural households to have between 3 percent to 7 percent of all land for *ziliudi* (private plots).[73]

Even during the Cultural Revolution, farmers continued their resistance against Mao's *Dazhai* commune system. Dali Yang's analysis shows that Mao could not achieve the big communes that he had dreamed of, despite the extreme measures he took to give them life. During the Cultural Revolution, localized resistance was able to maintain a less centralized "[production] team-based rural institutional set-up" in charge of distribution and accounting, and reduced the amount of resources extracted from the rural sector to serve urban needs.[74]

Even herdsmen in Inner Mongolia spontaneously started *liandi yijia* (the two contracts and one award system) in the early 1970s when Mao was still alive. This system of innovation gave herdsmen independent control over ten to fifteen cattle and sheep, a small but important step toward decollectivization. As one later remarked:

> If one searches the web for the words, *liandi yijia*, they are often linked to *baochan daohu, dabaogan* (contracting system in all) or *shengchan zirenzhi* (responsibility system). Due to the unique nature of animal husbandry, one household is often in charge of a herd (cattle, sheep and horses). Thus *liandi yijia*, the contracting production and labor and the award system, was in fact *baochan daohu*. It is difficult to imagine that as early as 1972 a Communist party directive contained this kind of individual based production method. [75]

Most party leaders took it for granted that people, especially the uneducated, rural masses, were ignorant. It was the duty of the Communists, they believed, to help ignorant farmers to understand their real self-interest, so they could unite to transform from a "class-in-itself to a class-for-itself,"[76] which is to say, to achieve solidarity through class-consciousness. Party members conceived of themselves as pioneers, representing the "real interests" of the people because the poor, rural uneducated were incapable of understanding their own best interest.

Farmers throughout China showed their preferences by working hard on their small private plots while shuffling their feet on collective land. Villagers made clear choices by their interest and labor. The green crops on the private plots contrasted sharply with the yellowish crops on the commune land, a contrast noticed by leaders like Zhao Ziyan, Wan Li, and Deng Xiaoping, who cared about productivity and later realized that those villagers' choices were rational.

In 1962, nearly 80 percent of rural households in Anhui adopted *baochan daohu*, while 70 percent of Sichuan, Gansu, and Zhejiang rural households adopted the same practice. More than 20 percent of rural regions also started to secretly adopt *baochan daohu*.[77] By October 1961, two-thirds of the counties of Guizhou province (which had been regarded as the showcase province for the Great Mess Hall) adopted *baochan daohu*. Within a few months, the famine-ravaged rural countryside regained so much energy that even many urban state workers wanted to return to farming.[78]

After leaving the collective communes, rural workers regained interest in working. Many rural people began to buy farm tools and equipment. In one commune in rural Sichuan, "farmers lined up to buy farm tools. In the commune shop, a thousand hoes were sold so fast one morning that the sales clerk had to go to the warehouse to get another 800 to meet the demand." Blacksmiths were busy making new tools and fixing old ones. Farmers preferred not to use the government's "new tools" and had their blacksmiths convert them to traditional ones. Although the government would wait until 1961 to announce the end of the Great Mess Hall, farmers knew its fate much sooner and were busy preparing a new life. Dong Fu, a Sichuan writer, found that in 1961, farmers in Pei County who practiced *baochan daohu* increased animal husbandry 320 percent, vegetable productivity 740 percent, and grain production 100 percent.[79] According to Deng's speech on July 7, 1961, more than 20 percent of rural people started all sorts of *baochan daohu*.[80]

After investigating in Sichuan, Mao's secretary, Tian Jiaying reported to Mao, "around 30% of rural areas farmers adopted the practice of *baochan daohu* and *fentian daohu* (contracting land to the household)." Tian suggested to Mao, "it is better for the state to take the lead than the spontaneous movement of farmers. If results prove positive, *baochan daohu* and *fentian daohu* can comprise 40% while collective and half-collective occupy 60%. When production reaches the normal level, we can lead them back to a collective economy." Mao did not utter a word until Tian finished, and then his first question was "Do you advocate collective or private ownership?" Tian did not know how to reply. [81]

Mao was concerned about the reemergence of capitalist tendencies both in the countryside and in the city, and regarded those 30 percent of rural households as signs of retreating to old China. In February 1964, Mao informed the visiting North Korean leader Kim Il-sung that, in China, "there are about 10 million bad people doing 'underground work.' Out of 650 million Chinese, such bad people have the ratio one of every 65 people."[82] Mao used all his political capital to contain rural resistance by launching the socialist education campaign in 1963, the Campaign of Learning from Lei Feng, the Four Clean-ups Campaign in 1964, in Agriculture Learn from Dazai in 1964, and the Cultural Revolution in 1966.[83]

Facing farmers' resistance, Deng Xiaoping reacted differently and stated his now well-known *bon mot* about the color of cats, "whether they are yellow cats or black cats, whatever catches mice is a good cat....I support further research on the problems of *fentian* (contracting land) or *baochan daohu*. If you say they are bad, you must give them a reply. We must do a thorough investigation of *fentian daohu*. The masses have demanded them and must have reasons for doing so. Do not negate them all at once. Do not assume a negative attitude before investigating the case. At this transition period [correcting the mistakes of the Great Leap Famine period], we must adopt many different kinds of methods of doing things. Right now it is time to retreat. Only through retreat can we make progress. In short, we must seek truth from facts and not follow the same pattern." [84] Deng and Liu Shaoqi felt guilty when they realized that their policies led to the massive famine. Their more pragmatic approach brought confrontation with Mao and his associates.

The party-state practice of deifying Mao meant that any systematic reform had to fit Mao's vision. Very quickly, Mao took control by setting up the twenty-three party guidelines, making the main target of the Four Clean-ups Campaign those local leaders who went along with mass movements of private economic initiatives (local markets and black market trading). Facing local resistance, the central and local governments sent more than 135,215 work teams to rural communes to carry out the four clean-ups from 1963 to May 1965. Some 171,620 local party organizations were transformed. Another 5,760 organizations were labeled "anti-party" and "anti-socialist." About 275,000 people were labeled "enemies of the state," while another 558,220 were determined to be close to the enemies of the state. The difference between their ideological crimes was the equivalent of the difference between felonies and misdemeanors. Another 5,032,750 people were criticized, corrected, and carried out public self-criticism. In the cities, 4,128 people were persecuted to death, while in the countryside 73,432 died of persecution.[85] However, although Mao was able to use those political campaigns and persecutions to weaken the *baochan daohu* movement in the countryside, he was never able to bring the People's Communes back to the glory days of 1958. Collectivization in most rural areas remained at the small team level.

Even during the high tide of the Cultural Revolution, a few rural people participated in black market activities. The state was so alarmed that in many places a special government bureau called *Daji touji daoba bangongshi* (The Office of Attacking Trading Opportunists) was established to curtail private trading of grain, grain coupons, raw building materials, cotton, lumber, water buffalo, fertilizer, and other agricultural items. In some parts of Shaoxin, Zhejiang province, people openly engaged in black market trading despite government attacks.[86]

The *Baochan Daohu* Movement in the Late 1970s

After Mao's death, the largely unofficial grassroots-liberalization movement created the foundation for officials like Zhao Ziyang, Wan Li, and Deng Xiaoping to support liberal practices in the late 1970s. "Instead of meekly submitting, however," remarked Dali Yang, "peasants took advantage of the more liberal environment to fight, often literally, for their own interests…"[87] The fact that Sichuan and Anhui, two provinces with high famine death rates, became the pioneers of the grassroots movements for agricultural reform shows the influence of history on people's enthusiasm for rural reform. The famine experience created "incentives for de-collectivization, which became a reality when the Chinese leadership jockeyed for power following Mao's death."[88] Since many farmers, especially those in famine affected regions, experienced the fruits of *baochan daohu*, they came to the forefront of those advancing the movement.

Elsewhere we have written that farmers risked their lives to make deals with local government officials, secretly contracting production to households (*baochan daohu*).[89] The only documented secret deal making took place in Xiaogan Village of Anhui province. Twenty years of collective farming had devastated the village. Before collectivization, in 1953, there were 175 people and 34 households. The Great Leap Famine reduced the population to 39 people and 10 households. Some 76 people left the village and 60 others died of starvation. In 6 households of the village everyone had died, which is called *juehu* (family line ended by famine, the worst fate according to Chinese family ethics). [90]

On December 18, 1978, heads of 18 households held a secret meeting to attempt contracting production to households. All 517 mu of land was contracted to the 18 households. Ten water buffalo were contracted for the households, with two households sharing one animal. Each household promised to submit the state grain quota and sideline production quotas (vegetable oil seeds, soybeans, and others) and to provide the commune and the brigade leaders monetary compensation and grain (this was crucial for the success of the deals). After this submission, the households were able to keep the rest for themselves. Their method was called *manshang bu manxia* (deceive the leaders at the top but be open with the villagers). The Deputy Leader Yen remarked, "if you agree with my condition, I will agree to do this. First, you must meet the state grain quota and that of the collective for both the summer and fall harvest [there are two harvests for both seasons]. No one should try to avoid this. Second, we will pretend that we work for the small team but in fact the household will be the production unit. We will be conducting *manshang bu manxia*. Do not tell this to the leaders at the top or to any outsiders. Whoever informs on us will be the enemy of the whole village." At this moment, a village elder commented: "I think we should add one more condition. If the team leaders are put into prison because of *baochan daohu*, we should carry his family's farm work and raise their children until they are 18."[91] All swore to obey the three rules by signing the pledge, using their thumbs.

At night they decided on land, farm tool, and farm animal allocations by lot. The next morning, all were fit to work as house units, thus creating autonomous individual farmers.[92] The combination of the corruptibility of local village leaders and the unorganized farmers' secret deal making allowed numerous farmers to breach the collective dike. If the cadres had not been corruptible and if the farmers had organized (making themselves vulnerable to the seizure of leaders), the farmers could not have succeeded. To some extent, the poorer the area, the easier it was for farmers to make deals like the Xiaogang Village, for the village heads were more susceptible to the farmers' offerings. A year after the changes to household production were made (1978 to 1979), the overall grain output in Xiaogang Village shot up from 15 to 90 tons, and average household incomes increased from 18 to 400 Yuan a year. "For the first time in decades we were able to feed ourselves, have warm clothes and even manage to have some surplus grain," Yan Junchang, ring leader for *baochan daohu* in the village, told a *South China Morning Post* reporter in 2008.[93] Within one year, the farmers had a harvest and submitted the state grain quota. The demonstration effect of Xiaogang's de-collectivization spread like wildfire across China. [94] As one Anhui farmer saying goes: *"Baochan daohu* is like a chicken pest. When one family's chicken catches the disease, the whole village catches it. When one village has it, the whole county will be infected." [95] When this illegal practice spread throughout the country, agricultural productivity increased.

Baochan daohu was essentially a movement of independence and autonomy from the state. Local innovations in Guangdong, Inner Mongolia, Sichuan, and other places led Zhao Ziyang to realize that the rural masses (*minzong*) were wiser than the government officials when dealing with agricultural production. Farmers always knew that their decisions were superior to those of central planners when it came to agricultural production. A Hubei farmer remarked, "rice does not grow out of the heads of cadres but out of our blood and sweat. Why have they [government officials] tried all means to make it harder for us to make a living?" [96]

Baochan daohu was developed first by Sichuan farmers in Guanhan County. In 1975, farmers in some localities in Guanghan divided the existing production into small groups (about six to ten households per group). Each group was responsible for supplying a required quota to the state and the collective and, in turn, group members would be allowed to keep the rest of the harvest. Given the fact that relatives often lived close together, farmers were able to form groups along kinship lines. This was an illegal action because it departed radically from the commune system, which focused on *yida ergong* (first, big commune; second, public ownership). [97]

Baochan daohu increased farmers' work incentives and productivity. In 1978, seeing the success of Guanghan farmers, Zhao Ziyang began supporting the Guanghan practice. The twelve guidelines of the Sichuan government in 1978 established *baochan daohu* and *ding daowu* (contracting for the crop production), which formally institutionalized farmers' local initiatives in some parts of Sichuan. Productivity soared: in 1976, per mu productivity increased from 473 jin per mu to 637 jin. The per capita annual grain harvest increased from 369 jin to 522. [98] The majority of rural people in Sichuan began to have sufficient food. On June 26, 1978, facing the "illegal" spread of the private raising of rabbits, chickens, ducks, geese, and water buffalo, the Sichuan provincial government issued a directive banning "*tu zhengci*," (local policies) of "limiting, beating, poisoning, and fining farmers who practiced private animal husbandry in Sichuan." [99] Support from provincial leaders like Zhao Ziyang was important for the grassroots movement to gain momentum.

At the same time, in an effort to gain more control over subsistence, Anhui farmers began making deals with their local party bosses to be allowed to farm on their own. As this practice spread throughout the country, agricultural productivity increased dramatically, leading to eventual central government acquiescence to this grassroots-initiated policy. [100] As a result, resources (primarily labor, but also capital in the form of farmers' savings) were released from agriculture, stimulating commercial activities and trade (both long-distance and local). [101] To appreciate the significance of this occurrence, one must remember that the farmers' actions were self-motivated and took place well before the now famous government-initiated reform.[102] This became a trend that would continue throughout the reform era to the present day.

In other places in Shanxi, farmers secretly adopted *baochan daohu* at the same time. For example, farmers in Tienjiajie Village of Hongcha People's Commune, Shanxi Province, increased production when they started the household contract system.[103] Likewise in Zhejiang, farmers made deals with local government by leaving collective commune land to do petty trade.

The overall result was that farmers took advantage of the power vacuum left by Mao's death in 1976 to abandon collectivization and to reestablish family-centered production units. It was the farmers themselves, not action by the state, who achieved de facto liberation from total state control. Our finding that Chinese peasants illegally abandoned the commune for the reestablishment of de facto family farming is confirmed by several scholars, such as Feng Xinyuan and Zhou Xiaohong in Zhejiang and Jiangsu provinces. Thus, Zhou Xiaohong remarks: "[The success of] *baochan daohu* illustrates the fact that the road to liberty was paved by the farmers themselves. They themselves sought freedom. Through resistance, they themselves gradually won the struggle to throw off the chains of the People's Communes. This struggle lasted until the close of 1982 by which time most farmers became free men, which led inevitably to further liberties."[104]

Even a Chinese reform official, Bao Tong admitted that there was no reform agenda at the so called reform meeting of the Third Plenum of the Eighth Party Congress in 1978 in Beijing: "In fact, reform wasn't discussed at the Third Plenum. Reform wasn't listed on the agenda, nor was it mentioned in the work reports. No one passed a motion calling for it, and there was no investigation into a possible reform program."

At that time, Wan Li in Anhui was implementing his policy of "household responsibility" for farmland, while Zhao Ziyang was trying out his policy of "reforms to expand the self-determination of farmers and enterprises" in Sichuan. But they were local leaders at that time. The word "reform" wasn't even in the vocabulary of central government leaders. The fact cannot be concealed or changed that reforms weren't the theme of the Third Plenum.[105]

After submitting a quota to the collective, the farmers could reap the fruits of their hard work and productivity. Under the commune *gongfeng* (work points) system, rural people were denied wages except for grain allocation which was deducted from total annual work points. Since the state devalued the grain price, the real labor value was further reduced in this system of work points when the state delayed payment to the rural people until the next fiscal year. The new system allowed farmers to keep the fruits of their labor.

The formal recognition of the farmers' movement came in the 1982 reforms, which provided institutional support for the new system. Farmers' lives improved rapidly with rural households enjoying an 18.3 percent annual growth rate between 1979 and 1983. Increasing numbers of farm households began to possess durable goods like bikes, sewing machines, radios, and watches, all of which had previously been the exclusive privileges of urbanites.[106]

The party-state reacted to the grassroots farmers' innovation by gradually extending the term of the family contracting system, from one year to three years (1982) to fifteen years (1990s) and to thirty years in 2000. The farmers' movement started as secret and gained local government recognition and later the central government's approval. In 2002, the passage of the Land Contract Law formally legalized farmers' household responsibility, allowing farmers to gain land use rights. What is more, it promised the farmers that such practice will be allowed in perpetuity.[107] This official recognition firmly established the results of the farmers' movement.

Impact of *Baochan Daohu*

Economic incentives helped spread the *Baochan Daohu* movement from just 1 percent in 1979 to 14 percent in 1980; to 80 percent in 1982; and 98 percent in 1983.[108] No government teams were sent to supervise this grassroots movement, although government recognition in 1982 played a role in institutionalizing the practice. This outcome stood in marked contrast to the government-enforced Land Reform (1949-53), People's Communes (1958), and Socialist Education (1963-65) movements where millions of urban bureaucrats and educated elite were sent against their will to the countryside by state fiat.

Agricultural reform increased productivity and released farmers' energies: total grain production in 1978 was 30,477,000 tons but by 1984 had reached 407,310,000 tons. Cotton production in 1978 was 21,670,000 tons but in 1984 reached 162,580,000 tons, and cooking oil was 521,800,000 tons but reached 119,100,000 tons.[109] These figures show that the cash crops under little state control enjoyed the largest growth. These data unquestionably sent a strong signal to the top leadership that less control meant more production.

Since the close of the commune era, rural people have gained greater autonomy to determine their own economic activity and increased their production for the market and mobility. According to one UN report, between 1978 and 2007, rural poverty fell from 30.7 percent to just 1.6 percent.[110] Fan Jie *et al* also argue that the party-state's power is being eroded by the nature and effects of rural urbanization and industrialization. The dramatic growth of towns in the countryside and their role as commercial hubs has increasingly allowed them to serve as mediators for new technologies and innovations for the rural population as well as sources of non-agricultural employment.[111]

To a great extent, most Chinese reform started with private contracting with the government and gradually gained the private share of products and even means of production. As rural entrepreneurs later on moved to the cities, more non-state sectors increased. Such a grassroots privatization is the basis of the Chinese market economy.[112]

It is important to note that the limited liberty gained after the collapse of the commune system brought about a variety of social problems, including environmental pollution, land misuse, vice, crime, the resurgence of traditional forms of organization (such as clans and secret societies), localism, reliance on *guanxi*, and vast income disparities between the affluent and the poor.

The Chinese farmers' movement is an example of the phenomenon that Hayek described as "spontaneous order" generated unintentionally by individuals pursuing their self-interest.[113] The incentives to improve one's family life were the engine that drove farmers to abandon the commune yoke that constrained their life. The fact that de-collectivization led directly to a vast proliferation of markets, rural industries, and migration is discussed below. Farmers obtained independent decision-making in terms of crop diversity, new industries, market activities, and the power of allocation of rural laborers and capital. Farmers had no intention of overthrowing the government, but they did leech away the government's control over farming, markets, industries, migration, and even family reproduction. Without firing a shot, without raising any placards, without posting ideological statements on any wall, the farmers' de-collectivization movement spread like the wind across the nation, fundamentally altering the course of Chinese history in the twentieth century.

Notes

1.   Chen, Weixing (1998), "Economic Reform and Social Inequity in Rural China," in Zhang Jie and Li Xiaobing, ed. *Social Transition in China*, (University Press of America, 1998), p. 95.
2.   Chen Jianyuan, *Zhongguo shehui: yuanxing yu yanhua* (Chinese Society: Original Pattern and Transformation), (Shenyan: Niaoning renmin chuban she, 1988), 142.
3.   *Xinwen wubao,* China.com, "The New China's Oppression Campaign against Counter-reactionaries" (*xin zhongguo de "zhenfan" yundong: ge dixia dachujue renfan zhibiao),* 2006, 11/2.
4.   Bo Yibo, *Ruogan zhongda juece yu shijian de huigu* (A look back at various important policy decisions and events), 2 pt, (Beijing: Zhonggong zhongyang dangxiao chubanshe, 1991, 1993), p. 538.
5.   Li Yingsheng, "*Woguo chengxiang eryuan shehui gejiu de dongta kaocha*," *Zhongguo shehui kexue,* (China's Social Science) 2 (1993), p.113-126.
     http://www.sx.gov.cn/portal/main/sxsz_msg_list.jsp?catalog_id=20050411001896.
6.   Helen F. Siu, *Agents and Victims in South China: Accomplices in Rural Revolution*, (New Haven and London: Yale University Press, 1989), p. 150. Zhonggo Shaoxin (Shaoxin, China), "*Gongxiao xingzheng*" (History of Industrial and Commerce Administration), Vol. 3.
7.   Wang Genjin and Zhang Xuansan, *Woguo nongye xiandaihua yu jilei wenti yanjiu* (A Study on Agricultural Modernization and Capital Accumulation in China), (Tanyuan: Shanxi jingji chubashe, 1993), p. 93.
8.   Helen F. Siu, 1989, p. 150.
9.   G. B. Talovich posted the online book review of Jasper Becker, *Hungry Ghosts: Mao's Secret Famine*, (New York: Owl Books; Reprint edition (1998), 2002).

10. For a good discussion of Chinese rural markets before the People's Republic of China see John Winthrop Haeger, *Crisis and Prosperity in Sung China,* (Tucson, AZ: The University of Arizona Press, 1975); Dwight H. Perkins, *Agricultural Development in China: 1368-1968,* (Chicago: Aldine Publishing Company, 1969); Dwight H. Perkins, *China's Modern Economy in Historical Perspective,* (Stanford, CA.: Stanford University Press, 1975); Yoshinobu Shiba, *Commerce and Society in Sung China,* (Translated by Mark Elvin) (Michigan Abstracts of Chinese and Japanese Works on Chinese History, 1970); G. William Skinner, ed. *The City in Late Imperial China,* (Stanford, CA: Stanford University Press, 1977).

11. Wang Gengjin and Zhang Xuansan, *Woguo Nongye Xiandaihua yu Jilei Wenti Yanjiu,* (Study on Agricultural Modernization and Accumulation in Our Country), (Shanxi: *jingji chubanshe,* 1993), p. 93.

12. ZGTJNJ (State Statistical Bureau), *Zhongguo tongji nianjian* (Statistical yearbook), (Beijing: *zhongguo tongji chubanshe,* 1984).

13. Nicholas R. Lardy, "State Intervention and Peasant opportunities," in William Parish, ed., *Chinese Rural Development: The Great Transformation,* (Armonk, NY: M. E. Sharpe, 1985), pp. 33-56.

14. Research Office of Central Communist Document Center, *Chenyun nianpu,* (The Chronologies of Chen Yuan), vol.2, (Beijing: *zhongguo wenxian chubanshe,* 2000), p. 418.

15. Chen Yun. *Chen Yun wensuan (1949-1956)* [Selected writings of Chen Yun, (1949-1956)]. (Beijing: renmin chubanshe, 1984.) p. 23.

16. Mao Zedong, *jianguo yilai Mao Zedong wengao* (The Selected Works of Mao Zedong since the Foundation of the PRC), vol. 5, (Beijing: *zhongguo wenxian chubanshe,* 1991), p. 538.

17. Mao Zedong. *Mao Zedong wenji* (Selected Works of Mao Tsetung), vol. 6., (Beijing: renmin chubanshe, 1999), pp. 432-433.

18. Chen Yun, *Chen Yun wensuan (1949-1956)* [Selected writings of Chen Yun, (1949-1956)], (Beijing: *renmin chubanshe,* 1984), p. 276. David Bachman, *Bureaucracy, Economy, and leadership in China: The Institutional Origins of the Great Leap Forward,* (Cambridge: Cambridge University Press, 1991).

19. Wu Li, *guoyou buji de jiannan xuanzhe* (Excess Policies and Hard Choices for Reform), *Zhongguo jingjishi yanjiu* (Journal of Chinese Economic History), (2000), p. 2.

20. Helen Siu, 1989, p.166.

21. *Hukou,* which can be rendered as a household registration certificate, is the government's control tool to place and target people. For a good discussion on *hukou* see, Wang, 2005. *Liangpiao* (food coupons) were often used together with *hukou* to control rural-urban migration. See Zhou, 1996, Mark Selden and Chen.

22. See Zhou, 1996, Chapter 2.

23. Susan Shirk, *Competitive Comrades: Career Incentives and Student Strategies in China,* (University of California Press, 1982).

24. Daniel Kelliher, *Peasant Power in China: the Era of Rural Reform 1979-88* (New Haven: Yale University Press, 1992), p. 103.

25. Helen Siu, 1989. p. 291.

26. Chen, Weixing (1998), "Economic Reform and Social Inequity in Rural China," in Zhang and Li, *Social Transition in China,* p. 95.

27. Lynn White, *Policies of Chao,* (Princeton: Princeton University Press, 1989).

28. Personal interview with Wang Wenhua in Tongxin, Jingshan County, Hubei Province, summer, 2003. For a good description of the mass campaigns against the four harmful things in *Dongfu, maimiao qingcai huahuang—chuanxi dayujing jishi*

(Records of Actual Great Leap Forward Events in Western Sichuan).
http://www.360doc.com/showWeb/0/0/263510.aspx.

29. R.J. Rummel, *China's Bloody Century*, (New Brunswick, NJ: Transaction Publishers, 1991).

30. Kelliher, *Peasant Power in China,* (1992), p. 101. The emphasis is mine.

31. http://www.cass.net.cn/zhuanti/y_party/yd/yd_a/yd_a_016b.htm.

32. Tian Jiyun, "The Recalling of Chinese Rural Reform" (*Huigu zhongguo nongcun gaige licheng*), *Yanhuang Chunqiu* (The History of China), No. 6, 2004. Posted on line March 30, 2007, pp. 4-5.
http://www.ls11.com/Article/ShowArticle.asp?ArticleID=14449.

33. Gao Wangling, "The Peasants' Reactions in the Great Leap Forward," *Modern China Studies,* Vol. 13, No. 2, 2006, pp.106-117. p. 108. Dali Yang, *Calamity and Reform in China: State, Rural Society, and Institutional Change Since the Great Leap Famine,* (Stanford, CA: Stanford University Press, 1996). Li Debin, Lin Shunbao, Jin Bilhua, He Fengqin, and Jin Shiying, *Xinzhongguo noncun jingji jishi* (Major Events of New China's Rural Economy), 新中国农村经济纪事, pp.186. Bo Yibo, *Ruogan zhongda juece yu shijian de huigu* (A look back at various important policy decisions and events), 2pt. (Beijing: *Zhonggong zhongyang dangxiao chubanshe,* 1991, 1993), p. 749.

34. Gao Wangling, "The Peasants' Reactions in the Great Leap Forward," *Modern China Studies*, Vol. 13, No. 2, 2006, pp. 106-117. Note 27, p. 117.

35. The Xushui model of allowing only a pair of chopsticks and a rice bowl was used as an example to push the People's Commune. Gao Wangling, "The Peasants' Reactions in the Great Leap Forward," *Modern China Studies*, Vol. 13, No. 2, 2006, pp. 106-117.

36. Dong Fu, *maimiao qingcai huahuang—chuanxi dayujing jishi* (Records of Actual Great Leap Forward Events in Western Sichuan), http://www.360doc.com/showWeb/0/0/263510.aspx; Ding Shu, *Cong dayuejing dao dajihuang* (From Great Leap to Colossal Famine), http://www.dqjj.com/bbs/dispbbs.asp?boardID=17&ID=16292; Feng Xianzhi, *Mao Zedong he tade mishu Tian Jiaying* (Mao Zedong and His Secreatry, Tian Jiaying), (Beijing: *zhongyang dangxiao chubanshe*, 1989), p. 36.

37. Personal interview with Cao on July 6, 2006 in Chengdu.

38. Personal interview with five Chengdu famine victims on July 6, 2006 in Chengdu.

39. Feng Xianzhi, *Mao Zedong he tade mishu Tian Jiaying,* (Mao Zedong and His Secreatry, Tian Jiaying), (Beijing: *zhongyang dangxiao chubanshe*, 1989), pp. 31-37.

40. Dong Fu, *maimiao qingcai huahuang—chuanxi dayujing jishi* (Records of Actual Great Leap Forward Events in Western Sichuan), http://www.360doc.com/showWeb/0/0/263510.aspx; Feng Xianzhi, *Mao Zedong he tade mishu Tian Jiaying,* (Mao Zedong and His Secretary, Tian Jiaying), (Beijing: *zhongyang dangxiao chubanshe*, 1989), p. 36.

41. Ding Shu, *Cong dayuejing dao dajihuang* (From Great Leap to Colossal Famine), http://www.dqjj.com/bbs/dispbbs.asp?boardID=17&ID=16292.

42. Jung Chang and Jon Halliday. *Mao: The Unknown Story*. (New York: Knopf, 2005).

43. Ding Shu, *Cong dayuejing dao dajihuang* (From Great Leap to Colossal Famine), http://www.dqjj.com/bbs/dispbbs.asp?boardID=17&ID=16292.

44. Guanyin mud was believed to be left by the female Guanyin, the bodhisattva associated with compassion so that the hungry could eat to fill their stomach. Many became sick and died after eating too much mud.

45. Raymond Li, "Farmers who provided the spark in Beijing," Nov. 17, 2008, *SCMP*.

46. Ding, Xueliang, "The Tome You Must Read," *Financial Times*, (Chinese version), 09/28/08, http://www.ftchinese.com/story.php?storyid=001022231

47. Ding, Xueliang, "The Tome You Must Read," *Financial Times*, (Chinese version), 09/28/08, http://www.ftchinese.com/story.php?storyid=001022231.

48. Yang, 2008.

49. Hu Xingdou, "Dizhi maoxiejiao, fansirenhou jiaoxue" (Resist Mao Cult and Learn from Human Disaster), Chinese Studies blogger, http://www.huxingdou.com.cn

50. Laszlo Ladany, *The Communist Party of China and Marxism, 1921-1985: A Self-Portrait.* (Stanford: Hoover Institution Press, 1988).

51. Jasper Becker, *Hungry Ghosts: Mao's Secret Famine.* (New York: Owl Books, Reprint edition 1998).

52. Yang, 1996.

53. The author lived in Tongxi Village, Jingshang between 1968 and 1971 and since visited the village five times. The visits to Jishou and Yue Yang were conducted in 1981, 2002, and 2006.

54. This slogan was created by Mao. During the Great Leap Forward, no private plot or private ownership of animals was allowed. The collectivization left *ziliudi* (a tiny private plot) for farmers to grow vegetables for family consumption. For a good discussion on the coercion of collectivization see Mark Selden, "Cooperation and Conflict," in Mark Selden and Victor Lippit, eds., *The Transition to Socialism in China,* (Armonk, New York: M. E. Sharpe, 1982), pp. 32-97.

55. The Chronics of Anhui People's Government's Political Records. 安徽省人民政府政务纪略., http://61.191.16.234:8080/was40/detail?record=86&channelid=33995.

56. Gao Wangling, "The Peasants' Reactions in the Great Leap Forward," *Modern China Studies*, Vol. 13, No. 2, 2006, pp.106-117. p. 109.

57. The author was present and was shocked that several local rural people started to use the political study session to complain about how the commune winds (*gongchan feng*) in 1958 to 1959 were hurting the rural people. Such kind of open attack against the state's imposed Great Leap Famine was quite common throughout late 1960s and early 1970s when the educated youth were forced to go to the countryside. They had to listen to the *yikusitian* (remember the bitter past and appreciate the current good life) report from poor farmers.

58. Vladimir Lenin, *Lenin xuaji* (Selected Works), Vol. 4, (Beijing: *renmin chubanshe*, 1972), p. 181.

59. Mao Zedong, *jianguo yilai Mao Zedong wengao* (The Selected Works of Mao Zedong since the Foundation of the PRC), vol. 5, (Beijing: *zhongguo wenxian chubanshe*, 1991), p. 357.

60. The name of the article was "*nongye hezuohua de yichang bianlun he dangqian de jieji dongzheng*," ("Current Debate and Class Struggle Concerning Rural Co-operatives," Jiang in Jiang Jianfang,"*20 shiji liushi niandai baochan daohu yaozhe yuanyin zaitan*," (The Reason behind the Failure of *Baochan Daohu* in 1960s), zhongguo xiandai shi (*The Journal of Modern China*). 2006.12 http://economy.guoxue.com/article.php/11709.

61. Zhou, 1996.

62. Wills, Garry, *Inventing America: Jefferson's Declaration of Independence.* (Garden City, New York: Doubleday, 1978).

63. Dali Yang, *Calamity and Reform in China,* (1996), p. 7.

64. Liao Bokang, "*Lishi changhe li de yige xuanwo*," (One of Historical Whirlpools). 历史长河里的一个漩涡--回忆"萧李廖案件." http://www.ybbbs.com/bbs/dispbbs.asp?boardID=126&ID=215079&page=1.

65. Tian Jiyun, "The Recalling of Chinese Rural Reform," (*Huigu zhongguo nongcun gaige licheng*), *Yanhuang Chunqiu* (The History of China), No. 6, 2004. Posted on line March 30, 2007, pp.4-5, p. 4, http://www.ls11.com/Article/ShowArticle. asp?ArticleID=14449.

66. Hu Yaobang once remarked: "In terms of *baochan daohu*, Wan Li was no. 1; Zhao Ziyang was the second place; while Zhou Hui was the third." In Xiao Guocai, "*bufix pinyin*," (Do not fight against doing it but cannot write about it), *Xuexi yukan* (*Study Monthly*, No.1, Issue 233, 2005), p. 55.

67. David L. Shambaugh, *The Making of a Premier: Zhao Ziyang's Provincial Career*, (Boulder, CO: Westview, 1984). For an excellent discussion on the topic, Edward Friedman, Paul Pickowicz, and Mark Selden, *Chinese Village, Socialist State*, (New Haven: Yale University Press, 1991). Dali Yang, *Calamity and Reform in China: State, Rural Society, and Institutional Change since the Great Leap Famine*, (Stanford, CA: Stanford University Press, 1996).

68. Roderick MacFarquhar, *The Origins of the Cultural Revolution*, Vol. 3, (Columbia University Press, 1999), p. 3.

69. Wei Li and Dennis Tao Yang, "The Great Leap Forward: Anatomy of a Central Planning Disaster," *Journal of Political Economy*, Vol. 113 (2005), pp. 840-877.

70. The Chinese goes: 出工一条龙，干活一窝蜂，收工打冲锋.

71. Wei Zhao, "The Life of Zhao Ziyang," (1989), p. 112-113.

72. Wei Zhao, (1989), p. 116.

73. See Jianming Zhou, *Geren zai jingji zhong de quanli* (Individual Rights in the Economy), (Beijing: *renmin chubanshe* (People's Press), 1989), p. 151.

74. Dali Yang, (1996), p. 98.

75. An anonymous author on line, "Something about Comrade Zhao's Work in Inner Mongolia," Boxun.com, Feb. 14, 2005. www.boxun.com.

76. Karl Marx and Friedrich Engels, *Communist Manifesto*, (New York: Penguin Group, USA, 2002).

77. Huang Zheng, *Wang Guomei fangtanlu* (The Interview of Wang Guomei [Liu Shiaoqi's Wife]), (Beijing: *zhongyan wenxian chubanshe*, 2006).

78. Gao Hua, "*Dazaihuang yu siqing yundong de qiyuan*," (The Origin of the Great Leap and the Four-Clean ups Campaign), *Zhongguo dangshi yanjiu* (Studies of Chinese Communist Party's History), 09/03/83, http://www.usc.cuhk.edu.hk/wk_wzdetails. asp?=5.

79. Dong Fu, *maimiao qingcai huahuang—chuanxi dayujing jishi* (Records of Actual Great Leap Forward Events in Western Sichuan), http://www.360doc.com/show-Web/0/0/263510.aspx.

80. Ross Terrill, *Mao: A Biography*, (Stanford, CA: Standford University Press, 1999).

81. Yue Qingshan, Mao *Zedong lun baochan daohhu—Li Rui fei Mao* (Mao Zedong on *baochan daohhu*—Li's Critics of Mao), May 16, 2006, http://www.xncxnc. com/data/2006/0516/article_281.htm.

82. Feng Kaiwen, *Hezuo zhidun bianqian yu chuangxin yanjiu*, (Research on Transformation and Innovation of Cooperative System), (Beijing: Zhongguo nongye chubanshe, 2003).

83. Few studies on this period have been published in the West. John P. Burns, "The Election of Production Team Cadres in Rural China: 1958-74," *The China Quarterly*, No. 74 (Jun. 1978), pp. 273-296.

84. Ross Terrill, *Mao: A Biography*, (Stanford, CA: Stanford University Press, 1999).

85. Chinese Fanlan Alliance, (*zhongguo fannan lianmeng*, 中国泛蓝联盟), "Chapter 11, The Unprecedented Cultural Revolution Terror," in *Critique of Political Cult, zhengzhi xiejiao piban*, 政治邪教批判 (神本正义论.下卷) 第十一章 史无前例 的文革暴政, http://boxun.com/hero/2006/fanlan/86_2.shtml.

86. The father of one of the author's high school classmates was caught doing long-distant trade and was fired from his state job in Wuhan in 1969. See more on the rise of black market in the cultural revolution in Shaoxin, Zhonggo Shaoxin (Shaoxin, China), "*Gongxiao xingzheng*," (History of Industrial and Commerce Administration), Vol. 3. http://www.sx.gov.cn/portal/main/sxsz_msg_list. jsp?catalog_id=20050411001896.

87. Dali Yang, 1996.

88. Dali Yang, (1996), p. 252.

89. Zhou, 1996.

90. Southern China Weekend (*nanfang zhoumo* 南方周末) December 18, 1998, p. 18.

91. Yang Xun and Liu Jiarui, *The Road to Chinese Rural Reform (zhongguo nongcun de gaige daolu)*, (Beijing: Beijing University Press, 1987), pp. 12-13.

92. Liang Caiheng, "The Pulse of Farmers, Rural China and Rural Migrant Workers in 1978—2004 (*sannong dadongmai*)," http://www.people.com.cn/GB/news/37454/37461/3090357.html.

93. Raymond Li, "Farmers who provided the spark in Beijing," Nov 17, 2008, *SCMP*.

94. Zhang Guangyou, "*gaige fengyun zhong de wangle*" (Wang Li in Reform), (Beijing: *renmin chubanshe* (The People's Press), 1995), pp. 154.

95. The Chinese goes: "*Baochan daohu xiang jiwen, yihu wenle, jiu quancun wen; yicun wenle, jiu quanxian wen*," Kate Zhou, 1996.

96. Farmer Pan, in Tongxin Village, Hubei Province, interview took place on Feburary 5, 1986. This is common expression among many farmers.

97. The collectivization left *ziliudi* (a tiny private plot) for farmers to grow vegetables for family consumption. The total amount of *ziliudi* was only 3 percent to 7 percent of all the land. See Jianming Zhou, *Geren zai jingji zhong de quanli* (Individual Rights in the Economy) (Beijing: People's Press, 1989), p. 151. For a good discussion on the coercion of collectivization see Mark Selden, "Cooperation and Conflict," in Mark Selden and Victor Lippit, eds., *The Transition to Socialism in China*, (Armonk, NY: M. E. Sharpe, 1982). pp. 32-97.

98. Wei Zhao, "The Life of Zhao Ziyang," Zhong, p. 228.

99. Wei Zhao, "The Life of Zhao Ziyang," Zhong, p. 222.

100. Kate Zhou, *How the Farmers Changed China*, (Westview, 1996).

101. Kate Zhou, 1996.

102. Daniel Kelliher, *Peasant Power in China: the Era of Rural Reform 1979-88*, (New Haven: Yale University Press, 1992), p. 103.

103. Zhang Hongwei, *Mimi baochan daohu gei Tienjiajie cun de bianhua* (The Secret *baochan daohu* Brought Great Transformaton to Tienjiajie Village), http://blog. voc.com.cn/sp1/zhanghongwei/112832112486.shtml.

104. The present author has already published the same conclusion in Kate Zhou, 1996. Zhou Xiaohong, *zhuangtong ye bianqian* (Tradition and Change), (Beijing: Sanlian Press, 1998), p. 227.

105. Bao Tong, "A Pivotal Moment for China," broadcast on RFA's Mandarin service. Director: Jennifer Chou, translated by Luisetta Mudie, edited by Sarah Jackson-Han. December 12, 2008, http://newsblaze.com/story/20090106100021zzzz.nb/topstory. html.

106. Lu xueyi, ed., *Dangdai zhongguo shehui jieceng yanjiu bao* (Study of Social Stratification in Contemporary China), (Beijing: *shehui kexue wenxian chubanshe*, 2002), p. 207.
107. Zhou Qiren "What Did Deng Xiaoping did Right?" *China Economist Forum,* July 28, 2008, 10:09, http://chinaeconomist.org/archives/236.html.
108. Wu Li, *guoyou buji de jiannan xuanzhe* (Excess Policies and Hard Choices For Reform) *Zhongguo jingjishi yanjiu* (*Journal of Chinese Economic History*), 2000, p. 2.
109. Government statistics but also in Gong Yuzhi, Dangshi Liji, (Records of Party History), (Hangzhou, *zhejiang renmin chubanshe*, 2002).
110. Michael Bristow, "Chinese 'living longer than ever," BBC News. November 16, 2008, http://news.bbc.co.uk/1/hi/world/asia-pacific/7731566.stm.
111. Fan, Jie, Thomas Herberer, and Wolfgang Taubmann (2006), *Rural China: Economic and Social Change in the Late Twentieth Century,* (Armonk, NY: ME Sharpe), pp. 281-293.
112. Zhou Qiren, "What Did Deng Xiaoping do Right?" *China Economist Forum*, July 28, 2008, 10:09, http://chinaeconomist.org/archives/236.html.
113. F. A. Hayek, *The Fatal Conceit : The Errors of Socialism* (The Collected Works of F. A. Hayek), (Chicago: Reprint edition, 1991).

2

Struggling to Move Freely

Women are like water, flowing everywhere and find-
ing a home everywhere. We look weak and soft but
water can be very powerful.
—*Xiang Xiang, a local female vendor[1]*

Introduction

An internal migration, unprecedented in pace and scope, has been unfolding in China over the last twenty-five years. Even conservative estimates put the number of migrants at between 150 and 250 million.[2] Attracted by the desire for more control over their lives, rural residents defy government regulations and, breaking tradition, leave their *laojia* (old home) for urban areas. The effects of such a drastic increase in the populations in and around cities have transcended the socio-economic and political boundaries erected by the state. Millions of migrants have entered the labor force, helping spur the growth of both domestic and global industry.[3] In the coming years, hundreds of millions more are expected to follow, as improved technology and increased efficiency decrease the number of individuals required to work on farms.

Although movement between cities also occurs, we focus our attention on the rural to urban flow, as this is the predominant migration pattern in post-reform China. More specifically, in characterizing this movement, we will follow Wenbao Qian's definition that considers "all the people who leave the countryside for the purpose of gaining better social-economic opportunities in the cities (including towns at the county level) as rural-urban migrants."[4] Despite the scale of this rural exodus, it is important to understand that it is has been a spontaneous, unorganized, leaderless, non-ideological, apolitical movement.[5] Even the Chinese government referred to the early migrants as *mangliu* (or random migrants), suggesting the spontaneity of their actions.

The reason that migration merits separate treatment as an important part of the China's rights acquisition movement, is that it represents more than just mobility of labor—it represents the desire of the individual for more control over the decisions affecting his life. Consequently, its socio-political dynamic is as

33

important as its socio-economic dynamic. The other factor that we emphasize is that the movement itself lends credence to the bottom-up nature of the reform. Proof of this will be provided throughout the chapter in describing numerous examples of the government's attempt to stop the movement.

In other industrializing nations, the government facilitates migration to cities through coordinated housing projects, transportation, and the construction of other forms of infrastructure designed to support growth. In China, the situation was quite different, as government regulations designed to prevent the movement of the masses were left in place. Had the government been successful in preventing migration as such, we would be looking at a very different China today.

Finally, in our continued discussion of the development of civil society, we espouse that the unrestricted flow of individuals is essential for the free exchange of ideas and the establishment of non-governmental associations. In looking at the establishment of migration policy, the positive and negative effects of its unraveling, and the individual strides being taken by rural migrants to acquire their inalienable rights, we document how this movement is changing the social, economic, and political landscape of China. Apart from published sources, we rely heavily on personal interviews conducted over the past seven years with ninty-six migrant workers, migrant vendors, and migrant entrepreneurs.

Population Control: The Foundation of Control and the *Hukou* System

To understand the uphill battle waged by early migrants leaving their homes in the country, one must begin with a basic knowledge of the system in which they lived. In China, this system is known as the *Hukou* (or Household Registration) system. The *Hukou* is a residence-based registration system, with strictly segregated rural and urban areas. It was formally established with the passage of the *Hukou Registration Regulations of the People's Republic of China* on January 9th, 1958, by the Standing Committee of the People's Congress. Holders either received either an "agricultural" or a "non-agricultural" designation as well as a residence status, which dictated what services the government would provide them.

Hukou provided urban residents with accessibility to employment, a place to live, a pension, school for their children, and many other subsidies not available to rural residents. The key impetus for this system came when food rationing began in urban areas in the late 1950s. The rationing was in response to food shortages created by the depression of food prices, and was implemented by directly connecting food rations with *Hukou*. If you possessed an urban *Hukou*, you could only receive rations in an urban area; with a rural *Hukou*, you received food in the countryside. Fourteen additional structural barriers were built into the Chinese socialist system, preventing any sort of equality in this rationing.[6] We highlight access to food because of its exemplary nature in showing that the state controlled everything. Consequently, rural residents lost the freedom to move to the cities, as they had no means of subsistence. Thus, the urban-rural divide was institutionalized. As the government made clear its intention to guarantee the welfare of urban residents, the city became a more appealing place to reside.[7]

In the countryside, individuals were organized into communes, and received food rations based on membership. These organizations became effective institutions for carrying out the government's economic as well as socio-political plans, "Because the control of labor flows was necessary for implementing the developmental strategy, *Hukou*, in effect, created a caste system, which enforced occupational and social apartheid."[8] Therefore, between the mid-1950s and late 1970s, rural-urban migration in China was almost non-existent, and "the only rural-urban migration that occurred was allocated migration, which means that all of the movements were arranged or approved by the government rather than initiated by the migrants themselves."[9] However, even the few who were authorized to go to the cities as temporary workers were deprived of the services and benefits that the urban residents received. This would continue to be the case even when the system began to break down.

Early Attempts at Reform and the Survival of *Hukou*

There are some who contend that the massive flow of migrants resulted from government policy initiatives.[10] We disagree, since the state policy was more of a reaction to an already existing situation. In addition, the government's reactions were not consistent. As a result, in the 1980s, the majority of those who went to the cities to work were still considered illegal and, thus, neither authorized to stay in hotels, nor able to acquire government housing. Most had to live in shanty-suburbs, on building sites, or with relatives. For a short period of time, the government permitted farmers to settle in small towns outside of the cities, but this policy was quickly abandoned due to fear of mass migration.[11] The first real step in allowing individuals to move from rural to urban areas occurred in the 1990s, when it became possible to buy an urban *Hukou* in the form of temporary work and residence permits. For example, for a brief period of time, one could purchase an urban Beijing *Hukou* for 10,000 Yuan ($1,200). Despite the high fees, this practice became quite popular. In fact, the government was so alarmed by the high number of transactions that it abandoned the program and restored its previous policy of only issuing temporary permits.

This precarious choice of limited control versus zero control of mobility explains why throughout the reform period, the government was never willing to abandon the *Hukou* system. "Since the Chinese state system is formed by the urban interest, most Chinese leaders are afraid that rural migrants will take jobs from urban people, putting additional burden on limited social services."[12] For government officials, the primary concern has been and will continue to be social stability. In their minds, losing their primary means of control over the more than 800 million rural residents is not the best way to achieve this goal. However, this view must be taken with a grain of salt. Solinger also notes that

government bureaus are, in varying degrees, concerned with both the maintenance of "public order" as well as the revenue-generating possibilities associated
with migrant management.[13]

Policy Override: *Baochan Daohu* and Freedom of Mobility

In the absence of government reform, how were the floodgates to the cities
opened in early post-Mao China? Although the movement is too varied and
complex to be traced back to a single event, we have found that there is a direct correlation between the *baochan daohu* movement and that of freedom of
mobility. This is primarily due to the fact that *baochan daohu* allowed farmers
to sell to the market those products remaining above and beyond the quantity
required by the state. The new farmer-led system ended the People's Commune
control system and the procurement system while at the same time weakening
the *liangpiao* (food rationing and coupon) aspect of *Hukou* system.[14] A China
scholar, Cai Cai, calls the three government control mechanism *sanjia mache*
(a three-horse pulled carriage).[15]

The early migrants traveling to the cities during the late 1970s and early 1980s
were primarily traders. Although this migration was successful in improving
the quality of life in most rural areas, it did not close the income gap between
these workers and those in urban areas. It addition, it provided neither current
benefits nor a pension system for the future. What it did accomplish was an
eventual process of "marketizing" the food sector in China. When food became
abundant to the point at which coupons were no longer needed, one of the major
anti-migration tenets of the *Hukou* system—access to food—lost its power over
would-be migrants. Once food could be bought on the market, people were
more willing to take a chance and move in search of work, regardless of the
legality of such decisions. The conditions were set, the people responded, and
"by 1985, more than one-fifth of the farmers had already changed their occupation, their residence, and their status."[16] Between 1980 and 2005, 189 million
Chinese relocated, with 66 percent constituting intra-province migration and
34 percent inter-province migration.[17]

Economic Influence

In the process of seeking new opportunity, migrants have increased more
than their prosperity. First of all, migrants helped China's transformation to an
industrial society because the migrant workers participate in non-agricultural
work. Before 2000, most people migrated because of job related (most urban
industrial jobs) and business while more than 60 percent of inter-province migration were in production industry.[18] In a 2005 survey, 53 percent of migrants
responded that they did no agricultural work; 37 percent helped out on farms
during the busy seasons; 7 percent spend only 3 to 6 months in the fields; and
only 3 percent spent half a year on the family farm. "Migrant rural labor has

Figure 2.1
Change of Urban Labor Market: Formal Sector versus Informal Sector

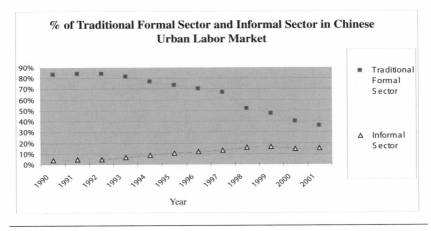

% of Traditional Formal Sector and Informal Sector in Chinese Urban Labor Market

Source: Zeng, World Bank, 2005

become a significant component of China's industry, accounting for 58 percent of the manufacturing workforce, 52 percent of service industry employment and 68 percent of processing workers. In the construction sector, the ratio is as much as 80 percent, official figures show."[19]

Few in this generation of young migrants intend to return home. They have cast their lots into the unknown future of an urban China they struggle to be part of, rejecting the state-mandated rural *Hukou* status.

Second, migrants have played a key role in the rise of the informal labor market in China because it is in informal markets that most migrants work, operate, and survive. The informal market often takes the form of services such as "restaurants, retailing, construction, repair, housing and delivery services." As a result of the inflow of migrants into the service industry, the structure of employment has undergone rapid change while employment in China's formal sector has decreased enormously from 83.6 percent in 1990 to 36.1 percent in 2001, while its counterpart in the informal sector has shown a tendency toward increase from 4.0 percent in 1990 to 15.3 percent in 2001 (see Figure 2.1).[20] Further, it is estimated that the informal labor market will continue to increase despite the government's attempts at prohibition since there is still great room for service industries to develop in the near future (Zeng, 2005, 20-21).

Third, unorganized migrants have brought pluralism to the closed urban planned system. There is no doubt that their life is full of struggle and that they have turned their backs on valuable aspects of their lives: their local dialect, familiar food, local customs, family and village support networks, and a familiar way of life.[21] Almost all migrants we have interviewed feel nostalgic when speaking of their hometown, but few wanted to return. Furong Zhou, a migrant from Baojing, rural Hunan expresses such a spirit: "Becoming a migrant is like buying a one-way train ticket. When I said goodbye at the bus station, my mother told me with tears, 'Take care of yourself and never return to this place of poverty. I am too old and sick, otherwise I would have joined you. Bite your teeth to overcome difficulties. Do not do things to harm others but watch out for everyone in the city.' My mother's words keep me facing tough times. I miss home but will not live there for a long time. The city life is hard but interesting and exciting."[22]

Wherever migrants flood, the economy booms. Economist Thomas Rawski's study shows that the labor market (fueled by illegal rural migrants) played an important role in increasing "both the marginal profit of labor and the marginal profit of capital."[23] As confirmed by the *Beijing Review*, "The prosperity of the private sector in these eastern and southern coastal cities is for [the] most part attributed to the cheap migrant labor, and the expansion of the manufacturing-based economy has provided job opportunities for millions of surplus rural laborers."[24] Thus, they are an integral and necessary part of continued growth. When looking at the numbers across the board, rural migrants are making a difference. Although hard figures are difficult to come by due to the questionable status of many migrant workers, it has been documented that whereas rural workers accounted for 70.5 percent of the workforce in 1978, this number had fallen to 50.1 percent by 2001.[25] These workers had to go somewhere and clearly had migrated to the cities. In addition, "the number of people working in tertiary trades has increased by 140 million, with the proportion growing from 12.2% percent in 1978 to 27.7% (in 2001) ...During the same period the proportion of primary industry in GDP decreased 10.1%, but its labor productivity grew by 11%."[26] The people were adapting to the changing economic landscape much faster than government policy.

Most Chinese businessmen recognize that rural migrants provide the back-bone of cheap labor for export industries, ensuring that the "Made in China" label adorns products in stores around the globe. It is an indisputable fact that migrants are the reason for the boom in China's labor markets, both official and unofficial. Before this quasi-freedom of mobility, the state was the sole agency in charge of job allocation. It would have been quickly overwhelmed had it tried to match workers with the expanding market economy. Instead, an informal system developed; day laborers would gather each day in front of train stations, bus stations, and other public places to offer themselves to employers. Most of China's construction workers, painters, plumbers, handymen, maids, cleaning workers, and caregivers acquire their jobs in this manner. This market is simple and convenient for both employers and migrants.

In addition to rural-urban labor movement serving as sources of economic growth, their effect on developing rural areas must also be considered. With the money they send or bring home, migrants make great contributions to agricultural investment, helping to reduce the income gap between regions. In addition, as the economy continues to expand, the price of food has continued to rise. "A major component of China's 5.3% inflation rate is higher food prices for grain, meat, and eggs. That means higher incomes for farmers. Indeed, rural incomes were up 16% in the first half of this year (2004)."[27] Finally, migrants who return to rural areas bring back newly acquired knowledge and skills, fostering further technological development in these regions.

Chinese migrants show that economic development can be internally driven. Many development theories project that economic growth comes from external stimuli.[28] But in China, it is the poor and uneducated rural people who took the lead by taking risks and seeking challenges.

Migrants, Street Entrepreneurs, and State Control

In the Chinese economy, the low-status farmers become the engine for growth. The movement of free labor from the countryside provided millions of jobseekers to private firms and rural factories. By 1987, there were about 88,000,000 persons working in rural factories, producing more than 50 percent of total rural production value.[29] This was the turning point for China's industrial take-off.

Migrants are both workers and movers of the new market institution in China. Rural migrants are the backbone of street entrepreneurship. But when the state started to allow individually operated private small businesses in the early 1980s, street vendor licenses were reserved for unemployed urban youth (*daiye qingnian*). Migrants without an urban *Hukou* were not allowed to acquire such licenses. The rise of the migrant-dominated Hanzhenjie and Dachenglu markets illustrates that migrants had to create their own markets. Hanzhenjie and Dachenglu were at one time ghettos in Wuhan, Hubei Province. Before the founding of the PRC, as lower class urban residents, most eked out a living on the streets by selling small food-related and handicraft commodities. After the PRC was founded, the government abolished all local street markets. Most residents worked either in small neighborhood factories or in poor collective enterprises. The local people were well known for their boorish culture and rude language.

However, even throughout the most anti-private business periods, such as the Cultural Revolution, a few private vendors (mostly from the countryside) somehow managed to appear in the Hanzhenjie and Dachenglu, providing services and selling products in tiny quantities. After 1979, many rural peddlers, especially women, came to dominate the street markets by selling agricultural products. Since they were close to the Yangtze River, rural people came by boats to swamp the streets with products. At first, the local government used force to protect state grocery stores and to get rid of the "capitalist" way of doing things. Police arrived randomly to catch illegal vendors and fined them heavily. In some cases, vendors were even jailed. But they kept coming despite these hardships, as there was a shortage of goods and services in the city, creating a demand that needed to be filled. Very quickly, shoe and pot repairmen appeared on their wooden boxes, loudly advertising their services. Hundreds of migrant vendors selling vegetables on street corners, and old and handicapped local urban residents cooked breakfast, rice noodles, sweet buns, and dumplings for a steady flow of people at small, makeshift sidewalk breakfast stands.

Migrants are the engines of entrepreneurship in China. Through the past ten years, an increasing number of migrant workers have returned to their native provinces to settle down and to start their own businesses with the hard-earned savings, knowledge, and technologies.[30] For example, in Yangxin County alone, between 2005 to 2008, about 2,500 former migrants set up more than 500 businesses, generating 3.5 billion Yuan in industrial output and 180 million Yuan in tax revenue in 2007 alone.[31] In Jishou, Hunan, most small businesses were set up by migrant workers.[32]

Rise of the Dachenglu Night Market

In mid-1985, thought they were unable to obtain licenses, rural migrant vendors and urban residents began to sell clothes and small commercial products at Dachenglu Street. Every night the street was full of vendors and night shopping became a popular activity, particularly during the summer when daytime temperatures were unbearable. Almost every night, *shirong* (city appearance maintenance) police also appeared to drive the vendors away. But the vendors, most of them women, developed strategies to deal with this situation. The police pulled down the awnings over *reganmian* (dried and spicy noodles) and *youtiao* (fried bread sticks) stands, throwing chairs, tables, dumplings, and bowls of noodles into the street. This led to a fight between the stall owners and the *shirong* police. While the fight went on, a relative or close friend of the owner escaped with the money.

Night and day, across Wuhan small markets popped up in all major streets and mobile vendors hawked their wares along the city's streets, alleys, and courtyards. Each day the *gongshangju* (industrial and commerce department), *shuiwuju* (the tax bureau), *chengguansou* (urban management bureau), the *shirong* police, and local police attempted to manage these "disorganized" and omnipresent markets through licensing, taxing, fining, chasing, and confiscating. This open and public struggle between government officials and street vendors who daily seek to improve their lives through trading and commerce is part of a larger fight across China over who can partake legally in what kind of markets and where and how this can take place.[33] In most of urban China, such small, spontaneous street markets can be formed in a few minutes, and then dismantled just as quickly. Such activity became known as "guerrilla markets," with illegal occupation of public spaces becoming conventional marketplaces.

Contestation over Street Markets: Street Vendors and State Officials

Local government officials generally realize the importance of small-scale, private businesses as key to economic development and reduction of the rising urban unemployment rate. Nevertheless, for several reasons, they often harass migrant-dominated street markets. Most importantly, government officials disliked the unorganized flow of migrants to the cities, and felt that migrants defied their authority. As a Shenzhen state company official remarked, "Migrant vendors are *wufa wutian* in their eyes there is no law and no one is assigned to control them. *Chengguan* (urban management bureau) was created to control them. But they do not have a fixed stall, making management difficult. I am glad that local police are involved to bring some order to the street vendors. But there are more vendors than police."[34] Interviews with thirty officials in Wuhan, Hunan, Shenzhen, Changsha, Guangzhou, and Beijing revealed that most officials placed social order above the market and economic growth. They repeated Deng Xiaoping's political slogan, "*wending yadao yiche*" (social stability prevails over all else). In other words, their first priority is political control over unorganized migrants (those not attached to formal state organizations) rather than the economic growth that they bring.

Several observations can be made about the urban migrant markets. First, urban street vendor markets overflow are so crowded that policing is difficult. Second, local government officials are often resentful towards these vendors, regarding them as competitors for the jobs of urban residents. Thus, whenever possible, local government officials did not hesitate to destroy such women-dominated street markets. For example, in 1983, when the central government in Beijing started an "Anti-spiritual Pollution" movement, the Wuhan police used force to dismantle the Hanzhenjie Market. "With no warning, the police came and smashed my small jewelry store one day in 1983,"one tearful female vendor recalled. "I did nothing wrong. The government people at that time were still very conservative and thought that private business was criminal. I still do not understand where the hatred towards us poor migrant small businesspeople comes from."[35] Third, local officials attempted to use their authority to extract money from migrant vendors. Although street vendors do not pay taxes, interviews with many of them show that they paid a variety of fees (management fees to the local government, hygiene fees, vendor fees and fines) at least five times a year. "The Big Hats Men (*dayanmao*) just came to demand money but they did not provide services or protection for us," sighed a vendor from Tianmen, Hubei. "I have to spend money to make sure that I will have no trouble with the local government. Since I was not raised here, I have to pay a local person to carry money to deliver this protection money for me. Thus, I pay the government people in this way. Why should I pay taxes again? I try to avoid being seen by government officials. They are only trouble for us."[36]

Faced with the rapid increase of migrant street peddlers throughout the 1980s, a web of local government organizations was set up to contain the growth. After the 1989 student movement, all large public gatherings alarmed the state. Thus, the urban administration in local governments played a role in regulating non-state growth in street markets. In Changsha, a *chengguanban* (Office of Urban Management) was established in 1989. Lower level of district *chengguanban* mushroomed in major cities such as Wuhan, Shanghai, Guangzhou, Shenzhen, and Beijing in the early 1990s. The key guiding principles were *du* (stop) and *su* (regulate or dilute). Between 1989 and 1993, the role of local government was to attempt to stop the flow of migrant peddlers. But after 1994, many urban unemployed and laid off workers joined the street market brigade, forcing the government to face reality by adopting *su*, the regulatory principle.

Most urban Chinese dislike the way local government urban planners dealt with migrant workers because both methods made it hard for migrant peddlers to reach urban residents. Most urban people were uncooperative with the *cheng-guan* (urban management office) police and officials dealing with unlicensed migrant peddlers. *Chengguan* were puzzled about this attitude of the urban residents. One director of Yuhua *chengguan* in Changsha remarked, "When we try to manage the urban streets, most urban people do not support us. They only care about their own conveniences. But we have to worry about the interest of the majority of the people. We must carry out the regulations and laws passed by the government. Most Chinese people do not have the concept of law. Such a public disobedience has made it hard for us to carry out our work."[37]

Migrant peddlers and workers have also put the resentment of the urban residents to good use by providing convenient and sometimes door-to-door sales to the urban households, and also informing urban residents of harassment by Chengguan officials. The following is the dialogue between a migrant soybean milk peddler and a retired urban resident in Changsha:

"Why is the price higher than last week?" asked the retired lady.

"Do not even mention it. *Chengguan* caught me leaving the morning market five minutes later than the required time and demanded a fine of 500 Yuan. I did not have that much money. Out of anger, they poured the milk onto the ground and destroyed my cart," replied the peddler.

"They behaved like teenage thugs, making the street dirty. Why do not you go to the office to report?" asked the retired lady.

The peddler replied, "Me? How could a rural migrant accuse the urban officials? They may create more problems for me. I do not have urban *Hukou* and no business licenses. I run in the opposite direction when I see them."[38]

Only in early 2007 did the Shanghai government issue an edict allowing non-licensed peddlers to exist, though still regulating the places for their businesses.

Since migrants cannot use the power of the media and politics to reduce local government officials' power and seek help, they have to resort to informal means of self-help. It was under this kind of pressure that networks of vendors, such as the Tongxianghui (village club), Chahui (Tea Party) and Majiang Clubs were formed. It is interesting to note that most merchants formed their businesses according to the origins of their birthplaces. With such village networks, street vendors shared information, labor and sometimes took care of each other's businesses. These network set up a new kind of worker-employer relationship.

Migration and Social Stratification:
The Rise of Merit-Based Working Class

The rural-led movement created a new social stratification. For more than twenty years, the most important social identity was the urban and rural *Hukou*. Due to the omnipresence of migrant workers, the most rigid identities have been replaced by new, social identities within the traditional urban/rural boundaries. Within the rural *Hukou*, new classes formed as new occupations emerged. Most rural migrants entered occupations in industrial or commercial services.

This change has great structural importance: with its 200 million migrant workers, China has been transformed from an agricultural society to an industrial society. Since most migrants are members of rural elites (relatively better educated and more capable), they have set an example for other young people to follow. In most villages we visited, it was difficult to find people between sixteen and forty years old. Most rural youth do not inherit the occupations of their parents. For many, economically speaking, "the sky is the limit." Having no welfare in the rural system, farmer migrants have become the most mobile group in China. Their individual abilities are measured by habits of hard work, education levels, cultivation of personal networks or *guanxi*, and possession of work skills. Such non-hereditary social mobility is relatively more modern than that of urban workers, whose career paths depends more on family background and state job allocation. This social reality makes China unique because, in most societies, rural people tend to have a more inflexible social status than urban people. This means that they tend to inherit their social status, while it is urban people who tend toward a merit-based status.

This example of social stratification departs from the theory of modernization that tends to view rural society as traditional, which means they tend to stay in the same place and refuse to take risks. But in China, the most entrepreneurial and the most risk-taking groups come from rural China. Given the fact that farming has been the lowest paid group, this migration means that upward social mobility is taking place in the Chinese countryside. According to Li Qiang, one of China's leading migration scholars, most farmers experience upward social mobility when they first migrate from farming and non-farming jobs, but such upward mobility becomes limited when they change jobs due to continuation of the state's *Hukou* discrimination.[39]

The Evolution of Tradition

The idea of choosing one's occupation and domicile, as currently being accomplished by rural migrants, is at odds with both the traditional Confucian ethic and the more modern values of the communist state. For more than 2000 years, Confucianism dictated that children remain close to their families as part of the traditional social fabric that defined Chinese culture. Yet the rural citizen, who often carries more traditional values than his urban counterpart, was the first to break away from this ethic. The contemporary term to describe this new ethic is *chuang tianxia* (good children may dare to venture into the world). Interestingly, this new ethic combines self-interest with the pursuit of individual rights, themselves entirely new concepts that challenge the traditional values among those who were previously Confucianism's most devoted followers. This is not to say that rural migrants do not still carry on strong traditions. On the contrary, they are generally more religious, more patriarchal, and more focused on family values. Consequently, the process of change we are witnessing is more evolution than revolution. This redefinition of values—those that influence the decisions of individuals—is the driving engine of the Chinese freedom of mobility movement.

The ability to move is one of the most significant indicators of Chinese liberalization. It is important to realize that this liberalization, however limited, is propelled by rural migrants themselves and not by government decree. Most migrants have depended on their own social network for job and housing information while on the road. Migrants have used the old tradition of *guanxi* networks with their schools, villages, and relatives. Migrants themselves have provided help and information to newcomers to the city, creating informal groups of support that help define this new China.[40] Most scholars in China have attributed China's economic growth, urbanization, and structural transformation to migrant workers.[41]

Migrant Women

The classic 1970 study by Danish economist Ester Boserup, titled *Women's Role in Economic Development*, initiated a new line of thought in the examination of economic, or more specifically capitalist, development on the lives of women. In this portrayal, women were described as victims of capitalism, as development was imposed upon them. Along this line of thought, it was said that multinational corporations employ women because they are "a docile, manipulable, easily replaceable work force" and that "flexibility of this kind is good for business."[42]

In China, such analysis has been turned on its head, as women have been at the forefront of many post-reform rights movements, including freedom of mobility. Our view, more in line with those expressed by Rae Lesser Blumberg, et al. in the book *Engendering Wealth and Well-Being*[43], is that women have been equally or even more successful than men at seizing economic opportunities in the newly capitalist China because they respond more strongly to a relatively small rise in income. Migrant labor has been a classic case in point. By 1993, female workers comprised 42 percent of the entire rural industrial labor force.[44] "According to the Labor & Social Security Ministry survey, 80 percent of Fujian textile plants report they only hire young female workers."[45] Never before in Chinese history have so many women worked outside the family and the village production model. This was a result of their seizing the opportunity to leave their village and pursue an independent life.

Migrant women have played an integral role in the massive freedom of mobility movement in China. In addition to helping the areas to which they migrate, they themselves receive the social benefits gained by leaving a male-dominated existence. Once outside the familiar environment, women must learn how to become independent. For example, Ms. Yasheng Zhou, a migrant from rural Hunan, had this to say: "The first year was hell. I was so afraid of even talking to the city people who were so arrogant towards me. But I had to leave; my husband in the village constantly abused me. After five years and many different experiences, I became strong and now know how to handle a situation. It is a great life to be able to live without a man. In a village, it is impossible for a woman to be independent economically. Now my village sisters admire me and know that they can become *duli* (independent). Today, fewer men dare to beat their wives because they may run away. I have already helped five other wives run away."[46]

In addition to the effects on individual women, the migrant movement is helping transform society as it facilitates creation of secondary associations. For instance, due to the difficulty of life as a female migrant, networks of women vendors have formed socio-economic groups such as *Tongxianghui* (village club), *Chahui* (Tea Party) and *Majiang* (Chinese card game) clubs. It is interesting to note that despite the evolution of this culture, most of these networks were formed on the basis of common birthplace. Women use these networks to share information and labor and, on occasion, even look after each other's businesses when needed. These bonds exist outside both government and familial contexts and are, thus, important for the social growth of women as individuals.

The experience of women, though unique in certain aspects, is also representative of the migratory movement as a whole. Of the twenty women street vendors we interviewed, all of them had moved their stalls at least once when the *dayanmao* ("big hats," a term used to refer to government officials) became too difficult for them to handle. Some referred to their strategies as guerrilla warfare to highlight their battle against the immovable bureaucracy. Interviews with women migrant vendors in Wuhan, Beijing, Shenzhen, and Shijiazhuang all reaffirmed that they felt the experience had empowered them. As self-empowered persons, they were proud of their ability to outwit government officials and were very willing to tell stories of how they did so. At the end of the day, they were realistic as well as proud. One such vendor from Xiangfan summarized the issue succinctly, "When the *dayanmao* are not looking, we spread; when the *dayanmao* come, we hide; when the *dayanmao* is strong, we flee."[47]

Urban State Control and Conflict

China's planned economy sought to controll urban growth. Before rural migrants began to invade the cities in the late 1970s, the urban share of the population was less than 17 percent but reached 26 percent in 1990 and to 40 percent in 2003, as demonstrated in Figure 2.2, largely due to migrants.[48] As soon as the rural migrants began to move, rapid urbanization followed. For the first 10 years 1979 to 1990, migrants contributed more than 76 percent of urban growth.[49] In other words, the migrations of rural people caused the rural population to shrink.

This was achieved despite the state's *Hukou* restriction. Most migrants found non-statement employment, higher income, and started a new life through their own efforts and with the help from kinship network members, *tongxiang* persons of the (same place of origin), and tongxue (former classmates).[50]

As a result of this rise in freedom of movement, Chinese migrants have, in effect, created urbanization without central planning. Cities and towns attracted more than 80 percent of migration in China according to the China 2000 Population Census Data.[51] In the eyes of the government, the migrants are still residents of rural areas, despite the fact that "the agricultural labor force had dropped more than 20 percent from 1979 to 2001, showing that the country has

Figure 2.2
The Ratio of Urban and Rural Population of the Total Population in China

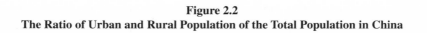
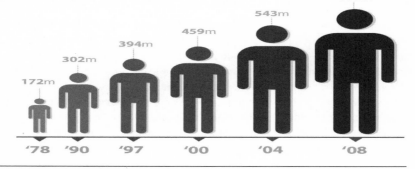

Urban Population in China

606m

543m

459m

394m

302m

172m

'78   '90   '97   '00   '04   '08

Source: 2004 China Statistical Yearbook

been experiencing a major urbanization movement."[52] Migrants are everywhere, too apparent to be ignored. The United Nations estimates that about 200 million more people will leave the agricultural hinterland by 2010.[53] In the end, this growing reality will force the hand of the government into dealing with this massive migration phenomenon, despite the fact that they did not initiate nor approve of it.

Because government policy and societal attitudes have not kept pace with their movement, migrants often find themselves at odds not only with the state, whose laws they are violating, but also with urban residents, whose space they are "invading." Although most urban residents depend on rural workers for "dirty jobs," many urban residents resent the "country folk" that compete for jobs and create rival businesses. For the local governments in many cities, this migration is a double-edged sword. They value the important contribution of the rural migrants, but they do not like sharing the government-provided services with migrants, making those services more expensive. Thus, they make every effort to ensure that these individuals are not entitled to the social safety nets provided to urban residents. "Most migrants have a lower level of education and thus lower social rank (*dichenci*)," one high-ranking government official in Wuhan remarked without hesitation. "The *Hukou* system helps us to legally differentiate those migrants from the urban residents. Without *Hukou*, we would have more chaos. With *Hukou*, we have a lot of chaos already. Thus, it is in the interest of Chinese civilization and the urban people that we keep the *Hukou* control."[54] Many others share this sentiment, fearing that the government would otherwise not be able to handle the increased burden.

The result of such concern is inevitable inequity. For example, almost all urban areas have a public school system based on *Hukou* status. Since rural migrants are not legal permanent residents, their children (even those born in cities) do not enjoy this same right of education. Those few who are permitted to attend are charged higher fees than their urban counterparts. "According to official statistics, there are 20 million migrant workers' children who are of school age but cannot attend because of financial difficulties and exclusion from urban education resources."[55] Without education for their children, it becomes more difficult for the migrants to break the cycle of poverty within the family. In many cases, migrants established their own schools. But in the 2000s, many urban city governments worked hard to close down those schools fearing the growth of civil society.

The State Continues to Contain Migrant Flow

By keeping rural people away from from urban formal institutions, China's government has sought to protect their own political and economic interests. Central, local governments and urban residents have solidified an "iron triangle" and restricted the peasants' rights for free residence.[56] Governments govern not by their social values but by their calculation of political interests.[57] China's state was afraid of getting rid of the anti-rural *Hukou* system because uncontrolled migration would lead to social chaos, and congestion of public good provision. These fears cause the central government, local governments, and urban residents to seek to limit migration from rural areas to urban centers.[58]

The government policies seek to control migrants. When the migrants created a more stable community, the government often destroyed the new communities. For example, since 2000, governments in major cities tried to contain the uncontrolled migration by demolishing migrant villages in the cities.

When the number of migrants in Shenzhen reached 14 million in 2007, the government used harsh measures to clean up migrant living quarters. On September 1, 2007, armed police set fire to one hundred low rent houses of migrants in Shangwu Village.[59] Shanwu was one of the early migrant villages that attracted Chinese migrant workers, professionals, and Hong Kong business people.

Although there is conflict between the two groups, some urban residents applaud the drive and self-sufficiency of their rural counterparts. As state support dwindles, they realize that they must also adapt to the changing economic environment or they may find themselves unemployed with minimal resources due to state-owned enterprise restructuring. Given the uncertainty of the economic landscape, these urban residents find themselves learning from the migrants. They have come to realize the importance of self-reliance and rights acquisition. In addition, some have begun to place more money into savings in preparation for the day when the government no longer sustains them.

Figure 2.3
The Scene after the Government Set Fire to a Migrant Workers' Community in Shangwu Village in Shenzhen.

Source: Zhang Junyan, *Southern Metropolis News*, September 1, 2007, http://news.qq.com/a/20070901/000172.htm. Photo by Xu Wenge.

The Present, the Future, and Beyond: A Challenge to State Control?

The increased population mobility has greatly challenged the very basis of the traditional *Hukou* system, forcing the government to respond. To curb migration, or at least attempt to control it, the government has instituted new and more drastic measures. Since 1995, the Ministry of Labor demanded that every migrant obtain an Employment Card to be considered a legal temporary resident. This card is issued by labor bureaus of destination cities showing proof of employment in the cities, and in order to obtain this card, the migrant must obtain and present three additional certificates:

- Identification Certificate: Issued by the police station of the migrant's home county; usually valid for 10 years.
- Temporary Resident Certificate: Issued by police stations in destination cities; must be renewed each year.
- Employment Certificate: Issued by the labor bureau of the home county to certify eligibility for employment.

In addition to these administrative requirements, the financial burden of migration is substantial. In the mid-1990s, a migrant had to pay 223 Yuan ($28) per year for these cards; the average wage for migrant workers was between $400 and $500 per year.[60] Thus, many migrants remained illegal because they could not afford the payment. The intention of the certificates was to create an official record with which to control the migrant population, but it often led to abuse by local governments and police. In addition to the workers themselves, many urban residents know that migrants have been abused, rounded up, and fined under a special set of government regulations outside normal criminal procedures. The existence of the detention centers is evidence that the Chinese state had no intention of giving rural residents freedom of mobility anytime soon.

In one example, in the summer of 2003, a young college student from a rural area, Sun Zhigang, was walking on a street in Guangzhou when he was detained for not having the appropriate documentation.[61] He was then brought to the police station, where he died while in custody. This incident caused much outcry and ill-feeling towards the government from all socio-economic classes and triggered a call for a more liberal policy. When the story was published on April 25, 2003 by the *Southern Metropolis Daily* in Guangzhou, the rights to move became a national issue. Sun's father's words spoke volumes about the lack of rights for migrants in China, "If he hadn't gone to university, he wouldn't have been so bookish as to argue about his rights, and he wouldn't have been killed."[62] When the report was circulated over the Internet, the public was enraged. Frantic internet activity resulted in millions of complaints about the unfair treatment and political oppression against the very people who contributed to China's economic growth. This public outcry gave lawyers and activists sufficient amunition to force the Beijing government to turn migrant detention centers into voluntary service centers, abolish the temporary residence permit requirement and mete out heavy sentences to the detention police. The provincial government arrested two liberal editors at the newspaper for corruption in an attempt to stop the tide of the newspaper's investigative journalism and discourage future whistle-blowers.[63]

Although being beaten to death is the extreme end of a wide spectrum of outcomes, those without the appropriate certificates are often abused and placed in *shourong suo* (detention centers). These facilities, in which rural migrants suffer both physical and mental abuse, were still in use as of 2004. In interviews with some thirty rural migrants who have experienced the detention centers, we quickly realized that migrants were treated like criminals and afforded no rights whatsoever. "I have done nothing wrong except trying to find a better job to support my daughter [so she can] go to school," remarked Jiang, from rural Jiangxi, who was detained in Beijing in 2001.[64] Jiang was forced to do hard labor in the periphery of Beijing for a month before the police sent him to a train station with instructions to return home. "[The police] said that this hard labor was to pay for my train ticket. But they took my money and possessions. I was not able to get my things at Beijing's construction site. They would not listen to us and rounded us up as if we were criminals. The detention center workers did not care about the law. No one could help us in there."[65]

Migrants' Impact on Society and Government

After more than three decades of non-sanctioned migration, some local government officials have begun to see the important link between freedom of mobility and economic prosperity for all. They realize not only that the state is unable to stop the flow, but also that urban services would collapse without migrants. "We Wuhan residents realize the importance of migrant workers and street vendors when they go home during the Spring Festival. All of a sudden, the city household services cease to exist," said Mr. Liu from Wuchang Urban Management Bureau. "…We could not live without migrant women."[66] In some cities, the local governments ignore the *Hukou* restrictions in order to attract and compete for productive rural Chinese. Because of massive non-compliance, state authorities regularly mount crackdowns in which migrants are forcibly cleared. However, in the end, even a constant series of sweeps cannot budge the millions of migrants who either remain in defiance of the regulations or move out temporarily only to return.

According to the *Human Rights in China Report*, the *Hukou* system "means that up to 20% of the poorest residents of China's cities are virtually without rights and subject to violence, intimidation and extortion at the hands of officials."[67] With so many disobeying the law, the pressure is building within the party and in Chinese society to stop the unjust treatment of rural migrants. Recently, the new leadership created under Hu Jintao and Wen Jiabao has asked urban residents to show more respect for rural migrants. They also issued a statement in early 2004 prohibiting job discrimination based on residency, potentially opening all jobs to rural migrants. Such actions are positive signs for the future, but real reform must continue with the end result being a call for the elimination of the *Hukou* system altogether.

The migration of millions creates social space for the rise of civil society and entrepreneurial spirit, which makes China excel in innovation, work ethic, and economic growth. Migrants have brought with them country folkways—self-reliance, entrepreneurial spirit, hard work ethic, and even food habits—that have remained ingrained in urban centers across China. With wide-ranging differences in culture and different heritages, migrants challenged "the one shoe fits all" planned socialist urbanization. The army of 150 to 200 million Chinese rural migrants has created a culture of freedom that is more open and expansive than any unitary tradition alone could possibly be.

Freedom of Movement and the Rise of Self-Help Organizations

After thirty years of civil disobedience, the right to move freely has become a social habit. According to the government's Fifth Population Census in 2000, there were about 121 million internal migrants, most of who came to the cities without government approval, as regulated by the *Hukou* system.[68] This is the largest instance of civil disobedience confronting the state. Although most migration takes the form of individual action, there are informal organizations guiding the flow of this, the largest human movement in the world.

The most important example of this is when migrants create villages within the city (called *chengzhongcun*). *Chengzhongcun* are sort of like Chinatowns in the U.S., where people composed mostly of migrants from a particular place. They can stay there because the land is controlled by the local government and farmers, not the central government. The rise of *chengzhongcun* came about because the government *Hukou* system made it impossible for rural migrants to find housing in the city.[69] *Chengzhongcun* is a self-help sheltering solution attempting to reduce the harm and barriers created by China's anti-rural migration state policies. This Chinese style grassroots urbanization is unique in that it is the rural migrants who are the pioneers for urbanization and grassroots urban planning without state finance and support. The very existence of *chengzhongcun* is a defiance of state discrimination policies.

Chengzhongcun in major cities across China have, through informal organizations and "with little in the way of government resources and assistance," successfully accommodated "millions of rural migrants because of their social accessibility and affordability..." In present day China, *Chengzhongcun* act as innovative and positive agents to promote urbanization by housing massive numbers of rural migrants and assimilating them into cities.[70] There are several thousands of such *chengzhongcun* in major cities.

These small migrant villages provide key services, like schools, legal aid, medical clinic, etc., to rural migrant communities. The rise of *chengzhongcun* also indicates the growing importance of Chinese civil society because the existence of these migrant projects resists much government urban development plans, generating a wide range of new interest conflicts and confrontations. Facing discriminatory policies, migrants must resort to basic market principles to confront the state head on, resulting in the pursuit of citizenship rights. The state's strategy towards *chengzhongcun* has met strong grassroots resistance (see land disputes below).

In recent years, grassroots legal aid groups have appeared.[71] This is especially true in Anhui, Sichuan, and Hunan provinces, where the majority of migrants have originated. In 2005, Tong Lihua founded a legal "first aid" station in Beijing to assist migrant workers in receiving back payments of wages. Everyday, numerous migrants applied for such assistance. In 2006, such successful grassroots legal aid stations encouraged the China Legal Aid Foundation and the All-China Lawyers Association (official NGOs) to launch China's first legal aid initiative for protecting the rights of migrant workers.[72]

Sometimes, informally organized migrant workers have taken the hard way, publicizing their situations to make their case. In July 2005, thirty migrant workers in the city of Shenyang, Liaoning Province, "climbed onto the roof of a tall building and threatened to jump off if they did not get the 1.2 million Yuan (US $150,000) back wages owed to them."[73] Trade union representatives spent nearly an entire day negotiating with their employer, who was having financial difficulties. The workers eventually came down safely "after the employer raised sufficient funds to pay them," said Zhang Jincheng, deputy president of Shenyang Municipal Trade Unions. "Dealing with such emergencies is part of the grassroots trade unions' work." Asked why their boss borrowed money to pay the workers, Xiaowu Chen, a Liaoning businessman, replied, "If any death occurs due to defaulted wages, he would be executed. He had to choose between his money and his life."[74] In interviews with Liaoning government officials, we discovered that the government officials were afraid that any migrants' death would get the attention of the central government, eventually culminating in their dismissal. This case illustrates the desperation to which migrants are driven as well as the political tactics used by migrant workers to gain justice.

In 2005, according to the official Chinese trade union ACFTU, 1.31 billion Yuan (US $163.75 million) in back wages were paid to 2.8 million migrant workers. The most promising grassroots migrant workers rights groups are often the ones established by migrants themselves. Thus Wei Wei, who migrated to Beijing to work and found pervasive anti-migrant regulations and environment, set up *Xiao Xiao Niao* (Little Little Bird) in an attempt to help migrants to get back wages, act as an information center, and provide aid with other legal issues. To avoid political problems, Wei's center is formally called the "Little Little Bird Cultural Communications Center."[75] With money coming mostly from other migrant workers, and none from the government, Wei and ten full-time workers have created a network of two thousand professional volunteers across China. Working with volunteer lawyers, NGOs, journalists, and businesses, this small center was able to recover "nearly 90 million Yuan (US $11.25 million) of back wages for about 11,000 migrant workers in the past seven years."[76] This cross-class formation of informal networks for migrant rights provides evidence that a critical mass for migrants' rights is forming in China. This formation is possible because more and more educated Chinese no longer find tolerable the unfair treatment of migrant workers who have substantially contributed to China's growth but have in return been systematically exploited and discriminated against.[77]

Wei's migrant consulting center receives nearly a thousand calls per month dealing with contract writing, payment default, medical insurance, social security, children's education, and related issues. Wei's case suggests that the most effective grassroots NGOs are those that provide solutions and help to one sector of society. The very fact that Wei was once a migrant himself is significant, since it provides him the experience to understand migrants' real needs. Because it has grown larger, Wei has been required to register *Xiao Xiao Niao* with a government organization. Once affiliated with the state, the organization will also be required to answer to the state's concerns. In an attempt to protect the independence of his still small organization, Wei has directly linked it with international NGOs and the foreign press, making it difficult for the government to close it down without receiving embrassing publicity.

Another effect of rural migration is that migrant Christian evangelists have been effectively evangelizing displaced migrant factory workers in South China. Converts from such factories are returning to their home provinces to continue evangelizing. Migrants themselves have also set up schools for their children in major cities where *Hukou* restrictions prohibit their children from attending public schools. The state finds the growth of such nongovernmental schools threatening. Thus in 2005, the Beijing city government began a campaign to shut down some 239 unregistered migrant schools attended by more than 95,000 children.[78]

Attainment of constitutional rights will assuredly be neither quick nor easy. Growing awareness of these rights has been paved with the death, blood, and imprisonment of untold numbers of brave Chinese who have helped to make substantial progress towards freedom of movement.

Until the death of Sun Zhigang, urban Chinese as well as urban governments, had become inured to rural migrants' habitual violation of *Hukou* regulations, while the migrants had to endure both public policy and social discrimination, including random raids that put migrants in urban *shou rongsou* (detention centers once found in all major cities) or labor camps. But exposure of official abuse of power in the Sun Zhigang case led to grassroots efforts to induce the government to close the detention centers. In May 2003, three young Chinese legal scholars wrote a petition asking the state "to enforce personal rights that are guaranteed by the Constitution, starting with the protection of downtrodden migrant workers in the cities."[79] This effort led to top-down change of some policies towards migrant workers. All urban detention centers were closed that year. Speaking to a *New York Times* reporter, Xu Zhiyong remarked,"We hope that by taking up this smaller, concrete issue, we can advance the cause of constitutional rights in general."[80]

The tipping point for freedom of movement in China has arrived as millions continue to violate *Hukou* regulations and increasing numbers of migrant workers take both public officials and employers to court seeking justice and equal treatment. Nongovernmental organizations that help migrants have mushroomed after 2003. In most urban cities, informal associations for migrant workers can be found, operating mostly among those from the same home province. The largest such associations are the Sichuan and the Anhui Migration Associations.

Governments, at all levels, are concerned about the migrants' ability to organize. In December 2006, the government of Shenzhen, where several millions of migrant workers have congregated, imposed a ban on two groups, the Shenzhen Association for Migrant Workers and the Shenzhen Laborers Mutual Help Association.[81] This ban has driven the two groups underground, transforming them into potential dissenting challengers to the Communist power monopoly.

The Virtues of Personal Choice

Despite often being described in such terms, the massive migration should not be regarded simply as an economic phenomenon. Freedom of mobility represents an individual's control over his or her own life. Although migrants still face formal and informal discrimination, more residents, both rural and urban, now have the opportunity to lead a life that is more independent of state control due to the rights movement currently underway. It is impressive that this movement developed primarily unplanned and leaderless. It is what Hayek called the spontaneous growth of individual actions.[82] With so many involved, the movement gradually evoked a coordinating effect of its own, impacting both economic and socio-political structures. When rural migrants violated the *Hukou* restrictions, they helped advance the liberty of all Chinese. As millions of migrants move across China, they are spreading the new value of personal choice. Their exemplary action has become what Johann Most called "action as propaganda," for the new values of independence and liberty and for the new people of China.[83]

By 2000, there were two hundred underground migrant schools for about forty thousand migrant children in Beijing alone, since the Beijing urban government public schools refused to take in those migrant children without Beijing *Hukou*.

Concluding Thoughts

The freedom of movement, the rise of a free labor market, and the rise of civil society shows that what might be a good course of action for an individual, when aggregated by millions, can lead to significant social change. In the Chinese case, unplanned migration was a departure from the norm of state allocation of labor, of control over mobility and resulted in the habit of self-employment or non-government employment.

Millions of migrants are the source and engine of Chinese growth, the basis of Chinese capitalist development, which depended on free labor. The life of every Chinese is affected by the commerce and presence of millions of rural migrants. Rural migrants used their feet to vote for a new society in China while at the same time building the new China from $199 per capita in 1978 to $2360 per capita in 2007. What is more, they achieved this migration despite the regime's continued discrimination and oppression.

Throughout the history of urbanization and industrialization, there have been many social problems, ranging from worker abuse to unsanitary living conditions. These circumstances helped facilitate many socialist movements in Europe and elsewhere, which influenced the development of Communism in China. Although China has experienced some of the same problems with this vast movement towards its cities, its situation is unique due both to its population size and to the *Hukou* system. Institutionalized restrictions on mobility have in turn institutionalized the problems that come with it. As a result, by law there are over 800 million people officially denied access to the new China that they themselves helped to build. In the short term, this may be providing the government with more stability, but in the long term, it will make the resulting problems of social and economic integration harder to fix.

Rather than waiting for the government to fix this problem, 100 million-plus rural residents have taken the situation into their own hands and moved in violation of the law. They are no longer willing to accept the socio-economic status afforded them by China's once all-powerful Communist Party. As described in the Introduction to this book, the social explanation for why such a large number of people decided to move in pursuit of rights, without any unified direction, can best be explained by Anthony Giddens' theory of "cluster of class situations with common mobility"[84] and Max Weber's ideas on "life chances."[85] Because their situation in the countryside offered so little in the way of a better life, like-minded individuals pursued common objectives without the need for leadership or ideology. The economic explanation is much simpler: the cities offer more opportunity to make money. They had a magnetic force.

Despite the simplicity of the economic explanation, the decision to move, as we define it, is far more complex. It crosses cultural, economic, and social norms, some of which have been in place for centuries. Although many have suffered greatly, their very existence shows that limited rights can be acquired from the state through direct action. Thus, millions of rural migrants have been able to overcome social and institutional barriers to find a better life. Although there is much well-deserved focus on the difficult path encountered by many of these migrants, the benefits must also be discussed. Increased economic prosperity, more opportunities for women, and greater freedom in decision-making are just a few of the positive aspects affecting both the migrants and others. By choosing where to live and where to work, they have advanced not only their own interests, but also those of society as a whole by creating an environment of decreased reliance on government. Migrants have played a key role in the structural transformation of China in terms of labor markets, market expansion, and the declined importance of the *danwei* (urban work unit) and *Hukou* systems of social control.[86] One of China's leading sociologists, Yanjie Bian, attributes to rural migrant workers the total collapse of the old socialist controlled stratification in terms of workers-cadre identity. Migrants have affected all Chinese.[87]

Migrants are true libertarians, relying primarily on themselves and informal markets to survive. They have created secondary associations for support, gone on strike over workers' rights, and created a tremendous labor pool on which China's continued growth is dependant. In addition, their maltreatment has drawn domestic attention to human rights abuses in general. Through all of this, migrants are part of a great human story of individuals' desire to attain more rights and shape their own future. The migrant path in China is the road to freedom—not only to migrant's freedom but to a more general and universal freedom. Their impact enters *Zhongnanhai* (the headquarters of the regime) in Beijing as well as in China's vast provincial hinterlands. Serving as a powerful engine of change, this vast army of long-suffering and persevering migrants will undoubtedly play an influential role in the future of the new China.

Notes

1. Interview with Xiang Xiang, a local woman vendor, July 11, 2000.
2. According to a survey by the State Council's Research Office, the number is 200 million, including 120 million migrants plus more than 80 million migrants who work within the local rural industries. Research Office of the State Council, *Guowuyuan yanjiushi ketizu,* (The Investigative Survey of Chinese Rural Migrant Workers), (Beijing: *zhonggguo yanshi chubanshe* [Chinese Yanshi Press], 2006), pp. 3-4. 国务院研究室课题组。中国农民工调研报告[M].北京：中国言实出版社，2006. p. 3-4. Also see website, "China shifts policy on rural migration," http:\\www.ipsnews.net/migration/stories/migrant.html.
3. Hu Jingbei, "China's Economic System Patterns after the Reforms: From Ideal to Scientific," *Journal of Shanghai University of Finance and Economics*, No.2, (Shanghai, China, 2000), pp. 3-11.
4. Wenbao Qian, *Rural-Urban Migration and its Impact on Economic Development in China*, (Aldershot: Avebury, 1996), p. 25.
5. Kate Zhou, *How Farmers Changed China,* 1996.
6. Guo Shutian and Liu Chulin, eds., *Shehen de Zhongguo* (Unbalanced China), (Shijiachuang: Hebei People's Press, 1991), p. 16.
7. The Chinese *Hukou* system has been the focus of many studies and books. The pioneers in this field include: Tiejun Cheng and Mark Selden, "The Origins and Social Consequences of China's Hukou System," *The China Quarterly*, 1994; Hein Mallee, "China's Household Registration System under Reform," in *Development*

and Change, vol. 26-1 (January 1995); Dorothy J. Solinger, *Contesting Citizenship in Urban China: Peasant Migrants, the State, and the Logic of the Market*, (Berkeley, CA, University of California Press, 1999); Delia Davin, *Internal Migration in Contemporary China*, (New York, Palgrave, 1999); Lei Guang, "Reconstructing the Rural-Urban Divide: Peasant Migration and the Rise of 'Orderly Migration' in Contemporary China," *Journal of Contemporary China*, vol. 10-28, 2001, 471-493; David Bray, *Social Space and Governance in Urban China: The Danwei System From Origins to Urban Reform*, (Stanford, CA: Stanford University Press, 2005); Fei-Ling Wang, *Organizing Through Division and Exclusion, China's Hukou System*, (Stanford, CA: Stanford University Press, 2005).

8. Sulamith Heins Potter and Jack M. Potter, *China's Peasants: the Anthropology of a Revolution*, (New York: Cambridge University Press, 1990).

9. Wenbao Qian, p. 53.

10. Kam Wing Chan and Li Zhang, "The Hukou System and Rural-Urban Migration in China: Processes and Changes," *The China Quarterly*, 1999, pp. 831-840.

11. More on this see Zhou, 1996. For the 1984 No. 1 document from the central government see: *Zhonggong zhongyang wenjian yanjiushi*, ed., *Shi er da yilai Zhongyao wenxian xuanbian* (Selections of Important Documents Since the Twelfth Party Congress) Vol. 1 and Vol. 2 (Beijing: *renmin chubanshe*, 1986), pp. 424-38; and State Council, "The State Council: Information on Peasant's Settling into Towns 13 Oct., 1984," in *Zhongguo nongcun fagui 1984* (Chinese Agriculture Regulations 1984), (Beijing: *nongye chubanshe*, 1986).

12. Solinger, 1999.

13. Solinger, (1999), pp. 67-71

14. Zhou, (1996). Chapter 6.

15. Cai Cai, "*Zhongguo liudong renkou wenti*" (The Problem of Chinese Migrants), *Henan renmin chubanshe* (Henan People's Press, 2000), p. 15.

16. *Fazhan Yanjiusuo* (Development Research Institute), *Gaige mianlin zhidu chuangxin* (Reform and System Innovation), (Shanghai: *sanlian chubanshe*, 1988). Quoted in Kate Zhou, (1996), p. 158.

17. Anqing Shi and Shuming Bao, "Migration, Education and Rural Development: Evidence from China 2000 Population Census Data." *Journal of Chinese Economic and Business Studies*, 2007, Vol. 5 (2): 163-177.

18. Bao, Shuming, Shuanglin Lin, Changwen Zhao, eds., *China's Economy after WTO Accession*, (Ashgate).

19. China Daily, "Government reacts to return of rural migrants," Nov. 19, 2008. http://www.chinadaily.com.cn/china/2008-11/19/content_7219957.htm.

20. Zeng, Douglas Zhihua. 2005 "China's Employment Challenges and Strategies after the WTO Accession." *World Bank Policy Research Working Paper 3522*, pp. 20-21. http://info.worldbank.org/etools/docs/library/137740/Zeng3522.pdf.

21. Fei-Ling Wang, *From Family to Market: Labor Allocation in Contemporary China*, (Rowman & Littlefield Publishers, 1998).

22. Personal interviews with Zhou Furong in Shenzhen on June 29, 2005.

23. Thomas Rawski, ed., *How to Study China's Economy Today*, (Hongkong: Chinese University Press, 1991), p. 8. Fei-Ling Wang, *From Family to Market: Labor Allocation in Contemporary China*, (Rowman & Littlefield Publishers, 1998).

24. "South Coastal Industries Short of Migrant Labor," *Beijing Review*, August 5, 2004, http://china.org.cn/english/2004/Aug/103105.htm.

25. *Zhongguo tongji nianjian (China Statistic Yearbook)*, (Beijing: Zhongguo tongji chubanshe, Various years from 1980 to 2002).

26. *People's Daily Online*, Sept. 10, 2002.
27. "Is China Running Out Of Workers?" *BusinessWeek Online,* http://www.business-week.com/magazine/content/04_43/b3905075.htm.
28. Edward C. Banfield, *The Moral Basis of a Backward Society.* (New York: Free Press, 1967).
29. *Zhongguo tongji nianjian* (China Statistic Yearbook), (Beijing: *zhongguo tongji chubanshe*, 1994).
30. Prof. Hu Jingbei, Tong Jing University, Shanghai. Personal interview July 12, 2007 in Jishou, Hunan.
31. China Daily, "Government reacts to return of rural migrants," Nov 19, 2008. http://www.chinadaily.com.cn/china/2008-11/19/content_7219957.htm.
32. Personal interview with Gong Ruizhen, Director of Human Resource Department, Jishou Government, Hunan in Jishou City, on August 3, 2004.
33. Matthew G. Ferchen, "City Appearance and Market Order: Understanding Conflict between the State and Street Vendors in Nanjing," at the International Conference on Globalization, the State, and Urban Transformation in China Hong Kong Baptist University, December 15-17, 2003.
34. Personal interview with Lou Dongxia in Shenzhen, August 16, 2006.
35. Interview with Erer, local female vendors, July 12, 2000.
36. It is clear that all twenty vendors we interviewed used informal means to pay off government officials.
37. Personal interview with Yang Yong in Changsha, July 30, 2007.
38. Personal observation in *zifa shichang* (spontaneous market), Changsha, Hunan, July 23, 2007.
39. Li Qian, *Nongmingong yu zhongguo shehui fengcheng* (Migrant Workers and China's Social Stratification), (Beijing: *shehui kexue wenxian chubanshe*, Social Science Document Press, 2004), p. 155.
40. Yaohui Zhao, "The Role of Migrant Networks in Labor Migration: The Case of China," *Contemporary Economic Policy*, 2003, pp. 500-511.
41. Bai Nansheng and He Yupeng, *Huixiang haishi jincheng* (Return Home or Entering the City?). Peiling Li, ed. *Nonminggong (Migrant Workers)*, (Beijing: *shehui kexue wenxian* Press, 2003). Zheng Gongcheng, *Kexue fazhan yu gongxiang hexie* (Scientific Development and Shared Harmony), (Beijing: People's Press. 2006).
42. Kelly, p.194. Hu Jinbei.
43. Blumberg, et al., provides cross-regional studies covering Latin America, Asia, and Africa. This book demonstrates that women in developing countries, especially poor women, may in fact benefit from globalization.
44. *Zhongguo tongji nianjian* (China Statistic Yearbook). (Beijing: *zhongguo tongji chubanshe*, 1994).
45. "Is China Running Out Of Workers?" *Business Week Online,* http://www.business-week.com/magazine/content/04_43/b3905075.htm.
46. Interview with Yasheng Zhou, summer of 1999, Shenzhen, China.
47. Interview with Xiang Xiang, a local woman vendor, July 12, 2000.
48. Shenjing He, Zhigang Li, Fulong Wu, "Transformation of the Chinese City, 1995-2005: Geographical Perspectives and Geographers' Contributions," *China Information*, Vol. 20, No. 3, 429-456 (2006).
49. H X. Wu, "Rural to urban migration in the People's Republic of China," *China Quarterly* 139 (September 1994), pp. 669-98.
50. This is confirmed by my own interview with 120 migrant workers throughout the years between 2000 and 2007.

51. Anqing Shi and Shuming Bao, "Migration, Education and Rural Development: Evidence from China 2000 Population Census Data." *Journal of Chinese Economic and Business Studies*, 2007, Vol.5 (2): pp. 163-177.
52. *Zhongguo tongji nianjian* (China Statistic Yearbook), (Beijing: *zhongguo tongji chubanshe* [China Statistic Press], 2002).
53. "China shift policy on rural migration," http://www.ipsnews.net/migraiton/stories/migrant.html.
54. Interview with Cadre, Wuhan, July 13, 2000.
55. Ren, Fan. "Reforming Rural Education. An idealist encounters both resistance and indifference in challenging the current educational system." *Beijing Review*, 30 September 2004.
56. Jonathan Gruber, *Public Finance and Public Policy*, (NY: Worth Publishers, 2005), pp. 467-8.
57. Robert H. Bates, *Markets and States in Tropical Africa,* (Berkeley: University of California Press) p. 5.
58. Dorothy J. Solinger, 1999.
59. Sun Shou, "Shuwei Shenzhen sanlai yibu shengyuan" (Who Corrects the Wrong Suffered by the Export Enterprises), September 30, 2007, http://www.aboluowang.com/comment/data/2007/0930/article_5999.html.
60. Interview with Mr. Ye Huabao, a Shenzhen government official, summer 1999, Shenzhen, China.
61. Zhang Yinghong, "Sun Zhigang zhisi yu zhidu zhier" (The death of Sun Zhigang and the evil of the hukou system), April 28, 2003, www.mlcool.com.
62. Jing Xiaohua, "*Daxuesheng yingwu zhangzhuzheng bei shourong bin bei duida zhisi* 大学毕业生因无暂住证被收容并遭毒打致死," (College Graduate Was Beaten to Death at Detention Center Due to Lack of Temporary Resident Permit), *Southern Metropolis Daily*, April 25, 2003, http://news.sina.com.cn/s/2003-04-25/09501015845.shtml. The interview of the father was translated by Human Rights Watch in, "Southern Metropolis Daily Article on the Case of Sun Zhigang," http://www.hrw.org/campaigns/china/beijing08/sun.htm.
63. Personal interview with two reporters from *Southern Metropolis Daily* in Guangzhou on July 26, 2005.
64. Interview with Jiang Rongmao, July 4, 2004.
65. Personal Interviews with rural migrants Guangzhou railway stations, July 10, 2002.
66. Interview with Mr. Liu, July 10, 2000.
67. David Lague, "Migration Restricted Movement," *Far Eastern Economic Review,* January 9, 2003.
68. (Population and Social Sciences Department, National Statistic Bureau of China, 2001).
69. Kate Zhou, 1996.
70. L. Zhang, Simon X. B. Zhao, J. P. Tian, "Self-help in housing and *chengzhongcun* in China's urbanization," *International Journal of Urban and Regional Research* 27 (4), 2003, pp. 912-37.
71. Xiang Biao, *A Village beyond Borders*. (Chinese by Sanlian Press, 2000; English by Brill Academic Publishers, 2007).
72. China Daily, "Legal aid fund to help migrant workers," January 20, 2006, http://english.people.com.cn/200601/20/eng20060120_236915.html.
73. China Features, "Trade Unions Play New Role to Safeguard Migrant Workers' Rights," November 13, 2006, http://www.chinagate.com.cn/english/news/49260.htm.

74. Personal interview with Chen Xiaowu, Shengyang, Liaoning, August 8, 2006.
75. China Daily, 2007-03-03 14:19:00.
76. China Features, "Trade Unions Play New Role to Safeguard Migrant Workers' Rights," November 13, 2006, http://www.chinagate.com.cn/english/news/49260.htm.
77. See good discussions on anti-migrants policies in Solinger, 1999.
78. BBC NEWS, "clashes sparked by closure of Shanghai migrants' school," January 9, 2007.ff, http://news.bbc.co.uk/go/pr/fr/-/2/hi/asia-pacific/6243997.stm.
79. Erik Eckholm, "Petitioners Urge China to Enforce Legal Rights," *New York Times*, June 2, 2003 (Internet version).
80. Erik Eckholm, "Petitioners Urge China to Enforce Legal Rights," *New York Times*, June 2, 2003 (Internet version).
81. Hu Xingdou, "China must legalize charity," www.huxingdou.com.
82. F. A. Hayek, *The Fatal Conceit : The Errors of Socialism* (The Collected Works of F. A. Hayek), (Chicago: Reprint edition, 1991).
83. Johann Most, "Action as Propaganda," *Freiheit*, July 25, 1885.
84. Anthony Giddens and David Held, *Classes, Power, and Conflict: Classical and Contemporary Debates,* (Berkeley, University of California Press, 1982).
85. Hans Heinrich Gerth and C. Wright Mills, *From Max Weber: Essays in Sociology*, New York, Oxford University Press, 1958.
86. Zhou, 1996.
87. Yanjie Bian. "Chinese Social Stratification and Social Mobility," *Annual Review of Sociology*, 2002, 28, pp. 91-116.

3

The Chinese Entrepreneur: Challenging the Status Quo

[Each man] is willing to join in Society with others
for the mutual Preservation of their Lives, Liberties
and Estates, which I call by the general Name,
Property.[1]
—John Locke

Introduction

It is only through the perseverance and initiative of individuals that societies can transform. In China, as people struggled through the early days of the reform period, one (disconnected) group pushed the limits of the existing socio-economic order more than any other. This collection of individuals, known as entrepreneurs, has had such a tremendous influence on both the lives of the average citizen and the continually evolving role of the government, that if any group can be given credit for pushing reform over the hump, this would be the one. To examine their role is to witness the power of human resolve. Whereas government policy must be developed and implemented, individual actions and grassroots activities skip this process and can be enacted shortly after conception. The nature and speed with which China is transforming is thus testimony to the role of grassroots activities, since policy-led reform has moved at a snail's pace.

Entrepreneurs are the engines of growth in most countries. But in communist countries, entrepreneurs have played a role in the institutional destruction of planned economies, while creating market opportunities. In 1942, economist Joseph Schumpeter described the process of transformation that accompanies radical innovation in capitalism as "creative destruction."[2]

In China, entrepreneurs have begun creative destruction because they had to destroy socialist institutional barriers before they could engage in market activities. Following David Li, we define Chinese entrepreneurs as those who try to destroy state institutional barriers in order to identify market opportunities and gather resources (financial, technological, political, and social). Entrepreneurs

61

are the primary force behind economic growth in this Communist Party-controlled country. To generalize, they test state limits, analyze demand, and then create markets. In China, however, this is more than just an economic process, as the market being created is often for a product or service whose existence was previously restricted or at least exclusively managed by the government. As such, the actions of these individuals are not only accomplished without the protection of the law but are often in violation of existing regulations. Thus, Chinese entrepreneurs must try to make "use of institutional rules, frequently represented as contingent government regulations, and manipulating the rules. An entrepreneur in China is someone who can handle the two missions of making profits and obtaining sociopolitical security in a way that the two can mutually benefit from rather than destroy each other."[3] By sketching the tales of entrepreneurs who have taken big risks in the context of a planned authoritarian communist state, this chapter shows that the entrepreneurs have not only created wealth but also undermined the socialist planned economy through private enterprises and individual entrepreneurship.

As referenced in the introduction, other scholars have documented the role of entrepreneurs and have marveled at their success, given the lack of government assistance to the private sector. Tsai's work, to cite one example, provides extensive detail on how state financing failed to reach the most productive private entrepreneurs, whose funding came primarily from non-government sources.[4] Building on this and other works, we wish to demonstrate that, in actively seeking expanded social and economic freedom, entrepreneurs have not only spurred private industry, but also lessened general reliance on the government and reinforced independence of thought and action among new workers in the private sector and freelance writers and opinion makers. As such, many entrepreneurs are representative of the liberalization movement we are analyzing. The initial entrepreneurs, as will be described in this chapter, thus were not beneficiaries of economic liberalism, but rather its grandfathers, a subtle, yet crucial difference.

Despite our rights-oriented approach, we fully concur with the scholars mentioned in the introduction that in the end, one of the most important developments of the reform era has been the rise of markets outside of the state planned economy and the subsequent rise of the private sector. Chinese entrepreneurs are the ultimate facilitators of the Chinese economic miracle and their importance should not be understated.[5] In 1978, state-owned enterprises generated about 80 percent of China's gross domestic product.[6] By 1997, there were 961,000 private enterprises and 28,500,000 *getihu* (small family private firm), which comprised 18 percent of all workers employed by the non-farming private sector.[7] By 2002, the non-state sector's share exceeded two thirds of the GDP with "the share produced by truly private activity comprising comfortably more than half."[8] By mid-2004, there were more than three million private companies in existence employing more than 47 million workers.[9] Much of this growth would not have taken place without the impetus of entrepreneurs. It clearly was not led by the central government, which did not even legally recognize private enterprise until 1987, nor grant state permission for united private household enterprises until 1993.[10] By 2008, there were "29 million private businesses, which employ over 200 million people and generate two-thirds of China's industrial output."[11]

Entrepreneurship has become a preferred road for social mobility in China. According to a 2006 survey by Qinghua University and Beijing Science Bureau, 16.2 percent of Chinese adults between 18 and 64 years old participated in setting up a private business, making China rank sixth in the Global Entrepreneurship Monitor (GEM).[12] The data suggest that for every six or seven Chinese, there is an entrepreneur, nearing the American level. Is entrepreneurship in conflict with the Communist state? What has made China the land of entrepreneurship? How has China turned from red to black?

The Rise of China's Entrepreneurs and the Story of Modern China

Chinese culture has always valued entrepreneurs. But this culture was lost for thirty years until the grassroots *baochan daohu* revived it.

There is a direct relation between *baochan daohu* and the development of China's private businesses. First of all, this new system brought a degree of autonomy to those affected. Farmers could decide what to do with their savings, labor, and harvest after they submitted their grain quota to the state and the local officials. Second, rural private saving provided the initial capital for China's development. The annual growth rate of rural production between 1979 and 1984 was around 18 percent.[13] By 1984, just 3.5 percent of all rural households had become *nongcun zhuan yehu* (rural commercial specialized households), with an average annual income of 7408 Yuan—6.1 times the average income of rural households.[14] A few rural households, about 0.56 percent, had become *wan Yuan hu* (ten thousand Yuan households). Much of the subsequent rural investment came from this source. Third, the new system released rural labor previously controlled by grain rationing, *Hukou* and the People's Communes system. An army of rural migrants rushed to job sites, simultaneously creating new jobs and businesses.

Before 1980, entrepreneurial activity in China was illegal. Today, there are over 40 million entrepreneurs, whose businesses employ over 200 million people and generate two-thirds of China's industrial output.

China's rapid economic development is testimony of the power of entrepreneurs who stepped into gaps left by the planned economy and profited while helping China to transform. The *baochan daohu* movement formed new tastes and habits, making rural Chinese the first group to undertake commercial and industrial occupations banned under the PRC's planned economy. After being locked in poverty for so many years, it was natural for the rural poor to apply themselves to occupations that held out hope for a better standard of living.

This rural drive was the nation's initial engine of economic growth and rural industrialization. The rural entrepreneurial surge helped transform China from an agricultural to a more industrialized society that encourages commerce and manufactures. Stories of Chinese entrepreneurs show how entrepreneurship can empower the poor to overcome obstacles and how entrepreneurial activities have alleviated poverty more effectively than government welfare programs and the state-imposed commune system. Throughout the 1980s, the social scene in China was replete with individuals with little capital but tremendous vision and persistence. These energetic individuals created new markets and improved the standard of living for millions by providing them with employment.

Chinese entrepreneurial pioneers tend to come from the least-privileged segment of society. Most entrepreneurs at the grassroots level are poorly educated, have no political backing, and started from abject poverty. But they have created some of the most remarkable enterprises in China. The richest Chinese in the 2007 *Hurun China Rich List*, for example, was the Yang family, owners of Country Garden, a property development company worth $27 billion. Yang Guoqiang, once a poor farmer from the southern province of Guangdong, became wealthy after acquiring large tracts of land and distressed assets in the countryside in the early 1990s where there was no real estate business. In 1997 he grasped the housing market opportunity and developed affordable townhouses and holiday homes for China's growing middle class.[15]

Malu tianshi (Street Angels) and *Jishi* (Farmers' Market)

Among the heroes of the market-creating process, and the subsequent public to private transformation, is a group referred to as rural merchants, or *tu laoban* (rural entrepreneurs). These initial entrepreneurs migrated to urban areas in the early 1980s to provide services and food products to urban residents. They arrived from rural China at a time when market activities were not only informal, but in most cases illegal. Their story is truly one of overcoming formal and informal barriers to better their lives. By defying legal barriers and moving about freely, they altered the system. Since there were no markets in a centrally planned economy, non-state entities were excluded from participating in most economic exchanges. The central government sought to act as the coordinating mechanism, determining and allocating financial as well as real flows of products and services.[16] As part of this process, cities, under the control of the state, issued coupons to urban residents allowing them to procure certain quantities of consumables ranging from sugar, grain, and oil to clothes, matches, and soap. In Wuhan, an industrial city of 4 million, there were nearly one hundred coupons used in the purchasing of various products. As in the Soviet Union, the average woman stood in line for hours each day waiting to use her family's coupons, often only receiving rotten food for her trouble. The process became such an entrenched part of one's daily existence that it became a significant part of the role of an urban working woman.

As this system weakened after 1978, the development of markets continued to be hampered by migration control policy, which limited the mobility of workers. Without an urban *Hukou* and a letter of introduction from their party boss, rural residents were not even allowed to stay in hotels in the cities. Thus, they were prevented from accessing potential urban markets. They circumvented this economic disadvantage while overcoming the restrictive social policy by either staying with friends and relatives or constructing temporary shelters on the outskirts of the cities.[17]

The government's inability to handle rural abundance sparked initiatives from farmers, including the independent marketing of their own goods. After farmers gained control over production and most of their harvests, some tried to make up for the inefficiency of the state by marketing goods on their own. Farmers had always contested the boundaries of households and markets, even under the collectives system. But after *baochan daohu,* farmers opened up markets with a vengeance. If unplanned *baochan daohu* fundamentally weakened the political structure of the Communist state in rural China, unplanned commercialization weakened its marketing power. Like *baochan daohu*, the process of commercialization centered on the struggle between farmers and the state, altering the patterns of politics in the Deng era.[18]

The original entrepreneurs were rural merchants, whose efforts transformed Chinese grocery markets from long food lines dominated by the state to a domain of private sellers with an abundance of food. With so many rural people selling their products, prices were relatively low. With such huge demand, rural people (street merchants, peddlers, repair services workers, and business people of all kinds) flooded the streets and open spaces in both cities and towns. The local governments in most urban centers sought to either shut them down or confiscate their products, but urban demand and rural supply were so high that the ban was impossible to implement. Urban people in many cities called street merchants *malu tianshi* (street angels). Facing this reality, governments in many cities began to officially authorize farmers' markets, usually placing them in less desirable areas. This movement progressed so rapidly that *jishi* (farmers' markets) quickly dominated the urban grocery market. By 1983, the majority of the people in major cities purchased their products in the *jishi* rather than in government grocery stores. For ordinary urban Chinese in the 1980s, *jishi* meant free markets. Within one year (1979 to 1980), most state vegetable markets (with the exception of the ones in Beijing and Shanghai, in which the state heavily subsidized urban residents) were out of business.

Having been denied access to government-issued coupons for consumption goods, rural merchants seized the opportunity and focussed their energies on supplying that demand, thus creating thriving markets across China. By circumventing the planned system, whose default functioning revolved around a shortage of goods,[19] rural merchants put the central government in a dilemma. The new situation lessened the government's burden by allowing everyone access to more food, but at the same time it straddled the dangerous boundary between non-government markets and private enterprise. Eventually the government accepted the reality and effectiveness of the farmers' markets.

The rural entrepreneurs' role in ending long food lines convinced urban residents, as well as government leaders such as Zhao Ziyang, of the power of grassroots entrepreneurial activities. It also affected government thinking about how it could curtail such activities without inflaming the entire populace. As rural people increasingly engaged in (then illegal) long-distance trade, ordinary people ceased to perceive such trade as illicit. *Jishi* blossomed all across the country. In 1983, the number of *jishi* reached 48,000, constituting 14 percent of wholesale transactions. In 1989, *jishi* sales accounted for 70 percent of the goods bought in cities, supplied mainly by rural merchants and industrialists. By 1991, there were 6,390,200 rural, non-state marketing organizations involving some 13,980,800 rural merchants, who controlled one-third of the agricultural products at wholesale markets. With the exception of grain, cotton, oil, tobacco, and silk cocoons, by 1990 almost all agricultural products came from *jishi*, while in 1979, only 15 percent of all products had come from this source.[20]

One of the largest *jishi* is the Changshu Garment Market in Jiangsu Province. This market evolved from a street clothing "market" in the 1980s to become the largest garment market in China. In Shanghai, *Qipu jishi*, one of the more advanced copycat products markets, and *Shilipu jishi* (fish and fruits "market") also evolved from *malu* (street) markets.

Linked with *jishi* development was the rise of private hotels. As mentioned previously, rural residents were not authorized to stay in government-run hotels (which amounted to practically all hotels in the late 1970s). These establishments only accepted guests with a government letter of introduction. Since most rural residents existed outside of the state welfare system, however, they could not acquire such letters. To meet the demand of these transient food sellers who had limited options for temporary residence, other rural entrepreneurs established the first privately managed hotels. Similarly, China's restaurant market boomed as newly mobile and prosperous rural entrepreneurs increasingly served as both owners and patrons. As these enterprises blossomed, other rural entrepreneurs became landlords, shopkeepers, and peddlers.

Although landlords may seem out of place in this process, they were actually indispensable in helping to keep the system from collapsing. By staying in the villages and continuing to oversee the farming of the plots left by transient entrepreneurs, they ensured that the government still received its agricultural quota. Without this, it would have been much more difficult for local government officials to look the other way, regardless of bribes. More and more rural merchants began to join the movement, and twenty-five years later, nightclubs, bars, restaurants, food stands, and other small shops now dominate both urban and rural landscapes. No letter of introduction besides money is needed in order to be served.

Hobos (Homeless Bourgeoisie/Migrant and Rural Entrepreneurs)
Seizing Market Opportunities:
China's Rags-to-Riches Rural Entrepreneurs

Of the original entrepreneurs, most had farming backgrounds or, at a minimum, had fathers who were farmers. After their release from the communes in the early 1980s through the *baochan daohu* movement, rural people with an entrepreneurial spirit left villages to search for greener pastures for themselves and their families. A few rural migrants established laundry businesses in major cities such as Shanghai, Wuhan, Beijing, and Guangzhou. Other rural merchants soon followed. We asked a Wenzhou entrepreneur who had set up a dry cleaning business in Beijing, "How could a farmer imagine a dry cleaning service, since most rural people do their laundry by hand?" The woman replied with a big smile, "My neighbor set up a small laundry shop in Shanghai and made some money in early 1990. My brothers and I borrowed 80,000 Yuan from relatives and friends, plus our 21,000 Yuan in family savings. When we went to Shanghai in 1995, we found out that there were already too many shops of this kind. This is why we turned to dry cleaning, a new type. In the beginning, our business targeted only foreigners, but now professional and business people are using our service. But competition is high. I do not know if we can survive here. We have to figure out what to do next."[21] The demonstration effect of the success of other migrant businesses has played an important role for the spread of entrepreneurs. Like entrepreneurs elsewhere, most Chinese private entrepreneurs set up their businesses through the three "Fs"—friends, family, and fools.

Theories of economics and development explain many things, but they cannot explain why those "uneducated" Wenzhou rural women would devote their lives to produce a service that they had neither used nor seen. If freedom has a chance to survive in an authoritarian society such as China's, it is not only because it works, but because entrepreneurs such as those Wenzhou women and millions of other small entrepreneurs chose to live a life that follows a principled path of a "small tradition" of entrepreneurship.[22] While most of the urban Chinese tried to hold on to their government jobs, the entrepreneurs' staunch and principled risk-taking actions were a major influence in creating the limited freedom Chinese enjoy today. Given the fact that economics and politics are linked in a Communist planned society, entrepreneurs have played a key role in undermining the planned socialism which smothered individual liberty.

Private businesses had to develop strategies in order to survive in China's planned economy. Entrepreneurs had to bribe their way into the system. For example, in 1978, almost one full year before the Third Plenary of the Eleventh Party Congress, the creation of *lianhu jizi* (united households capital formation) led to the formation of 190 independent rural enterprises in Chenlu Commune, Jinjiang County, Fujian Province, all of which were licensed under the collective enterprises of the commune organizations.[23] This fact is worth noting, since it helps in tracing the roots of the initial entrepreneurial spirit. The same year in

Jinxiang, Changnan County, farmers marched into a government officials' cantina, demanding food or work. Their action led to quasi-recognition of existing private enterprises.[24] As a result, by the end of 1979, out of 4369 households, 2920 (69 percent) had become de facto family businesses, employing 8098 people.[25] The movement was on, and the government was already in reactive mode. By 1982, as this process continued to expand, so many rural family units had become household production units that a large group of potential entrepreneurs now had a basic understanding of small-scale business and an economic incentive to engage in further entrepreneurial activities. So much was missing from the daily life of all citizens that opportunities were boundless. Even if only 5 percent seized this initiative, when dealing with a rural population of 800 million, one can see how explosive such a situation could become.

Since most entrepreneurs in the 1980s had to violate several government policies to create and sustain a business venture, they were generally risk takers. An example of such risk taking is the evolution of long-distance trade. After 1949, the state regarded long-distance trade as a speculative, capitalist activity and branded those involved as criminals. In the early 1960s, many people were labeled *huai fengzi* (or bad elements) after they were found engaging in such trading (mostly in food) during the famine periods. Some "bad elements" lost their jobs and were sent to labor camps while others were put on the neighborhood watch lists to be supervised closely.

Figure 3.1
A Struggle Meeting against Four "Bad Elements," in the Four Clean Ups Campaign in 1964.[26]

"四清"中每逢开会,民兵都把"四类分子"押解到场听会

Even in the late 1970s and early 1980s, the urban police constantly harassed traders. The sight of policemen chasing and confiscating a rural peddler's goods was quite common.[27] Although in 1979 the state reformed its policy somewhat, allowing rural farmers to trade at the local markets, this did not amount to the legalization of long-distance trade. The political risk was tremendous. Thus, although these traders did not have many options (the main alternative was a return to farming), they still required an adventurous spirit to continue after experiencing harassment and witnessing many of their peers being sent to prison.

Shortages in the urban areas also created market demand for rural products, making it difficult, if not impossible, for the state to successfully enforce the ban. Since so many people were involved in this illegal industry, identifying and catching the criminals was no easy task. To compound the problem for authorities, in addition to buses, farmers also used bicycles to bring their goods to the cities. Throughout the early 1980s, farmers in northern Jiangsu packed their bikes with chickens, ducks, and other fowl, crossed the Yangzi River, and shipped their products by rail to Nanjing, Shanghai, Ningbo, and other urban centers in the Yangzi basin. "A million roosters cross the mighty Yangzi" was the expression of the day, suggesting the ubiquity of rural to urban entrepreneurial activities.[28] In Guangzhou in the late 1970s and early 1980s, rural peddlers with "entrepreneurial vigor" gingerly negotiated themselves around bureaucratic power.[29]

The surge of small rural merchants and peddlers not only brought changes to the lives of urban people by ending the long food lines, but also helped to create market institutions, which in turn changed the perception of some government officials toward the need for market reform. Rural peddlers helped build China's economy and transformed the planned economy: the share of state and collective ownership among commercial entities dropped from 97 percent in 1979 to 70 percent in 1991.[30]

A rural minority woman from Baojing County, Hunan Province named Minghui Zhou began her business by buying shoes in major cities—in Wuhan, Changsha, and Guangzhou—and selling them in her hometown, Baojing. She had to leave her three children behind during her one- or two-month journeys. Zhou and her family lived frugally, saved much of their money, and invested in building new houses. When returning from her mountain sales trips, she bought herbs, mushrooms, and other local goods and resold them in county markets. After ten years of hard work and helping two of her children get college degrees, Zhou settled down and collected rent every month from the six houses her family built over the years. She is one of the *nouveau riche* in her hometown, Baojing.

Peng Xiaobia (pseudonym), a farmer, lived in Xiaogan about fifty miles from Wuhan, and he rose each morning at 4:00 AM. After packing his heavy-duty bicycle, Peng started his enterprise by taking chickens to sell in Wuhan. His wife packed his lunches and bought chickens from other villages. By 1985, Peng had saved enough to build a roadside hotel.[31]

The more rural merchants there were, the more private companies appeared, the richer the economy became, and the more the government was able to earn through taxation. As a group, the best-known rural merchants came from Wenzhou, a mountainous region in Zhejiang Province. Wenzhou residents have a historic tradition of trading and mobile peddling. Even under Mao, in an effort to supplement their meager incomes, they often attempted to evade the ban on rural-urban migration, leaving their villages to sell handicrafts. Thus, it should not be surprising to learn that after the creation of the household-based economy, the Wenzhou entrepreneurs took the lead in the development of further private entrepreneurship. As a result, Zhejiang had an annual growth rate for private enterprises of 13.5 percent, the highest in any province.[32]

Like their counterparts in nineteenth century America, Chinese entrepreneurs mix prudence with daring and hard work with frugality. One of the best-known rural entrepreneurs in China today is Wang Feiyu, nicknamed Wang Ba (this is a pun, since phonetically the Chinese can be translated as either an Internet bar or a bastard, depending on which characters are used). Wang grew up in rural Shanxi, a poor province in western China. After making some money as a rural industrialist, he decided to move to Beijing to try his luck at other endeavors. There, in 1997, he opened the city's first Internet cafe, although at the time he could not use a computer.[33]

The impetus for setting up the cafe was an observation similar to one made by all entrepreneurs—perceived high demand, with limited or no supply. In this case, his observation was that many students needed to use computers but few had access to them. Consequently, he borrowed some money and set up an Internet cafe close to Beijing University. As the cafe became popular, several government officials became concerned about the potential uses of such establishments by students and the possible consequence of another Tiananmen Square-like incident led by students after reading too many things on the Internet. They attempted to force him to move.

Wang knew that fighting directly with the officials would be fruitless. However, he had his own political connections, which he used to fight his battle. In the spirit of *guanxi* (using one's connections), one of Wang's friends arranged an opportunity for Wang to meet Vice Premier Li Nanqing, who happened to be from Shanxi. Although the vice premier was viewed as a conservative leader who held strong reservations about market development and the Internet, he intervened on Wang's behalf. To understand the reason why is to understand the complexity of the Chinese entrepreneur's environment. Because so few entrepreneurs from Shanxi could have made it this far, had Li turned Wang away, he would have "lost face" in the eyes of his home province, and he would not have been able to face his fellow citizens when he returned to Shanxi because Wang was the pride of Shanxi people.[34] This would have been far more detrimental to his future than acting counter to conservative feelings. Thus, Wang was saved and allowed to open a bigger Internet cafe close to Beijing University. Wang was subsequently elected a delegate to the National People's Congress in 2003. Ironically, he represents Shanxi Province and not Beijing, despite having lived in Beijing for a decade because he did not have a Beijing *Hukou*.

Two of the main reasons that most early Chinese entrepreneurs hailed from the countryside are, firstly, they were less controlled by the state after the household became the production unit; and second, they were less involved in the political campaigns of the Communist state. Eroding the state controlled planned economy in favor of private enterprise had become an integral part of rural life.

A leading Chinese sociologist, Lu Xueyi, has said that, "private enterprise owners started in the countryside first. Before 1991, 80% of private enterprises existed in the countryside; there were fewer private enterprises in the city. But after 1992 [Deng's southern tour and the state's new policy], private enterprises grew at a faster rate while, at the same time, large rural private enterprises also moved into cities and towns. Now [in 2000], 60% of private enterprises are in the cities and 40% in the countryside."[35] Another scholar, Jie Liping, found the same pattern in Zhejiang province, the engine of China's private sector development: "In 1989, of all registered private enterprises, 71.48% were rural firms but [...] by 1998 the percentage had dropped to 50 percent."[36]

The data show that the rural entrepreneur invasion was the principal reason for the emergence of private enterprise in China. This contradicts the common perception that the emergence of private enterprise was the aim of the old communist elite.[37] In short, the Chinese government has been always lagging behind rural entrepreneurs' action.

Although the *liangpiao* used to ensure cheap grain supplies to urban residents became useless for most Chinese in the early 1980s, the state did not formally abrogate the grain and oil supply coupons until May 2001. Only then did leaders in provinces such as Guangdong, Hunan, Hebei, Fujian, Jilin, and Zhejiang begin to reform the *Hukou* (registered residence) system. However, *Hukou* is still a sort of *apartheid*—separate development—system that for decades has marked rural people as second-class citizens by strictly distinguishing between rural and urban residence and forcing rural people to stay on the collective land.[38]

Wearing a Red Hat *(dai hongmaozi)*

Literally, *dai hongmaozi* means "wearing a red hat." This name is used to describe the practice of registering one's family business as a part of a formal legal organization in order to engage in economic activities. Another common name is *jiajiti* (sham collective enterprise). It is also called *guahu* (attaching one's household to someone else's). Those "in name only" collective or state enterprises use formal organizations for *sandai sanjie* (three substitutes and three borrowings): to issue receipts, keep books, pay taxes, to issue letters of introduction, write contracts, and open bank accounts. The formal legal organization (i.e., the organization that provides the cover) gets a certain percentage of the profits from the private rural entrepreneurs, varying from 8 percent to 15 percent in Zhejiang and 1 percent to 5 percent in Hubei.[39] Like *baochan daohu*, *dai hongmaozi* was a subterfuge to circumvent official patterns. Government officials call those sham collective businesses *sisunzi* (illegitimate children).

According to one government investigation in 1987 (the year before the government formally allowed private enterprises to be established), 50,000 private enterprises were using the names of rural collective enterprises. In Zhejiang more than 30 percent of private enterprises registered as rural collectives.[40] The *Chinese Industrial and Commercial News* estimated in 1996 that 70 percent of enterprises in villages, townships, and neighborhoods consisted of such *Potemkin* (fake) collectives.[41]

In his 1988 book, Wang Kesi showed that most private firms on the east coast of China were established in1984 and 1985, several years before the state first legalized such activity in 1988 (see Table 3.1 below). This table shows that more than half of the interviewed private enterprises were established between 1984 to 1985 in Wenzhou and Shanghai, while more than 93 percent of 5556 Anhui rural private enterprises were founded between 1984 and 1987, several years ahead of the government's 1988 legal recognition.[42] This shows that the 1988 law, important as it is, merely accepted the social reality of already existing private enterprises.

Rural entrepreneurs in Wenzhou were most successful in adopting the practice of "wearing a red hat" on a large scale. In 1980, when farmers in other places secretly made deals to leave the commune system, Wenzhou farmers used the same method to achieve contracts for small village industries. For example, villagers in Jingxin negotiated with local officials to contract production with a previously money-losing office supply factory. At first, they divided the factory into four shops and carried out a policy of *sitong shizi* (four similarities and

Table 3.1
Timing of Private Business

Founding Time	Anhui (5556)	Wenzhou Shanghai (120)	Nation as a Whole
1979	-	9.35	
1981-1979	-	6.26	-
1983	6.62	19.79	25.80
1984-1985	34.82	43.76	40.20
1986 – 1987	58.72	20.84	34.00

Source: Wang Kesi, *Zhongguo jieduan siying qiye tansuo (An Exploration of Current Chinese Private Enterprises)*, (Shanghai: Fudan University Press, 1988), p. 2.

nine independences). *Sitong* roughly refers to the same leadership, the same factory name, the same bank account, and the same tax rate (7 percent); *shizi* can be summarized as voluntary cooperation, independent work contracts, self-improvement of technology, independent production, self-investment, independent instruments, independent production quotas, and independent responsibility for profit and loss. In this way, private control of production was clearly guaranteed but the appearance of a commune entity avoided political attention from both the government and people. Other villagers imitated this model. Within less than a year, 2500 village factories were using the *dai hong-maozi* approach. This factory cluster model was originally the innovation of the Wenzhou entrepreneurs.[43]

When profits soared, local officials allowed village households to take over the management but demanded fees in return.[44] By using the commune's name, these early private firms survived the anti-capitalist wind within the party.[45] The demonstration effect of "wearing a red hat" attracted villagers in other rural places and became widespread in the countryside. Starting with a few hundred or thousand Yuan, many rural entrepreneurs became millionaires or even billionaires in less than twenty years, a typical story of rags-to-riches in contemporary China. Wenzhou in 1988 was one of the busiest places in China. Street dealing was a way of life for Wenzhou people in the early 1980s.

There were several reasons for the development of *guahu* in the countryside. First, the social and political environment in China was hostile to private business. The regime upheld Four Cardinal Principles (Socialist Road; Marxism, Leninism, and Maoist Thought; the People's Dictatorship; and the Leadership of the Communist Party) under socialism as the only proper social structure. As soon as it attained power in China, the Communist Party began killing the rich and powerful elements of society. In February 1950, under Mao's sway, the Central Committee established a quota of killing one out of every thousand persons. Mao personally instructed leaders in Shanghai and Nanjing to carry out the killings:

> Shanghai is a huge city with a population of 6 million. Only 200 have been killed and 20,000 arrested. I believe in 1951 at least 3000 people, including bandit chiefs, strong [wealthy] men, bullies, spies and heads of organized crime gangs should be killed. At least 1500 should be killed within the first year of [1951]. Only slightly more than 200 people got killed in Nanjing, the former capital of the Guomintang and a city with half a million population. We should kill in Nanjing...As people have remarked, killing the counterrevolutionaries is as soothing as a nice rain.[46]

The killing was massive. In 1950 and 1951, 712,000 were executed, 1,290,000 were imprisoned, and 1,200,000 were sent to labor camps. The percentage killed surpassed the government's target quota: 1.24 out of 1000. Many of the victims were killed for the crime of being rich. In the 1960s, the Four Cleanups campaign further scared anyone with an entrepreneurial spirit. The government did not give legal recognition to *siying* (private enterprises) until 1988.[47] Thus, rural entrepreneurs feared becoming the targets of political campaigns.

When five local entrepreneurs were asked why there were so few private enterprises in Xiangxi, rural Hunan, in the 1980s, three of them replied that the fear of imprisonment and the fear of confiscation were the main reasons.[48] During the crackdown period in 1950 and 1951, 4600 people were killed in Xiangxi, a small minority region with a population smaller than 400,000. Often, rural entrepreneurs had four fears: fear of confiscation; fear of being forced to take on new employees and new leadership when efficiency improved and wages grew; fear of becoming targets if they made any mistakes; and fear of being forced out of business if they were successful.

Since the Chinese regime constantly changes its policies towards private business, few trust the government. Although the government has allowed the private sectors and entrepreneurs to exist, the state has at times made a conscious effort to devalue private entrepreneurs. In August 1989, the Central Government issued a document (No. 9), Directives to Strengthen the Party, specifying, "The relationship between the heads of private businesses and their workers is exploitative. No head of any private business will be allowed to join the Communist Party."[49] Party members working in private firms automatically lost party status. In 1983 and 1989 the government attacked private businesses as the root cause of corruption. After the 1989 Tiananmen "incident," the government launched a national campaign to attack private businesses. All major Chinese newspapers criticized private entrepreneurs as an exploitative class which caused instability.

The *guahu* practice helped the private sector to survive. When the government began to relax its policies in 1992, privatization became a major trend. By 1999, in coastal regions such as Wenzhou and Zhejiang, more than 90 percent of all rural businesses were private. The sham collective enterprises helped rural entrepreneurs get around government restrictions on private businesses. For example, regulations established in 1983 prohibited private businesses from hiring more than five workers. Although the state did not specify the punishment for those who violated it, this regulation made many rural entrepreneurs reluctant to expand their private business. "Wearing a red hat" enabled small private businesses to go beyond government regulations by hiring more than five persons. Although rural specialized commercial households ignored this regulation, with 50 percent of them hiring long-term rural workers in larger numbers, the entrepreneurs' fear of state confiscation led some rural industrial enterprises to utilize the formal organizations to avoid legal problems. For example, in Chongqing, Sichuan Province, private enterprises hired two hundred workers by "wearing a red hat."[50] When the former party secretary of a village in Heilongjiang tried to form a private construction firm, he had to use the collective name to register the business, since the provincial government did not allow private businesses.[51] In 1988, the private company made a profit of 4 million Yuan. Clearly, *guahu* enabled rural entrepreneurs to break through state restrictions on the size or scale of private businesses.

Moreover, "wearing a red hat" helped rural enterprises and merchants gain access to bank transfer notes and checks that they would otherwise have been denied. Rural entrepreneurs had to carry cash for business transactions. Some had to pay police for protection if they carried large sums. One rural entrepreneur, Zhou Minghui, from Baojing, Hunan Province, tired of paying police and attached her businesses to a formal organization in her county seat, saying, "With *guahu,* I get checks from the bank and do not carry cash with me all the time. Although I have to pay the county government use its name, I can get bank loans and have bank accounts, just as collective firms do."[52]

"Wearing a red hat" overcame other restrictions on banking and borrowing as well. In Shuqian County of Jiangsu Province, village collective enterprises received small loans (less than 5,000 Yuan) without going through an approval process. A private business, on the other hand, required approval from the county bank if the loan was more than 1,000 Yuan.[53] While a private enterprise could never issue a receipt acceptable to a government entity that they did business with, a collective could issue such receipts easily. Banks either refused to give loans to private business people or charged them high interest rates. In some places, the interest rate for loans reached as high as 18 percent for private loans.[54] No state-owned enterprise would take receipts from private enterprises, especially rural ones, and exhibitions refused entry to non-state enterprises. "Wearing a red hat" overcame the structural barriers and enabled rural entrepreneurs to acquire the social cover of collective enterprises.

A further advantage of this strategy was that its legal status brought about direct economic benefits to rural entrepreneurs through tax and economic privileges. For one thing, collective enterprises paid lower taxes than private ones. According to the state 1986 tax law for private businesses, private firms were taxed 60 percent of earnings if their net earnings did not exceed 30,000 Yuan and were taxed 84 percent, if they earned more.[55] When a private firm wired money through the collective firm's account, the legitimate firm would deduct 7.5 to 8 percent. But for many village firms, additional fees of 2.5 percent (supposedly for the village community, but actually used by local officials) would be added.[56]

Since this heavy tax did not include enterprise taxes and management fees, the state progressive tax law made it virtually impossible for private business to make money legally. "Wearing a red hat" enabled rural entrepreneurs to make use of government policies, especially regarding tax privileges for collective enterprises. Many rural private businesses could not have survived the tax burden without pretending to be a collective firm. For example, two farmers in a village of Fujian Province who gathered 140,000 Yuan to set up a packaging factory owned everything personally. Everyone in the village knew that the factory belonged to these two farmers but the factory had to carry the name of a village collective. By using the name, the private village factory paid lower taxes to the state and received low-interest loans. After paying 5,000 Yuan in management fees to the village head and another 1,000 to the township government, the village factory went about its business unhampered.

To cite another example, in some places in Guangdong, collective enterprises paid no taxes for the first three years of operation. Even in the less developed region of northeast China, when the manager of a private tractor repair shop in Heilongjiang Province heard that collective enterprises that hire handicapped people would be granted a tax exemption, he immediately recruited several handicapped people and attached the factory to the Civil Affairs Bureau.[57] With good management and a reduced tax burden, this village-based private business grew into an enterprise with capital assets of more than one million Yuan. Apart from paying a 30,000-Yuan management fee, the company had no real connection to the Civil Affairs Bureau, despite its official attachment.[58]

Moreover, private businesses had to pay management fees to local governments. By becoming *guahu*, the rural entrepreneurs were able to avoid tremendous fees aimed at private business. An example from a rural factory in Jieshou of Anhui illustrates the benefits of *guahu* for rural entrepreneurs despite the fees.

> In 1980 a farmer applied for permission to establish a factory in the county seat. At that time, private persons were not allowed to use land in town, nor could they open bank accounts for their firms. The law was sidestepped by designating the business a TVP at the commune level under the direct control of the county. This status made the firm eligible for more liberal bank loans than ordinary private enterprises and exempt from taxes. In addition, it obtained easier access to low-cost inputs through the government channels that served rural industries, advantages in obtaining fiscal assistance from the government (such as a Y5000 interest-free loan for working capital), better credit standing because of being able to use the county's name, and the privilege of selecting a plant site anywhere in the county...We were amazed to find that the firm had just bought 1 mu of land at the new site for Y10,000, although China's constitution forbids private ownership of land. The purchase would have been impossible had the firm not been designated a township enterprise. In return for all these privileges, the enterprise pays 1 percent of its gross sales as a management fee to the county business administration every year.[59]

Rural entrepreneurs in Henan have an expression to describe this rent-seeking behavior: "Small and medium size enterprises depend on *san ju* (three government bureaus), the district government branch office for tax, the neighborhood police bureau, and the local commercial office; the large ones depend on the county magistrate." To some extent, the fees became a form of local government taxes imposed upon the private sector. According to one survey, today there are more than sixty-seven state bureaus collecting eighty-nine different taxes and fees from private businesses, of which forty-one have no legal basis.[60] As the *People's Daily* reported on April 10, 2003, "the total fees imposed on township village enterprises are about 20% of the profits, 3% of the total sales of a firm."[61] This suggests that entrepreneurs have to pay a price for entering into the market.

The new business model also helped enterprises avoid the mistrust that the public had for private businesses, even though government leaders sometimes made remarks like those of Deng Xiaoping in the 1980s and Jiang Zemin in late 1990s to encourage some people to become rich first. "In China, for so long the government had educated everyone that making money was an evil act," Lei Tao, a Shenzhen trader, remarked. "The government agencies would not deal with private businesses and the people would not buy products from private businesses in the 1980s. Thus we had to use the *gongjia* (public-owned) name to conduct private business. It was a norm in the 1980s."[62] Lei set up a trading company by attaching his company to the Shenzhen Education Bureau in 1985.

Interviews with four rural entrepreneurs in 2004 showed that many Wenzhou private businesses used the system of "wearing a red hat" to gain national recognition. One local Wenzhou government official remarked:

> Jinxiang rural household factories were producing plastic *liangpiao* (grain coupons), badges of all sorts, trademarks, and plastic certificates. There was no way that governments at all levels in China at that time would buy anything so important from private rural family businesses. But there was a strong need for this kind of product. Thus, Jinxiang people used *guahu* to deal with governments outside our district. The result was that within less than two years, Jinxiang products supplied more than 50% of China's demand for badges, plastic covers, and other related products.[63]

According to leading Chinese economists who studied Wenzhou, sixteen of the largest Jinxiang factories all carried the names of a commune or collective in the early days of their businesses.

A further benefit of "wearing a red hat," apart from economic benefits and political protection, was the increased social status of rural enterprises, especially the ability to legally transfer from a rural to an urban designation. Once a rural enterprise enjoyed the legal status of a county or township collective enterprise, entrepreneurs and sometimes workers gained urban *Hukou* and other privileges of urban residents. Politically, entrepreneurs may have been promoted into formal cadres, enjoying life tenure appointment in the government bureaucracy. Even their family members were be able to obtain *Hukou*. William Byrd also found that moneymaking was not the only concern of rural entrepreneurs:

> Non-pecuniary goals include providing employment and a secure future for [immediate] family members and, to a lesser extent, other relatives; improving one's social and official status (for example, by becoming a second-class urban resident as many Jiezhou entrepreneurs did); and even contributing to local community welfare and employment.[64]

As a result of those benefits, many rural business people tried their best to seek *kaoshan* (a reliable mountain, i.e., a big shot) or *zaopojia* (a mother-in-law). The practice of "wearing a red hat," thus, flourished. By the early 1990s, it became a common method for farmers to expand their businesses. In Sixia County of Henan Province, sham collective businesses comprised 36 percent of all *getihu* (individual private firms) and 30 percent of all private enterprises were sham collectives.[65] In Wenzhou in 1988, only ten of ten thousand enterprises would dare to register as private enterprises. But in truth, all of them were private.[66] Today, in Changle County of Fujian Province, 80 percent of rural industries are *guahu*, and in Shantou, Guangdong Province, *guahu* enterprises constitute 90 percent of all enterprises.[67]

"Wearing a red hat" also occurred when a collective firm facing difficulties asked a private rural company to take it over, assuming its debts. This was especially true in rural areas where industry was undeveloped. According to Lou Xiaopeng, in the 1980s, 50 percent of all private companies in less-developed areas took over collective enterprises but used the collectives' legal status to retain their privileges.[68] The old collective enterprises continued to exist in name and receive various benefits from the government, but the enterprises became private, enjoying independence. Since it saved rural enterprises from bankruptcy, local government leaders often ignored this practice so long as the firms continued to pay local taxes. This was another form of *baochan daohu*. The protection furnished by "wearing a red hat" sheltered private enterprises. This practice best illustrates China's mixed economy or so-called "socialism with Chinese characteristics" where Communist Party officials and entrepreneurs coexist to gain access to resource allocation. *Guahu* is an example of what Victor Nee has called a hybrid form of organization, which "represents a solution to the problem of weak market structures and incomplete market transition."[69] These hybrid forms provide entrepreneurs political protection while at the same time helping them gain privileged access to local authorities, and through them, to resources.[70]

Since ownership structure is blurred, there have been documented cases of coercion and property confiscation. In some instances, when *guahu* businesses grew, the local government gave in to the temptation of taking over the businesses. But in general, the practice in the beginning provided institutional protection for rural entrepreneurs. Once the situation became relatively favorable after 1993, many rural private businesses openly emerged from their *guahu* closets.

Moreover, numerous rural industries established relations with urban factories through *guahu*, greatly increasing the interdependence between the rural and urban residents. While state factories benefited from the efficiency of rural industries, rural factories gained new technology from their urban state cousins.[71] In Suzhou, Jiangsu province, several hundred rural enterprises attached themselves to the State Foreign Trade companies, accounting for a third of the exports from that city in 1985.[72] *Guahu* enabled many private rural enterprises to march into urban markets under disguise of legality. In fact, the emergence of rural corporations in the cities in the early 1990s resulted from *guahu*.

The diffusion of the *guahu* phenomenon provided important paths of expansion for private businesses on the one hand and the erosion of the state's power on the other. In November 1986, the national state business and commercial administration bureau issued a document attempting to halt the spread of *guahu*. The document pointed out that between 80 percent and 90 percent of cooperatives were in fact private partnerships and demanded that the local government change their licenses into private business licenses. However, *guahu* was so important for the growth of rural industries that the state could not undo the status quo without giving up its economic benefits, which it was loathe to do.[73] While *baochan daohu* restored family farming, *guahu* facilitated and expanded the growth of private businesses, which absorbed the surplus labor released from agriculture. For the transition of China's economy from Communism to privately owned businesses, the key ingredient has been the entrepreneurial risk-taking behavior that created market opportunities from previous non-market conditions. In this sense, Chinese rural entrepreneurs resemble the "pure entrepreneurs" proposed by Israel M. Kirzner.[74]

Rural Industrial Entrepreneurs

The rise of entrepreneurs and the spread of private ownership produced values outside, or even starkly opposed to, those of Maoist Communism. Some were traditional values (trust, diligence, thrift, self-reliance) but others were new, such as risk and initiative taking, venturing outside accepted norms. These values are best described by the Chinese term, *chuang*, whose Chinese character is a house within a gate, but the gate door is open. The most daring group was rural entrepreneurs.

The sudden rise of rural industrial entrepreneurs has had far-reaching significance for the Chinese political economy. First of all, rural industrial entrepreneurs altered the ownership structure of Chinese socialist industrialization. The non-state sector, led by rural industrial entrepreneurs, changed the landscape of industrialization from state-owned domination to non-state, challenging the dominance of the state industrial sector and forming the backbone of Chinese industrial production. This competition forced the state to reform some of its dying industries that were predominantly unprofitable.

Before the take-off of rural industrialization, the state took virtually "all of the surplus generated by industry, including profits and indirect taxes, and local governments were able to retain only a portion of the profits of selected local enterprises."[75] But the rapid growth of rural industry changed this pattern. Rural industries eroded the state's main source of revenue: monopoly profits of state-owned industries. As a result, the central state budget shrank from over 40 percent of national income in 1978 to only 22 percent in 1989.[76]

It is important to emphasize that private enterprises emerged in rural China several years before the government passed its 1988 permission regulation. This is especially true in places like Wenzhou and Zhejiang where there had been a tradition of commercial trading and family business even prior to 1978. For example, before 1986, 23,302 rural households (90 percent of the total) in the Yingshan district of Changnan county, Zhejiang, had already begun to operate family-owned textile factories. Not a Yuan of initial investment capital originated from the government-owned banks. Second, rural industrial entrepreneurs have pioneered market development across China. Entrepreneurs saw gaps in the planned economy and exploited them to their comparative advantage. With the planned economy, shortages were the norm. Urbanites lined up for hours for bad products, while rural Chinese were cut off from most commercial exchange. The rural industrial revolution resolved this issue.

They have led China's Industrial Revolution. For example, in Zhejiang and Guangdong provinces, many small commodity markets mushroomed. The largest and most famous in China is the Yiwu Small Commodity Market run by rural merchants and rural industrial entrepreneurs. Our interviews with scholars and officials in Zhejing found that the development of the Yiwu Small Commodity Market by private entrepreneurs meant that in the 1980s, more than 70 percent of industrial and agricultural production was already in private hands.[77]

This farmer-led market transformation resulted from the struggle between farmers' desire for more liberty and the state's tendency towards total control. The story of the development of the Liushi electronic market illustrates the innovative entrepreneurship of rural farmers and the government's attempt to control market development. In 1970, a farmer, Chen Qingyao, visited a friend in a mining town in Anhui and found out that there was a shortage of sockets (used to link mining machines). Since a planned economy meant that all machines were produced and sold in complete sets, no spare parts were produced anywhere in China. Chen then hand copied a drawing of the sockets and returned to his home in Liushi to start production. He invited a technician from a local lock factory and used his home as a workshop and his family members as workers. Thus, in Liushi, the first *dixia jiating gongchang* (underground family factory) was born. In 1972, with another farmer, Chen Weisong, Chen Qingyao established Tiaodong Metal Electronics with 19 workshops and 125 workers. But when, in 1976, the factory received a letter of credit for 35,000 Yuan to order products, the county office of Attacking Opportunist Trading forced all the workers in the factory to attend political study sessions, declaring that "anyone who made 1000 Yuan would be labeled *huaifengzi* (a bad element); anyone who made 5000 Yuan would go to prison; and anyone who made 10,000 Yuan would be executed."[78] This attack forced the factory to close, but other small-scale family factories remained.

When the political environment became more relaxed after *baochan daohu*, electric parts production in Liushi boomed, with three hundred households engaging in production in 1981. The business was so successful that other businesses, such as metal processing, screws production, index card printing, electronic wires production, casting, marketing, mining lights factories, and second-hand equipment markets spun off. In order to sell their products across China, an army of ten thousand salespersons was created. In 1982, however, the central government took notice of this perceived industrial and marketing challenge and issued a directive to contain its development. On May 20th, 1982, the provincial government sent a work team to Liushi to stifle this outbreak of capitalism. Facing prosecution, a number of well-known rural entrepreneurs, whose market domination in China earned them fame as the "Eight Kings," all faced imprisonment, fines, and the loss of their businesses.[79]

But in 1984, when the local government began losing money due to revenue losses from factories, it released the eight big entrepreneurs. From this point on, Liushi embarked upon a new wave of entrepreneurial activity. By 1984, there were one thousand shops and fifty thousand sales staff specializing in marketing various electrical products.[80] This was four years ahead of the state's endorsement of private enterprises given in 1988.

In Guangdong, rural industrialists adopted the export development strategy called the Zhujiang Model or the Pearl Delta Model. Both physically and culturally close to Hong Kong, rural Zhujiang entrepreneurs were able to cultivate clan and family relations to help market the output of the factories they set up. With a significant international presence in the region, rural industrial entrepreneurs cared more about export contracts outside of China than about China's internal market.

In terms of overseas Chinese investment, rural industries in this region received very little before 1990. After 1990, however, the share of overseas Chinese investment increased rapidly, especially in the Pearl Delta region. Rural entrepreneurs tried to attract overseas Chinese investment by using their village and family connections. Unlike other places, most capital in this area arrived from external sources after 1993, largely from Hong Kong business people with close family and blood ties to rural industrialists in Guangdong.

Regardless of the developmental model, family-centered rural industrial clusters were effective in promoting economies of scale. When one family succeeded, other families soon followed suit, as expressed in a 1980s rural saying, "*yihu dai yicun; yicun dai yipian; cuncun dianhuo; huhu maoyan*," (one household influences one village; one village affects one district; every village has an [industrial] smoke stack; every household emits smog).[81]

As might be expected, rural industry developed unevenly in China, varying from region to region. The eastern and southern rural regions developed faster than the rest of the country. This uneven development complicates the analysis of Chinese farmers' industrial development. Nonetheless, rural industrial development in less-developed regions has also been crucial. Even in Gansu, one of the country's poorest provinces, rural industry made up 26 percent of overall output value by 1986.[82] Nowhere in China is rural industry irrelevant to development, although geographically, the scale of impact varies considerably.

Rural influence threatened the state's planning to such a degree that in his 1989 government report, then-Premier Li Peng called for a reduction of rural industrial development and advocated the return of *sanjiudi* (that local development should be contained).[83] However, as happened in its attempts to curtail *guahu*, the rapid development of rural industries and the changes that accompanied it made it impossible for the state to stop the growth of rural industry without injuring its own interests.

Despite the great achievement of rural industries, much of the world's attention has focused either on the elite (especially Deng Xiaoping) or on overseas Chinese investment. There is no doubt that state permission for rural people to set up small-scale industries opened the gate for farmers. However, the main goal of the official elite was to stop rural-urban migration. Their real concern was for the state factories. Since their power base was built upon the state industries, the elites, including Deng, often attempted to constrain rural industries, especially when state factory revenues were shrinking. This sudden erosion of state revenue startled Deng. As late as 1989, according to Joseph Fewsmith, Deng Xiaoping's support for rural industries was still wavering. In 1989, when state industry dominance was threatened by competition from rural industries, Deng remarked in a Politburo meeting that "it is all right to shut down inefficient or wasteful village and township enterprises."[84]

The Chinese experience makes clear that the rural population is not inherently antagonistic to modernization. The marginalization of rural people in Chinese elite politics may have also benefited rural industrialists because the leaders paid little attention to rural people. The state apparatus has continued to run under the urban planned model but has become increasingly irrelevant by doing so. During the entire reform period (1978-93), state rural investment in fact declined from 10 percent of all capital investment in 1978 to a little over 2 percent in 1992. State leaders knew little about the farmers' industrial development until it gathered too much momentum to reverse.[85]

Rural entrepreneurs took full advantage of the central leadership's ignorance of or lack of interest in them to develop industries with a vengeance and, above all, on a spontaneous, unorganized, leaderless, non-ideological, and apolitical basis. Robert C. Tucker, a leading scholar on political leadership, has pointed out that politics must take account not only of leadership by those in state authority, but also of sociopolitical movements for change that act as vehicles for attempted leadership of political communities. The rural industrial entrepreneurs, in fact, became political leaders from the grassroots level even though they did not set out to lead a movement.

Due to the nature of the Chinese Communist regime's control over organizations, grassroots liberal movements often take a particular form, that of non-state businesses. In this way, rural entrepreneurs were also early leaders. It is important to distinguish between unconscious de facto "leaders" and *designated* leaders. Rural entrepreneurs can be called entrepreneur leaders "in themselves," which makes them different from social movement leaders "for themselves"—like the underground Christian house churches activists. However, both have contributed to the emergence of China's civil society.

Development of the *Jimao* Industrial Wholesale Markets (JIRMs)

Rural industrial entrepreneurs have been linked to another unique market development in China, the *jimao* (farmers' commerce) industrial wholesale markets. This kind of market, at first, evolved from *jishi* (farmers' markets) but later evolved into wholesale markets for small commodity industrial products. There are five features of JIRMs in China. First, the markets focus on an individual commodity such as clothing, electronics, shoes, buttons, or the like, distinguishing the JIRMs from comprehensive markets, supermarkets, and department stores. Second, wholesale dealings predominate though retail also exists. This feature differentiates the JIRMs from *jishi* (farmers' markets) and other commodity markets. Third, the salespeople exhibit a high level of market specialization, which means that the JIRMs achieve a certain economy of scale. The JIRMs thus differ from specialized commodity stores. Fourth, they consist of over-the-counter trading. Fifth, both the daily and weekly trading hours are longer than those of ordinary markets.

The development of the JIRMs has arisen out of a struggle between the rural people's desire to improve their lives by diversification of production and the state's fear of rural industrial and market competition with the state industries. Almost all early JIRMs evolved from *malu shichang* (street markets) and *heishichang* (black markets). For more than twenty years, all street market exchanges were labeled as *touji daoba* (illegal trading opportunism). Thus, the only surviving *malu shichang* and *heishichang* were located in deep mountainous regions and islands where, proverbially, "the sky is high and the emperor is far away."

Even during the high tide of the Cultural Revolution, a few rural people participated in black market activities. The state was so alarmed that in many places a special government bureau called *Daji touji daoba bagongshi* (Office of Attacking Trading Opportunists) was established to curtail private trading in grain, grain coupons, art, building raw materials, cotton, lumber, water buffaloes, fertilizers, and other agricultural sidelines. In some parts of Shaoxin, Zhejiang Province, people openly traded in illegal markets or black markets despite the attacks.[86] Even in the 1970s under Mao, rural people in Wenzhou, Zhejiang, took advantage of the Cultural Revolution's chaos to initiate underground private construction contracts, private transportation, *minjian shichang* (local free markets), black markets for raw materials, and other forms of trade.[87] From the table below, we can see that the number of illegal traders (*wuzheng shangfan*) in 1976 was estimated at 11,115. By 1976, more than 90 percent of the total commercial sales in Wenzhou took place in the black market, even though at the time China was still explicitly Maoist.[88] In 1976 Mao's wife Jiang Qing launched an attack against the development of capitalism in Wenzhou, saying, "if you want to see capitalism, go to Wenzhou."[89] The central government subsequently adopted the policies of *jin*, *du*, and *gan* (ban, stop, and chase).

Yasheng Huang points out as early as 1985, 10 million businesses classified as collective were in fact private.[90]

Rural Women Entrepreneurs

Chinese rural women played key roles not only in the decollectivization movement but also in the widespread appearance of entrepreneurialism. In the early days, rural female merchants dominated most free markets in both cities and the countryside. Some have been very successful. An example is one Jiang Guilan, who after completing middle school, migrated to the city where she learned the basics of plastic production. In 1991, after a decade of working in different factories, she borrowed 200,000 Yuan from friends and family members to set up a plastic products company. After only four years (1995), she was able to rent a space from a state company at the Annual Guangzhou Commodity Trade Show and signed her first contract with a foreign company. Before 2000, private companies were banned from direct foreign trade. Like most other private firms, Ms. Jiang had to pay a high price to a state foreign trade company in order to have her products show. Here corruption became the price of entry into foreign trade for the private companies. Gradually, most export manufacturing sectors became private in the 2000s. In 2005, employing more than a thousand workers, Jiang's company became KFC'S main suppler for plates and eating utensils, requiring six hundred sea-going containers annually to transport them.[91]

Illegal and Black Market Traders in Wenzhou in the 1970s

There are several additional points to be made about the JIRMs. First, the early market activities described above trained a generation of Wenzhou people, making them pioneers of the JIRMs in the 1980s. Thus, by 1982, non-state capital investment in Wenzhou reached 49 percent when the political environment was less hostile toward private local trading activities.[92] Fei Xiaotong, a well-known sociologist, confirmed our findings in Fujian and parts of South Jiangsu:

> During the ten-year chaos [the CR], the whole nation suffered. But in the countryside, rural industries in villages and communes were able to develop because of the chaos, turning bad luck into good fortune. I was surprised when I first heard that the commune and village factories were like a famous Chinese saying, *luashi chuyingxiong*, (heroes grew in times of chaos). After listening to the history of rural development, one realizes that the horror of urban violence [the CR period] and of the forced exile of "urban cadres" and high school students to the countryside provided two key conditions for rural industrial development: educated urbanites provided both market information and technology know how.[93]

Second, the development of the JIRMs overcame systematic discrimination against non-state industrial organizations in the planned economy, enabling rural industries to gain market shares and access to raw materials. China's socialist economy meant explicit state control of all marketing and distribution of raw materials and goods. The government did not allocate raw material, loans, and credit to rural industries, nor would the state's commercial departments help them sell their goods. Thus, many specialized commodity wholesale markets were developed to fill this gap in the sale of raw materials. Of 95,000 existing wholesale entities, some 6,200 dealt in raw materials alone.[94] The JIRMs thus helped rural industries gain access to raw materials and markets, bringing competition into China's industrialization process. A rural saying has this to say about rural industrial development: "*Qianjia wanhu, piandi kaihua*" (literally, "digging under the foundation," i.e., undermining the planned economy).[95]

Third, the JIRMs eliminated the traditional system of wholesale trading, which required the approval of three levels of government planning bureaucracies. The JIRMs provided three "fixes," enabling both consumers and producers to buy and sell with few restrictions. A JIRM is a system of *tanwei zhi* (stall ownership responsibility). In many JIRMs there are thousands of *tanwei* (stalls) where each *tanwei* has many different channels for commodity production. Thus, the JIRMs had more means to bring more diversified products to the markets than the traditional system of wholesale trading.

Zhao Yunsheng, a merchant from Nanyang, a rural community in Henan Province, was able to use a JIRM to market traditional handmade rugs. When the government was in charge of selling the rugs, sales were low and inefficient, which meant less material benefits for rural handicraft makers. Frustrated, Zhao began selling the products first in the street markets and then in a JIRM, rapidly increasing the sales revenue to millions of US dollars. This expeditious increase has not only made Zhao rich but also improved the life of many rural families. He is currently treated like a king in his local community in Nanyang because his marketing has enabled more than one hundred Nanyang rural households to become non-agricultural workers and concentrate on rug making. "I am just one drop of water in the sea of JIRMs," Zhao said modestly when we met him trying to start a JIRM in the United States in 2006. "JIRMs enable me to link to the global market. I was grateful and surprised to see that there is no fixed JIRM in the United States, the world's headquarters of markets. I tried to organize my JIRM friends to come to set one up, but the American Embassy would not grant them a visa. Now I have to drive across the United States to look for marketing opportunities by visiting museums and artists' associations. It is inefficient, time-consuming and exhausting."[96]

Fourth, JIRMs have led to clusters of village industries. Villages close to JIRMs produce for the wholesale markets while merchants from throughout China provide new styles and innovative ideas to local rural industries. At the same time, JIRMs tend to become established in regions where clusters of industries are situated. This interaction facilitates development of both non-state industries as well as marketing networks.

Fifth, the development of JIRMs ended the monopoly of the state's big department stores. All the major state department stores had to reform to meet the competition from JIRMs or face bankruptcy.

Sixth, JIRMs are competitive because of their economic independence. Each vendor is private or non-state, making it easy for vendors to organize their merchandise according to market demand. As independent entities, they attend to their costs and to the market, following the needs of consumers and the demands of seasons and fashion. JIRM merchants became formidable competitors for urban state sales organizations and, in a short ten-year span, JIRMs took over a substantial part of the wholesale market.

As a result of the JIRMs' successes, nearly all state sales organizations were soon running in the red. For example, 26 out of 29 state commercial organizations in Yinde County of Guangdong Province lost a total of 480,000 *Yuan* in 1985. In the same year, one rural merchant in Changsha, Hunan Province, could match the sale volume as a dozen workers in a state shop.[97]

Finally, the rise of rural merchants transformed social mobility in China. Trading became the fastest way to climb the social ladder for the poor as well as for the more prosperous and politically connected. In contemporary China, where the pursuit of wealth dominates ideology, the merchant route has become the preferred one. This has long-term social and global implications, since Chinese merchants are destined to play a major role in both the Chinese and the global economies.

Probos (Rags-to-Riches Urbanites)

When describing early Chinese rural entrepreneurs, one must also discuss their urban counterparts, the *probos* (proletarian bourgeoisie). The *probos* (including former convicts and youth who were forced to go to the countryside during Cultural Revolution) lacked the connections to obtain state jobs in cities. Another push factor was the failure of the planned economy to provide jobs for urban youth. Under Mao, the elite tried to solve the urban unemployment problem by forcing 20 million urban youth to go to the countryside. This practice, however, created resentment among urban working families who suffered when their families were split apart and among rural people who perceived urban youth as parasitic on their limited resources, especially grain.

In the 1980s, this pressure led the elite to begin running small family household private businesses. In Beijing, the first entrepreneurial scene was the large tea stalls set up on busy street, run by unemployed youth returning to the countryside in the early 1980s. Some became successful and started to expand, challenging the communist state, whose stated aim was to eliminate the exploitation of the workers. To understand the origins of this group one must look back to the first few years of newly communized China. After 1949, political attacks against members of the private sector were so severe that most people were afraid to attempt any activity that would put them in this group. Private entrepreneurs were regarded as the scourges of society. Even in the early 1980s, street market business licenses were reserved for unemployed youth (*daiye qingnian*). As a result, even though the state allowed small individual enterprises to exist in the early 1980's, few dared to take the opportunity due to structural fears of political backlash. Thus, in the cities, the urban downtrodden, or the future *probos*, were generally the only ones desperate enough to jump at the chance of earning money and taking control of their lives.

Although there are many examples of successful *probos*, one of the most celebrated is Mu Qizhong. Mu's story starts (and nearly ended) during the Cultural Revolution, when he was sentenced to death for criticizing government actions. He succeeded in avoiding this fate, however, and was released from prison in 1980. At that time he took a job at a glass factory, which he quickly left to participate in entrepreneurial activities. Mu borrowed three hundred Yuan from friends and relatives to establish the first private commercial agency in his hometown located in Wan County, Sichuan Province.

When Mu discovered that the bamboo chairs in his county were cheaper and more attractive than those made elsewhere, he organized the sale of bamboo chairs across the country, in the process becoming one of the first Chinese entrepreneurs to engage in long-distance trading of a non-food product. Later, with the help of friends, he was able to set up what at the time was the largest privately owned company in China, the Land Corporation. His road was not an easy one. To pursue his dream, Mu had to overcome institutional discrimination against private businesses. Besides many other impediments, the government refused to grant his company permission to use a round-shaped company chop like those used by state companies. So Mu used small square ones. The difference discouraged private businesses from competing. As a result, no state organization in the city would deal with his non-sanctioned organization. Although this example may seem trivial, it is representative of the difficulties he faced at every turn.

Unlike entrepreneurial start-ups in mature market economies whose primary concerns are business failure, complicated regulations, and market competition, Mu's worst fears were related to government interference and police harassment. As a Chinese saying goes, "Policies of the state are like the moon—they wax and wane." Mu compared his early business ventures to an untrained acrobat walking a tightrope. "I was excited about the huge market opportunities while scared to death of returning to a prison cell. I lived a life of constant sweat, sleepless nights, and thumping heartbeats."[98] Mu's marketing skills stimulated the private production of chairs within Wan County. The newly employed former farmers were so grateful for Mu's marketing and trading of their products that they allowed him to pay them three months after the sale of the chairs. Mu's company was able to retain substantial capital for reinvestment. As Mu proudly proclaimed, "Wherever there are markets and profits, there am I."[99]

In addition to the chair venture, Mu engaged in other activities. His biggest success was a well-publicized airplane barter trade involving the Russians in 1990. Although non-governmental commerce between China and the former Soviet Union existed in the 1980s, the trade was in a very primitive stage, limited to small quantities in and around the border area. When Mu discovered that there was a huge demand for consumer goods in Russia, especially food and daily necessities, he became determined to trade Chinese food and consumer product surpluses for Russian goods. "Think big and act decisively," was Mu's business motto. In the end, he decided that he wanted to trade Chinese surpluses for Russian airplanes.

For Mu, the fundamental tenet of a successful business venture was the benefit of both parties involved. Although it was obvious that Russians would buy consumer goods, Mu's belief that Chinese consumers would use Russian airplanes was bold, since at the time ordinary Chinese people were banned from purchasing airplane tickets. "People with money should have the right to fly," Mu said, "but the state's monopoly has constrained the development of the airline industry."[100] Mu had to bribe both Russian and Chinese officials to gain final authorization for the deal. In the end, five hundred cargo loads of consumer goods were traded for four Soviet jets. After this success, many energetic Chinese entrepreneurs like Mu began to make money with a vengeance. The rise of the entrepreneurial class demonstrates that the desire and determination the common man puts forth in an effort to improve his life is at least as important as any government policy in promoting market development.

There is a common perception among certain groups of foreign scholars that the government has supported the rise of entrepreneurs. Nothing could be further from the truth, as many entrepreneurs learned the hard way. Mu realized early in his career that there is a double standard when the government interacted with those involved in private enterprise as opposed to those in government-owned enterprises. This is true not only when entrepreneurs attempt to conduct business but also when they attempt to recover from mistakes. Since his release in 1980, Mu has been sent back to prison twice for offenses that were more harshly prosecuted due to his dealings in private enterprises. Because of the lack of legal protection facing non-state enterprises, his activities were easy targets once his business became profitable. When Mu was finally sentenced to life in prison in 2001, it was primarily the result of his engaging in speculative enterprises and failing to repay government loans on time. Although such activities are illegal, the punishment hardly fit the crime.

Mu's initial rise and eventual fall represents both the promise and the shortcomings of China's developmental course. Although the initial years of Mu's entrepreneurial experience are proof of the power of these risk takers, his later years are representative of the long road China still has to travel to reach a transparent market economy. As Mu became increasingly involved in the engrained corruption of the Chinese marketplace, it was only a matter of time before he crossed the wrong official and found his entrepreneurial run in ruins. The fall of Mu encouraged private business people to seek political protection from government officials, pushing for widespread rent seeking activities of most private business people. The rise and fall of Mu illustrates the love-hate relationship between businesspeople and the state. To a great extent, the number one job for most private businesses in China is to make friends with government officials.

Although some *hobos* (migrant and rural entrepreneurs) and *probos* have gone bankrupt or been thrown into prison, others have developed stable private companies based on sound economic principles. Some companies have even started to undertake research and development. For example, Zhentai Corporation in Zhejiang, formerly a *hobo*-run entity, spends 3 percent of its income on research and development.[101] In an interview with Zhentai's CFO, we learned that the corporation started as a typical *hobo* venture whose founder was a migrant shoe salesman. Within five years, he was able to build a small electronics factory, which became a leading domestic producer. As seen from Table 3.2 below, such a story is representative of *hobos* and *probos* in general, who seem to have one recurring trait of which they are very proud; namely, that they are mostly self-made, with little or no political backing.

For example, the new Chinese billionaire Chen Rong was a low-class mechanic in a Shanghai textile factory. In 1984, he asked to have work leave (*tingxin liuzhi*) to start his own company. With his life savings of $250, Chen made his first pile of gold, $12 million, in Shanghai's the stock market in the early 1990s. Chen used this money to set up Zhonglu Enterprises focusing on tenpin bowling equipment. By 2003, Zhonglu was the largest manufacturer of such equipment in China.[102]

One of the most successful homeless entrepreneurs was Anhui Province sunflower seed producer, Nian Guangjiu. Nian lost his opportunity for education because of poverty from his earliest years. After the Great Leap Famine (1959-61), a small group of Chinese tried to conduct long distance trade to seize the opportunity caused by food shortages. Nian and his family tried to sell fish in 1962 through long distance trade on the black market since at that time independent trade and market activities of any kind was banned.

In 1963, Nian was caught and was sentenced to a year in prison for profiteering ("long distance trade" was a criminal act). Three years later when the Cultural Revolution started and millions of mad Chinese were running around ransacking urban households and confiscating valuable ("bourgeois") goods, Nian tried to sell cooked chestnuts on the street and was immediately imprisoned for about three weeks. Nian called himself a student of economics when interviewed in 2008: "You kept asking me why I had guys [working for me] and where I learned how to do business. Let me tell you. The economics I learned at a very young age required no formal schooling. You learned through practice. You must know what goods you have in the warehouse. You try to sell high but buy low. These are basic economic rules. At that time, almost everyday I was caught by police. But I was not afraid. My cost was low," so he was not afraid of having his things confiscated.[103] Nian often lost everything and many times had to beg to survive.

Nian's stubbornness earned him the nickname *shazhi* (idiot) since he seemed unconcerned with being targeted by the overpowering state. Seized by the power vacuum left by Mao's death, Nian started to make sunflower seeds to sell. He even gave the brand a name, Idiot Sunflower Seeds. Paying attention to taste, Idiot Sunflower Seeds became popular first in Wuhu city and then spread across the nation. In 1982, two years after becoming a private business man, Nian made his first million Yuan. With nearly 7 million Yuan, he hired 140 workers. Like many other early rich businesspersons, Nian tried to hide his wealth by stuffing the money under his bed. But during the rainy season some of the money became moldy. When he dried it under the sun, he attracted the attention of the authorities. Fearful of becoming a political target, Nian donated 5,000 Yuan to a region in his province damaged by flooding. According to the Chinese Marxist standard of the political elite, anyone who hires eight workers is a capitalist and intends to exploit his workers.

When Nian's story reached Beijing, a reform leader, Du Rensheng led a group of young economists to write a report strongly sympathetic to Nian, since Nian hired the urban unemployed youth at a time when such unemployment worried the top elite.[104] One leading young economist, Zhou Qiren, recalled why he supported Nian in drafting the report to Deng: "Nian Guangjiu hired 140 workers who could not find jobs in the state companies; Nian pays them the same wage as the local state factories; Nian provides a good service to those unemployed workers or those whose prior jobs paid less than Nian's company. What is more, the market success of 'Idiot Sunflower Seeds' gave incentives to the supply chain for the products. This competition is a blessing not only for consumers but also for workers!"[105]

After reading this report linking Nian's story to the farmers' grassroots de-collectivization movement and to increasing employment that aided political stability, Deng Xiaoping remarked, "Let us wait and see what happens next." This wait-and-see attitude saved Nian's business. After the June 4th, 1989 crackdown, Nian's and many other small private businesses became political targets. Two years later, in 1991, Nian was charged with hooliganism and given a three-year sentence in an attempt to destroy his spirit. But when Deng mentioned his name again in 1992, Nian was rehabilitated.

The story of Nian's entrepreneurialism illustrates how ordinary and even illiterate people created markets in the socialist China. Friedrich A. Hayek's "The Use of Knowledge in Society," published in the September 1945 issue of *The American Economic Review* pointed out that sensibly allocating scarce resources requires knowledge that is dispersed among many people. No individual or group of experts is capable of acquiring all of such knowledge. Informed economic decision-making requires allowing people to act on the information of "time and place" that only they have, while providing a system of communication that motivates them and informs them about how best to behave.[106] It is through entrepreneurs like Nian that market exchange and prices generate the information and motivation required for economic efficiency. Planned economy, however, required centralized knowledge.

Moreover, with millions of entrepreneurs come the millions of new ideas. The market is essential precisely because it allows people to benefit from widely dispersed knowledge when no one has more than the smallest fragment of that knowledge, not even government planners. The abundance produced by an entrepreneur-driven economy contrasts sharply with the shortages of China's centralized, planned economy, where long lines of would-be consumers were the norm.

The table (Table 3.2) shows that most Chinese entrepreneurs before 2000 came from humble family backgrounds, with rural entrepreneurs comprising more than half of all entrepreneurs. This makes China different from other developing countries where most come from urban centers.

The stories of *hobos* and *probos* have also influenced privileged urban state workers. After viewing the success of these risk takers, some state workers became restless and yearned to explore entrepreneurial activities. They saw the models of success as having more freedom and control over their lives. They had to balance these desires, however, with the reality that they already had a job and the fact that life in the private sector is anything but stable. In what amounted to a compromise, some urban state workers became entrepreneurs by gaining the status of *tingxing liuzhi* (those whose salary stops, but whose

Table 3.2
Previous Occupation and Father's Occupation of Private Entrepreneurs
(percent)

Previous Occupation	(N=1,440)			
	Entrepreneurs		Father's Occupation	
	Rural	Urban	Rural	Urban
Farmer	53.5	17.2	68.9	35.2
Cadre	17.0	22.1	7.9	19.4
Industrial Worker	11.6	25.2	7.9	17.4
Technical Personnel	4.1	12.1	3.5	9.4
Peddlers/Small Business	6.1	9.2	—	—
Commercial staff	2.7	7.6	6.0	10.1
Soldier	0.7	1.2	—	—
Other	4.1	5.5	5.8	8.5

Source: Li [107]

employee status continues). This was similar to leave without pay, which enabled them to reduce the worry of losing a lifelong job when starting a small business. Although this may have seemed like the best of both worlds, this situation had its drawbacks. In the eyes of the state managers and government officials, these workers were not *anfen* (those who stay put and are obedient) and thus were not loyal to the state. Some gave up their secure and familiar environments to create businesses for themselves or join others doing the same. These entrepreneurs contained both a bourgeois and a bohemian spirit, never knowing what lay around the next corner.

One of the most important urban market centers is that of the Hanzheng Jie Commodity Market Street in Wuhan, where thousands of small family businesses from throughout China sell their products. Wuhan is situated in central China, easily accessible by the Yangtze and Han rivers as well as by rail. Hanzheng Jie was the location of government offices during the Ming and Qing dynasties (1368-1911). After the abolition of the private sector in 1956, the location became the worst slum in the city and went on to become the center of black markets in the late 1970s, when rural merchants came to Wuhan to sell their wares and buy products unavailable in the countryside. At that time, many consumer products were only sold in urban centers and urban residents needed coupons to buy such products as soap, matches, bicycles, sewing machines, washing basins, and furniture.

In the eyes of the urban people of Wuhan, those working on Hanzheng Jie Commodity Market Street were inconsequential riff-raff. Before 1985, residents of this street found it hard to find a spouse in the city due to the location's negative image. Thus, in 1983, the local government in Wuhan was completely surprised to find that a street of just 1600 meters had overtaken the state department store in sales and ordered a crackdown, forcing many small stores to close. Through the *xiadian shangzhu* (downstairs for selling, upstairs for living) strategy, merchants together with local residents set up a privately owned housing market, linking the services of migrants with businesses, making it difficult for the local government to confiscate their property or eliminate the market exchange activities. The volatility of the merchants was so high that, in the words of a local law enforcement officer in Hankou, "Migrant merchants are like mice, running fast and disappearing quickly. This makes it difficult for us to fine them. Thus we often make landlords take responsibility for the bad behavior of migrant merchants, since they share the same interests, like wearing the same pants."[108] Many local residents resented this practice but had to bribe police to look the other way. "I have to pay protection fees to local government officials, including police, during major Chinese holidays and to *heilaoda* (the underground organized crime head)," remarked Xiang Xiang (not her real name). "The difference between the two groups is that *heilaoda* often keep their word, but the officials change personnel a lot and are thus more unpredictable. If they demand too much, I'll have to leave here and move elsewhere. I have a network of 100 suppliers across China. I can take my market anywhere."[109] Standing next to a small store of less than twenty square feet with more than one hundred different kinds of bras, Xiang Xiang, a woman in her late forties and less than five feet tall, represents a new, more assertive Chinese person who creates markets while engaging in cat-and-mouse games with local government officials. Since the 1990s, *chengguan* (urban management bureau) officials and police have worked together to impose sanctions and management fees upon small businesses and vendors, increasing conflicts.[110]

One newspaper vendor in Beijing has this to say about *chengguan* officials: "They are very strict with the categories of things you can sell. They charge me 500 Yuan a year as an administration fee. We are not allowed to extend the booth's display stand and sometimes must sell things they print, like calendars. They require the best display area and specific sales numbers. Usually we buy all the leftovers ourselves."[111] Although *chengguan* can make it hard to run a small business, they cannot force them to sell the party newspapers that no one wants to read.

Because of male and female merchants and peddlers like Xiang Xiang, between 1979 and 2000, Hanzheng Jie Commodity Market Street was transformed from a 1600 meter-long urban slum into the largest commodity market in central China. With the street providing 21 percent of wholesale business in Wuhan by 1994, even state and collective commercial businesses have had to swallow their pride and open stores on Hanzheng Jie. By 1996, there were 12,968 private businesses, 1480 state and collective stores, and 30 specialized markets along Hanzheng Jie, with a daily flow of 150,000 people and 8 billion Yuan—more than 1 billion USD.[112] The private businesses also paid the local government more than 70 million Yuan in taxes and created more than 420,000 jobs, which benefited both the central and the local governments. By 2000, many major international and domestic brands had entered this small street. The development of Hanzheng Jie Commodity Market Street is another example of the spontaneous order outlined by Hayek. In his book, *The Road to Serfdom*, Hayek points out that the market is better than the central government to communicate vast amounts of complex information. The Chinese case confirms Hayek's prediction that the loss of economic liberty under command-and-control regimes can eventually lead to totalitarianism while at the same time supports Hayek's theory that the government is inferior to the market's ability to generate economic growth and prosperity because the market routinely brings to order millions of evaluations undertaken by each individual participant. The Chinese entrepreneurs have played a key role in innovation while looking for a wide range of possible opportunities to make profit.[113]

The Development of *minjian rongzi* (Grassroots Capital Formation)

Without land as collateral, Chinese rural people have developed informal financial institutions over the past twenty years, which have existed in defiance of state rules that establish a strict government monopoly over finance and banking. As would be expected, the transaction costs are very high.

Prior to the Communist era, an informal system of finance had already existed in China for hundreds of years, but it only became crucial to the development of Chinese enterprises during the 1980s. Even during Mao's time, however, informal financial capital formation was a regular part of life since the government did not formally allow a private person to borrow money. The resultant urgent financial need drove people to form informal institutions across China. The most common form, which is still widely found in rural China today, is called *hui*, a traditional self-help association organized specifically for money lending, which usually consists of a rotating financial arrangement. Due to the variation among Chinese dialects, the same phenomenon has been called *lai hui* (Hubei and Hunan), y*ao hui* (Zhejiang), *tai hui* (Zhejiang and Jiangsu), *piao hui,* and *he hui* (Guangdong, Zhejiang, and Fujian). *Hui* are networks built on mutual trust, social relations, and financial capacity. The more central an individual's position is in the cognitive trust network, the more people one will have in one's *hui* and the more funds that *hui* will be able to amass. In recursive fashion, the wealthier one becomes, the larger one's network size grows as more people are willing to become members of one's *hui*, and the more potent one's network influence becomes. Thus, the size of a *hui* depends on the *hui* network's ability to gather and recruit members. During the Mao era, *hui* were a common source of funds for workers who needed money for their children's weddings and other unexpected family expenses. In the countryside, *hui* were regularly formed among neighbors and relatives living in the same village, while in the cities, *hui* also tended to form among members of the same *danwei* (work unit). During Mao's time, most urban *hui* did not require interest to be paid, but in the countryside it varied from region to region; when interest was paid it was usually low.

Informal financial arrangements took on new meaning and significance when *baochan daohu* enabled millions of rural households to start saving and millions of rural entrepreneurs needed to borrow money to develop and expand their businesses. Thus, the development of *baochan daohu,* a grassroots act of dissolving the communes, was accompanied by another grassroots innovation—the creation of more advanced informal financial institutions, including *dixia qianzhuang* (underground banks), new and more developed versions of *hui* such as *juhui* (a combination of multiple forms of *huis*), *gaolidai* (high interest loans) groups, *qiye jizi* (enterprise deposits where workers and their families invest money to earn interest), *gongfen jizi* (a company which sells shares to gain capital), and *yinbei* (literally "silver backs" or money-lending men).

In the late 1970s and early 1980s, as more and more rural entrepreneurs started small businesses, usually in the trading and manufacturing sectors, the capital needs of these rural entrepreneurial households became a serious issue, since the state-owned banks and rural financial cooperatives were not allowed to lend to private enterprises or individuals. As a result, informal lending and borrowing practices spontaneously developed without the aid of any organizational and institutional processes.

As private enterprises became widespread and branched into the industrial sectors throughout the 1980s, however, *hui* and other informal forms of lending became unable to meet the demand of rural industrial entrepreneurs. This rural demand only increased after 1989, when the government tightened its financial lending in rural areas, and various grassroots organizations blossomed even though they proved ultimately incapable of supplying the vast amounts of financial demand. In Zhejiang, for example, these informal institutions became the lifeblood of private industrial development, especially in Wenzhou, where recently, *juhui* lending alone reached several hundred million Chinese Yuan and involved up to 100,000 people.[114] In one instance in 2005, Wang Xiaolan of Liushi became the head of one of the big *huis*. Making use of her good reputation and *guanxi* (personal relationships), Wang was able to start 190 *hui* of different kinds, 50 of which incorporated 100 people, with each member contributing 10,000 Yuan.[115] High interest rates drove many rural industrialists and entrepreneurs to her *huis*, and in 2006, she was reported to possess 3.8 billion Yuan, becoming one of China's new tycoons. However, her lending was mostly in the real estate sector, and a bull market later that year lured away many of her investors, causing her *huis* to collapse and the government to arrest her and charge her with criminal activity. Notably, when the government asked creditors to claim their debt in the government offices, only small depositors came forward; no big lenders stepped forward for fear of similar imprisonment. Wang Xiaolan's example serves as a reminder of the perils and vulnerability of financial operations without land and other assets to act as basic collateral.

Another case highlighting the unreliability of informal and unregulated financial lending involved a well-known twenty-six-year-old Dongyang woman entrepreneur, Wu Ying. Wu utilized a network of *yinbei* to gather funds and used this money to invest in stock and raw materials and to broker loans herself. She charged remarkably high interest rates to those who were desperate for money, in some cases charging as much as 0.7 percent per day for loans of one million Yuan. These high interest rates attracted the attention of wealthy people in her hometown, and in 2006, she had accumulated 3.6 billion Yuan. Her ability to attract savings eventually also caught the attention of the local government, which arrested her in late 2006 for illegally taking deposits.

Although self-help and non-interest paying *huis* do exist in China, people are often attracted to a *hui* expressly in order to benefit from high interest rates.

The interest levels of *hui* lending are often explicitly stratified; for example, the hierarchy of a particular *hui* in Zhejiang consisted of five levels of interest rates, with the highest level set at 25 percent monthly interest, the second highest at 20 percent, the third at 15 percent, the fourth at 9 percent, and the lowest at around 2 to 3 percent. Even this lowest level of 3 percent surpasses regulation levels.[116] As was the case with the financial behavior of Wang Xiaolan, these irregularly high and unstable interest rates can be attributed to the lack of financial collateral such as land.

In addition to *hui*, *yinbei* (silver back) comprise another highly significant grassroots financial institution. *Yinbei* rose to prominence during the 1980s when both the average savings rates of and the demand for startup capital from private enterprises and rural entrepreneurs began to increase. Since the state-owned banks left both groups unsatisfied, with their low interest rates and reluctance to lend to the private sector, *yinbei* developed to meet the needs of both sides. The practices of *yinbei* are dependent on different interest rates offered to lenders and borrowers. According to government regulation, the interest rates should not be 4 times higher than the official bank interest rate and the loan amount should not exceed 100,000 Yuan.

In 2004, we interviewed a *yinbei* we will call Jia Laoban. Entering the elegant offices of his real estate consulting company in Hangzhou, one could not help but feel impressed. The firm, a front for his *yinbei* operation, is privately owned by two entrepreneurs with extensive close ties to private enterprise bosses throughout the Zhejiang Province. The real business for this company is to lend money to business people who need cash to meet urgent needs. To meet collateral requirements, the borrower must transfer the ownership title of an apartment or house to the company. The lending amount is often half the market price of the collateral. The firm's business depends heavily on referrals from friends and business partners. If the borrower fails to repay the loans with 3 percent monthly interest, the property is forfeited to the company.

This 3 percent monthly interest is more than 30 percent per year, much higher than allowed by law. Many entrepreneurs are willing to pay such rates to cope with emergency situations or other important obligations. Jia told a story of a businessman who needed $70,000 to meet government regulations for the seafood he ships to the United States. The government requires that an amount sufficient for purchase, (in international currency only) be placed in the company's account before the seafood can be shipped. But American companies will not pay until the seafood arrives on US soil. Jia wires the funds through his Hong Kong account. The three-month rate is about 30 percent per month, allowing Jia a tidy profit. Conversations with two entrepreneurs who have dealt with Jia convinced us that both sides welcome this kind of high interest arrangement.

In this episode, private ownership of the apartment and office building used is the key for the *yinbei*. In other cases, the *yinbei* challenges the state banking monopoly. One *yinbei* in Wenzhou has this to say about why he can attract more deposits than the state banks: "At that time, for each 10,000 Yuan, the bank gave out 0.2 Yuan per day but if the money was at my control, depositors could get 1 Yuan, fives times than the state. The annual interest after tax would be 180 but *minjian* (informal bank) interest would give out 840 Yuan. That is why many people trust their money in me."[117]

Due to the lack of legal protection for their operation, informal institutions like *hui* are vulnerable to politicking and inconsistent policies, enforced by a central government concerned about grassroots development of any kind. In the 1980s, the government threatened imprisonment for anyone caught engaging in high interest loan practices. When more and more private enterprises began to obtain capital from private sources, the state passed a law in 1995 to criminalize anyone who tried to procure capital from ordinary people with savings deposits in the banks. "The Central government found informal lending practices to be objectionable," Feng Xinyuan, a native of Zhejiang and an economist specializing in rural finance and rural development at the Chinese Social Sciences Academy, pointed out. "The government tried to put a stop to it first. For example, the State Council issued a directive, No. 247 on 30th of June 1998, called the 'Method of Abolishing Illegal Financial Institutions and Illegal Financial Businesses.' When such legal enforcement failed to contain the development, the new phrase the government used to contain grassroots financial institutions is '*biaozun hua*' (standardization). Many people working in the government have realized the important contribution these informal banks have made to China's economic growth by providing needed capital to China's most productive private sector and in the countryside. Compared with the state banks, the default rate is much lower and is often absorbed by people involved."[118]

In 2004, the Hebei court sentenced farming entrepreneur Sun Dawu to three years in prison for *feifa jizi* (illegally taking deposits from his workers at his enterprise), when all who participated did so voluntarily. "The court accused me of wrongdoing based on a 1999 law," Sun stated, "but in fact, the local government officials in our region were corrupt and tried to force me to 'sleep together' with them, otherwise I would not get any financial loans. I refused to cooperate and was thus singled out. However, most people in my town have already known for a long time that I am involved in grain banking and *qiye jizi*. The so-called *feifa* practices are the lifeblood of most rural private enterprises since the government-owned banks have closed their doors to people like me who have no connections."[119]

Sun Dawu started his business in the early 1980s, when the *baochan daohu* movement led farmers to increase their food production, by creating a grain bank for farmers to deposit their grain. Sun promised to pay the market value of the grain plus a small percent interest to the farmers by the end of the year. As a result, farmers sent their grain to his factory, which Sun used to make chicken feed. After selling his chicken feed at the market, he usually had more than enough to pay the farmers back. Local farmers liked the system because it not only saved them the effort of having to sell their grain at the market themselves but also paid a bit of interest in addition. Following his established model, Sun used the same idea to gather funding for his rural factories by asking his workers to either buy shares of his company or deposit their wages in the factory accounts, at an interest rate higher than that of the state banks. This form of deposit taking has been common practice for small business in China, but in an effort to eradicate the competition, the government has issued many regulations against high interest loans, deposit taking, and underground banking activities—all in the name of security.

Conclusion

China's story shows that economic growth was the result of private entrepreneurialism, not governmental fiat. A latecomer to modernization, China has been dependent on entrepreneurs as key players in economic development, since individual initiative, not ideology, has become the driving force in Chinese society. Entrepreneurs in China have now increased to some 40 million persons.[120]

Entrepreneurship is essential because in it is a central aspect of the individual liberty that has been the catalyst in China for economic empowerment and development. It allows anyone to work for him- or herself, which is highly motivating. Private business energizes the Chinese economy. As a result, the power is not centralized in the hands of the few officials.

Notes

1. John Locke, *Second Treatise on Civil Government,* (1690).
2. Joseph A. Schumpeter. *Capitalism, Socialism and Democracy.* (London: Routledge, 1942).
3. Keming Yang, "Double entrepreneurship in China's economic reform: An analytical framework," *Journal of Political and Military Sociology,* Summer 2002. Douglas North, *Institutions, Institutional Change, and Economic Performance,* (Cambridge University Press, 1990).
4. Kellee Tsai, *Back-Alley Banking: Private Entrepreneurs in China,* (Ithaca, NY: Cornell University Press, 2002); Zhang, Li, *Strangers in the City,* (CA: Stanford University Press, 2001).
5. For more analysis, see books such as Barry Naughton's, *Growth out of the Plan: Chinese Economic Reform, 1978-1993,* (Cambridge University Press, 1996) and Ted Fishman's *China, Inc.: How the Rise of the Next Superpower Challenges America and the World.* (Scribner, 2006); Victor Nee, "Peasant Entrepreneurship and the Politics of Regulation in China." In Victor Nee and David Stark (eds.), *Remaking the Economic Institutions of Socialism: China and Eastern Europe,* (CA: Stanford University Press, 1989), pp. 169-207. Mary C. Brinton and Victor Nee, (ed.), *The New Institutionalism in Sociology,* (New York: Russell Sage Foundation, 1998). "A Theory of Market Transition: From Redistribution to Markets in State Socialism," *American Sociological Review,* 1989, 54(5), pp. 663-81. Victor Nee and Yang Cao, "Path Dependent Social Transformation: Stratification in Hybrid Mixed Economies." *Theory and Society,* 1999, 28, pp. 799-834.
6. Guojia Tongjiju, *zhongguo tongji nianjian 1987* (Statistical Yearbook of China), (Beijing: *zhongguo tongji chubanshe,* 1988).
7. According to an Asian Development Bank Report. Centennial Group Holdings for Asian Development Bank, "The Development of Private Enterprise in the People's Republic of China," Asian Development Bank, 2003, http://www.adb.org/Documents/Reports/TAR3543/default.asp.

8. "People's Republic of China: The Development of Private Enterprise," http://www. adb.org/documents/studies/PRC_Private_Enterprise_Development/default.ap.

9. "Private enterprises expanding quickly," *People's Daily Online*, February 04, 2005. http://english.people.com.cn/200502/04/eng20050204_172945.html.

10. The "privately owned enterprises," or *siying qiye*, were formally allowed to exist as a category in 1988 with the state directing "Tentative Stipulations on Private Enterprises." Those privately owned enterprises were defined as for-profit organizations owned by individuals and employing more than eight people. Only after the amendment to the Constitution of the PRC, passed in 1998, did both categories become "private economy." Private economy includes private enterprises and individual, industrial or commercial households. Centennial Group Holdings for Asian Development Bank, "The Development of Private Enterprise in the People's Republic of China," (Asian Development Bank, 2003), http://www.adb.org/Documents/Reports/TAR3543/default.asp.

11. Kellee S. Tsai, "China's Complicit Capitalists," January/February 2008, *Far East Economic Review*.

12. *Qinghua Daxue he Beijing Kewei* (Qinghua University and Beijing Science Burea), Global Entrepreneurship Monitor (GEM) (*Quanqiou zhuanye guancha zhongguo baogao*), 08/20/07, 15, p. 51, http://club.cn.yahoo.com/bbs/threadview/200087545_5__pn1.htm.

13. Cao Jianshan, "*Gaige kaifang de lishi jincheng*, (The History of Reform and Opening up)," 04/04/05, China Economic History Forum, http://economy.guoxue.com/article.php/5321.

14. Lizhi Ming and Zhang Houyi, eds, *1999 Zhongguo siying qiye fazhan baogao* (1999 Report of the Development of Private Enterprises in China*)*, (Beijing: Social Science Press, 1999), pp. 259-260.

15. Robin Kwong, "China's billionaires begin to add up," *Financial Times*, October 22, 2007, http://us.ft.com/ftgateway/superpage.ft?news_id=fto102220071307209730.

16. Raphael Shen, *China's Economic Reform: An Experiment in Pragmatic Socialism*, (Westport, CT: Praeger Publishers, 2000), p. 18.

17. Zhou, 1996.

18. Zhou, 1996.

19. Janos Kornai, *The Socialist System: the Political Economy of Communism*, (Princeton, NJ: Princeton University Press, 1992).

20. Liu Xuemin, "Speech on National *Jishi* Conference," (1990). Kate Zhou, 1996.

21. Personal interview with Wu Jialing (not her real name), Beijing, summer 2000.

22. Feng Xinyuan refers to state domination as a major tradition and entrepreneurial culture as a minor tradition of people. 2005. Personal communications with Feng since 2006.

23. Shuxun Liu and Zixi Wei, *Zhongguo guoqing congshu_Jiniang* Juan (Chinese National Achives), Jinjiang Volume, (Beijing: *zhongguo dabaike quanshu* Press [Chinese Encyclopedia Press], 1992), p. 393.

24. Wenpu Liu and Yang Xun, *Zhongguo guoqing congshu Changnan Juan* (Chinese National Achives), Changnan Volume, (Beijing: *zhongguo dabaike quanshu* Press [Chinese Encyclopedia Press],1996), p. 594.

25. Ibid.

26. Haiguang Wang, "*Shandong: liushiniandai chengxiang shehui zhuyi jiaoyun yundong*," (The Socialist Education Campaign in 1960s Shandong Urban & Rural areas) *Shandong Shiji caoxi*, April 18, 2007, http://www.cdds.chengdu.gov.cn/detail.asp?id=3452

27. The struggle between urban police and street vendors was common in major cities. On many occasions, the author personally witnessed police chasing and then beating street vendors in the early 1980s in Wuhan and Beijing (1983 to 1984).

28. Kate Zhou, 1996.

29. Helen F. Siu, "Socialist Peddlers and Princes in a Chinese Market Town," *American Ethnologist*, Vol. 16, No. 2 (May 1989), pp. 195-212.

30. Yang Xueye, *"Jueqi de zhongguo siying jingji* (The Rise of China's Private Economy)," *Modern China Studies*, No. 63, Vol. 4.1998, http://www.chinayj.net

31. Personal interview with Peng and his wife in 1997, July in Wuhan.

32. Mingzheng Zhou, *"Jiedu zhejiang mingying jingji* (The Analysis of Zhejiang Private Economy)," *Zhongguo Gaige* (China Reform), no. 8, pp. 4-10.

33. Personal Interview with Wang, July 2000.

34. The Chinese goes: *"wulian jian jiangdong fulao;"* the unsuccessful cannot face their elders in the hometown. Personal interview with Wang summer in Beijing.

35. Lu xueyi, ed., *Dangdai zhongguo shehui jieceng yanjiu bao* (Study of Social Stratification in Contemporary China), (Beijing: *shehui kexue wenxian chubanshe*, 2002), p. 195.

36. Jie Liping, et. al, *Zhejiang Siying Jingji Yanjiu* (Economic Studies on Private Enterprises in Zhejing), (Hongzhou: *zhejiang renmin chubanshe* [Zhejiang People's Press]), p. 162-3.

37. Jean C. Oi, *Rural China Takes Off: Institutional Foundations of Economic Reform*. (Berkeley: University of California Press, 1999). Andrew Walder, "Local Governments as Industrial Firms." *American Journal of Sociology*, 1995, 101, pp. 263-301. Nan Lin, "Local Market Socialism: Local Corporatism in Action in Rural China." *Theory and Society*, 1995, 24, pp. 301-54. Yanjie Bian, "Bringing Strong Ties Back In: Indirect Connection, Bridges, and Job Search in China." *American Sociological Review*, 1997, 62, pp. 266-85.

38. Sulamith Heins Potter and Jack M. Potter, *China's Peasants: the Anthropology of a Revolution*, (New York: Cambridge University Press, 1990).

39. Wang Xiaoqiang, et al., "The New Trends" (1985). Data in Hubei is from my own investigation in Wuhan fringe areas and in Jinshan of Hubei Province, 1984 and 1985.

40. Jie Liping, et. al, *Zhejiang Siying Jingji Yanjiu* (Economic Studies on Private Enterprises in Zhejing), (Hongzhou: *zhejiang renmin chubanshe* [Zhejiang People's Press]), p. 73.

41. *Zhonghua Gongshang Shibao* (The Chinese Industrial and Commerce Times), January 6, 1996.

42. Wang Kesi, *Zhongguo jieduan siying qiye tansuo* (The Exploration to Current Chinese Private Enterprises), (Shanghai: *fudan daxue chubanshe* [Fudan University Press], 1988), p. 2.

43. Kristen Parris, "Local Initiative and National Reform: The Wenzhou Model of Development," *The China Quarterly*, No. 134 (June 1993), pp. 242-263.

44. Personal interview with Ye Zong (not his real name), a Wenzhou underground banker, Wenzhou, July 7, 2004.

45. *Nongmin Ribao (Farmers Daily)*, Sept. 23, 1987.

46. *Xinwen wubao*, China.com, *xin zhongguo de "zhenfan" yundong: ge dixia dachujue renfan zhibiao*, 2006, 11/2.

47. According to official definitions, a *siying* enterprise is different from *getihu* in that the foreman hires more than five workers where *getihu* is often a family or an individual business. While the state in the early 80s lifted the restrictions on *getihu*, the formal recognition of *siying* remained in force until 1987.

48. Personal interviews with Zhou Yasheng in March 2003, Xu Zuoming, Shi Gang, Zhou Minzhu, and Zhou Minhui on July 30 2004.

49. *"Nongyebu jingji zhengce yanjiu zhongxin* (Economic Policy Research Center of Agricultural Ministry)," *Zhongguo Nongcun: Zhengce yanjiu beiwanglu* (Rural China: the Memorandum of Policy Research) , Vol. 2. (Beijing: *nongye chubanshe,* 1991), p. 312.

50. Zhang Jinjiang, "An Preliminary Analysis of Private Enterprises Under the Name of the Collective," *Social Sciences in Chongqing,* 1, 1988, pp. 60-4.

51. Ibid., p. 97.

52. Personal interview with Zhou Minghui from Baojin of Hunan Province in 1985 in Wuhan.

53. *"Nongyebu Jingji Zhengce Yanjiu Zhongxin* (Economic Policy Research Center of Agricultural Ministry)," *Zhongguo Nongcun: Zhengce yanjiu beiwanglu,* (Rural China: the Memorandum of Policy Research), Vol. 1, (Beijing: *nongye chubanshe,* 1988), p. 375.

54. *"GuowuYuan yanjiu shi geti siying jingji tiaochazu"* (The State Council Investigation Team), *Zhongguo de geti he siying jingji* (Chinese Private Enterprises), (Beijing: *gaige chubanshe,* 1990), p. 17.

55. GuowuYuan, *Chinese Private Enterprises,* (1990), p. 289.

56. Huang Jiajin, *"Wenzhou de guahu jingying jiqi wanshan wenti"* (Improvement of Wenzhou's Guahu Management System), *zhejiang xuekan* (Zhejiang Academic Journal), Vol. 5. 1986.

57. Ibid., p.57, 98, 102.

58. Zhou, 1996.

59. Lou Xiaopeng, "Ownership and Status Stratification," in Lin and Byrd, ed., *China's Rural Industry,* (1990), pp. 147-62.

60. Liu Jixin, *"Woguo feigong youzhi qiye jin qunti jiben xianzhuang"* (An Analysis of None-state Entrepreneurs and Their Basic Conditions), *Shehui Xue Yanjiu (Sociological Research),* 6, (1992), pp. 13-20.

61. *RMRB (People's Daily)* of April 10, 2003 quoted from Xueguang Zhou. "Rethinking Property Rights as a Relational Concept: Explorations in China's Transitional Economy," International Economic Association Round Table on Market and Socialism In the Light of the Experiences of China and Vietnam, January 14-15, 2005.

62. Personal Interview with Lei Tao, December 24, 1994 in Shenzhen.

63. Personal interview with Ye on July 9, 2004 in Wenzhou.

64. William A. Byrd, "Entrepreneurship, Capital and Ownership," in Lin and Byrd, ed., *China's Rural Industry,* (1990), p. 199.

65. *The People's Daily,* July 3, 1993.

66. Kristen Parris, "Local Initiative and National Reform: The Wenzhou Model of Development," *The China Quarterly,* No. 134 (June 1993), pp. 242-63.

67. *"GuowuYuan yanjiu shi geti siying jingji tiaochazu," Chinese Private Enterprises* (1990), p. 7.

68. Lou Xiaopeng, "Ownership and Status Stratification," (1990).

69. Victor Nee, "Organizational Dynamics of Market Transition: Hybrid Forms, Property Rights, and Mixed Economy in China." *Administrative Science Quarterly,* (1992), 37, pp. 1-27.

70. Chun Chang and Yijiang Wang, "The Nature of the Township-Village Enterprise." *Journal of International Business Studies,* 19, (1994), pp. 434-52. Martin L. Weitzman and Chenggang Xu, "Chinese Township-Village Enterprises as Vaguely Defined Cooperatives," *Journal of Comparative Economics,* 18, (1994), pp. 121-45.

71. Kate Zhou, 1996.
72. *People's Daily*, May 16, 1985.
73. Nongyebu, *Rural China,* (1988), p. 378.
74. Israel M. Kirzner, *Competition and Entrepreneurship.* (Chicago: The University of Chicago Press), p. 47
75. Andrew Walder, "Local Government as Industrial Firms: An Organizational Analysis of China's Transitional Economy," *American Journal of Sociology*, 101(2) (1995), pp. 263-301. Christine P. W. Wong, "Fiscal Reform and Local Industrialization: The problematic Sequencing of Reform in Post-Mao China," *Modern China,* 18 (April 1992), pp. 197-227.
76. Ibid.
77. Personal interview with Chen, in Hangzhou, Ye in Wenzhou, Hu in Shanghai, and Feng in Shenzhen.
78. Luo Weidong, *Zhidu bianqian yu jingji fazhan: wenzhou moshi yanjiu* (Institutional Transformation and Economic Development: A Study of Wenzhou Model). (*Hangzhou: zhejiang daxue chubanshe* [Zhejiang University Press], 2002), p. 158-159.
79. Ibid. Those entrepreneurs were Liu Dayuan the screw manufacturer; HuJinlin of metal production; Ye Jianhua the index card maker, Zheng Qianqing who made electric wires; Cheng Buqing of the mining light factory; Li Fangping of the sales network, Wu Shiqian the head of metal casting and Wang Maiqi of used products sales. This research finding was confirmed by personal interviews with five Wenzhou government officials in 2004.
80. Ibid.
81. Kate Zhou, 1996, Chapter 5.
82. *Jingji Ribao* (Economic Daily), August 11, 1987.
83. Li Peng states: "Rural industries must appropriately reduce their pace of development in accord with the state's macroeconomic demands and the market requirements. They should also rectify, improve their operational work style, pay attention to readjusting their product diversity, improve product quality…The township and village industries should concentrate on developing the processing of agricultural and sideline products, the production of certain raw materials, and production of export commodities that earn foreign exchange. The capital needed by the township and town enterprises should mainly come from their own accumulations." "Report on the Work of Government," Beijing Domestic Service, (March 20, 1989); FBIS-Chi-89-053, (March 21, 1989): 11-13, at p. 18.
84. Fewsmith, *Dilemmas of Reform in China,* (1994), p. 247.
85. Kate Zhou, 1996.
86. The author's high school classmate's father was caught doing long-distant trade and was kicked out of the state job in Wuhan in 1969. See more on the rise of black market in CR in Shaoxin, Zhonggo Shaoxin (Shaoxin, China), *"Gongxiao xingzheng,"* (History of Industrial and Commerce Administration), Vol. 3, http://www.sx.gov.cn/portal/main/sxsz_msg_list.jsp?catalog_id=20050411001896.
87. Luo Weidong, *Zhidu bianqian yu jingji fazhan: wenzhou moshi yanjiu* (Institutional Transformation and Economic Development: A Study of Wenzhou Model), (Hangzhou: zhejiang daxue chubanshe [Zhejiang University Press], 2002), p. 65.
88. Ibid.
89. This was well known in China in the late 1970s. Personal interview with local Wenzhou officials in the summer of 2004, confirmed by online discussion in Zhejiang, China, http://book.94888.net/连载/人文社科/社会/温州评判/问姓氏是是非非.
90. Huang, Yasheng, *Capitalism with Chinese Characteristics: Entrepreneurship and the State*, (MA: Cambridge University Press, 2008).

91. Zhou Qiren, "What Did Deng Xiaoping do Right?" *China Economist Forum*, July 28, 2008, http://chinaeconomist.org/archives/236.html.

92. Luo Weidong, *Zhidu bianqian yu jingji fazhan: wenzhou moshi yanjiu* (Institutional Transformation and Economic Development: A Study of the Wenzhou Model), (Hangzhou: *zhejiang daxue chubanshe* [Zhejiang University Press], 2002).

93. Fei Xiaotong, *Xingxing chong xingxing* (Travel and Discorvery), (Yingchuan: *ningxia renmin chubanshe* [Ningxia People's Press], 1992), p. 24.

94. Hong Tao, *"Woguo xiao shangpin pifa shichang mianlin de tiaozhan he fazhan qvshi* (Challenges and Development Trends of Our Country's Small Commodity Retail Market), *Journal of China Commodity Circulation Economy, zhongguo liutong jingji*, December 2005, http://www.kesum.cn/zjzx/mjzl/beijin/hongtao/200512/8802.html.

95. Zhou, 1996, Chapter 5, p. 152.

96. Zhao Yunsheng, interviewed in Honolulu, October 10, 2006.

97. Diao Xinshen, *"Shichang Xing Cheng Zhong di Gaige Renwu"* (Task of the Reform in Market Forming), *Jingji Yanjiu* (Economic Research), 8, (1986), pp. 43-48. Kate Zhou, 1996, Chapter 4.

98. Personal interview with Mu in July, 1997, Beijing.

99. Ibid.

100. Ibid.

101. Personal interview with Mr. Zheng Lihua, the CFO of Zhentai in Wenzhou, July 15, 2004.

102. Personal interview with Xiangling Ma, the Senior Research of Shanghai Management Institute, 2005, July 27 in Shanghai.

103. Jia Yunyong and Jiang Yingshuang, *"Shazhi Nian Guangjiu"* (The Idiot Niang Guangjiu), *South Metropolis News*, March 24, 2008, http://www.sina.com.cn. Wu Xiaopo, *Jidang sanshi nian* (The Surging Thirty Years), (Beijing: Caijing Press, 2006).

104. For a good discussion on the role of Du and young economists, see Joseph Fewsmith, *Dilemmas of Reform in China: Political Conflict and Economic Debate*, (Armonk M. E. Sharpe, 1994).

105. Zhou Qiren, "What Did Deng Xiaoping do Right?" *China Economist Forum*, July 28, 2008, 10:09, http://chinaeconomist.org/archives/236.html.

106. Friedrich A. Hayek, "The Use of Knowledge in Society," *The American Economic Review*, XXXV, No. 4; September 1945, pp. 519-30.

107. Li, Cheng, *China's Leaders: The New Generation*, (New York: Rowman & Littlefield Publishing, 2001).

108. Personal interview with Li Caisheng (not his real name), a local police chief in Jiaotou District, Wuhan, July 2, 2001.

109. Personal interview with Xiang Xiang, July 3, 2004 in Wuhan.

110. The list of additional official bureaus that were created to regulate private sectors includes: *gongshang* (the Industrial and Commerce Bureau), *shuiwu* (tax bureau), *chengguan* (urban administration bureau), *huanbao ju* (environment protection bureau), *jicha dadui* (the inspection special force brigade), and *fangbao* (armed police for emergences).

111. Jay Xie, "Newspaper vendor paid a high price for his city venture," *South China Morning Post*, Dec 30, 2007

112. *Hanzheng Jie xiao shangpin shichang guanli wei Yuanhui zonghe guanli bangongshi* (Comprehensive Management Office of Hanzheng Jie Small Commodity Market), *Wuhan Hanzheng Jie xiao shangpin shichang* (Hanzheng Jie Small Commodity Market in Wuhan), February 15, 2006, http://info.china.alibaba.com/news/detail/v5000180-d5541697.html.

113. Friedrich Hayek, *The Road to Serfdom,* 50th anniversary edition, (University of Chicago Press, 1994).

114. Luo Weidong, *Zhidu bianqian yu jingji fazhan: wenzhou moshi yanjiu* (Institutional Transformation and Economic Development: A Study of Wenzhou Model). (Hangzhou: *zhejiang daxue chubanshe* [Zhejiang University Press], 2002), p. 206.

115. Ibid.

116. Jin Shaoce, "*Qingbeida di jiedai shengyi* (The Loan Business of The Money Middle Men)," May 2, 2007, http://jinshaoce.blshe.com/post/495/44909

117. Ibid.

118. Personal interview with Feng Xinyuan in May 24, 2007 in Honolulu.

119. Personal interview with Sun Dawu in July 5, 2005 in Xushui, Hebei.

120. George Zhibin Gu and William Ratliff, *China and the New World Order: How Entrepreneurship, Globalization, and Borderless Business are Reshaping China and the World*, (Grand Rapids, MI: Fultus, 2006).

4

Capitalism with Chinese Characteristics and the Basis of Civil Society

Although the discussion thus far has only dealt with the entrepreneurs who created something from nothing and filled voids left by an inadequate socialist economic system, more players entered the game as time passed and the entrepreneurs' successes continued. These ranged from former state workers and rural employers looking to safeguard their businesses to children of the elite looking to profit from the commercial dynamics of a newly evolving China. In varying degrees, they all played their roles as entrepreneurs, creating both positive and negative attributes of the new economic landscape.

In the late 1980s and early 1990s, especially after the Tiananmen Square incident, many rural entrepreneurs became subcontractors for state firms, rather than compete directly for every lucrative offer that presented itself. This allowed them to avoid a certain amount of direct confrontation with state and international companies while also expanding their businesses into the cities. Throughout the 1990s, contracts became common features in most rural industries, laying the groundwork for further privatization. Although this system worked fairly well and many companies profited, it did not alleviate private owners' fear of the government. As a result, many entrepreneurs continued to "wear a red cap" as discussed above.

The trigger for China's millionaire boom was first led by the poor people. The majority of China's wealthy are first-generation, self-made entrepreneurs. When Deng Xiaoping's pronouncement, "let some people get rich first," became accepted in the 1990s, the politically connected individuals, especially children of high-ranking officials, grabbed the opportunity and some of them became billionaires.

Also existing in the twilight world of the socialist market economy were the *combos* (Communist bourgeoisie). The *combos* or "intrapreneurs" are managers in state-owned enterprises (SOEs) and government bureaucrat/technocrats who hold shares in private enterprises. Although many of the *combos* run their businesses with little innovation, competition from non-state firms has pressured some to reform in an effort to remain profitable. These are new Chinese-style state *chaebols*.[1] One of the most successful of these organizations is the Shenzhen Investment Holding Corp. (SIHC), a powerful but little-known holding company for most of the city government's vast business empire. SIHC's 1,000-odd companies cover the gamut of the city's economy, including an airport, a textile mill, a food distributor, a commercial bank, a computer-parts maker, and a petrochemical plant. It has a combined turnover of over $4 billion and, because it is public, it also has many private shareholders in addition to the state.

The most successful Chinese *combo* is Zhang Ruimin, the head of the Haier Group. Haier has become a global corporation with annual sales exceeding $3 billion.[2] As proof of their global success, Zhang's companies have established a factory in South Carolina[3] and produce 25 percent of the medium size refrigerators sold in the United States.[4]

Red Capitalists and the Imperial Family Corporation

Further down the rungs of the entrepreneurial ladder (as measured by degree of politicization) are the *hongse zibenjia* (red capitalists). *Hongse zibenjia* are businessmen with strong capital backing and political connections. Although the red capitalists were relative latecomers to market development in China, their political contacts provided them with the capital, connections, and resources needed to become wealthy in a short period of time.[5] Some of the red capitalists are bureaucrats who have intentionally used government resources for personal gain; others include the so-called red princes and princesses, whose family connections to government officials have allowed them to become tremendously successful.

Since the state legitimized private business in 1987, one of the most powerful entrepreneurial groups has been these red princes and princesses, the children of senior officials. These offspring of current leaders are often the first to strike deals with foreigners and mobilize national and local resources to set up factories and other ventures. For example, Chen Weili, the daughter of Chen Yun, a leading state planner in the 1980s, is deputy chairwoman of China Venturetech, one of the most profitable venture firms in China. Chen Yuan, her brother, became the governor of the People's Bank of China in the 1990s. Another example is in the area of energy. Li Xiaolin, daughter of Li Peng (former Chinese premier), is chairwoman of China Power International Development while her brother, Li Xiaopeng, is chairman of Huaneng Power International—giving the Li family control of 15 percent of China's power generation industry.[6]

Deng Pufang, Deng Xiaoping's elder son, is president of Kanghua Development and is one of the richest entrepreneurs in China. Deng Zhifang, Deng Xiaoping's younger son, is CEO of Shifang Group, Ltd. Deng Xiaoping's daughter, Deng Nan, is vice-minister for the State Science and Technology Commission and has used her position to finance entrepreneurs in exchange for an interest in their business. Deng's son-in-law, He Ping, is the largest arms dealer in China. Bo Xicheng, son of Bo Yibo, Mao's minister of commerce, is chairman of the Board of Directors at Beijing Luhe Hotel.[7]

According to government research by the Research Office of the State Council, the China Academy of Social Science, and the Research Office of the Party School, "90 percent of China's billionaires are children of senior officials. There are about 2,900 senior officials' children in China, with total wealth amounting to two trillion yuan. Their businesses mainly cover 5 areas: finance, foreign trade, real estate development, large-scale projects, and bonds and securities. They either own their businesses or are senior managers in big companies."[8]

The Chinese state awarded monopolies for international trading. For example, the Pioneer Iron and Metals group was founded by Diana Chen, whose late grandfather, Lu Dong, was China's metallurgy minister in the 1960s and 1970s. With this connection, Chen was able to gain exclusive contracts to provide imported iron ore to several state-owned enterprises, making her company one of the largest private importers of iron ore into China, and making her into one of the nation's richest tycoons. In 2007, *Forbes* magazine estimated Ms Chen's wealth at $216 million. People like Ms. Chen can gain state loans at low interest. If they make a profit, they repay the loan; but if instead they lose money, they declare bankruptcy. Due to her grandfather's connections, several top steel producers only use the iron ore imported by Chen's company. This family monopoly is one of the main complaints against the ruling party state in Chinese society today.

The princely red capitalists are important because of their influence. Although they have created the Chinese version of crony capitalism by taking advantage of their political positions to enrich themselves, their behavior has helped ensure the continued existence of Chinese capitalism. When the elite and their children gain from such developments (as twisted a form of capitalism as it may be), the trend toward capitalism becomes almost unstoppable. Consequently, despite the nepotistic aspect of their success, they are helping to carve out non-governmental spaces in which people can interact, thus reducing overall reliance on the state. However, since their new economic power comes from political connections, these new red capitalists are anti-democratic in nature, creating tension between business people who have no political backing and those who do.

Extortion of the State and Party-State Oligarchy

As this new breed of entrepreneur has become more common in the marketplace, so too has a new form of corruption. As the situation became less politically volatile in the late 1990s, a number of government officials began running their own enterprises. Seizing China's open-door environment, people with political connections became wealthy by getting high legal or illegal commissions when they introduced foreign investments either to local governments or to local businesses.

Children of the top elite used numerous tricks to benefit from their political connections. For instance, the party controlled state factories and government agencies can import equipment at highly inflated prices (between 60 percent to 300 percent higher than market prices). According to one estimate, rent seeking and official profiteers occupied between 20 percent to 30 percent of China's GDP, reaching 4 to 5 trillion.[9] This money flew into the pockets of the politically connected, enlarging Chinese inequality while decreasing the state treasure. Such corruption, however, forced the authorities to gradually end the system of state-controlled commodity prices.

Widespread corruption added to the marketing skill of merchants made it costly for the government to continue the double price system. Thus, the top elite wanted to stop the two-truck system of price to save the government revenue. Under the leadership of Deng Xiaoping, in 1993, 95 percent of retail commodities, 90 percent of agricultural side products, and 80 percent of raw materials had prices determined by market prices, systematically altering the nature of the Chinese economy.[10] To a great extent, entrepreneurs taught the Beijing elite the power of the fabled "invisible hand."

Others used their previous experience in state managed enterprises and official positions to take on such tasks as consulting, supplying, or distributing for large companies. Government managers also began to devise their own form of privatization, accumulating capital by looting the assets of state enterprises. Because of the poor financial accountability that characterized SOEs and the non-transparent methods by which many were sold off or downsized, this was not a difficult practice. In the short term, stripping assets aggravated the financial problems of the SOEs, though most were unprofitable in any case. In the long term, the practice created a situation in which corruption once again was a cornerstone of economic activity.

Ever since private vendors and migrant merchants made their appearance in major Chinese cities in the early 1980s, *hobos* and *probos* have played cat-and-mouse games with the government. The government "cats" crack down on entrepreneurial "mice" by confiscating their wares. However, the "mice" pour back into the cities with new wares as soon as the "cats" are not in sight.

Before 1987, even *hobos* would regard official attacks against private businesses as normal for government officials in *gongshang ju* (industrial and commerce bureaus), *shuiwu ju* (tax bureaus), *pachu suo* (local police), *shirou jingcha* (hygiene police), *weisheng ju* (health departments), and *ju weihui* (neighborhood committees). Although in June 1988 the central government allowed private enterprises to exist, an anti-private business attitude still dominated government officials' practice in making bank loans, licensing, and extorting high fees. The goal of the "Temporary Rules on Private Enterprises of the People's Republic of China" was to limit the existing growth of private enterprises. This included setting limits on investment ranges, profit sharing, production development fund use, organization formation, labor conditions, capital formation, salaries for senior managers, and the size.[11] The guiding principle was to stem the private enterprises' growth, even though the law did legalize private enterprises.

Hobos and *probos* complained that anyone working for the government wanted to control them the way he or she likes.[12] Since the entrepreneurs could not challenge government officials and demand identification, anyone dressed in an official uniform could demand fees or bribes. One popular way for entrepreneurs to pay off government officials has been to become "losers" at *majiang* (the Chinese game played with tiles). Large numbers of Chinese are *majiang* players, gambling from a few dollars to several thousand. It is common knowledge across China that local police and government officials undertake random neighborhood inspections to uncover such illegal gambling. Much of this inspection, however, is done by officials attempting to cover their own gambling debts (especially at *majiang*) by shaking down other players. The author witnessed one such occasion during the summer of 1999 when two local government officials went to a relative's home to demand a fine for playing *majiang*. Handing over the money, the uncle complained: "*Ni de shouqi zenmo zhemo chou? Lianzhe shule lianngtian?* (What a sticky hand [bad luck] to lose two days in a row!)." Thus, the government regulation banning *majiang* has created an open-ended cash cow for local officials to enrich themselves.

Deliberately losing to officials at *majiang* is the most common way for private entrepreneurs to pay bribes. The author's own brother, a private entrepreneur, informed her in December 1994 that losing to government officials to keep them happy had become his night job. "Sometimes, my luck was very good, with runs of great cards. [But in the end] I had to put all the winning coins on the table and could not leave the table until all my money was gone. On an average night, I would lose about 10,000 to 30,000 Yuan. During holidays, I lost more."[13] Such practices have been amply confirmed by friends and government contacts in Wuhan, Jishou (Hunan), Jingshang County (Hubei), Baojing, Beijing, and Shenzhen during more than a decade of summer travel, from 1995 to 2006.

With private businesses catering to corrupt officials, some local officials have become even more predatory. Many officials have adopted the habit of using rules and regulations to enrich themselves, as described by an old Chinese proverb: "To want the horse to be the best runner, but to demand that the horse not eat anything."[14] By adopting a "flexible" attitude, political officials encourage private businesses to develop fast to boost the local economy, which also allows them to gain wealth from the private sectors. Entrepreneurs have responded using venal officials to get rid of competition. In March 2007, central government officials in the National People's Congress of 2007 realized that the private sector is the current engine of growth for jobs and passed the Property Law of the People's Republic of China. The most important aspects of the law delineates the creation, transfer, and ownership of property.[15]

Will the central government enforce this law as energetically as it enforces the "one child" law? If so, this law will provide legal protection for private entrepreneurs who lack political backing from the arbitrary harassment of government officials at all levels. However, the honest enforcement of the law would necessarily reflect a rule of law that places the party beneath the law, something the party-state is by no means prepared to do. Still, two leading Chinese economists, Feng XinYuan and Hu Jingbei, predict that knowledge of the existing law will drive ordinary Chinese to sue government officials and institutions, and that the resulting grassroots legal battles which attempt to hold the government accountable for the laws it passes will positively affect the content of the regime and strengthen constitutional liberalism within the state.[16]

Fearful of the competition from Chinese entrepreneurs, the state gave favorable tax treatment and land to foreign companies including HK and Taiwanese businesses at the cost of Chinese private companies while, at the same time, the government-induced red capitalists in the 1990s and early 2000s used their political power trying to monopolize key industries. The result was China's dependence on foreign trade (more than 60 percent).

Although corruption was the price of freedom for most entrepreneurs in their initial stage, the continuation of corruption and rapid growth of income disparity led to anti-market social sentiment that challenges the political system and the market economic system. Lucrative commodity trading involved several elements of fraud and rent seeking. State officials also offered discounted awards to politically linked people to buy state assets, fueling popular resentment.

The most common form of institutional corruption is the common practice of giving a "red bag" (*hongbao*) to tax bureaus and other government agencies, such as police, environment, and health agencies. Interviews with 50 entrepreneurs in Hunan, Shenzhen, Shanghai, Beijing, Wuhan, and Liaoning in the summers of 2005 and 2006 showed about 10 to 20 percent of profits went to pay off government officials: the poorer the region, the higher the payment.[17]

But institutional corruption does not always lead to predictability because political appointees at local levels change frequently due to change among the top elite.

Technology Entrepreneurs and the Rise of Internet Traders

A subsection of the previously mentioned groups who deserve further examination due to their rising importance are technology entrepreneurs. Among them are Internet entrepreneurs. Not all of these individuals are technical geniuses, but they are pioneers who solve problems and learn from experience to further expand the technology sector. Some started out with little knowledge about the industry but were able to recognize opportunity and understand how to take advantage of it. They possess a powerful curiosity fueled by the desire to find new and better ways of providing people access to the world via the Internet.

In 1997 there were about 100,000 privately owned, technology-intensive firms in China, with a total of 270 billion Yuan in assets. The income of 675 of the firms surpassed 100 million Yuan each.[18] In 1999, China experienced tremendous growth not only in the number of Internet users, but also in the number of e-businesses. Wholesale e-businesses increased from around one hundred at the start of 1999 to over six hundred in January 2000, roughly a 500 percent increase in one year. According to the State Council of China, China's Internet companies are being established twice as fast as American Internet companies.[19] During the same period, the number of Internet subscribers on the mainland hit seven million, more than tripling the two million users of the previous year. With such a small percentage of China's population currently able to access the Internet, this kind of explosive growth is expected to continue for the foreseeable future. A secondary, and potentially highly significant, consequence of this boom is the rise of a new social space in which people are free to interact with those both inside and outside of China, the effects of which will be discussed in later chapters.

Online Traders Revolution

With the rise of the Internet, online commerce has also made its appearance in China. The Chinese online merchants have become middlemen between producers and consumers. Rather than trade in products, the new merchants sell information. Since the new merchants depend on ad fees, they do not demand payment from consumers. These new traders will likely pose challenges for existing merchants, especially JIRM merchants, who tend to be less educated.

Another subcategory of entrepreneur is the *daiban* (a Chinese representative of a foreign firm, or a Chinese executive in a large-scale joint venture). These individuals assist foreign businesses targeting both domestic and international markets. Although we will not discuss their contributions in detail here, they must be mentioned as a group affecting change in the economic landscape. Their influence is detailed more specifically in the chapter on globalization and foreign influence, which examines the importance of the exchange of culture and ideas.

The Rise of the New Landlords and the Real Estate Boom

Chinese entrepreneurs have also played a key role in the rapid growth of private ownership of housing in China. The planned economy of the communist regime was inherently anti-consumption.[20] In China, the national slogan was "*xian shengchang, zia shenghou*" (production first and consumption second). Thus, little was spent on housing and light industry. Housing was not distributed through markets. Instead, housing units in the cities were assigned to employees by their work units (*danwei*) or the local housing management bureau (*fang-guangsou*) at very low rent. As the large-scale owner and rent controller, the government banned the independent housing market. Due to the state's control of land and capital used for construction, there was no such thing as a real estate market in China before 1985. This started to change informally, however, during the reform period as people began to wean themselves from government control. A limited real estate market emerged in the early 1980s when farmers began to build private houses across China, leading to a construction boom. It continued at a much more rapid pace in 1992 after Deng's Southern Tour, as people became increasingly confident that the new system would survive. Real estate markets in the cities boomed and thousands of real estate agents and other related businesses appeared.

As the majority of property rights (land, housing, and capital) had been noticeably absent from the reform up to this point, legitimization of private businesses created ample opportunities for government officials to line their pockets. So long as government officials still controlled essential economic elements (capital goods, financial capital, land, and information), they were able to embed themselves in the corresponding economic markets. For example, children of senior government officials were able not only to get cheap land deals but also to grab large-scale infrastructure projects. "Eighty-five percent of freeways were contracted by private companies, which were owned by children of senior officials. One can reap seven million to eleven million yuan from constructing one kilometer of freeway."[21]

The local governments openly sold land in order to gain revenue. A higher percent of China's new rich is linked to political networks at all levels of government starting from 1993. Politically linked individuals were able to develop and sell land with government bank loans and zero costs. "Twelve large property developers in Guangdong Province are owned by senior officials' children. In Shanghai, nine of the ten largest property developers are owned by senior officials' children. In Jiangsu, children of senior officials control the 22 largest property developers and the 15 largest project contractors."[22]

Jane Duckett has demonstrated the role of these cadres in real estate and commercial development in Tianjin. Their role in the market expansion was so important in the 1992 real estate boom that Duckett referred to them as the "entrepreneurial state."[23] The state government traded politics for money through land deals, helping to create the new Chinese magnates. Among the 500 magnates in China, 128 are from the real estate industry.[24]

In addition to under-the-table profits, government officials expanded their bureaucratic power to profit from the development of real estate. A new bureaucratic organization, *Guotuju* (State Land Bureau), was established and quickly became one of the more lucrative state bureaus. With official support at all levels, real estate businesses boomed. By 1992, there were 12,400 real estate development companies, 4,700 repair and management companies, and numerous mediation agencies employing 2,500,000 workers.[25] This development was phenomenal given the fact that the government had initiated land development fewer than eight years earlier. In 1992, real estate investment increased 117 percent over the previous year, reaching 73 billion Yuan.[26]

The real estate market development, together with housing reform, led to a situation in which half of all urban people became the de facto owners of their own homes, creating the biggest growth rate of home ownership in the world. To support this sudden increase in ownership, there was a rapid development of homecare services, home design and remodeling, painting, cleaning, and plumbing services. The significance of this ownership movement was that it was initiated from below as a blatant act of rights acquisition, specifically property rights. As people began to carve out non-governmental spaces, they wanted these spaces protected. The desire for increased self-sufficiency thus fed upon itself, leading to a desire for further rights acquisition. Once again, the pursuit of liberty and economic gain became intertwined.

Realities of the Chinese Entrepreneurial Landscape

As the economic landscape continues to change, several observations on the impact of the entrepreneurial spirit and the future of Chinese business can be made. First, it is evident that the entrepreneurial spirit is vital for the transformation of the Chinese socialist economy. Entrepreneurship anchors the new economic landscape, making it nearly impossible to reverse the trend towards markets.

Second, *guanxi* is essential for entrepreneurial startups to overcome the uncertainty of the Chinese marketplace. We have seen that Chinese culture is an inseparable component of the new entrepreneur class. Businessmen have always drawn from, and will continue to draw upon, social resources as a means for success. The only difference now is the environment in which they are succeeding. Although making money was traditionally viewed as a self-serving pursuit, Chinese entrepreneurs cannot escape another aspect of their traditional past, which tells them to care for their relatives, friends, and even downtrodden strangers. Although entrepreneurship development varies from region to region, the culture of Chinese entrepreneurs, with its emphasis on family, has become a small tradition struggling against the elite tradition of authoritarian state building. There is no doubt that the ability of officials to shake down entrepreneurs has made government jobs more attractive than entrepreneurial ventures. The struggle between small private businesses and big government administrators will dominate China so long as one-party rule continues. However, by combining traditional and modern values, these individuals are reshaping China's social and economic environments.

Guanxi seen in its more positive light allows successful people to positively affect the lives of those to whom they are closest. As people work together, this web expands to encompass a large number of family members, friends, and those lucky enough to be part of an inner circle. Our prototypical Chinese *probo*, Mu Qizhong, refers to himself as a Confucian entrepreneur who was able to build a web of personal connections designed to enhance and expand his business opportunities. Most business people we interviewed related that personal relationships (such as those with former classmates) were crucial to their initial capital accrual and market development. While *hobos* and *probos* depend upon their families and friends, the red capitalists and *combos* rely on political connections.

Third, Chinese entrepreneurs live a life between the planned state economy and the free market, and between rationalism and irrationalism. In the daily life of many entrepreneurs, belief in rational markets melds with *fengshui* (geomancy—divination by lines and figures) and playing *majiang* with government officials. In fact, gambling is an important part of entrepreneurial life, both figuratively and literally. Thus, many have tried to increase their chances of success with traditional "good luck" charms. Some have *shoucaishen* (deities that protect wealth) in their offices or homes. Others have chosen different ways of ensuring luck and happiness. For example, to take advantage of the lucky number 8, the new rich will spend to ensure an "8" appears in their address and phone number. Since both the market and the government are so unpredictable, Chinese entrepreneurs are simultaneously becoming more superstitious and more realistic. Irrational faith is rooted in rational calculation. Interviews with many Chinese entrepreneurs resulted in the following composite sentiment: "If there is no money-protecting god, I will not be hurt by believing in one. If there is one, I will be in big trouble if I do not worship it." Another term for this is calculated superstition. This is much like Pascal's wager!

Fourth, becoming *guanshang* (businessmen with strong official backing) is still the preferred path for some, implying that the transition to independent entrepreneurship is nowhere near complete.[27] Whether it is import subsidies, export rebates, or land allocation, benefits given to government-tied enterprises still exist. Regardless of the business, to become successful in today's landscape, Chinese entrepreneurs have to work with the government in one way or another. Given continued state influence over access to the new economy, some business people still regard *guanshang* as the easiest (although not ideal) model. Even *hobos* often envy official businessmen. "Government people have the power to mobilize social resources," remarked Lei Tao, a private Shenzhen businessman. "I wish I would have that legal power to market my product and avoid problems with local government officials."[28] Such envy has historical roots. In the past few years, one of the books widely read by Chinese entrepreneurs depicts the rise and fall of Hu Xueyan (1823-85), a legendary businessman who used his government connections wisely and subsequently became the richest man in China during the Qing Dynasty.[29]

Lastly, in today's market, even small-scale entrepreneurs are aware of global competition. Nearly all Chinese entrepreneurs strive to compete one day in the global market. The well-established relationships between overseas Chinese; Hong Kongese; and, recently, Taiwanese provide today's entrepreneurs with a unique comparative advantage to market their products abroad through these overseas Chinese merchant networks.

The reorganization of ownership, the creation of private property laws, and the emerging entrepreneurial mindset led to the economic boom. To sustain this arising entrepreneurial attitude, as well as China's increasing involvement in the international market, however, China needs major reforms with regard to the rule of law and a reduction of governmental habits of oppression. Here entrepreneurs are in a dilemma. Most want the stability required for successful engagement in their businesses. This desire coincides with the regime's desire to stay in power. Thus, from the outset entrepreneurs seem to support the one party rule status quo. But this attitude is contingent upon government adoption of measures meeting some of their needs. But in the long run, as the private sector gains dominance over the economy, entrepreneurs as a "strategic group" with economic clout and attendant political bargaining power, present a potential rival social stratum opposed to one party rule and its political elite.

From the political viewpoint, Chinese entrepreneurs have had a structural effect on Chinese politics. Politically connected entrepreneurs (mostly real estate developers, state enterprises, children of political elite) have used political connections in support of their economic interests, forming what Kellie Tsai calls "the implicit pact": continued growth ensures support for continued one-party rule.[30] The party-state has been responsive to the needs of such "red capitalists," encouraging rent-seeking behaviors from businesses of every variety. In engaging in discreet collaboration with local officials, entrepreneurs have created a range of informal adaptive institutions including corruption, which in turn, have fundamentally altered China's political and regulatory landscape.

This "pact" will create problems for China's future democratization because parties to the pact want to retain the status quo. Entrepreneurs do not seek a new regime but instead defend their interests within existing institutions or constitutions. When the state's interest matches with theirs, entrepreneurs tend to support the status quo. If they are in conflict, they confront the state.

A majority of entrepreneurs who are the victims of the state with respect to taxes, loans, and regulations are working hard for more transparency and the rule of law. Some have joined the 2008 Charter Movement, urging the Chinese government to take responsibility for the laws they created themselves.[31] Still others try to reduce the harm by allying with international companies by going overseas.

The Impact of Entrepreneurs and Private Sector Development

In China's transition to a market economy, private businesses are "institutional entrepreneurs." According to Li, *et. al*, "such entrepreneurs are at the forefront of destroying existing bureaucratic rules in many creative ways…In many cases, they are destroyers of old and inefficient institutions and pioneers of new market institutions. Therefore, they have to be more versatile and possess more skills than their counterparts in mature market economies."[32]

Entrepreneurs, especially rural industrial entrepreneurs, led China's rapid privatization movements in both ownership structure and labor allocation. Several million rural entrepreneurs started businesses in transportation, construction commerce, and trade, the bedrock of China's private businesses.[33] Early rural entrepreneurs also transformed China from an agricultural society to a modern industrializing society. Rural industrial entrepreneurs have hired millions of workers; by 1988, more than 86 million persons labored in rural industries.[34] By the end of 2005, the private sector accounted for 50 percent of GDP, while foreign companies (mostly Taiwanese, along with Hong Kong capital) made up another 35 percent and the state-owned share dropped to 35 percent.[35] By 2007, the private sector contributed 66 percent of GDP and 71 percent of tax revenues, despite the fact that the government invested little capital or support. Entrepreneurs are the main source of new jobs: "between 2002 and 2006, the private sector created almost 44 million urban jobs, 70 percent of all new job creation, whereas employment in state-owned and collective enterprises shrank by nearly 11 million.[36] Chinese entrepreneurialism led to competition with the state, forcing many publicly owned factories to close, even as new private firms rapidly sprang up with a 35 percent growth rate after 1993.

Entrepreneurs have also influenced the structure of the PRC by redefining the role of government cadres. The local government receives substantial income from "wearing a red hat" practices and other fees. The China scholar Dorothy Solinger labels such interaction between entrepreneurs and government officials as "joint dependence" and a "symbiotic relationship."[37] Other scholars point out that the self-interests of entrepreneurs and local government officials involve a pattern of "interest convergence."[38] Local governments prefer to give a red cap to such private businesses to collect added management fees. In fact, these enterprises have become *xiaojingui* (small gold treasure boxes) for local cadres. This new form of patron-client relationships is different from the old one in that the participants all try to weaken the state's economic power for their personal benefit and local interests. So long as private enterprises pay management fees to local governments and officials, they receive the same lower tax status as other collective enterprises in the countryside. Local taxes make it difficult for the state to collect more from these sham collective enterprises, while simultaneously strengthening the power of local governments and local entrepreneurs.

Starting in 1993, increasing numbers of local enterprises started shareholder management systems. For example, rural entrepreneur Lu Guanqiou provided 25 percent of his own company shares to the local government. According to Lu, this is the strategy of *huaqian mai buguan* (spending money to buy a lack of interference). For Lu and other entrepreneurs, the shares secure the government's interest in helping the company.[39] By so doing, the former political cadres themselves become gravediggers of the socialist planned state.

Rural governments are therefore motivated to reduce state taxes and increase the revenues of local enterprises. Since local government budgets come from local industries, more development means more money for local cadres.[40] Thus, cadres have become monetary dependents, rather than controllers, of rural industries. Such mutual dependence has transformed local cadres from political commissars into economic parasites. Some of them have even become patrons of rural entrepreneurs. Of course, local cadres still retain political control. What is important is that the new power base combines politics with money. When the state launches a campaign against private businesses, rural entrepreneurs are often protected by their formal organizations. For example, when the 1983 anti-spiritual pollution campaign destroyed many private businesses, rural entrepreneurs with sham collectives remained intact. This also explains the surge of red hat businesses when the state attacked private businesses after the 1989 Tiananmen massacre. In addition, the very success of red hat businesses permits local cadres to take part in private enterprise. When the state lifted restrictions banning government officials from participating in private businesses, rural cadres often became de facto owners or partners of rural enterprises.

In short, the "red hat" strategy has changed the role of local governments within the greater framework of the Chinese economy. Local deal-making with officials has become uniquely Chinese in that the process of interaction between entrepreneurs and local government officials has created what Xueguang Zhou has called "negotiated property rights involving a tradeoff between decision rights to income flow and securing a stable, protective environment."[41] Negotiated property rights has become the key for transition economies like those of China, Russia, Cuba, North Korea, Vietnam, and other formal socialist states in less developed countries.

The rise of entrepreneurs has not only created an eruption of economic competition but has also altered the nature of the Communist regime from socialism to state capitalism. Private sector development laid the foundations for the rise of civil society, since people in the private sector are less dependent on the state. Their autonomy is the principal factor in explaining the mushrooming of dissenting voices within society. Entrepreneurship under Communist rule means living and working independently of the state. This independence is key to the formation of free enterprises and civil society, both of which depend on dispersed innovative actions and self-reliant women and men.

The Elite Learning Curve

Grassroots entrepreneurs' successes have also taught the ruling elite a lesson about the power of the "invisible hand." When Jiang Zemin became party boss after the June 4, 1989 Tiananmen Square crackdown, he gave an anti-private business speech on July 1, declaring that he would fine private households into bankruptcy and let them bleed to death: "There are two reform views: one is socialist reform view; the other is the capitalist one. The Party's education job is to carry out anti-peaceful transformation to the end."[42] But on July 1, 2002, Jiang proposed the so-called "Three Representations," inviting capitalists into the party.[43] As entrepreneurs and private businesses have set about altering China, many government officials also benefited from the competition with the state brought about by private sector growth. The elite are learning how to go with the flow, reluctantly passing laws to protect the private property laws promulgated in 2003 (passed into law in 2007). Thus, after a forty-year struggle, founding a business has become a new right for most Chinese.

Chinese entrepreneurs have produced and offered social value and produced considerable profit during the reform process. Since every step was full of hard struggles, making money was the driving force behind those entrepreneurs because the government's control made transaction cost high. As Adam Smith explained in *The Wealth of Nations*, "It is not from the benevolence of the butcher, the brewer, or the baker that we expect our dinner, but from their regard to their own interest."[44] Driven by the economic necessity for survival, entrepreneurs undertook both economic and political risks, as in the example of the "idiot" Nian.

Limits to the Emerging Entrepreneurial Class

Despite the emergence or rural and urban entrepreneurs, we do not want to give the false impression that in the 1980s, or even today, it has ever been easy to operate a privately owned business in China. In fact, with the exception of the red princes and princesses, almost all stories of the entrepreneurial road are strewn with tales of constant struggle. Everyone has experienced both success and failure. All have had to deal with a government bureaucracy that was designed without private enterprises in mind. They are living in two worlds: an emerging market filled with seemingly endless opportunities on the one hand and a declining, but still powerful, planned economy and all of the restrictions that come with it on the other. The transitional economy is not an easy environment in which to conduct business. Despite its open door and reform policies, China's economy is still rather inhospitable. In many ways, it is still one of the most restrictive in East Asia.

Rural entrepreneurs became successful precisely because they violated the government rules and regulations. Corruption played a key role for the rural industrial take off. But corruption cuts both ways. But this habit of paying the officials to look the other way was the price of freedom in China early on but may create a structural barrier due to the social habit of violation of rules, which makes it difficult for rule of law to take root in the people's hearts. Both Chinese people and officials have a hate and love relationship with corruption. It has become an unwritten rule, guiding businesses and daily life.

State officials also offered discounted awards to politically linked people to buy state assets, fueling popular resentment.

The Chinese arbitrary political system not only leads to economic corruption but also legal problems for business people. The perils of doing business in a one party state is that the party state can put business people in prison often without following the rule of law. "There are now more than 50 Americans in prison in China [in 2008], many for economic crimes. There are many Europeans in prison as well. The number of Hong Kong Chinese in mainland prisons for alleged economic crimes probably exceeds 1,000. Very few are the focus of media attention. Their families suffer in silence, and no one speaks for them...Mr. Shao [American Chinese business man] was denied access to a lawyer until he was brought to trial, 26 months after his detention. For most of the time he was detained he was kept in solitary confinement. His trial took less than a day. On appeal, he recovered documentation that his firm had paid the taxes he was accused of evading. The evidence was ruled inadmissible. A group of distinguished Chinese legal scholars examined the case and advised that at the very least Mr. Shao should be granted a retrial. They were ignored. The Supreme People's Court rejected Mr. Shao's petition."[45] Taiwanese, Korean, and Japanese business people have also suffered under the arbitrary legal system without rule of law.

Since government officials are above the law, they pay little attention to the rule of law and property rights, prompting business people into politics in order to mitigate such risks. In this way, corruption weakens the entrepreneur class because some are siphoned off to politics, driven there by the need for political protection and fear of market competition, which gave rise to the wide spread rent seeking and hurting the long-term development in China.

Chinese entrepreneurs have not gained power to pursue their interests due to the degree of their political dependence. Even those who have grievances tend to use unofficial and informal channels to deal with their problems due to lack of rule of law in China. According to one survey based on a national survey of private entrepreneurs and extensive fieldwork in 10 provinces, Kellee S. Tsai found out that "only 5 percent of business owners regularly rely on more assertive modes of dispute resolution—such as appealing to the local government or higher authorities" or "appealing through judicial courts."[46]

Given the social impact of restructuring state-owned enterprises, the government will not be out of the business of subsidizing large companies any time soon. In addition, many leaders still fear that private entrepreneurs will become too powerful and will hold the economy hostage while demanding political reform. In fact, in addition to standard new business obstacles, Chinese entrepreneurs have to deal with government officials who have either tried to take advantage of them or disrupted their operations. Thus, entrepreneurs are often forced into a short-term business strategy of "take the money and run." This short-term business strategy destabilizes the evolution of a truly open market economy while exacerbating problems such as piracy and inattention to worker abuse.

Another area of concern arises from the role of the *combos*. Although they helped push the development of capitalism in China, due to their monopolistic nature, they have erected barriers to continued market development. Most of China's monopolies are spin-offs created from state sector restructuring. Thus, in many cases, they started with 100 percent of both the market share and the government's backing, both official and unofficial, making it difficult for competitors to gain a foothold. In the 1990s, the old state-run enterprises (electricity, aviation, railway, and telecommunications industries) became newly successful. According to Chinese economist Hu Angang, state monopolies used their political influence to "divide and swallow up economic resources in the name of the state" and otherwise acted in ways that, though detrimental to public welfare, benefited the monopolies themselves.[47] As a result, private individual owners have suffered.

In addition to these problems, there are still many institutional obstacles faced by private firms. These barriers include limited access to financial services, limited market access, double taxation, and legal vulnerabilities.[48] As a result, it may not be surprising to learn that by the close of 1999, "the private sector accounted for only 1 percent of bank lending, and only 1 percent of the companies listed on the Shanghai and Shenzhen stock exchanges were non-state firms."[49]

It must also be kept in mind that the grassroots liberal movement has its own limitations as well. It has been effective in transforming the old system but has not been able to generate real institutional change. The lack of support at the elite level means that China has become two societies: one composed and driven by grassroots liberal movements from below and another driven by the formal illiberal tendencies of the Chinese Communist state.

According to Sinologist Bai Nansheng, most reform measures did no more than recognize the social reality which rural migrant entrepreneurs had already created.[50] Professor Zhou Qiren, a former adviser to deposed Premier Zhao, has openly called for privatized rural property and land rights.[51] However, no leader to date has answered his call because collective ownership of land provides the commercial basis of enriching local governments and officials. Due to this lack of leadership and formal liberal social movements, China will be caught in a tug of war between a nascent liberal society and an entrenched authoritarian state for the foreseeable future. By studying Chinese entrepreneurs and economic growth, however, the elite in Beijing should gradually learn that growth occurs when people have more freedom. When this message is positively received, the ideas of Smith, Hayek, Friedman, et. al. will finally have arrived in the People's Middle Kingdom.

In a different setting, Stark points out that socialist transitional economies often led to the emergence of the "recombinant property" characteristic of "persistence of routines and practices, organizational forms and social ties that can become assets, resources, and the basis for credible commitments and coordinated action in the post-socialist period."[52] For the time being, the state's continued control strengthens one-party domination politically while entrepreneurs used their political backing to simultaneously gain private property and personal wealth. The love and hate relationship between business and politics will create a structural problem for China in the long run. The political interference makes China rank low in economic freedom while Hong Kong gains its number 1 ranking because of its, "open trading system, low taxes, sound money, minimal government regulation, and the rule of law."[53] This will have enormous implications for "China's future."

Chinese entrepreneurs have played an important role in weakening the planned economy, but they are still not strong enough to bring about a property rights regime because too many try to explore and benefit from the rent-seeking appetites of officials and find ways to deter competition.[54] According to economic theory, property rights refer to the "residual rights of control" over assets and properties—the right to make decisions concerning the asset's use or transfer that are not explicitly controlled by law or assigned to another by contract.[55] In other words, they are the so-called rights of exclusivity and alienability.[56] Together with government officials who also attempt to profit from the ambiguity of ownership, Chinese entrepreneurs create barriers for the institutionalization of property rights which clearly delineate the boundaries of ownership. As noted by Xueguang Zhou, "interestingly, such relationships are built on some compromise of the bundle of property rights among the parties involved."[57] Thus, China has a long way to go before the efficient allocation of risks and incentives through market mechanisms become attached to a property rights regime.[58]

Despite legitimating private businesses, the one-party state bureaucrats have used their hold on key elements of the economy to serve their own interest. Thus China's fundamental flaw remains its self-serving bureaucracy. Government tax rates have increased rapidly during the past years and created problems for millions of new entrepreneurs.[59]

Government does not support private businesses since 75 percent of loans from state banks continue to flow into money loss state factories to buy political stability. Private businesses have to depend on high interest from informal loans or borrow with usury. The success and failures of Chinese entrepreneurs show that the Chinese state still strangles the most productive sector in society. Unless the government can release its grip on the people and the market, the Chinese capitalist revolution will never be complete. The fundamental problem in China is still the state that chokes the freedom and liberty that is linked to rule of law.

Entrepreneurs Are Forcing China to Transform

Despite all the aforementioned problems, Chinese entrepreneurs have played and continue to play an integral role in China's structural transformation from an industrial to an information economy without the one-hundred-plus years that most Western countries took to accomplish the same task. Too many studies have focused on their economic role, however, while neglecting their equally important role in social and political transformation. Some of these effects of the evolution of entrepreneurs include:

1. Diversified Ownership Structure

Entrepreneurs play an important role in the structural transformation of ownership. The most fundamental tenet of the traditional socialist system was public ownership of the means of production and distribution. In 1978, the state controlled almost all industry. But by 2005, that share declined to about 38 percent, while at the same time, "the number of SOEs fell from 118,000 in 1995 to 27,477 in 2005.[60] Also in 2005, the private sector's share of GDP reached 50 percent while Hong Kong and Taiwan took another 15, forcing the state's control over the economy to 35 percent.[61] As a result of the efforts of the entrepreneurs, this system changed at such a rapid pace and with such a broad scope that by the time the government fully understood what was taking place, it was too late (and would have been too devastating) to attempt to reverse course. This explains why there still exists such a diverse economic structure in China today.

2. Rapid Development of Markets

The rapid growth of entrepreneurs is largely responsible for the speed and scope of market development in China. Gone are the important indicators of socialism: state monopolies on foreign trade and domestic circulation of goods; cooperative production in agriculture and handicraft industries; planning of industrial production; state control of finance and credit; state determination of virtually all prices (including wages); and state-planned allocation of labor.

3. Reduced Dependence on the State

The rapid rise of Chinese entrepreneurs has lessened the individual's dependence on the state. Rural citizens have partially broken through the constraints that have kept them down for so long and urban residents are challenging the psychology of social dependence that characterized their lives for half a century. People increasingly realize that there is a life apart from state direction and control and now desire privacy and space between state and society.

4. Job Creation

The Chinese government is trying to reduce its welfare burden, not increase it. Thus, the state sector is not a net creator of jobs. Consequently, small businesses and new ventures contribute substantially to job creation and employ an increasing percentage of the working population. As state factories downsize and disgorge workers onto the streets, the rise of the private sector is the most effective path to new job creation—70 percent of all new jobs.

5. Government Learning Curve

The transforming economy in China has provided a lesson: limited government is better for economic development. One Wenzhou official explained the secret of the city's economic success: "To be honest, before the left ideology was cleared away, leadership's keeping their hands off was the secret. Because in the past, we severely attacked [the entrepreneur activities] who in fact were helping to rid us of poverty. On the contrary, social problems increased [with such attacks]. In this complex environment, we had to adopt an attitude of less control."[62] With so many entrepreneurs who can vote with their feet by going elsewhere for business ventures, local government officials may modify traditional party-state behavior to keep local business from relocating. A typical case is that of one Li in Zouping, Shandong Province. When Li, a local CEO wanted to move his company to another Shandong city, the local government granted land use rights at a price.[63]

6. Social Structural Change

Entrepreneurs have changed China's social structure. For thousands of years, merchants carried a lower social class image. The dream of the merchant was to have a son who passed the national exam to become an official who in the end would retire honorably. According to the late sociologist, Marion Levy, this cycle prevented China from developing markets.[64] It took the famine in China to break the cycle in the 1960s. The pioneers of risk taking are the poor rural people, former slaves of the planned economy. There are 40 million entrepreneurs in China, most of which had a rural background. Most early rich people in the 1980s had rural backgrounds, including some today. Former famine victims turned rural entrepreneurs have become the most daring and devoted group of risk-taking people unprecedented not only in China but in the world. This social background will make China powerful and strong because of the numbers. Few rural children today are doing what their grandparents were doing thirty years ago. We cannot say this about the untouchable class in India.

Today, the entrepreneur has become the preferred model for upward mobility among millions of Chinese, despite the barriers the state has created for business success. To obtain this ideal, an ideology advocating individualism, open society, and international involvement will be necessary. The ideas of entrepreneurship and personal liberty are the basis for economic development, which means that reducing traditionally oppressive government control is the first step for development. Chinese entrepreneurs have not been successful in eliminating the heavy hand of the state, but they have systematically altered the nature of this control.

Civil Society Building

The development of private businesses is also linked to the rise of civil society in China (to be discussed in a later chapter). The private provision of jobs reduces the fear of losing jobs while engaging independent activities. The business guilds have become relative independent. By the early 2004, there were already 114 business associations representing different industries in Wenzhou, the capital of Chinese entrepreneurs. Wenzhou Business Association has become national with branch offices in various major cities in China.[65]

In addition to these factors, entrepreneurs are proof of how ordinary citizens have gradually eroded the fundamental tenets of Communism that had been engrained in Chinese society. The ideas of Communism and egalitarianism are becoming almost irrelevant in the lives of those involved in today's commercial environment. The rise of a private sector and an entrepreneurial culture has undermined the control of the ruling party without directly contesting its power. This emerging situation will lead to a more balanced power structure between public and private spheres.

A small but representative indicator of this phenomenon lies in the fact that most private business owners are not party members. Not until Jiang Zemin's "Three Represents" speech in June 1, 2001, at the eightieth-year reunion of the CCP, did the party fully re-open its doors to entrepreneurs.[66] At this point, as Dickson states, the party devised and implemented "a two-pronged strategy of creating new institutional links and co-opting the newly emerging economic elites" in an effort to develop closer links to entrepreneurs.[67] This strategy, one of co-option, attempted to create more red capitalists and entrepreneurs with strong party ties. Individually, China's millionaires and billionaires have on occasion challenged Beijing's authority through shady business deals, tax evasion, and blatant theft of state assets, but few have confronted the government as Sun Dawu has. Ultimately, what is far more troubling for Beijing is that Sun has like-minded peers who want to change Beijing's policies—or, failing that, change the policymakers in Beijing.

Despite the 2001 elimination of the policy banning them from party membership, many entrepreneurs feel they can succeed without it. "What is the use of becoming a Party member?" replied a restaurant owner, Tang Xiaoling in Wuhan; "I would join the Party tomorrow if the state bank gives me a loan [otherwise]...I am busy...I don't have time for meetings."[68] A survey in a party journal discovered that "only 17 percent of private firms employed party members in 1999 and just 3 percent had any kind of party organization. Foreign-funded enterprises are often formed in partnership with state-owned firms, yet just 35 percent of them employed party members that year and a mere 17 percent had party cells."[69] One recent book on China's emerging new class structure, published by the Chinese Academy of Social Sciences, quotes a 2002 survey conducted by the central government showing that only 8 percent of private businessmen wanted to join the CCP.[70] By contrast, 31 percent indicated interest in belonging to local or national-level parliaments (420 are already members) or political consultative bodies (941 current members).[71]

However, despite the apparent loss of interest in party membership, some feel that the party is simply undergoing a transformation in which economic incentives will replace ideology as its cornerstone. As a result, Dickson's recent survey states that "membership in the party is still advantageous for many careers…[and is thus] highly sought after."[72] Hong also supports this view, claiming that CCP membership is the new entrepreneur's most popular means of "self-preservation and self-protection."[73] It is clear that entrepreneurs who can prosper economically from party membership will still desire it. The Communist Party thus finds itself in an interesting position. However, our belief is that with increased globalization, the balance of economic power will continue to shift away from the state, consequently reducing its ability to provide incentives for party membership.

Concluding Thoughts

In these two chapters, we have discussed the role that entrepreneurs play in the ongoing transition to a market-driven society and industrial development in China. Forty million Chinese entrepreneurs have created a new world order around the world in which a supply of capital, labor, technology and ideas are creating new business and manufacturing centers in developing nations and in poor regions in China.[74] Most states are going with the flow rather than leading this new industrial global revolution. Chinese economic success and the rapid growth of entrepreneurs point the way for those elsewhere in the developing world by demonstrating that entrepreneurship is the basis for industrialization and commercialization—as they were in the West. In short, China's economic rise has depended on individual initiative and entrepreneurship, rather than reliance on the government.

However, their impact is not limited to the rapid growth of the Chinese economy. The rise of Chinese economic development took place because entrepreneurs thrive despite major obstacles. It is rural entrepreneurship that liberated 400 million Chinese from starvation and led a genuine capitalist revolution. In his new book, *Capitalism with Chinese Characteristics,* Huang Yasheng argues that "Capitalism with Chinese characteristics is a function of a political balance between two Chinas—the entrepreneurial, market-driven rural China vis-à-vis the state-led and oligarchic urban China. In the 1980s, rural China gained the upper hand but in the 1990s, urban China gained the upper hand. When and where rural China has the upper hand, Chinese capitalism is entrepreneurial, politically-independent and vibrantly competitive in its conduct and virtuous in its effects. When and where urban China has the upper hand, Chinese capitalism is tending toward oligarchy and political dependency on the state and it is corrupt."[75] The majority of the much-touted poverty reduction occurred during the short, eight-year entrepreneurial era (1980-8) to a far greater degree than during the long, thirteen-year state-led era (1989-2002).[76]

Despite the different types of Chinese entrepreneurs, they have transformed socialist state policies. Although the Chinese state and other economic elite try to create an oligarchy, the foundation of entrepreneurship and the global linkage have created opportunities and choices for all Chinese people, which can reduce some degree of oligarchy. The shift from a monolithic state ownership society to a multiple ownership society has profoundly affected the lives, social relations, and value systems of many millions of Chinese citizens. The differing responses of state and society to structural reorganization have altered the trajectory of market transition. Entrepreneurs constantly contest the state's limits and in so doing, have altered the basic thrust of the Chinese state from a political Communist to an authoritarian regulative state.

The lesson of the Chinese entrepreneurs has global implications, in that most early entrepreneurs emerged without any special support, education, or training, yet still played an invaluable role in the process of economic development and social change. The fact was that many poor in China became "budding entrepreneurs whose greatest desire was not to bring down the market economy," but to create it.[77] The success of early Chinese entrepreneurs from the countryside shows that market development is linked to the degree of freedom people fought hard to gain so that they can pursue their own interests. Such entrepreneurship would have been impossible under the collective commune. Today, however, they are continuing to create employment and wealth, alleviate poverty, and raise the living standards of those around them in an effort to increase their basic economic and social rights. Studies like that of He Qinglian suggest that the role of red capitalists somehow negates the importance of the economic rise of the private sector. This view, however, ignores not only the impact of party members concerned more with capitalist entrepreneurship than ideology, but also the effect of such practices on the billion-plus remainder of the population.

We contend that unsanctioned rights-driven economic activity occurring from the very beginning of the reform era has resulted in a revolution that has transcended the economic arena to encompass the social and political realms as well. As such, we believe that the development of civil society—understood as a de facto autonomous social and economic sphere—must include private enterprise. Without it, no private space can exist and the state controls enough of the basic necessities (food, employment, welfare) that effective dissent is all but impossible. Chinese people have experienced wealth, health, opportunity, and choice. The rise of China's economic power came about because of the fruits of the ingenuity, curiosity, and perseverance of its entrepreneurs.

The Chinese entrepreneurs have helped China to create its economic miracle in a short time. As Hayek points out, sensibly allocating scarce resources requires knowledge dispersed among many people, with no individual or group of experts capable of acquiring it all.[78] Informed economic decision-making requires allowing entrepreneurs to act on the information of "time and place" that only they have, while providing a system of communication that motivates individuals and informs them on how best to do it. Market exchange and prices generate information and motivation. So does the desire to make money.

Thanks to the growth of a private sector, the competitive ownership structures (the private, state, collective, and global firms compete) are competing at almost all levels of interaction to accommodate the new economic power bases, thus lessening the state's control over society. This reflects Joseph Schumpeter's discussion about how the new structure "incessantly revolutionizes the economic structure from within, incessantly destroying the old one, incessantly creating a new one. This process of Creative Destruction is the essential fact about capitalism."[79]

This new Chinese capitalism kills the Communist ideology of eliminating private property. For example, in 2007, social pressure in China led to the Property Rights Protection Law. In addition, as proof of the cultural evolution that is occurring, merchants have become a preferred social class. This in itself is a veritable revolution for both the traditional and communist Chinese societies, in which merchants were the bottom rung.[80]

Many have given Deng Xiaoping undue credit for China's rapid economic development. If he was the primary driver, why was he not able to instill the same entrepreneurial spirit in state factory managers? Why were entrepreneurs harassed and arrested for three decades, despite being at the forefront of economic growth? Why, even in 1999, did private enterprises receive less than 1 percent of government loans? Indeed, Deng Xiaoping was not the main driving force of the economic development while he was in power. Deng can take credit only for not cracking down too harshly during the opening phases of the spontaneous, leaderless, and autonomous grassroots liberal movement that has brought China to the place it is today. The real heroes of the economic take-off were the common people who simply desired more rights, more self-sufficiency, and better lives—who wanted to ease the state's overwhelming hold on their lives.

While this transformation is in no way complete, it is amazing to consider the pace and scope of economic and social progress up to this point and to realize that the majority of this change occurred not only without support from the Communist regime, but in the face of its determined resistance. The entrepreneurs-led revolution in China is not a democratic revolution. Some entrepreneurs even fear a democratic revolution like the Russian one will create social chaos. But they have laid the economic foundation for the future liberal democratic China. "In order to run their businesses in a transitional and a politically charged regulatory environment, private entrepreneurs have created a host of adaptive strategies at the grass-roots level. The popularity and relative success of these strategies have, in turn, enabled reform-oriented elites to justify significant changes in the country's most important governing institutions."[81]

Entrepreneurs will continue to play a vital leading role in guiding China towards a new future that will challenge the status quo.

Notes

1. The term "chaebols" was used in South Korea as groupings of profitable family owned enterprises that have close ties with the government.
2. Mark, Landler, "In China, a Management Maverick Builds a Brand," *New York Times*, July 23, 2000.
3. Ibid.
4. *Chinese News Digest* (CND), 09/11/01, http://www.cnd.org/CND-Global/CND-Global.new.html.
5. He Qinglian, *Zhongguo de xianjing (China's Pitfall)*, (Hong Kong: *mingjing chubanshe*, 1998).
6. Shu-Ching Jean Chen, "China's Power Queen," Forbes.com, January 3, 2008, http://www.forbes.com/2008/01/03/li-xiaolin-china-face-markets-.
7. The list goes on. Fu Yan, son of Peng Zhen's (a former chairman of the People's Congress), is chairman of the Board of Directors at Beijing Fuli Ltd. Wang Jun, son of Wang Zhens (one of the Eight Immortals of the Communist Party of China), holds a leading position with China International Trust & Investment Co. Wang Xiaochao, son of Yang Shangkun's (a former defense minister), is general manager of the Poly Group, Ltd. Zhu Yanlai, daughter of Zhu Rongji, is head of the Bank of China International. Zhu Yunlai, her brother, is the head of China International Capital Corp. The sons of Jiang Zemin and Li Peng have all gone into business after studying abroad. The son of the late Marshal Ye Jianying, Ye Xuanming, is the general manager of the military-owned Kaili Corporation, an arm of the General Political Department of the armed forces. Wu Jianchang, chairman of the China National Nonferrous Metals Industry Corporation, is the son-in-law of Deng Xiaoping.
8. *China Digital Times*, "90 percent of China's billionaires are children of senior officials," November 2, 2009, http://chinadigitaltimes.net/2006/11/90-percent-of-chinas-billionaires-are-children-of-senior-officials/.
9. Wu Jinglian, "*shichanghua congnanlai? Daonanqu?*(Whither the Reform of Market?)" September 12, 2008. http://www.ias.fudan.edu.cn/news/messageInfo.asp?ID=112.
10. Zhou Qiren, "What Did Deng Xiaoping do Right?" *China Economist Forum*, July 28, 2008, 10:09, http://chinaeconomist.org/archives/236.html.
11. Zhang Jun, "*Feigongyoushi jingji falu diwei de bianlian jiqi qishi*, (Transformation and Lessons of Private Economic Sector's Legal Status)," *Xinhua wenzhai (Xinhua Readers' Digest)*, No. 395, Vol. 23, pp. 18-21.
12. The Chinese words were "*shi ge guan jiu yao guan, xiang ba ni zenyan jiu zenyan.*"
13. Personal interview with Lei Tao, on December 20, 1994.
14. *Youyao maer pao; youyao maer bu chicao.*
15. See English version of the Law in editorial, "Property law gets fine-tuned in latest round," *China Daily,* 03/09/2007, p. 6.
16. Personal interview with Feng XinYuan on May 25, 2007 in Honolulu, HI and Prof. Hu Jingbei telephone interview.
17. Personal interviews by the author in July 2005 and 2006.
18. Yang Yaqin and Shi Zhangzhong, "*Shanghai minying kejiqiye fazhan zhong de wenti jiqi zhiyue yinsu* (The Development of Private High-Technology Firms in Shanghai: problems and measures)," *Shehui kexue (Social Sciences)*, No. 8 (1999).
19. *China Daily, Business Weekly*, May 22-28, 1994, p. 1.

20. János Kornai. *The Socialist System: The Political Economy of Communism*. (Princeton, NJ: Princeton University Press, 1992).

21. *China Digital Times*, "90 percent of China's billionaires are children of senior officials," November 2, 2009, http://chinadigitaltimes.net/2006/11/90-percent-of-chinas-billionaires-are-children-of-senior-officials/.

22. *China Digital Times*, "90 percent of China's billionaires are children of senior officials," November 2, 2009, http://chinadigitaltimes.net/2006/11/90-percent-of-chinas-billionaires-are-children-of-senior-officials/.

23. Jane Duckett, *The Entrepreneurial State in China*, (London: Rutledge, 1998).

24. China Radio International, "China: Second largest billionaire population," 12/31/2007, http://www.wsichina.org/morningchina/archive/20080104.html.

25. Duckett, 1998.

26. Duckett, 1998.

27. Eun Kyong Choi Kate Zhou, "Entrepreneurs and Politics in the Chinese Transitional Economy: Political Connections and Rent-seeking," *The China Review*, Vol.1, No. 1, (Fall 2001), pp. 111-35.

28. Personal interview with Lei Tao, in Shenzhen on August 17, 1996.

29. Gao Yang, Hu Xueyan, *The Businessman with A Red Hat* (*Hongding shangren Hu Xueyan*, 红顶商人胡雪岩), (Beijing: Sanlian Press, 2001).

30. Bruce J. Dickson, *Wealth into Power: The Communist Party's Embrace of China's Private Sector*, (New York: Cambridge University Press, 2008); Kellee S. Tsai, *Capitalism without Democracy: The Private Sector in Contemporary China* (Ithaca, NY: Cornell University Press, 2007).

31. Several leaders of the charter 08 have been detained.

32. David Daokui Li, Junxin Feng, and Hongping Jiang, "Institutional Entrepreneurs," *American Economic Review*, Volume 96, Issue 2, (May 2006), pp. 358-62.

33. Yang Xueye, "*Jueqi de zhongguo siying jingji* (The Rise of China's Private Economy)", *Modern China Studies*, No. 63, Vol. 4. (1998), http://www.chinayj.net.

34. *Zhongguo tongji ju*, (State Statistics Bureau) *Zhongguo tongji nianjian 1990 (China Statistical Yearbook 1990)*. (Beijing: *zhongguo tongji chubanshe* [Chinese Statistics Press],1990).

35. Li Yining, "Chinese Economy Will Not Fall After the Olympics," *Beijing Daily*, February 5, 2007, http://www.sina.com.cn.

36. Jie Chen and Bruce J. Dickson, "Allies of the State: Democratic Support and Regime Support among China's Private Entrepreneurs," *The China Quarterly*, 196, (December 2008), pp. 1-25.

37. D. J. Solinger, "Urban Entrepreneurs and the State: The Merger of State and Society." In *State and Society in China: The consequences of reform*, ed., Arthur Lewis Rosenbaum, (Boulder, CO: Westview Press, 1992), pp. 121-141.

38. Yia-Ling Liu, "Reform From Below: The Private Economy and Local Politics in the Rural Industrialization of Wenzhou." *The China Quarterly*, 130, (1991) pp. 293-316.

39. Hong Caohui, "*Zhongguo xiangzhen qiye chanquan gaige yu zhongyang - difang quanli de hudong* (China's Rural Industrial Ownership Reform and Its Interaction with the Central State and Local Government)," *Modern China Studies*, No.46. Vol.2. 1995.

40. J.C. Oi, "Communism and Clientelism: Rural Politics in China," *World Politics*, 38 (2), (1985), pp. 238-66. "Fiscal Reform and the Economic Foundation of Local State Corporatism in China," *World Politics,* 45, (1992), pp. 99-126. Margaret M. Pearson, *China's New Business Elite: The Political Consequences of Economic Reform.* (California University Press, 1997). A. Rona-Tas, "The First Shall Be

Last? Enterpreneurship and Communist Cadres in the Transition from Socialism." *American Journal of Sociology,* 100, (1993), pp. 40-69.

41. Xueguang Zhou, "Rethinking Property Rights as a Relational Concept: Explorations in China's Transitional Economy," International Economic Association Round Table on Market and Socialism In the Light of the Experiences of China and Vietnam, January 14-15, 2005.

42. Zhou Qiren, "What Did Deng Xiaoping did Right?" *China Economist Forum,* July 28, 2008, 10:09, http://chinaeconomist.org/archives/236.html.

43. Jidang Zhu Xueqing, *sanshi nian* (*Thirty Year Surging: The Truth of Reform and Openness*), http://www.chinaelections.org/NewsInfo.asp?NewsID=120324.

44. Adam Smith, *The Wealth of Nations,* (New York: Bantam Dell, 2003), pp. 23-24.

45. John Kamm, "Free on the Fourth of July," *Wall Street Journal/ Asia,* July 4, 2008. John Kamm is founder and executive director of the Dui Hua Foundation. http://online.wsj.com/article/SB121511904579427751.html?mod=todays_asia_opinion.

46. Kellee S. Tsai, "China's Complicit Capitalists," *Far Eastern Economic Review,* Vol. 171, Iss. 1, (2008), p. 13-5.

47. He, Qinglian, "The Pit of China's Modernization," (1998), p. 76.

48. Allan Zhang, "Hidden Dragon: Unleashing China's Private Sector," *Price Waterhouse-Cooper,* http://www.pwcglobal.com/extweb/newcolth.nsf/docid/3D15C57A6D220BB985256CF6007B9607#2R.

49. Neil Gregory and Stoyan Tenev, "The Financing of Private Enterprise in China," *Finance & Development,* March 01, 2001.

50. *China Daily,* "Relocation for farmers faces snags," 2002-01-08, *Business Weekly,* http://www.chinadaily.com.cn/chinagate/doc/2002-01/08/content_246821.htmhome.

51. Zhou Qiren Blog, www.zhouqiren.com.

52. David Stark, "Recombinant Property in East European Capitalism." *American Journal of Sociology,* 101:993-1027, (1996), p. 995.

53. James A. Dorn, "Hong Kong's economic freedom," *Washington Times,* September 27, 2007.

54. Xueguang Zhou, Wei Zhao, Qiang Li, and He Cai, "Embeddedness and Contractual Relationships in China's Transitional Economy," *American Sociological Review,* 68, (2003), pp. 75-102.

55. Oliver Hart, *Firms, Contracts and Financial Structure,* (New York: Oxford University Press, 1995).

56. Harold Demsetz, *Ownership, Control and the Firm.* (Oxford: Blackwell, 1988).

57. Xueguang Zhou, "Rethinking Property Rights as a Relational Concept: Explorations in China's Transitional Economy," International Economic Association Round Table on Market and Socialism In the Light of the Experiences of China and Vietnam, January 14-15, 2005.

58. Ronald H. Coase, "The Problem of Social Cost." *Journal of Law and Economics,* 3, (1960), pp. 1-44. Keun Lee, *Chinese Firms and the State in Transition: Property Rights and Agency Problems in the Reform Era.* (Armonk, NY: M.E. Sharpe, Inc., 1991).

59. The central government early in 1994 enacted a new uniform tax law fixing the enterprise profit tax at 33 percent and imposing a flat 17 percent value-added tax (VAT) on manufactured goods. Revenues from the profit tax were to be apportioned between the center and localities on a 60:40 basis (a reversal of the 40:60 ratio the early 1990s); proceeds from the VAT were to be distributed between center and localities at a fixed ratio of 3:1.

60. EIU, *Business, Industry Overview, China Manufacturing,* January 12, 2007. Wayne M. Morrison, "China's Economic Conditions," CRS Report to Congress, Updated May 13, 2008.

61. Li Yining, "The Post-Olympic Games Decline Will not be Repeated in China, 奥运后滑坡现象不会在中国重演," *Beijing Daily*, February 5, 2007, http://www.sina.com.cn.

62. Zhang Renshou and Li Hong, *Wenzhou moshi yanjiu (Study of Wenzhou Model),*, (Beijng: *zhongguo shehui kexue chubanshe* [Chinese Academy of Social Sciences], 1990), p. 34. Caohui Hong, "*Zhongguo xiangzhen qiye chanquan gaige yu zhongyang - difang quanli de hudong* (China's Rural Industrial Ownership Reform and Its Interaction with the Central State and Local Government)," *Modern China Studies*, No.46, Vol. 2, 1995.

63. Personal interview with Li on July 10, 2007, in Zouping.

64. Marion J. Levy, "Contrasting Factors in Modernization of China and Japan." In Sunion Kuznets, Wilbert Moore, and Joseph J. Spengler, *Economic Growth: Brazil, India and Japan* (Durham, NC: Duke University Press, 1955), p. 544.

65. Cao Haidong and Zhang Peng, "The Amazing Power of Wenzhou Business Association (*Wenzhou shanghui de jingren liliang jiemi*)," *The Economics*, http://www.cat898.com.

66. Zemin Jiang speech, June 1, 2001.

67. Bruce Dickson, *Red Capitalists in China: The Party, Private Entrepreneurs, and Prospects for Political Change*, (2003), p. 55.

68. Interview with Tang Xiaoling on July 10, 1999.

69. "China: The withering away of the party," *The Economist*, May 30, 2002.

70. *Lu Xueyi, Dandai zhongguo shehui jaichen yanjiu baogao (Study of Social Stratification in Contemporary China)*, (Beijing: *shehui kexue wenxian chubanshe*, 2002), pp. 11-12.

71. Ibid.

72. Dickson, 2003, p. 167.

73. Hong Caohui, "*Zhongguo xiangzhen qiye chanquan gaige yu zhongyang - difang quanli de hudong* (China's Rural Industrial Ownership Reform and Its Interaction with the Central State and Local Government)" *Modern China Studies*, No. 46, Vol. 2, (1995), p. 32.

74. George Zhibin Gu, *China and the New World Order: How Entrepreneurship, Globalization, and Borderless Business Are Reshaping China and the World*, (Fultus Corporation, 2006).

75. Huang, *Capitalism with Chinese Characteristics*. (Cambridge University Press, 2008).

76. Ibid.

77. Hernando De Soto, *The Other Path: The Economic Answer to Terrorism*, (Perseus Books Group, 2002).

78. Friedrich A. Hayek, "The Use of Knowledge in Society," *The American Economic Review*, September 1945.

79. Joseph A. Schumpeter, *Capitalism, Socialism and Democracy*, (New York: Harper, 1975 [orig. pub. 1942]), pp. 82-5.

80. In traditional China, merchants were at the bottom of the social ladder behind gentry, farmers, and artisans. Under Communism they fared even worse, since many of their activities were labeled as criminal. Marion J. Levy, Jr., *Modernization and the Structure of Society*, (New Brunswick, NJ: Transaction Publishers, 1996).

81. Kellee S. Tsai, *Capitalism without Democracy: The Private Sector in Contemporary China*, (Cornell University Press, 2008).

5

Information Wants to Be Free

Satellite television was a threat to totalitarian
regimes everywhere.
—Rupert Murdoch

If liberty means anything at all, it means the right
to tell people what they do not want to hear.
—George Orwell, Preface to Animal Farm

Each time a man stands up for an ideal, or acts
to improve the lot of others, or strikes out against
injustice, he sends forth a tiny ripple of hope, and
crossing each other from a million different centers
of energy and daring, those ripples build a current
that can sweep down the mightiest walls of oppres-
sion and resistance.
—Robert F. Kennedy

Mao Zedong said that to have power you need two
things: the gun and the pen...The Communist Party
has the gun, but the Internet is now the pen. If they
lose control of it, something will happen to chal-
lenge their authority.[1]
—Guo Liang

Introduction

As China continues to reform economically, scholars as well as the media have focused their attacks on China's shortcomings regarding freedom of the press and enforcement of intellectual property law. The 2006 World Press Freedom Index ranked China 163rd of the 168 countries listed.[2] Although much of this criticism is valid, it fails to appreciate the extent to which people are successful in their daily struggles with government's restrictive information regime. China must be seen as two parallel parts: one of government institutions and the other of the rest of society, many members of which actively oppose the government's suppression of rights and liberties, in varying ways and with varying degrees of success.

133

In this chapter we will consider opposition to authoritarian party-state controls on the flow of and access to information. We will demonstrate the complexity of the state-society contestation over information by examining the evolution of this growing struggle, which has now reached the point where the general populace has made significant gains in the availability of information, even as the government has committed increasing resources to stopping these gains. Aspects of this struggle include illegal production of a variety of information-related products, development of informal markets, the commercialization and limited liberalization of state media, and the powerful impact of global media.

Authoritarian regimes maintain political power though the use of two principle weapons: the gun (the military and police) and the pen (media and other information distribution control). Mao used these weapons in his progressive ascent to power in the 1940s and consequently, after 1949, took control not only of the armed forces, but of media and information channels in their entirety, demonstrating his view that the pen is as decisive as the gun in controlling the mouths and the minds of the Chinese people. Even after the "opening" of China in the 1980s, the state has remained protective of its control over the media and publishing houses. As recently as 2006, the government arrested numerous journalists and fired several editors who dared to publish material on the "dark" side of Chinese society.[3] Given this situation, how is it that uncensored books and magazines are sold freely on nearly every street corner in conurbations, including Beijing, throughout the country? In addition to the spread of the unregulated printed word, why has the content of radio and TV programming also undergone change? In considering such issues, we have found that what prompted these dramatic changes was not government-induced deregulation, but rather the inadvertent collusion of various informal markets with a consumer-driven quest for information and entertainment.

The Early Foundation of Information Control

Historically, censorship has played a crucial role in the Chinese government's program of controlling information. The object of policy was to build and maintain the party-state's absolute domination over the media.[4] According to Gao Song, a *South China Weekend* journalist, for a long time the Chinese media could be described as the party's loyal eyes, ears, and tongues, which were "used to initiate policy shifts and provide ex post facto justification of the elite's policies. The media became a means to impose ideological hegemony on Chinese society, as well as a third channel to penetrate society and detect any potential crisis for the party."[5]

The party's control over the media was a key element of its total control of Chinese society. For one thing, the party-state had monopoly control over the media, which were state owned. Secondly, all journalists were state employees, who were controlled through the *danwei* (work unit) system in which urban working Chinese must seek permission for marriage, divorce, education, and access to goods and services.[6] This system has opened the door for despotism and corruption, leading to cynicism. Media workers and journalists became government officials (in Chinese *guojia ganbu* or later on *gongwu yuan*). Their financial dependence created self-censorship among journalists. Thirdly, a strictly enforced information distribution system ensured that information was controlled hierarchically. Thus higher levels of government were allowed to learn more than lower levels; the public was at the bottom of this hierarchy, with the least access to information.[7] Fourth, the CCP used the media to indoctrinate people with ideological programs. Ideology became a resource for the top elite to coordinate and enforce its priorities.[8]

In the 1960s and 1970s, in addition to the printed word and electronic media, censorship applied to other forms of expression, including symbolic expression of all kinds. During Mao's era, kissing (even in private), long hair, and clothing with conspicuous color or style were forbidden as profoundly counter-revolutionary. For the most part during this time period, China remained a closed society, its people dependent on the government for news and other information as well as approved modes of thinking. In essence, from 1949 until 1976, the Chinese people were passive receivers of action by the socialist state, never themselves actors. This situation was replicated in the economic system, where the state owned all means of production and distribution and controlled the allocation of work.

The relationship between the financial independence of media and their ability to express themselves freely is well known. From 1953 to 1958, when the Chinese state obtained complete control over media employees and (in keeping with the rest of the population) their access to food, espousing dissent in the media became difficult, if not impossible. When it did occur, it resulted, at a minimum, in a mandatory "struggle session," and at worst, a long-term prison sentence or even death.[9] During the Cultural Revolution, the government banned all forms of artistic expression, with the exception of six contemporary-style Peking operas and two Maoist ballets, collectively known as "Eight Revolutionary Model Dramas." Books were burned and statues, some of them thousands of years old, were destroyed. As with the rest of society, the state's monopoly over information blocked the development of independent civil society media organizations. As stated in the introduction, we define civil society as the sphere of autonomous voluntary intermediate associations not mandated by the state; and our concept of civil society also includes the private economic sphere.[10]

One of the many unintended consequences of the information control regime established after 1949 was the formation of public policies in the absence of accurate information, since much information was suppressed and in turn unavailable to top leadership; this occurred because only a one-way flow of information existed, and there were no secondary or unbiased sources to supplement, corroborate, or contradict this flow. According to economists who study the relationship between information and market development, information adds value to transactions in three ways: "it supports reputations, permits customization, and provides yardsticks." Like those practices in formal Soviet society, such information "was frequently not produced; if produced, it was often concealed; whether concealed or not, it was often of poor quality."[11] The Chinese planned economy was based on foundation of a low-value information stock. Thus, in many (and sometimes critical) instances, it was impossible for the Zhongnanhai elite to comprehend the reality of conditions across the nation.

The extreme example of elite ignorance was the 1959-61 Great Leap Famine, in which 20 to 30 million Chinese died of starvation.[12] Misinformation was so extensive that even though the famine affected the majority of people in China, internal news bulletins for the eyes of the Zhongnanhai elite from 1958 to 1961 failed to mention famine at all. During this time, the world was unaware that a catastrophic famine was proceeding. Moreover, so effective was information control that even hungry urban Chinese believed government reports that food shortages were caused by natural disaster and that no one had died.[13] The well-oiled and disciplined party bureaucratic machine was so effective in carrying the center's Great Leap policies that they brought about a nationwide catastrophic famine. Never before in Chinese history had such a national famine occurred; all others were regional in character, allowing victims to seek relief in unaffected areas. Mao's Great Leap policies, implemented effectively throughout the country, succeeded in creating the worst famine in human history. During this calamity, the international community was not even informed of the circumstances, much less able to provide relief. As a result, a bad situation became incalculably worse. Indeed, Premier Zhou En lai used scarce foreign currency, which could have saved numerous lives, to buy gold on the international market to augment China's gold reserves.

For rural Chinese, the Great Leap Famine was the watershed event in their experience of the socialist welfare system and the Communist state's management.[14] As it became clear that they had been systematically exploited and excluded from the state's welfare benefits, while being tied to the land of which they had little control, distrust of the government arose among the rural population. Many learned that non-compliance with state planning regulations often meant an improvement in family income and their overall ability to sustain themselves. This elemental distrust became the unique psychological background from which China's grassroots self-emancipation movement began.

In the absence of autonomous civil society institutions, ordinary people reacted by creating what scholars such as Perry Link, Richard P. Madsen, and Paul G. Pickowicz have referred to as an "unofficial" China—compared with the formal official China.[15] Ba Jin, arguably China's most famous modern writer, confessed as early as 1979 that to please the party-state he had lied both in what he said and what he had written.[16] The well-known Chinese actor Zhao Dan complained about the party's tight reign over the arts, but only dared to do so on his deathbed in 1980.[17] The entire situation was eloquently summed up by Deborah Davis:

> Because of the CCP leadership's repeated use of class struggle and pervasive censorship after 1949, Chinese artists and non-artists necessarily took their cues from party and government agendas out of concern for their security—even survival. Public identities were shaped to fit with the official ideas of sacrifice for the collective, hatred of the bourgeoisie, and in the extreme version that prevailed during the Cultural Revolution, rejection of all traditional art forms. In private, the tenacious or alienated individual might nourish a counter identity that celebrated the ethereal, the sensual, or the intensely private. But such pleasures and identities could not be displayed in public. Nor could they provide the link to draw peers together openly into communities of fellow connoisseurs or performers.[18]

Artists and writers surrendered to what Hungarian critic Milos Harszti referred to as a "velvet prison."[19] The contradiction between what such public figures felt and what they felt they could say was never resolved by the state, but rather is being slowly eroded, as we will see, by everyday resistance of ordinary Chinese.

Finding Liberation through Forbidden Literature

Censorship in the People's Republic has only been able to achieve a certain degree of success; even during the Cultural Revolution, when enforcement and enforcers were at an all time high, people copied banned books by hand and circulated them among themselves. The first wave of an underground reading movement appeared in 1967, during the high tide of the Cultural Revolution, when Red Guards occupied the nation's libraries, gaining access to banned books previously available only to top officials. The second wave came in 1968, when the government began sending young people, who in the end numbered more twenty-million, to the countryside at an increased pace.

During the 1968-78 period, many bored urban youths, away from the city for the first time, began setting up *dushuhui* (reading clubs) in villages and on military farms (*junken nongcang*). Xiao Yuan, a leader of the Tianmen *dushuhui* recalled, "Most of us came from intellectual families and had a habit of reading, but we lacked access to a library. We had only the books of Mao, Marx, Engels and Lenin. We read these classic communist works first. My initial enlightenment came when we carefully read the *Communist Manifesto* and the Paris Commune and discovered that Mao and his associates did not follow Marx's actual doctrines. We were desperate to find independent critiques of communism. Unfortunately, at the time I was unable to read Djilas great work, *The New Class* until in the 1980's, but when I did, it was mind opening."[20]

Across China, members of reading groups like Xiao's became anti-Maoist grassroots intellectuals. One of most famous reading clubs was Liyizhe Group, which in 1980 posted long articles on busy Guangzhou streets denouncing Mao as the worst dictator in Chinese history.[21] Some, like Xiao, became leaders of the 1989 student democracy movement. Xiao later became a professor in Wuhan and was sentenced to four years in prison after the June 4, 1989 crackdown. Another member of Xiao's reading group, Ai Xiaoming, after 1995 became one of China's leading human rights activists. Both Xiao and Ai attributed their political awakening to their experience in the reading clubs.

A third wave of underground reading spread throughout urban China in the mid- 1970s when millions of urban youths hand-copied underground literature such as *The Heart of a Young Lady*. The themes ranged from pornography to detective stories, cult thrillers, traditional knight errant fiction and triangular love stories. Their popularity among the urban youth showed a collective defiance against the state's control over printed materials and the media.[22] Such books, which contained sexually explicit descriptions of teenage sexuality, pushed descriptions of romance and sex far beyond permissible limits. A significant feature of such works was that youth did not simply copy them but also used their own creative imaginative to add new material and, in some cases, to cut what they considered inappropriate. Another hand-copied book was *The Club Party*, a Chinese version of the James Bond genre. These two books became so popular that between 1972 and 1976, in the midst of the Cultural Revolution, literally millions of young people participated in hand copying their contents. It is important to note that for some, reading the banned books was not simply a passive recreational activity but an active form of resistance to state censorship. Reading illegal books and articles became a respected pursuit among youth. This *samizdat* style of publication was known as *you yin ban* (mimeographed) or *shou chao ben* (hand-copied books). This underground literature is much like what James Scott calls "hidden transcripts."[23] The official publication was to indoctrinate people so that they could believe what the party-state wanted them to believe. But the act of copying and reading the underground apolitical literature was in fact to reverse the party-state social engineering by allowing people to express their feelings and their preference for reading. Thus, it was a grassroots political act of defiance. For many powerless Chinese at that time, reading *wuxia xiaoshuo* (knight errant fiction) also gave them a psychological empowerment when the heroes in the novels punished the powerful with magic and supernatural power.

For many young men and women, reading *The Heart of a Young Lady* was a direct attack upon state-imposed desexualized Puritanism. Ji San (not her real name), who read the book as a high school girl, stressed the importance of women's defiance of the state's imposed "blue ant" de-feminization campaign: "When I read *The Heart of a Young Lady*, I felt like a woman and desired men. I was brought up hating being a woman and craved complete equality with men. The book helped me to discover that I am a *woman* and not just another revolutionary."[24] Ji's words expressed the feelings of an entire generation of women who grew up wearing Mao jackets. Underground literature started to challenge the party-state. According to Perry Link, various hand-copied novels show mockery of the political system's rigid hierarchy. The story of a soldier who is handed a ticking time bomb and has to call in an official report to his superior before disposing of the bomb is widely distributed among Chinese fed up with the god-like powers of the petty tyrant who governed every aspect of their lives at their workplace.[25] Some Chinese, paid dearly—with their lives—for such defiance. Yu Luoke, for example, who wrote a hand-copied book to challenge the Chinese class-based discrimination in 1966 was executed in 1972. The regime, however, proved unable to cope with the situation; the defiant actions of millions alienated from the system, created a new social environment on a scale unmanageable by the party-state control machine. As the Chinese saying goes, when everyone is committing a crime, it is not a crime (*zuibu fanzong*).

The power vacuum that ensued after Mao's death in 1976 deepened popular defiance. One of the more important movements of the late 1970s and early 1980s involved underground art exhibitions and poetry writing groups. Abstract art and avant garde poems were circulated throughout urban China, especially among college students. Some of these new creations, which included nude paintings by the *Xinxin* (New Star, meaning a new direction to follow) group, were displayed in Beijing's parks. At about the same time, a controversial performance art exhibition took place at a Beijing Museum that challenged approved modes of expression and contributed to undermining state control over artistic expression. In the eyes of China's youth and the entire intellectual community, these artists were viewed as *zhengkui* (the essence of cool) because of the tremendous talent placed at the service of artistic defiance. This defiance, however, only served as a prelude to increased openness among the artistic community. Once again, open violation of formal government rules governing public displays of art had a liberating effect.

The grassroots liberalization movement deeped public cynicism, making Mao's style of ruling impossible to continue. In the late 1970s, the top elite could no longer to use ideology as a resource "to coordinate and enforce its priorities."[26]

Transgression and the Rise of Parallel Societies

The push towards free speech began with increasing displays of individual resistance. At first, such actions were quite modest, but during the technological explosion of the reform period, the spread of duplication equipment led to a boom in alternative media, which pushed the cause to a whole new level. Thus, the rise of rural industry and market development in the countryside resulted in an explosion in non-sanctioned publication of all sorts of reading materials. Simultaneously, China began to open itself to the outside world, mostly channeled through non-regulated sources without adherence to copyright law. As non-state sectors (informal and rural industry) boomed, the ability to reproduce books, videos, computer software, etc. spread so quickly that it was soon beyond the control of censors. Long-suppressed demand was finally being serviced. Chinese buyers began eagerly making up for the lost time by consuming everything from Hong Kong pornography to Kung Fu movies.

In addition to providing entertainment, the pirated books, music CDs, and bootleg videos that swept across China facilitated the formation of a parallel society independent of state ideology, a form, in essence, of civil society. By parallel societies we mean *two different social realities* (the state, on the one hand, and the people—"society"—on the other), two different information distribution systems (state versus non-state), and two different economies (formal versus informal). The informal parallel society welcomes Western ideas and values. More importantly, it has helped create the foundation for China's increasing liberalization.

During the reform period, public resistance to the state's control over information expanded, due in part to the rise of the private sector. Violations of government information rules, massive as these violations have been, are nevertheless no more than a small segment within China's much larger and encompassing rights movement. This grassroots anti-censorship movement was also linked to the liberalization movement in the countryside.

To a great extent, there was a close association between the spread of illegal and politically incorrect materials and the increased free flow of many other forms of information in China. How did illegal and informal publishing activities surmount the seemingly great obstacles the state placed in their paths? First and foremost, the government's long-term censorship of all categories of information and artistic expression created a social urge for access to unofficial and uncensored material. Consequently, a huge potential market existed in China even before such products appeared in the marketplace. Government bans on books and films were signs of future best sellers. Ambitious writers hoped they would be criticized by the government because subsequent state bans often enhanced sales far more effectively than even the most successful marketing strategies. Second, the spread of non-sanctioned printing was linked to the growth of the informal business sector and its corresponding markets. This sector includes everything from illegal black-market operations to night markets, populated by unlicensed street vendors. Although most informal markets existed in cities, most production took place in rural areas where the *baochan daohu* movement made the family an independent economic unit. As rural factories in Guangdong produced massive amounts of tape recorders, millions of Chinese households gained the ability to listen to whatever they wanted. In response, illegally run rural publication firms churned out tens of millions of unauthorized copies of popular foreign CD's, featuring Western performers from Michael Jackson to Madonna and Asian stars such as Deng Lijun (a popular Hong Kong-based Taiwanese singer) and Jackie Chan. The state's ban on "unhealthy" content, such as romance, crime, and sex quickly translated into more profits for private enterprise by eliminating state competition in a lucrative market. The state media, fearing being left behind were obliged to create Chinese-style tabloids exploiting sex-and-crime stories as well as "constructive," critical, investigative news.[27]

Reduction of state censorship was also linked to market development. Pirated music tapes and later CD's gradually became a part of life for ordinary people. To a degree, in addition to being places to purchase entertainment, the illegal markets also served as breeding grounds for subversive thought. Pirate industry gatherings often become focal points for spreading ideas of freedom and democracy. The majority of house churchgoers (estimated between 50 to 70 million), for example, used Bibles and hymns from unofficial publications. In fact, one of the most influential unofficial publications is a collection of house church worship songs, *Jianan Shixuan* (Canaan Hymns). Nearly a thousand traditional, beautifully written songs were composed by Xiaomin, an uneducated rural young woman.[28] Through illegal copying and publication, millions of house church worshippers have gained access to Xiaomin's indigenous Christian songs. We were amazed to find the same *Jianan Shixuan* DVD in house churches in Beijing in 2005 and in distant Lijiang, Yunnan, in 2006. Although these house churches have no communication with each other, their respective services began with the same Xiaomin song, "Five O'clock in the Early Morning." This Christian song deliberately counters "The East Is Red," the Communist Party's official song, which dominated China for more than thirty years. While "The East Is Red," blasted from loudspeakers in every village and hamlet in China, "Five O'clock in the Early Morning" emanates from the hearts of those who sing it.

The party state's reaction to unapproved publications like Xiaomin's songs has always been attempts at suppression. In 1998, the Supreme People's Court issued "An Explanation Regarding Certain Questions About the Specific Laws to be Used in Adjudicating Criminal Cases of Illegal Publications," which allows courts to use Article 225 of the Chinese Constitution to imprison anyone who "publishes, prints, copies, or distributes illegal publications."[29] In this case, the author, Xiaomin was imprisoned for about one year.

The government attempted to stop Xiaomin's songs by punishing its publishers and distributors as well. Those who attend unsanctioned churches are the most frequent targets of crackdowns. In 2004, after discovering more than 200,000 pieces of Christian literature in the Beijing home of church leader Cai Zhuohua, the government imprisoned him and his family. In 2005, Pastor Cai received a three-year jail sentence on charges relating to "illegal business practices" and was fined $18,500. His wife, Xiao Yunfei, was imprisoned for 2 years and fined 120,000 Yuan. Her brother Xiao Gaowen received an 18-month sentence and fined 100,000 Yuan.[30]

According to ChinaAid, a Texas-based Christian NGO, a home church leader in Xinjiang, Zhou Heng, was arrested in September 2007 when he was caught receiving three tons of Bibles from another city.[31] Home churches also sell banned traditional cultural products like old-style calendars and forbidden books. These high profile cases suggest that media suppression has not stifled the unofficial publication and distribution of materials deemed "unhealthy and dangerous" to the regime.

The Rise of Consumer Society and the Transformation of the Media Audiences

There is a relationship between the rise of a consumer society and demand for apolitical media content in China. As Chinese become consumers, the nature of the media has also been transformed because consumers' preferences dictate the media content and advertisement styles that censors still control.[32] For more than 4 decades, party officials composing less than 3 percent of the Chinese population dictated the content of all media, ignoring the interests, concerns, and tastes of the remaining 97 percent . This system of elite media dictatorship reached crescendo during the Cultural Revolution when a tiny handful of top officials decreed that only eight modern revolutionary dramas and nothing else could be watched by the 800 million-strong Chinese population.

However, like consumers elsewhere, Chinese consumers today are most interested in apolitical and non-ideological entertainment, as well as political views from a variety of independent non-party sources. Mass consumption has given rise to mass advertising, through the new outlets of radios, newspapers, and television, as products are offered with increasing emphasis on style, image, and brand. Since products have no ideology, this depoliticization of people's daily life is liberating in itself. In the past, most Chinese people lived a life submerged in party-state propaganda.[33] Such words and images appeared in homes, offices, classrooms, streets, public bathrooms, and on everyday products such as towels, basins, bowls, cups, matches boxes and chopsticks, book covers, shirts, notebooks, school bags, textbooks, and the ubiquitous Mao caps and buttons. In addition, party propaganda was spread by speeches heard daily through loud speakers in villages and cities. The pressure to conform was such that many Chinese actually feared dreaming politically incorrect dreams. Liu Xiaowu said the following about his horrifying boyhood experience: "When the Cultural Revolution took place, I was only eleven. The next year, for some reason, I often dreamed of touching girls' breasts and had wet dreams. When I woke up, I was so ashamed of myself, I dashed out in the middle of the night to punish myself by crashing trees. I thought this physical pain would cure my hooligan desires."[34] Omnipresent political force was so overwhelming that those whose most personal life diverged from the party line suffered intense anguish.

The retreat of high tide of party-state propaganda from its saturation of people's public and personal experiences constituted a qualitative change in their lives. When Chinese stopped being comrades and became consumers, the party's propaganda machine ran into trouble. At first, propagandists continued doing what they always did but soon found that they had to choose between losing all audience or to reduce censorship of information that would weaken the party state's monopoly on information.

When the government is silent about certain events, freelance writers and underground publications fill the void. In early 2006, the government and state-controlled media's silence over the Shanghai corruption scandal involving Party Secretary Chen Liangyu opened a lucrative market for a number of underground books. Titles like *The Path of the Rise and Fall of Chen Liangyu, The Shanghai Social Security Case,* and *Power behind the Scene* sold like hotcakes. "Most writers just wanted to cash in on the public's hunger for truth," said Lu Qing (not her real name), a Shanghai journalist. "But we received specific instructions not to print any stories about this case from Shanghai Media officials. The reporters and editors were frustrated. With rapid publication of those underground books and the Internet, the public seemed know the news a step ahead of the professional newsmen. It is a ridiculous situation."[35] In today's consumer society, "government media control creates the conditions in which rumors and unofficial books make up the void in public desire for accurate information."[36]

The end of the state's monopoly on the use of media means that publishers look to the marketplace in choosing what to publish. Non-state publications have provided consumers with a wide variety of products, from almanacs to anecdotal accounts of crime and prostitution. After thirty years of being force-fed politics, the Chinese public sought the relief of entertainment ranging from classic literature stories to folk fiction, sports to pornography.

Much of the initial supply of books produced to meet this demand was illegally copied from abroad. Over time, writers from Hong Kong and Taiwan entered the market with titles like of *The Hero with Arrows (Shediao yingxiong zhuan)* and *Sword of the Yueh Maiden (Yuenu zhuang)* by Jin Yong and *The Rainy Season Won't Come* and *The Story of Sahara* by the Taiwanese writer San Mao. The emergence of this market effected a qualitative change. Literature no longer had to carry a political message. As the informal market became the mass market, the institutionalized state control over print media was adulterated. The rise of such new markets has been accompanied by the spread of violations of intellectual property rights.

Apolitical literature has been inadvertently tolerated by Beijing because the state lacks resources to deal with the tidal wave of new literature production that has swept across China over the past twenty years. Thus censors' focus on dissident literature averted their attention from an emerging apolitical literature of romance and sex. A new tacit agreement is formed between publishers and the media censors: so long as the works are not attacking the party, they will be allowed to be published. Moreover, as early as the 1980s, entrepreneurs made good use of the party's monopoly on publication by selling ISBNs (International Standard Book Number) to make a profit. The newly emerging literary markets have liberated a new generation of writers. Loyalties of new markets have allowed publishers to attract works by famous writers such as Yu Luojing (a dissident writer) and Jia Pingmao.[37]

The consequences of this market-based separation of state and society are profound. Materials the government tries hardest to suppress (works on democracy, human rights) are made more alluring and thus more in demand. In addition, second tier violators (Kung Fu, sexuality) often escape censorship altogether, thus continuing to redefine what is deemed appropriate by what can be controlled and what cannot. In most urban *jishi* (farmers markets), unapproved books of all kinds can be found, such as politically incorrect, pornography, mystery, Kung Fu, fortune-telling works, and biographies. On the streets of Beijing, during the summer of 1998, the author could find accounts of the 1989 Tiananmen incident as well as copies of *The Private Life of Mao Zedong* by Mao's doctor, which was banned by the state. Indeed, the information market has reached such a size that book sales have become specialized, some merchants sell only detective stories, some romance, others classical Chinese literature. Opening to the outside world, those specialized booksellers realized that they have a global reach.

A trip to any large bookstore in a major Chinese city provides insight into the topics interesting to the average Chinese reader. Although bookstores, all of which are government controlled, are required to feature displays of the works of former supreme leaders Mao Zedong, Deng Xiaoping, and Jiang Zemin, the books remain untouched. Rather than perusing them, shoppers are perusing through foreign books translated into Chinese. Titles cover a variety of genres from technology and education, to art, business, and society-related books, such as: *Think Like a Manager*; *Take Charge Now, Powerful Techniques for Breaking the Blame Habit*; *Men are from Mars and Women from Venus*; *How to Become A Millionaire*; *Secrets for Positive Living*; *Privacy*, and Dale Carnegie's 1936 classic, *How to Win Friends and Influence People*. These books are more representative of the newly emergent urban culture than their dated, irrelevant, ideological counterparts.

Book publishing was not the only industry helping to lower institutional impediments to the free flow of information. The emergence of music production, initially underground, gradually evolved into a bustling industry, more consonant with the market-driven China. Before 1980, there was no recording industry. Only a few dozens songs were approved for broadcast or public performance: China's deep and rich folk music tradition was suppressed. Instrumental music was virtually unknown; even film soundtracks were drawn from revolutionary songs. Music was used exclusively by the party-state as a tool for social and political control.

After 1980, however, the music industry began to evolve. Even as early as 1978, two years after Mao's death, a few people began to listen to classic and traditional music as a form of resistance to the regime. But the most widespread, national, popular resistance occurred in the year 1980 when the

Taiwanese singing sensation Deng Lijun, already a household name in much of East Asia, swept the Chinese people off their feet. This phenomenon was remarkable because Deng Lijun, the daughter of a Guomingdang general, was openly and vociferously anti-Communist. Deng, who liked nothing better than to perform for the Taiwanese army, became the most popular artist in China. After suffering though the Cultural Revolution, many people who sought a more calm and relaxed environment, found comfort in Deng's love songs. Due to her popularity, singers began imitating her style. When cassette tape players became widely available in the mid-1980s, Deng's songs dominated the atmosphere in restaurants, department stores, and homes alike. The public immersed itself in her music, oblivious to the fact that most of it was pirated. Although she willingly acquiesced in the piracy of her music on the mainland, Deng declared that she would not perform in China while the Communist regime was in power. The very fact that this anti-Communist performer was so popular on the Communist mainland was a huge feather in her cap. Her influence was captured by a popular saying of the early 1980s, stating that "the old Deng (Deng Xiaoping) ruled China by day but the young Deng (Deng Lijun) ruled by night."[38]

In 1983, Deng Xiaoping launched an "anti-spiritual-pollution campaign" in an attempt to stifle the influence of the moral competition coming from non-party sources. Partly out of personal vengeance and partly out of political calculation, the elder Deng ordered police searches for tapes of younger Deng's music throughout China's major cities.[39] Deng's policy amounted to a little more than a minor setback, and an explosion of musical expression came in response.

Popular music in general, and Western popular music in particular, has a great capacity to subvert ideas and policies espoused by the authoritarian state. In 1996, Wu Meng, then a Chinese college student and rock music aficionado, summed up this subversive capacity as follows: "We love rock music because it expresses the frustration and dissatisfaction with the life we led in high school. It shuts up the noises from the state and our parents [discipline]. It is a really liberating experience."[40] Pirated sound recordings featuring the Beatles, the Police, U2, and Guns N' Roses helped spread the spirit of the youthful rebellion and captivated large numbers of young music fans across China. As one Hunan youth put it, "In the Rock 'n' Roll era, who's going to sing the boring and old *The East is Red* ?"[41]

In late 1980 the importation and increased sales of CDs and modern stereo equipment further expanded consumers' appetite for diversified styles of music. Illegal providers of CDs stepped up to meet this demand. The illegal producers had two advantages over official vendors. First, much of music they produced was illegal and, therefore, unavailable from other sources. Second was a matter of cost: a pirated CD could be produced cheaply and sold at a price one-tenth that of the legal copy (during the 1990s, pirated CDs sold for $1 to $2 while imported CDs cost at least $10). The fact that illegal vendors could provide these products with only a minimal decrease in sound quality made CDs a favorite target for pirating.

Beijing's five Haidian Electronic Streets, Shenzhen's Lao Jie Street, as well as Shanghai's Fuzhou Office-supply and Wujiaoyang Streets became marketing centers for pirated goods spawned by the underground technology industry. The streets are lined with vendors selling the cheapest and newest music CDs, CDROMs and American film DVDs. Marketing networks are so decentralized that distributors are often unaware of the identity of their suppliers. The tremendous profit and the number of those involved would greatly limit the effectiveness of government effects to curb pirating, even if it sincerely tried. Since pirating tends to benefit Chinese consumers, many Chinese did not consider buying or selling pirated CDs a crime, despite the government's objections.

With their ever-increasing availability, pirated CDs, DVDs, and tapes have become a normal part of life in urban centers and small towns. The activities involved in buying such CDs as well as listening to the music have created new venues for communication among individuals. Thousands of Karaoke bars providing such music can be found throughout China in both urban and rural settings. Karaoke bars have become important social gathering places where people make contact through the medium of songs. Such songs, freely chosen outside the state mission, have become a means of circumventing limitations of personal freedom imposed by the state. All those involved in pirated CDs, DVDs, and tapes have no ideological motivation but rather desire to make their own decisions what music should be produced and consumed.

Pirated music products introduced Chinese to a variety of music genres. To cater to youthful and elder middle-class listeners, local radio stations began to provide such music as American anti-establishment songs of the 1960s and 1970s. By 2000, Chinese radio stations swept up in the expanding market revolution had begun playing international songs (American, Taiwanese, Japanese, South Korean, and European songs) to attract listeners. Vivien Xu, a Shanghai News Corps TV manager explained why American music is popular among Shanghai radio stations: "As middle class people increasingly own cars, they want to listen to good music and learn English at the same time. Many industries buy ads targeting such groups."[42]

In short, practically all Chinese media have been transformed in non-political areas from party-state preferences of the few to consumer-driven preferences by the masses.[43] Thus, while pirating is theft that deprives producers of the fruits of their labor, it nevertheless has far-reaching positive effects. It reduces the strong hand of the state, shattering the power of censors and providing widely accessible cheap information and entertainment choices. The social revolution implied by the circumvention of censorship reaches back prior to 1990, when students of the democracy movement sang the anti-war and, therefore, anti-government songs of Joan Baez and Bob Dylan, and the sound of "Blowing in the Wind" wafted across Tiananmen Square before June 4.

Decline of the Party Line in the Media: Competition for Commercial Ads

As the standards for what qualifies as interesting or entertaining have risen tremendously across the gamut of sources of information and artistic expression, state television stations and newspapers have had to adjust their content in order to keep their viewers and readers happy. Regardless of their formal hostility towards considering the illegal sector as legitimate, they have had to compete with it in order to survive. The process of accommodating themselves to the transformed tastes of viewers and readers was further solidified when multinational companies began to advertise according to the audience size and market sentiment. In a change of business strategy, state media that previously served only party-state interests began to concern themselves with their bottom line, since state support was insufficient to cover increasing costs. Before 1985, newspapers were distributed not via the market but through party-state bureaucracies. After 1985, individual subscriptions surpassed the urban *danwei* distribution with close to 100 million copies in daily distribution, the world's highest newspaper circulation. Facing this new market challenge, subsidiary party newspapers (*zibao*) were published to help the old party newspapers to survive. Prior to the appearance of *zibao*, the old party had few readers. But the appearance of *zibao* transformed the situation by creating a new generation of newspaper readers in all major urban centers. Newspapers stands began to appear in Chinese cities for the first time since 1949. This competition led to the proliferation of newly founded newspapers and magazines, which experienced a tenfold growth with 1,900 newspapers and 9,700 periodicals in print in 2006.[44]

The story of *Sichuan Daily* is exemplary. *Sichuan Daily* is a mainstream, provincial party newspaper paper covering the capital city of Sichuan Province, Chengdu, but also other cities and rural counties of the province. In 1995, in order to attract advertising and to avoid political difficulties, editors in *Sichuan Daily* set up a daily subsidiary paper, *Huaxi Metropolis News* (*HMN*), with a focus on the daily interests of ordinary people. Within a year, *HMN* became profitable; by the third year, profit reached a billion Yuan ($130 million).[45] This huge profit shocked not only the paper's editors but also newspapers throughout the country. As a result, *zibao* fever swept through China. Party newspapers (*zhubao*) survive to satisfy the party-state propaganda machine, but subsidiary papers (*zibao*), whose profits eclipse their parent papers, exist for their profitability, 70 percent of which must be remitted to the *zhubao*.[46] Since subsidiary papers and party newspapers depend on commercial advertisements to survive, they are forced to cater to urban readers' interests. This attention to urban readers has greatly diluted the level of ideological bombardment directed towards urbanites.

A similar situation has been created with radio and television sources. Since most editors are still appointed by the party-state political machine, they must cope as best they can with the contradiction between their paper's function as the party's mouthpiece (*hongshe gongneng*) and their professional ethics as journalists (*zhiye gongneng*) demanding that the truth be told. In both cases, the voice of the party is weakened.

Editors wrack their brains to find ways of making use of media to enhance their profits. Although officially, gaming is illegal in China, lottery, nevertheless, is used for this purpose. For example, running lottery results are placed in the news captions that run at the bottom of the TV screen while the party news is being broadcast. The most shocking incident of this practice took place on the CCTV, China's largest television station, on September 6, 2004 when the new lottery was presented to viewers asking them to pick the number of hostages that would be killed in a school hostage drama that was taking place in Russia.[47] When asked why the TV station most closely controlled by the party would launch such a lottery, Wu Litang, a magazine editor in Wuhan replied: "CCTV was trying to cash in on the fact that it reaches nearly 400 million TV sets and one billion viewers. Nowadays, the media dare to try any new lucrative venture. The regime will look the other way so long as there is no politically incorrect message involved. They, too, have been sold out."[48] The fact is that Chinese TV media is composed of 400 million TV sets, 110 million cable subscribers, and fifty-one satellite channels transmitting programming from international media providers such as Star-TV, Phoenix, and MTV. Chinese media outlets are obsessed with this enormous market and try to take advantage of it without antagonizing the party watchdogs.[49]

Within the environment of consumer-driven media, the state media must change or face precipitous decline of readers, listeners, and viewers. The orthodox paper *Chengdu Wanbao* (*Chengdu Evening News*), for example, was one of the early urban newspapers carrying more party news than other papers. At its peak period, between 1990 and 1994, subscriber circulation reached 390,000. But after 1995, with the rise of *zibao* such as *Huaxi Metropolis News* and *Chengdu Commercial News*, its individual paid subscriptions declined rapidly: to 280,000 in 1998 and to 200,000 in 2000. The decline of commercial advertisements fell precipitously from 170 million Yuan in 1996 to 150 million in 1997; further to less than 100 million in 1999 and only 300,000 Yuan in 2000, a 2000 percent decrease from the 1996 value.[50] Finally in 2007, the paper had to change its political stand and went with the flow. This case shows that a form of economic democracy has insinuated itself in the operation of Chinese media. Richard Baum has also found that in the 1990s, *People's Daily*—the CCP's mouthpiece—saw its circulation drop by 40 percent, despite the fact that compulsory subscription is imposed on all government organizations. As a result, *People's Daily* found it necessary to diversify and enliven its content by starting new, eye-catching, commercial media spin-off ventures. "The latter include a highly popular tabloid-style newspaper, *Huanqiao Ribao* (Global Times), and a lively, interactive website, *Renmin Wang* (People's Net), featuring diverse editorial commentaries, interviews and an on-line public forum."[51] In 2008, even the party secretary, Hu Jingtao, had a lively, interactive website in order to reach people's eyeballs.

In its pursuit of advertising money, certain state TV stations became bolder, experimenting with news that pushed the limits of orthodox party state propaganda, and producing programs to compete with other forms of entertainment. Thus, along with increased media competition has come a corresponding rise in the influence of commercial advertisers. While it is true that the government retains a monopoly over the mass media, the core values of the government propaganda machine have been transformed by the addition of corporate advertising. Now, stations seeking maximum profits must cater to viewer tastes. As a result, Chinese media have been partially depoliticized, with official outlets forced to compete for audience share with black markets in a host of non-political areas everyday life.

Although some party officials such as Hu Yaobang, Zhao Jiyang, Hu Jiwei,[52] Sun Yanjun,[53] Liu Yunshan,[54] and Zhang Tao,[55] have pushed hard for these changes as a move towards reform—proposing such policies as separating the party of management of the press—to a great extent, concern for the bottom line has been far more important to decision makers than these reform initiatives of the elite.

Gone are the days when the media were only allowed to report positive news. Today, many television programs focus on corruption and other negative aspects of Chinese society. For example, Chinese versions of CBS "60 Minutes" (*Xinwen 60 Feng*), ABC's "20/20" (*Jiaodian Fengtai*), and other investigative reports (*Xinwen Diaocha*), have appeared to attract audiences. These news programs include such stories as: "Anti-corruption in Haier Bin," which exposed government corruption (aired on November 4, 1997); "Land and Farmers," which revealed local government officials' abuse of farmers (aired on October 24, 1997); and "Who is responsible for Lake Tai?" which concerned a badly polluted lake (aired October 10, 1997).[56] Such content is representative of the changes taking place in today's China. With the limit of what censors will permit shifting almost daily, further confrontations seeking to push the limits of government toleration even further seem inevitable. Such confrontations will play a substantial role in redefining the balance of power between the state and society.

Youxiao Faxing or Publishing to Maximize Profit

Notwithstanding what we have just said, the state still exercises formal control over the media. But the Chinese media have been fundamentally altered, as a majority of journalists and editors have adopted the new practice of *youxiao faxing* (publishing to maximize profit). In other words, rather than relying on government sources of revenue, media state workers have sought to gain extra money (in Chinese it is called *waikuai*). There are several ways for journalists to augment their income. First, journalists can demand cash from sources for writing specific stories, such as new companies seeking to establish name recognition or established companies wishing to generate positive publicity. For example, mining companies seeking to whitewash environmental or safety incidents pay for exculpatory reporting. Secondly, journalists also receive "gratitude" money (*dadianfei*) as middlemen for linking their clients and friends to government officials, especially in law enforcement agencies, to get out of legal difficulties. Journalists also play a role as commercial advertisement brokers taking commissions from advertising they generate. Some journalists also set up private businesses using state property to generate profits.[57] Finally, the share holding serves as another channel for the media to gain capital by lining up capital from some private and global companies. Commercialization of China's media is one aspect of the sweeping changes that have attended the country's rapid economic development. Since about 1995, the Chinese media industry has grown at an annual rate of 25 percent, nearly three times the country's GDP growth rate.[58] Most state-owned enterprises lose money, but media, along with telecommunication and energy, have become the first to generate profits. In 2003, television, newspaper, and magazine advertising revenues grew from about $13 billion to $18.6 billion, increasing by 39 percent in a single year.[59]

Market-generated income has had the effect of detaching media from slavish adherence to the party line. Although this new situation has not made the media autonomous, it has made them independent to a degree unimaginable just fifteen years ago. The pursuit of financial gain emboldens journalists who may otherwise toe the party line through self-censorship. This illustrates how the market has infiltrated politics and bids fair at least to a degree to alter the direction of politics.

Investigating Reporting

Two of China's most popular television news programs in the 1990s were "*xinwen toushi*" ("News Analysis") in Shanghai and "*Jiaodi fangtang*" ("Focused Interview") of the CCTV in Beijing. Both programs have exposed the abuse of power by local officials so much that many ordinary individuals, especially rural people, travel to Beijing to petition the program to investigate their cases. In the late 1990s and early 2000, two groups lined up at in CCTV's Beijing offices: in one line were ordinary Chinese seeking to report their cases to *Jiaodi fangtang*. In the other were government officials from throughout China flush with cash attempting to dissuade the program's producers from investigating their bosses.[60] Local governments send numerous representatives to Beijing in an attempt to stop the programs from damaging publicity by wining and dining those in charge, or offering material gifts. According to an official report, the top Chinese leaders, even Jiang Zemin and Zhu Rongji, watched "*Jiaodi fangtang*," a fact not lost on local officials. The success of the program is a sign of political change in China.

In the absence of an effective rule of law regime, such publicity acts as a second legal channel for aggrieved Chinese.

Strategies to Circumvent Censorship

Over time, media workers (editors, reporters, office clerks, party officials, and even censors themselves) have developed strategies to circumvent the ubiquitous Chinese censorship. One strategy in the publication world involves buying and selling ISBNs, which constitute an official imprimatur from the government. China appears to be the only country in the world in which ISBNs have a market value. In 2000 the government officially recognized the existence of private publishing houses. At the same time, the government acquiesces in an essential illegal aspect of the private companies' operations—the buying and selling of ISBNs. These ISBNs are often sold on the market by the publishing houses. By 1999, private publishing companies became well established. Finally, in early 2000, the government tacitly recognized the private publishing industry when the state professional publishing association created a Non-State Ownership Committee, representing eight thousand private publishing and distribution companies.[61] Thus, although the state still has official control over publishing, in fact, publishing business has been privatized.

Another frequent strategy for journalists seeking to evade censorship is *yidibaodao*. In this practice, when reporters in one locality cannot report on news in their region for fear of government reprisal, these reporters give the forbidden news to counterparts in a second locality, who can publish or broadcast the information free from censorship. This practice worked for many years because local governments are in competition against each other for market share of foreign investment, for example, and for favorable treatment by Beijing, and negative reports about one government can work to the advantage of competing governments. Party bosses, concerned principally with their own backyard, therefore will deal harshly with negative news about their own region in the press, but tend not to attempt kill negative stories about distant localities.

For example, in April 1998, 120 children and women became infected with HIV virus through unclean needles in Shenzhen. To protect the image of the Special Economic Zone, China's first and most prominent economic window to the world, the Shenzhen government, forbade the local news media to report the event.[62] The victims spent two years suing the government hospital but the judicial system sided with the hospital. Two years later, some of the victims traveled to Guangzhou to seek assistance from *South China Weekend (Nanfang Zhoumu)* and the *Southern Metropolis News (Nanfang Dushibao)*, over which the Shenzhen government did not have control. These two newspapers carried the story for nearly three weeks, enraging Shenzhen government officials. To bring the story coverage to an end, the Shenzhen government sought help from the vice governor of Guangdong, Huang Limang, former vice mayor of Shenzhen and a close friend of Jiang Zemin.[63] Using her considerable influence and working behind the scene, Huang was able to engineer a compromise. In return for the end to the publicity, the Shenzhen government would allow the court to adjudicate victims' lawsuits, allowing them small compensation.

The "Shenzhen Needle Case" demonstrated that ordinary Chinese could develop strategies for seeking justice by using the media as weapons to expose wrongdoing. In this case, it is the *yidibaodao* form of news reporting that proves partially successful. In today's China, *yidibaodao* is media coverage with Chinese characteristics because it short-circuited *tiao* ("strips," or vertical control from the center to the local) and *kuai* ("blocks" or horizontal control by the local government).[64] In 2006, dissenting journalist Mao Xiaoming told Radio Free Asia: "In the past year, the Chinese government banned *yidibaodao*. Why is there *yidibaodao*? Because the Chinese media are closely supervised by local bureaucracies. Local governments punish negative media reporting. To get around this supervision, journalists report negative news from different regions and journalists from these regions do the same. A place reports about B region and vice versa. In this way, we can escape the local government. But main control is still the party organization. The center can also ban reporting."[65] In 2005 this practice reached such a crescendo that embarrassed local governments persuaded Beijing to ban it. Nevertheless, though less frequent, the practice continues today.

For the past decade, Chinese journalists have increasingly practiced *yidibaodao* by exposing cases of corruption and major scandals such as the collapse of the Rainbow Bridge in Chongqing and the slave labor in Shanxi coalmines. The central government sometimes uses the *yidibaodao* information to both reduce local corruption and to encourage loyalty to the center. For example, the central propaganda ministry forced a complete leadership reshuffle when *Beijing News*, a popular and outspoken newspaper, became sufficiently emboldened to publish political commentary. The forced reshuffle led to a strike protesting the editorial takeover by one of its parent publications, the party mouthpiece.[66] According to interviews with two Beijing journalists (Zhang Zhijun and Liao Zhizhu), the December 2005 strike was the first time that hundreds of reporters and editors risked their careers and their lives to register their extreme discontent.[67]

Another strategy is to increase non-political news to meet consumer demand. A result of this strategy has been the rise in popularity of evening newspapers. Even cursory acquaintance with such papers reveals the party's declining role in people's daily existence. To satisfy readers' increasingly demanding fastidious tastes, papers now feature health and crime as two of the primary focuses. These depoliticized newspapers broaden cultural horizons of new urban residents increasingly conscious of their growing ability to escape the state. Focusing their attention on non-political as well as private matters, the Chinese progressively build a Chinese version of civil society, editors, reporters, and readers are bound together by apolitical affinities.

Through their loyalty Chinese readers have awarded publications, including newspapers, relative editorial independence and the practical capacity to tell the truth. In today's China, publications are more likely to attract readers and advertisers if they are known to be credible sources, especially in challenging the policies and honesty of government officials. Today, the most credible newspaper in the country is the *South China Weekend* (*Nanfang Zhoumu*). For the past ten years Beijing has attempted to mute the paper's relatively independent voice by frequently changing its editors. But China's current newspaper culture dares to push the envelope when it comes to reporting news that may or may not be acceptable to the regime.

Another strategy of professional journalists seeking independence is the gradual reduction of regime ideology in publications of all kind. Professional journalism that focuses on truthful reporting also affects the censors' behavior, especially the behavior of the younger censors. Every day, Zhongxuanbu (the Propaganda Ministry in Beijing) publishes a comprehensive list of banned subjects and distributes them throughout the country. But such lists cover an inordinately wide range of topics—from rural riots, urban demonstrations, minority issues, and high-level corruption, to a host of liberal ideas. If the lists were rigorously adhered to, nearly all publication would cease. As a result, most journalists consider themselves tightrope walkers. "The difference between us and tightrope walkers is that tight rope walkers usually have a safety net if they fall off," remarked Qiu Feng, a liberal columnist in China.[68]

More and more Chinese journalists are attempting to behave as professionals rather than mere party mouthpieces. For example, Huang Liangtian, a highly respected former editor of Bai Xing, a magazine known for its investigative reporting about official abuse in China remarked: "I stuck to my beliefs. This is the inborn quality of an intellectual—to tell the truth and never tell lies to please the bosses...I always told our colleagues that the guidelines issued by the propaganda administration were more like a rubber band—we needed to expand them to just before breaking point to create space for good stories. We avoided making comments, we listened to both sides, we presented the facts as reporters and left readers to judge...I am disobedient. I didn't worry about...guidelines from above. I just tried to do real stories based on [their] news value."[69]

In addition to the changing role of newspapers, alternative media sources, primarily on the Internet, have created new communication channels with which state media have trouble competing. For four decades, the media were dominated by the state, setting the agenda for the nation and the people. The state not only managed all major networks and newspapers but also ensured compliance through content approval and censorship. Early in the reform period, it was less that this system changed than that people's expectations changed. As they became less reliant on the government for their day-to-day existence, people sought more and different types of information from a wider range of sources.

The era of competition and choice has successfully challenged the state's monopoly over information. Facing competition from the market place, Peng Bo, the editor of *Zhongguo Qingnian* (*China Youth*, the party youth journal), has developed two survival strategies: the first involves changing the content and format of the journal to produce what the market wants most and second is to move readers by the journal's editorial sincerity.[70] This shift in policy at a top national journal has affected the decisions being made and risks taken by other sanctioned publication houses.

The case of the controversial book *Feidu* (*Decadence of the Metropolis*, published in 1993) is an example of cooperation between liberal editors and readers to confront censorship. Two years after the publication of the popular book, in 1995 the government banned its circulation and fined its publisher, the Arts Press in Beijing, and its editor-in-chief Xie Dajun, 810,000 Yuan for issuing a "corrupt" book. Xie paid the fine but also paid 270,000 Yuan in royalties to Jia Pingao, the author. When news of the incident broke the following year, subscriptions to Art Press's main journal, *Shiyue* (October) skyrocketed almost overnight.[71] The situation demonstrated that the publisher was concerned about both his company's reputation among its readership and perceptions to his loyalty to the party. This conflict of interests proves troubling to the Chinese government because it underlines the extent to which such editors' loyalty to the party has been diluted by the market.

Xie, however, has gained respect among many Chinese intellectuals, who take pride in his bold behavior in challenging censorship. This incident occurred within the state publication house. With the creation of countless new non-state publishers, including private and collective enterprises, educational centers, universities, and schools, the ability of censors to perform their function effectively is fanciful. Evidence that Beijing took notice of the media's "deviation" became apparent in January 2002 when the National Propaganda Ministry (*Zhongxuanbu*) circulated a national notice (*tong bao*) on ten problems with the media: [72]

1) The government has failed to control the media. Serious mistakes were made by the media. For example, some newspapers went so far as to encourage people to sue Party Committees;
2) The Party's principle of state secrecy and its policy of stratified news management have broken down through leaks of inner circle news to the public, causing social chaos. (For example, journalists reported a 30 percent salary increase for government officials, as well as confidential talks on reducing the state's share of the stock market);
3) The media has created a public frenzy about certain unexpected events (for example, the death of Princess Diana);
4) The media has caused social instability by reporting on important epidemics like AIDS;
5) Tolerance of irresponsible reporting on nationalities and religions that have suffered discrimination and harassment;

6) Sensationalization of oddities and distribution of false stories;
7) Publication of vulgar articles;
8) Leaked state secrets;
9) Frequent use of unreliable news from the Internet;
10) Propagation of Western reporting values such as "freedom of the press" and "all news is fit to print."[73]

By the late 1990s, the Chinese media began instituting a *shuangguo zhi* (dual-track) policy, in which the principal party newspaper continued the voice of the party while the commercial sectors created satellite newspapers to persue profit.

Blackmail Journalism and Corruption in the Media

In today's commercialized world, the media trends have been set by the flow of money. Among these new trends, "blackmail" journalism and other forms of corruption have been metastasizing throughout China's media.[74] For example, commercial enterprises bribe journalists to write false stories about their products and services. In one instance in Wuhan, a new glass factory paid journalists to write fictitious reports about their supposedly environmentally friendly product. When asked how journalists feel about selling themselves, Wu Qing (not her real name) replied: "The government media budget is small and we have to survive like anyone else. The party trained us to lie about serious news, and now we are only continuing to do what we were trained to do. The difference is that now our incomes increase. Many people are creating 'news' like this."[75]

As Edward Cody suggested, "In many ways, blackmail journalism grew naturally out of a system in which Communist Party censors control the news rigorously, barring reports that could be seen as unfavorable to the party or contrary to the government's political goals. If the ruling party distorts the news for political reasons, blackmailing reporters have concluded, why shouldn't they do it themselves for financial reasons?"[76]

Corrupt officials pay to prevent unfavorable stories from being published. Such behavior functions as a new form of censorship. But when reporters demand hush money in exchange for withholding of unfavorable news, the tables are turned. When money dominates, it is relatively difficult for the government to censor every article because doing so alienates media workers whose income derives mostly from advertisements and commercial bribes from enterprises and personal bribery from corrupt officials. When government officials have to pay to have the "bad" news killed, reporters have attained an edge over their superiors in deciding what is fit to print. Political control still exists for sensitive subjects.

Intellectual Property Rights

Up until now, we have demonstrated the many benefits to the Chinese people of being able to access banned and pirated material. Although some of the methods simply involve overcoming or circumventing censorship, others involve outright pirating, which understandably is not easy to justify. It is estimated that Chinese pirating costs the Microsoft Corporation $200-300 million each year. For example, Windows XP Professional, which sells for about $300, is available on the street for $1.[77] This is assuredly not a modus operandi for conducting business and ensuring continued innovation.

Our contention, however, is that during the initial phase of the reform era, given the economic status of the common man and the disposition of Beijing government, it is difficult to imagine other means of spreading information, ideas, and entertainment so rapidly. Theft in the form of piracy was not and is not an end state, but was an opportunistic first step in a complex process of delivering a critical mass of independent (non-state) information to the hands of ordinary Chinese. Pirated entertainment, including Hollywood movies, has provided widespread knowledge and awareness of alternative values, ways of life and social arrangements (e.g., the operation of American legal systems). This new consciousness has been a key factor in the Chinese people's unwillingness to accept the status quo under the Communist party-state.

When some Chinese found their own interests attacked by the near universal disregard for intellectual property, matters began to change. In today's China, although pirating is still widespread, respect for intellectual property rights (both foreign and domestic) is increasing. Independent (non-state) publication and distribution systems and the creation of domestic literature, arts, and cinematography markets in the 1990s have fostered a "homegrown" appreciation of the role of intellectual property rights. This development bespeaks a far more natural evolution than would have been possible without the first stage of the violation of these rights.

That Chinese sue other Chinese for intellectual property infringement illustrates increased consciousness of legitimacy of intellectual property. We contend that the rise of intellectual property consciousness in China is linked to the process of domestic creation, which would not have occurred without the previously discussed black markets. Companies and individual citizens are using these newly established mechanisms for protection of their intellectual property rights. According to one government report, from "April 1, 1985 to the end of 2004, the State Intellectual Property Office handled 2,284,925 patent applications with an average annual increase of 18.9 percent. Of these, 1,874,358 were domestic applications, and 410,567 came from other countries, accounting for 82 and 18 percent, respectively. Patent applications in China had exceeded two million by March 17, 2004."[78]

One case in Shanghai, *Wang vs. Dongfang Commercial Ltd.*, illustrates the spread of intellectual property rights of ordinary people. In 1992 the plaintiff, Wang Dingfang, a high school teacher, entered an advertisement slogan competition sponsored by the above company, a clothing manufacturer. Wang's phrase, "International Fashion with an Eastern Flavor," won second place in the competition, for which she received 500 Yuan. When the company subsequently used her phrase in television, newspaper, and radio advertisements, and placed it on rental cars and shopping bags, Wang sued the company for violating her right to the phrase. The defendant, a large state-owned company with strong political backing, defended its behavior, stating that advertising copy is part of the public domain and should therefore not be included in intellectual property right's protection. The case was settled out of court by arbitration. Wang was recognized as the owner of her phrase, but the company owned the advertisements. The company paid Wang 5000 Yuan in compensation. Although she received only half of the compensation she sought and did not receive a public apology from the company, Wang was one of the first individuals to successfully sue a state company on the grounds of upholding her intellectual property rights.

Using public media to restore or propagate one's reputation is often part of mediation and legal settlements. In most intellectual property rights cases, plaintiffs generally ask for an open letter of apology printed in the newspapers of their choice. Because reputation is so important in business, requiring public apologies works as a strategy for rewarding those who obey the law and for punishing those who violate it.

Another case involving software pirating in China, demonstrates the effective use of the media to force pirates to apologize publicly in a newspaper. In late 1992, the Weihong Software Research Institute in Beijing's Haidian District went to the People's Court to sue the Yuanwan Technology Company for unlawfully advertising and selling Weihong Unfox software products.[79] In October 1991, shortly after Weihong Institute created and marketed Unfox software, many companies began to sell unauthorized copies. On June 15, 1992, Weihong Institute applied for and received a computer software license stating that Weihong had sole ownership of Unfox. On June 16, 1992, Weihong put an ad in the newspaper, *Chinese Computer News*, stating its legal ownership rights. In September 1992, however, the Black Horse Company, which is attached to state-owned Yuanwan Technology, listed Unfox in its own product catalog without Weihong's permission. At two computer exhibitions, workers from Black Horse illegally reproduced and sold copies of Unfox. In response, Weihong asked for 18.6 million Yuan in compensation and demanded a public apology from Yuanwan Technology. The judge ruled that, according to the new Computer Software Protection Regulations, Yuanwan should immediately stop the reproduction of Unfox 2.1 software products, pay 46,000 Yuan in compensation, and place an apology on the front page of Chinese Computer News.

Although Weihong did not receive full compensation, as a member of the non-state sector, the victory itself was nonetheless very important. Moreover, the public apology increased its reputation among Chinese software companies. This case is representative of the changing dynamic between state and non-state commercial relationships. A non-state enterprise took on a state enterprise and came away victorious. In addition, the creation of China's first software copyright registration agency should help companies adhere to Copyright Laws and the Computer Software Protection Rules designed to protect their rights. The Chinese government has acceded to the major international conventions on protection of intellectual property rights. Although various government agencies have set up regulations, and decrees in the areas of trademark, copyright, and patent, the implementation is still problematic.

As part of this dynamic, as more Chinese companies are able to enter various markets and compete with foreign firms, prices drop and consumers can afford authentic (legal) products. Once prices become equal, people are faced with a decision. In the days when there was no alternative to pirated goods, the decision making process was simple. For example, SRS Information Technology created Richwin 97, a popular Chinese software package. The product was cheap enough that computer owners considered factors (anti-virus features, upgrades, repairs) other than cost in making purchasing decisions. In the end, of the five million copies of Richwin in circulation, half were paid for—a tremendous success at a time when perhaps 95 percent of software in circulation consisted of unauthorized copies.[80] This case shows how companies are sometimes able to compete successfully with black market products.

Global firms have also used franchise strategies to protect their intellectual property in China. For example, in 2005, the Chinese video game company Aomei Soft was able to obtain legal license to be official distributor of various French Vivendi video games. To protect its franchise, Aomei has been diligent in attempting to identify Chinese firms pirating these products. Thus, in April 2006, Aomei sued Nasdaq-listed Shanda in a Chinese court for "allegedly offering products under licence to Aomei without permission."[81] Although the court threw the case out for lack of evidence, the 120 million Yuan suit gave warning to competitors that they could expect to be sued under similar circumstances. Aomei's action illustrates how hard Chinese companies are working to gain and maintain exclusive rights to international brand name products. These profit-driven efforts may in time restrain the country's widespread industrial piracy.

It is not only corporations but also individuals are taking steps to protect their intellectual property interests. For example, in an August 1992 case, freelance songwriter Jiang (full name) was invited by a state film company to compose a theme song for a documentary film.[82] In the course of his relationship with the company, Jiang gave the company two other songs, hoping they would be used in future productions. Soon afterwards, without consulting Jiang, the state company signed a 100,000-copy production contract with a record company, including the two songs. Jiang went to court to demand financial compensation and eventually won. Similar cases involving copyright ownership of printed material have been won by writers even against the prominent state Xinhua News Agency.[83] Based on such successes, individual artists, understanding their ability to take disputes to court, are learning to be more protective of their intellectual property rights, even going so far as to confront the state.

Another well-known case involved a famous Chinese movie star, Liu Xiaoqing. In the early 1990's, Liu Xiaoqing sued various magazines for violating her rights by using her image on their covers without her permission. Liu argued that the use of her picture in this manner violated her sense of self and created the impression that she was being used. Her case attracted considerable attention and led to a national debate about intellectual property rights. Some argued that as an actress she could not limit the use of her picture and that her action violated freedom of expression. Others argued that she should be compensated for the use of her picture. This debate had the effect of raising public consciousness about such issues throughout urban centers.

These examples are just a few in the long and growing list of court cases involving alleged Chinese intellectual property rights (IPR) violations. In conducting interviews with Professor Liao at Qinghua University in 1998 and 2001, we discovered that of the court cases published by Beijing People's Court involving IPR violations between 1992 and 1996, nearly all accused pirates were found guilty.[84] As the Chinese have become involved in the creation and production of intellectual property, they are increasingly grasping the importance of the issue. The government has signed nearly every contemporary intellectual property rights treaty.[85] However, signing treaties is one thing; implementing them is quite another.

Local Compliance

Despite increased understanding of intellectual property rights and their importance, there is still a very central role to be played by the government, specifically the local government, in IPR enforcement. At the national level, adherence to international law is a much more straightforward process than at the county level. Consequently, at the local level, the introduction of intellectual property rights has intensified the complexity of local politics. In addressing the issue, local leaders often have conflicting goals.

Our investigations in Guangdong County revealed a local government official who appeared to genuinely wish to enforce intellectual property rights, but was conflicted in how to balance this with strengthening the local economy. He is often concerned with enhancing the prestige of the local government, proving his commitment to party policies at all levels, and maintaining his base of power. As protecting his prestige and political power frequently requires quite different behavior than enforcing intellectual property rights, he is faced with a dilemma. Because so many in his locale benefit from pirated products, he often ignores violations. When directives issued by the central government come, local governments often responds with well-publicized enforcement demonstrations, such as smashing thousands of copies of pirated DVDs with a military tank. But such actions are a far cry from effective enforcement across the board.

In some cases, local government officials seize pirated goods from manufacturers or distributors, fine violators (increasing government revenue), and
then resell the contraband back to the original owners (again raising their
revenue). Similarly, customs officials often resell confiscated pirated goods to
private retailers. Thus, venality among government officials makes it difficult
for government at all levels to fight IPR violations. The Chinese case suggests
that legal development, as with social development, is a gradual process with
its own logic, rules, and procedures, which is consistent with Carl Menger's
theory that the origin, formation, and ultimate processes of social institutions
follow a spontaneous evolutionary development.[86] Government officials, intellectuals, and many urban Chinese have begun to understand the function of
intellectual property rights in a modern market economy as they have become
that economy rather than simply receivers of economic output. As individuals
now increasingly use legal means to protect their interests, there is at least a
partial balancing force to the monetary incentives of non-compliance to intellectual property laws.

Growing Professionalism

Despite constant government's attempts to keep a lid on the media, journalists have increasingly become professional instead of being just the tool of the
state. When interviewed, Huang Liangtian, the ousted former editor of liberal
Baixing magazine, explained the impact Chinese journalists have on government
officials: "There has also been a recognition that there is a social attitude that
is specific to the media, which has its own existence, whether or not you try to
control it…Also, that sometimes you can control it, and sometimes you can't.
Now they are aware of the media as a social force."[87] Journalists have been able
to use news scandal to inform the public about the value of press freedom. For
example, journalists were able to use the 2008 milk powder scandal in Hebei
to highlight the public health crisis both to domestic and overseas audiences,
letting them know how the government's approach to information focuses on
its restriction, rather than its usefulness to ordinary people.

The local government helped the Sanlu Group, the Shijiazhuang-based state
company at the center of the scandal, cover up the extent of the problem in
the name of the social stability during the 2008 Olympic Games. Journalists
and editors at the *People's Daily* revealed the letter from Sanlu to enlist local
government's assistance in a cover-up: "Please, can the government increase
control and coordination of the media, to create a good environment for the
recall of the company's problem products….This is to avoid whipping the issue
up and creating a negative influence on society."[88]

More and more journalists dare to come out with demands for a free press.
One of the most vocal voices is Jiang Yiping, deputy chief of the Guangzhou-
based Nanfang Media Group, whose responsibilities included the *Southern
Metropolis Daily*. After she was demoted, she told Hong Kong's *South China*

Morning Post, "The paper has been dedicated to its path striving for democracy, science and the rule of law and I believe this line will not be changed."[89] Disgusted by the regime's jamming of international broadcasts, former state-run Xian television journalist Ma Xiaoming told (US-based) Radio Free Asia:

> We're not just talking about newsgathering. We're talking about freedom of opinion, the freedom to gather news, and the freedom to publish or broadcast it. On top of that there is the freedom on the part of the audience to read, hear, or watch whatever they like....It's the same with the Internet....There are a great many sites you can't access if you just use normal browsing methods, as opposed to special methods to get around the blockages...There are huge stories and small stories every day which just pass the Chinese people by. That's why I tell people that they shouldn't bother commenting on current affairs. I'm not even sure that I should be commenting. Because opinions are formed from the facts, right? If you don't even know the true situation, how can you have an opinion about it?[90]

Some journalists even call for transparency and democracy. For example, Li Datong, a former editor of *Bindian*, a magazine attached to the party-state's major newspaper *China Youth Daily*, who was removed from his post in 2008 over the magazine's daring coverage, argued that the party would gain more legitimacy and popularity if it became more transparent: "If it gives people the rights and democracy stated in its constitution, it will be popular...If it had subjected itself to the media's supervision, you would not have the current level of corruption that there is now."[91]

On December 10, 2008, journalists were among many who signed the 2008 Charter petition letter (*lingba xianzhang* [零八宪章]). Freedom of speech and freedom of the press top the list among other freedoms: "freedom of assembly, freedom of association, freedom in where to live, and the freedoms to strike, to demonstrate, and to protest, among others, are the forms that freedom takes. Without freedom, China will always remain far from civilized ideals."[92]

Global Influences

The global flow of information, media, capital, and technology have also played a role in the relative "liberalization" of the media environment as foreign magazines, international news, and electronic media flood China through the Internet, black market, and new technology such as cell phones (especially text messaging), computers, DVDs, electric games, MP3s, and CDs.[93] In this aspect, global trade facilitates the inflow of information and ideas as foreign investment in telecommunications represents 72 percent of the industry's output and accounts for 65 percent of the industry's total value. We will discuss this further in later chapters.[94]

Media analysts such as Chin-Chuan Lee regard the entry of global media as having given rise to a new coalition of interests in which Chinese elites and global capitalists dominate the Chinese working poor.[95] This view, however, ignores the positive role that the global media have played and are playing in reducing the domination of state media and by precisely breaking up their monopoly hold in ownership and content. They have introduced a large number of alternative voices and sources of information.

In the 1980s, only people in the Guangdong region had access to Hong Kong television. But in the early 1990s, high-end hotels were able to gain access to international channels. By the mid-1990s, new apartment buildings began to install international channels. Our visit to the Chinese Police Academy faculty and staff housing community revealed all apartments to be cable-ready for international channels like Japanese, Hong Kong, Taiwanese, and American channels such as CNN. Hong Kong-based Phoenix TV now reaches an estimated 140 million Chinese.[96]

Editors we interviewed in Wuhan, Shanghai, Guangzhou, and Beijing repeatedly stated that The *Wall Street Journal*, The *New York Times*, The *Washington Post*, The *International Tribune,* and The *South China Morning Post* are their models in both news content and format. When The *South China Weekend* (*Nanfang Zhoumuo*) copied many features from these papers in the early 1990s, it shocked the newspaper establishment with its daring content and design ideas. The *South China Weekend* transformed itself from a medium-sized local paper into a national one, attracting cutting-edge journalists, fresh from top schools like Peking University and Central University of Media and Communication. Wang Qinghong, a 1999 Peking University graduate, recalled, "Nearly all the graduates wanted to go to Guangzhou to work in *Nanfang Zhoumuo* [The *South China Weekend*]. Apart from financial consideration, relative media independence [less party interference] and the space to develop one's professional skill played an important role in our decision to move to the South. Now, best students from my department choose to work at *Nanfang Zhoumuo*."[97]

Another important influence of foreign sources is the coverage of international news. Starting in the middle of 1980s, major Chinese universities began to subscribe to foreign newspapers and magazines such as The *New York Times, Time, Newsweek*, The *Wall Street Journal*, The *Washington Post*, The *International Tribune,* and The *London Times*. Both the format and content of such papers influenced and continue to influence principal Chinese newspapers and magazines editors who have become skillful in presenting important events to heighten readers' interest in international news.

For example, *Nanfang Zhoumuo* and The *Southern Metropolis News* (*Nanfang Dushi Bao*) made strategic use of Princess Diana's tragic 1997 death to increase international coverage. Thereafter editors seized the momentum and began reporting more substantive international events. Deng Zhixin, a The *South Metropolis News* editor recalled, "The coverage of Princess Diana's death opened the world to the Chinese people. It was the first time that many major newspapers had in international event on the front page. Readers were fascinated."[98] The tragic date of August 31, 1997, marked the beginning of global coverage by the Chinese media. Thereafter, readers have become accustomed to reading international news, making it difficult if not impossible for censors to call a halt to international news reporting.

Television stations across China also follow the modern global media format in design and substance. The success of China's most popular television station, Hunan Star T.V. in Changsha, depends on its heavy borrowings of American, Japanese, Taiwanese, and Hong Kong programs. This imitation has become "originality with Chinese characteristics," because foreign media styles are something new to Chinese audiences. Just as McDonald's in China adds Chinese varieties to its standard international fare, television shows model their own formats after similar international programs. One such example is "Super Girl," a Chinese program formatted much the same as the American show "American Idol." Such entertainment formats may seem apolitical, but they can occasionally have implications for political change. When "Super Girl" received eight million text message votes from viewers to choose the winner of its program, the government in Beijing was so alarmed by the mobilization that to prevent the incident from having any demonstrative effect on the population, it banned future programs from using similar voting methods.

In a profoundly creative and dynamic interaction, foreign borrowing, commercialization, mass audiences, and key technological advancements (the cell phone, the MP3, the Internet, and the television) have weakened the voice of the state's political propaganda machine so severely that orthodox political jargon has gradually disappeared in Chinese society.[99] For example, slogans such like "Serve the People with all your Heart and Soul," "Do whatever the Party asks," "Politics in Command," and "I am just the cog in a socialist revolutionary machine," have disappeared along with many others. To attract global capital, Chinese entrepreneurs have formed joint ventures with more than fifty foreign magazines to launch Chinese editions including *People, Elle, Reader's Digest,* and *Vogue.* All these joint ventures, however, violate Chinese censorship regulations, which ban anything unrelated to science and technology. In some cases, foreign publishers have acquired entire Chinese publications but have disguised the fact by signing agreements with them to accept advice on advertising, marketing, design, and other production factors.[100]

In practice, with few exceptions, foreign magazines take over existing state publications, changing everything, including the title, and launch a repackaged Chinese language version. Foreign media with their experience in attracting commercial advertisement have become a favorite among Chinese magazine editors seeking to sweeten the bottom line. Considered the fate of *China Pictorial*, a monthly founded in January 1951 which served for generations as the model and standard of what a proper Chinese Communist should look like, including attire and hairstyle. Today, however, this bastion of Maoist asceticism has been transformed into one of China's most extravagant trend-setting publications. This transformation came about when, in 2004, the magazine used its commercial branch to set up a joint venture with Advance Publications Inc. to produce 服饰与美容, the Chinese version of *Vogue*. Mao and his associates are surely rolling in their graves over the *China Pictorial* complete makeover.[101] In 2005, the China Travel Bureau set up a joint company, Trends Group (with Hearst Communications Inc. and International Data Group), to publish a Chinese language *Cosmopolitan*. The inundation of ubiquitous foreign magazines has drowned boring and pedestrian state media in China.[102]

The interaction between global and local media helps dissenting voices to be heard in the outside world. Dissenters, moreover, are emboldened when information about social unrest and government suppression of resistance to its authority finds its way into the international media. Although Beijing vigorously attempts to maintain the control of dissent, it fights a losing battle. With the proliferation of global media and the presence of numerous reporters in China, the government may be successful in silencing some voices some of the time, but not all such voices all of the time. Thus, the truth of the adage that "information wants to be free" continuously asserts itself in the context of a China increasingly a full participant in today's shrunken world.

Beijing certainly realizes the danger of global media upon its regime, setting up rules and regulations to limit global influence. In the past few years, only a small number of transnational media firms, such as AOL Time Warner, Rupert Murdoch's News Corporation, and German firm Bertelsmann have gained limited access to the Chinese market.[103] But former licensing is just the tip of the iceberg.[104] An interesting development in 2005 was the entry to China of AGB Nielsen Market Research, a US-based media-rating corporation that implemented the UNITAM system by placing its "peoplemeter" in more than 11,000 households representing 471 million Chinese TV viewers.[105] This meter has been certified internationally to provide accurate TV ratings even in the most complex environments, including the overnight measurement of digital broadcasts. Its household TV view data will lead to ratings wars among TV stations across China competing for billions of Yuan in advertising revenue. The ratings wars will create fierce competition, giving incentives for producers to create programs catering to the viewing public rather than the party state.[106] How will the party's fading mouthpieces survive the "peoplemeter?"

Foreign media not only adds competition to the Chinese marketplace, but it also helps Chinese media workers to "establish a more financially rational and professionally constructive media system," a modern corporation, and a radical departure from lack of accountability that characterized socialism.[107] This financial learning is an important motive leading Chinese editors and producers to allow joint ventures to attract foreign capital. In February 2004, the government formally lifted its ban on foreign investment in television programming by adopting a "dual-track" policy. Used in the publishing industry since the mid-1990s, the "dual-track" policy separates the politically sensitive content over which the party maintains control, from the television commercial operation. Consequently, private companies, including foreign investors, have gained access to commercial sectors of state-controlled media outlets.[108] In addition to commercial influence, foreign government radio services such as BBC, VOA, and RFA (Radio Free Asia) have also provided alternative news and information.

With funding from private Chinese and international investors pouring in, a media relationship was formed between the party-state, editors, private investors, journalists, and audiences. So long as programming does not challenge the regime's political dominance, the parties in this new relationship have a degree of autonomy. "Just like the old days when state media workers paid close attention to the party boss because all their welcome and pay came from the state," remarked Wu Ying, a journalist from Wuhan News, "nowadays, we have to pay attention to what audiences, commercial advertising companies and private investors want. Of course, we have political boundary (*dixian*) that we can not cross."[109] Even foreign companies have to obey the *dixian* rule.

Fearing global media influences, in 2005 the government tightened control over new entry in foreign televisions, radios, and publishing.[110] The government has continued to demand that foreign media practice self-censorship. Critics of global capital in China rightly point out the continuation of state control in this new environment. But they fail to see the degree of freedom that this investment has underwritten. One thing is certain: the Chinese propaganda machine cannot practice business as usual when media outlets are linked with global capital and global markets.

Global audiences have also played a role in liberalizing China's arts and entertainment. For example, many banned films have been able to find global markets. Once given recognition by international society, ordinary Chinese are eager to buy pirated copies of banned movies on the black market. This linkage between global markets and Chinese black markets encourages writers and artists to dare to produce films, paintings, and music which are censored by the party-state. For example, Zhang Yimou's *To Live*, Chen Kaige's *Farewell My Concubine*, and some thirty other Chinese films won international awards but were banned inside China. Such bans have become useless, however, since copies can be bought for less than one dollar in most Chinese cities. This linkage is crucial in the rise of a new generation of underground filmmakers who have no intention of submitting their work to the state censorship. Thus, underground films like Liu Fendou's *Green Hat* and Zhang Yuan's *The Square* won international awards that facilitated their popularity among young Chinese. Their ambition is to produce films that gain recognition of fellow filmmakers around the world. For them, the popularity of pirated version is the final sign of professional success. Those artists seldom criticize the act of piracy in China.

The Internet Genie Is Out and the Civil Society Is In

This section discusses the emergence of Chinese civil society in the Internet age and how the Internet age and cell phones have become tools for Chinese to aid interaction among themselves which were previously constrained by geography and state media control. They have also aided in the formation of groups and associations that are increasingly independent of the state. This interaction has been beneficial in building social awareness around various issues (rule of law, political participation, environment, human rights, etc.). In the Chinese case, technology provides necessary conditions for the emergence of civil society.

The number of Internet users in China reached 260 million in 2008, representing an annual growth rate of 53.3 percent , according to 2008 figures of the China Internet Network Information Center (CNNIC), a state organization. Also extant are 620 million cell phones, all with instant and text messaging capability.

In China, the Internet has become the public sphere because it provided differing and contrasting opinions from a variety of sources competing to provide different perspectives and a differing slant.

What is more, Internet has enabled anyone to be published. That is good news for Chinese because of strong state censorship. The state media's control over news and information led to public mistrust. For many years, people would read the officials news the opposite ways. If the state newspapers suggested that there would not be inflation in China in the future, there would appear a buying panic because most people believed the opposite, that the government wanted to raise the price.

The rise of the Internet has created a variety of problems for the state propaganda machine. The *Zhongxuanbu* (Ministry of Propaganda) in Beijing and the network of state-controlled media must now compete with millions of new voices and sights. In 2008, even Party Secretary Hu Jingtao had a lively, interactive website in order to reach out to people's ever-gaping eyeballs.

Bloggers make the best use of the public's mistrust of the state media to create alternative voices in Chinese society. The flood of information on the Internet destroyed the lie of the state media machine. Today, with the Internet and the DVDs, many Chinese, especially young people, simply "don't give a damn" about the major (mostly state-controlled) media. Unless the state bans the Internet, cell phones, DVDs, and MP3s, the government can never shut down the growing chorus of alternative voices, including the voices of dissent.

To stifle information or comment deemed threatening, the government normally silences writers through imprisonment or shuts down websites. But the Internet provides a new world of infinite choices. It is impossible for the cyber police to shut all of them down.

Apart from traditional means of oppression, state bureaucrats are having a difficult time determining what to do to win back trust. They have had to adjust in order to survive, since Chinese netizens play hide and seekers with officialdom. Netizens search out and are proud to find unapproved material, such as pornography and voices of political dissent.

State Surveillance Meets Mass Bloggers

The government can use the police to scale back online civil liberty movements, but the movement will continue so long as the Internet exists in China. The state crackdowns spawn public interest, which then creates a new wave of methods to circumvent state restrictions.

The government uses the "Great Firewall of China" to block politically incorrect terms such as democracy and Falun Gong. But netizens find methods of searching for sensitive topics, such as news about the Tiananmen Square student democracy movement, terms banned on the Internet. Skilled Internet users can link their Internet browsers to route page requests through unblocked proxy servers outside China. It is difficult for censors to control the discourse of millions of Chinese bloggers. Bloggers are more critical than traditional media. An online survey by Prof. Ashley Esarey of Middlebury College found out that 61 percent of the Chinese blogs he studied carried criticism, while only 19 percent of Chinese newspapers did so.[111]

The widespread Chinese obsession with new telecommunication technology (the Internet, cell phones, text and instant messaging, and facebook) has helped form networks on a scale and with a speed that is beyond the party-state's ability to control. The Internet has thus become a place to expose official abuse of power. For example, bloggers spread the word when a forty-one-year-old Tianmen man, Wei Wenhua, was fatally beaten by local police while trying to use his cell phone to photograph a dispute between villagers and city inspectors. Blogs were full of angry messages from all over China, forcing the local government to detain a dozen local officials and remove the director of the Urban Administration Department.[112]

Exposure of abuse of all kinds through the Internet has become common in China. At times, ordinary people use the Internet to call for policy change. For example, open defiance against the government's "One Child" policy occurs only on the Internet. One Shandong province blogger calls him- or herself the "Birth guerrilla leader," sporting a banner, declaring: "I volunteer to overthrow the state family planning policy and return reproductive rights to the People."[113]

The Internet revolution has had the important effect of creating free, independent, critical netizens who cannot be manipulated and silenced by the strong machine of the one party state. Netizen activism has reclaimed the some information access with regard to news and provides an alternative to the state controlled media. In short, the Internet is a new public sphere with civil society-generating potential, because it allows the Chinese to openly express their interests, passions, and ideas exchange information, make demands on the state, and hold state officials accountable.

Politics of Sichuan Earthquake and the Emergence
of a New Chinese Media

The Chinese media have been transformed from the party's mouthpiece to a mixture of state and private content, although the state still attempts to exert control. The best illustration of this transformation is the freewheeling reporting of Chinese journalists following the May 12, 2008 earthquake that devastated Wenchuan in Sichuan Province. A few hours after the quake, the state Central Propaganda Department issued an order to Chinese media across the country: "No media may send reporters to the disaster zone."[115]

But many had already left for the disaster region. Some reporters were recalled but many others remained, including Yu Song and Wang Juliang, attached to the Shanghai-based newspaper, *Dongfang Zaobao (The Oriental Morning Post)*, a local and subsidiary (*Zibao*) newspaper, provided uncensored and unapproved coverage of the tragedy on the front page, breaking the hierarchical habit of news reporting through administrative ranks (the central party newspapers in Beijing first, the provincial party newspapers second, and the others third). The previous rule was that only Xinhua news agency was authorized to break important news.

In the immediate aftermath of earthquake, however, Chinese journalists were able to ignore the state's censors. Such independent reporting is normal in liberal democracies but is rare in authoritarian states such as China. But this time, China's heavy-handed propaganda machine bureaucrats, "found themselves uncharacteristically hamstrung when they tried to micromanage news coverage of the earthquake, as they do most major news stories in China."[116] Two days after the quake, *Zhongxun bu* (the Propaganda Department) had to swallow its pride and "rescinded its original order, replacing it with another, more realistic one, reflecting its temporary loss of control. "Reporters going to the disaster zone must move about with rescue teams," it announced. Like most government so-called reform policies that retroactively approved of social reality, this new order was in fact accepting uncontrolled news coverage. Like millions of migrants who ignored *hukou* constraints, millions of ordinary Chinese, thousands of online writers and hundreds of journalists collectively defied the state's goliath, *Zhongxun bu*.

What is more, journalists and scholars challenged the government by offering policy advice to the top leaders in open letters online and in traditional media. On May 14, 2008, Professor Hu Xindou asked the government in a blog to lower the flag to half-mast, stop entertainment activities, and investigate construction site-related corruption.[117] While the government did not adopt the final point, it accepted the other two. And Huang Fuping, in the Beijing-based financial magazine *Caijing*, challenged the state-sponsored Olympic torch relay during the rescue period: "Under these circumstances, the strategy of the torch relay of the Beijing Olympic Games should be adjusted. It should be suspended between the provinces. After decisive progress has been made in the rescue effort, then we should pass the torch directly from the affected areas of the quake to Beijing."[118]

Both online and printing news outlets called for an investigation about corruption in the construction of buildings because 95 percent of earthquake casualties resulted from the collapse of buildings. Other online writers seized the moment to challenge the forbidden subjects of government accountability and corruption. One wrote: "Why did all the school buildings collapse, while official [government] ones remained standing?" Another wrote: "How much of the donation money is flowing into the pockets of local government officials?" Still others blamed the government for failing to warn people earlier. Facing millions of angry online Chinese, on May 16, 2008, the state went so far as to hold a rare, real-time online exchange with ordinary Chinese to "answer angry questions about why so many schools collapsed in the quake."[119]

There are several reasons for this appearance of a critical anti-censorship mass. First and foremost, the Chinese are fed up with the state censorship. A 2008 World Public Opinion survey showed 66 percent of the Chinese public desire more media freedom, while 71 percent say that, "people should have the right to read whatever is on the Internet."[120] All journalists we interviewed expressed a sense of pride. Wu Han, a reporter based in Shanghai, remarked, "It is the first time I felt proud of my job as a reporter. For once I could be true to my profession and tell the truth. I hope this will last."[121]

Second, global influence has also played a role in forcing the Chinese state to greater information transparency. The party-state's concern about the Olympic games and Western criticism following the state's March-April mishandling of the Tibet protests brought pressure to bear on reducing information and news secrecy. In January 2008, the central government passed an Information Act recognizing ordinary people's rights to information. In April, Wen Jiabao formally declared the operation of the act. Two of four mainland journalists interviewed by telephone cited the new law as the reason for journalists' defiance of *Zhongxun bu*'s reporting ban.[122] Third, the event's apolitical nature added to overwhelming public concern encouraged journalists to take a firm stand against the censors. Government policy would backfire if journalists reporting the events were arrested.

Fourth, amid much heralding, China's top leaders traveled to the quake region, making it hard for censors to ban reporting. Journalists' positive reports about the visits also helped, because leaders realized that free reporting might not damage their image. They have learned that the media can be used to their advantage. Fifth, competition among media outlets for public attention helped motivate the media's defiance of the state.

Finally, China's earthquake coverage shows that the Internet became the single most important mainstream information medium for ordinary people. The new media rankings in China today are no longer determined by censors but by this powerful information network and its impact on 250 million online users and 600 million cell phone users with instant messaging, bulletin boards, and blogs. The constant updating of death tolls on the Internet and text messaging ended the state media's information monopoly once and for all. When in 1960 and 1976 the state had society completely in its grasp, 30 million Great Leap Famine deaths and 240,000 Tangshan earthquake deaths on Beijing's doorstep went unreported for years, treated instead as state secrets. Now all this is changing.

Exposure of Fake Olympics Production

The Beijing elite spent 300 billion dollars to send such messages to the world as "peaceful China," "harmonious China," and "happy Chinese people (under the CCP's rule). On August 8, 2008, they put on a spectacular show broadcast to an audience of billions worldwide. But the primary audience the Beijing elite had in mind was the Chinese people. Had the games been produced and consumed only in China, it could not have had the intended effect. Rather, the elite hoped that the world's reaction to a dazzling visual display of China's new-found power reflected back to China (a reflection controlled by China's media censorship, shielding the public from unwanted comment), would strengthen the regime's legitimacy, renewing and buttressing its mandate to rule. Since the Olympics Games are linked to regime survival, detailed preparation for them became a primary campaign of the Communist Party-state. When the Olympic torch rally revealed that the world was not reacting as the Beijing elite had planned, they flew into a moral panic, doubting their ability to achieve the "perfect" games they envisaged. The pursuit of "perfection" involved the art of counterfeiting at the very outset, with the opening ceremony singing faked, the electronic manipulation of the world's TV screens with prerecorded special effects of various kinds, the nation's flag unfurled, and waved smartly in a breeze created by a hidden fan, and so-called "minority children" were mostly Han youngsters in minority custumes.[123] The actual child singer, Yang Peiyi, was replaced by Lin Miaoke, who lip-synched the party's revolutionary song, "Ode to the Motherland," illustrating the fruits of such panic and its overkill response.

The regime has undertaken much other fakery in preparation for the Olympics Games. To show an immaculate host venue, the government cleaned up Beijing by kicking out *several million* migrant workers, whose toil and sweat, and in some cases blood, had made the Olympic facilities possible. In fact, the free movement of 200 million Chinese that has taken place over the past three decades constitutes a colossal showcase of the Chinese people's newfound mobility and entrepreneurial risk-taking spirit. China would have looked stronger and· more harmonious with some of these mobile workers sitting in the audience, enjoying the fruits of their labor. The developed world would have been greatly impressed. But like the two young girls, they must now be regarded as merely exploited pawns, kicked out of the great show. It is ironic that China, largest of Communism's "workers' paradise" states, has exploited its workers so openly and shamelessly before the world.

Another matter was China's promise to the International Olympic Committee (IOC) to clean up its human rights record prior to the 2008 games. With breathtaking cynicism, the regime openly turned its back on it pledge. To deter Chinese dissidents, state security police harassed "house churches" and, on August 10, 2008, detained home church activist Hua Huiqi (华惠棋) on his way to a church service to be attended by US President George Bush. The show of thousands of home churchgoers could have been shown as the strength of a new China with religious tolerance. To ensure that no troublemakers entered Beijing, foreigners voicing criticism of the regime or anyone (including business people) from "unsafe" regions such as Africa and the Middle East have been barred from China through unique Olympics visa restrictions, even if they had done business in China for years. Officials ordered Beijing's bars and upscale restaurants not to serve those with dark skin, revealing a preoccupation of a clearly racist cast. Given that China has entered Africa's and the Middle East's markets, this appearance will surely hurt China in the long run, should word get around.

Mocking its human rights commitments to the IOC, to control petitions and protests, Beijing government created more fakery—this time fake "protest zones," three parks, Beijing announced with great fanfare in July, that would be designated for protests. Five days in advance of proposed meetings, protesters were required to submit the names and addresses of participants, protest topics, and copies of materials. Midway through the games, no applications were approved. On the contrary, when Ji Sizun, a self-trained lawyer from Fujiang; Gao Chuancai, a farmer activist from Heilong Jia; Zhang Wei, a Beijing resident; and Ge Yifei, a well-known property rights advocate from Suzhou, attempted to submit protest applications for one of the designated zones, they were either detained, harassed, or arrested by the police. When a British TV journalist tried to cover a pro-Tibet demonstration, he was detained and roughed up. The Beijing elite again failed to understand that the eerie quiet of empty protest zones is likely to draw more attention than full ones. Instead of a ploy to quell critics seeking to highlight China's lack of free expression, Beijing should have used the occasion to show that in being allowed to demonstrate, ordinary Chinese have gained greater participation in the political processes. The very fact that these individuals took the risk of following stated protest procedures shows that the Chinese have pushed for constitutional liberty from below by focusing on making officials accountable for the rules they themselves create. The Olympic Games have allowed dissidents to push the envelope in this regard.

To ensure perfect security, the government made it difficult for visitors to reach the pavilions of Olympic sponsors, upsetting companies that have spent tens of millions of dollars on promotional campaigns.[124] What is worse, the accumulated effects of visa hassles, security jitters, anxiety about attending a major event in such a regimented police state, anti-foreign nationalism, and high hotel prices have deterred many foreigners from attending. Draconian control regulations (travel restrictions and other security precautions) and rampant violation of individual rights deterred many Chinese and foreigners from going to Beijing. When it became obvious that many of the sports events were half empty, the state bused cheerleading squads to fill unsold seats.

But the fake production is not the only China. The other China is contesting the official fake production to "live in truth." The discovery and exposure of official legerdemain in the opening ceremonies shows that China is being transformed. The Chinese are no longer the passive "blue ants" (so-called for once ubiquitous blue workers' uniforms) of Mao's malignant dystopia. Today, the Chinese use the Internet and cell phones to inform one another of shams of all kinds, in this case the lip-synched voice. My phone interviews with a dozen mainland contacts suggest that the Chinese consider the government to have badly overreached with its singing switch. "I wished the government had not done the switch," Liu Liu (not her real name), a Wuhan mother said. "The poor girl will always feel that she is not good-looking." Another mother, remarked that, "Miss Lin will be forever labeled as fake. The act harms both girls. This is not right."

Chinese who are becoming cynical about party-state antics do not like the political manipulation of the event when the highest leadership is involved in what amounts to production chicanery and when the primary audience is Chinese. The "national interest" rationale for the lip-synching reminds us that the elite always used "national interest" to explain away their oppression and exploitation of the people. This time, however, the exposure has had unintended consequences. Within minutes, Internet chat rooms, YouTube, cell phones, and text messages were spreading on the Internet, which the government Internet police attempted to block. Chinese, fed up with state control of information and the generation of lies on a vast scale, have used the opportunity to speak out, declaring that the elite has hurt China's image. One Internet writer put it, "Adults may lie, but leave the kids out of it." Another wrote, "Sometimes, the bottom line and principle are more important than national interests. If she were my child, I would not allow her to have such an opportunity."[125] Another wrote angrily, "You are destroying the soul of a beautiful and innocent girl. At school, you included her parents repeatedly telling her that outside appearance is not important. Beauty lies in the heart and soul. But what have you done in real life? I beg you, middle and upper class people, to be gentle towards that pure soul. Please do this so that you can remember your lost kindness and innocence."[126]

A blogger called Shiniankaicai criticized the lip-synched "Ode to the Motherland" saying, "Even that beautiful voice is faked. The motherland is never to be sung for, but to be cheated."[127] Another writes, "Motherf....r, this thing has already gone way beyond just lip-synching; putting in a stand-in singer is no…different from having a stand-in test-taker, and this is a huge misguidance to the youth of China. Zhang Yimou, you get your butt out here and apologize!"

Yang Binbin, a senior reporter from China's leading finance and business magazine *Caijing* wrote: "What are the Olympics? There's only one answer in the world, except in China, where the answer varies, but has nothing to do with justice, fairness and openness. For the Olympics, the Chinese ping-pong community has been playing fake games and it became an open secret; for the Olympics, those parents who lost their children were asked to accept compensation from local governments but not to pursue responsibilities of 'shoddy school buildings.'"

"Letting such young children lie in front of the whole world, this nation has no hope."[128] Yang's critical words represent a new China and unofficial production of a true powerful nation with individuals who challenge bogus official productions. Some even lent humor to criticism. A Chinese cartoonist/blogger, Guaiguai, posted an Olympics cartoon in which a child carrying a Chinese flag told another child: "I have learned a new curse word. Your look is violating national interests!!!"[129] This is the Chinese way of telling the government not to politicize the Olympics.

One Guangdong businessman sent a text message to his networks: "This fake production confirmed the dominant thinking in the West that the Chinese are cheaters. The person responsible should be fired." Tongue wagging by word of mouth, text messaging, and cell phoning from Yang's relatives, classmates, neighbors in Beijing University's affiliated school has already placed the Beijing authorities in an awkward position. The public's "voice-switch" discussion and the state's moral panic point up how China has changed. The government is worried about the Chinese people's reactions to its machinations. It is perhaps dawning on the government that the Chinese people are not a colony of ants captured by the power of the state. The Chinese public's reaction to the exposure shows that, despite entrenched party-state control including the tens of thousands of Internet police, large numbers of Chinese aspire (and dare) to live in the truth.

Concluding Thoughts

The Chinese information revolution is another example of Joseph Schumpeter's notion of capitalist "creative destruction;" in this case, leading to the crumbling of the party-state's control over society. In China this revolution is so gradual that it is invisible to those in its midst. Rampant violation of intellectual property rights, subsequent growth of illegal markets for books, videos, and other media, the rise of consumer culture, and decline of party media have replaced the old order of strict party-state control over information. In its place has arisen a new mixture of party mouthpieces and commercial media. The main function of the media has been transformed from its function as tool of party-state propaganda and mobilization of "the masses" to a dual function as both state propaganda and entertainment, an eclectic repertoire of choices to attract audiences. Profit-seeking has become a primary focus of the Chinese media. The foundation for this transformation has been the merging of China's despotic historical experience with a renewed pursuit of freedom of expression.

The resulting spread of countercultural ideas has provided the Chinese with a number of sources of information, including foreign sources, as well as an explosion of entertainment forms that the government is able neither to censor nor to regulate, resulting in two worlds of media. On the one hand, most Chinese struggle for freedom of information, more access to truth, and less intrusion from the government. On the other hand, the party-state is engaged in its own struggle to exercise what control it can to ensure the regime's survival.

Throughout this chapter, we have suggested that rampant violation of intellectual property rights, subsequent growth of black markets in books, videos, DVDs, and other media, the rise of a consumer culture, and the decline of state media have replaced the old order of complete control over information and its distribution media with a new mixture of party mouthpieces and commercial media. Only a tiny handful of purely political, non-commercial publications remain.[130] The media have been transformed from party-state devices indoctrinating the "masses" about what to think and exhorting them to action in political campaigns, to a combination of a small number of sophisticated regime mouthpieces and a far more varied commerce-driven repertoire of media choices designed to attract audiences.[131] Gone are the days of massive Maoist political campaigns such as the Great Leap Forward and the Cultural Revolution that roiled society for years at a time. Today, the regime's attempts to mount annual mass-mobilization exercises such as the "anti-pornography," "strike hard," and "anti-corruption" campaigns are largely ineffectual. It appears, therefore, that the regime is no longer able to use the media as it once did.

The Chinese media have become primarily profit-seeking enterprises. The process through which this situation has developed has been made possible by the merging of China's historical experience with despotism and with its contemporary renewed pursuit of freedom of expression both for its own sake and as means to material betterment. The resulting spread of countercultural ideas has provided the Chinese people with a veritable flood of information that government is able to neither censor nor regulate.[132] The Chinese increasingly crave access to uncensored information and the ability to pursue the truth as they see it without intrusion from the government.

Facing the information revolution, the Chinese government has been defensive and insecure and attempted "to rein in a newly vigorous news media by imposing draconian permits and licenses, or tests of professional ethics and procedures. Libel laws are strengthened to protect the powerful, and when all else fails, journalists are harassed, beaten and imprisoned."[133] The extent to which Chinese society and its government are able to reconcile their contradictory positions on these issues will be instrumental in shaping the country's future. The longer they remain divergent and the greater the degree of their mutual antagonism, the more dangerous the situation could become for both. There is no doubt that control over media content is the one of key battlegrounds in an ongoing protracted war between the authoritarian state and a society groping uncertainly for freedom. Since everyone knows that government officials themselves no longer believe in Communism, or even socialism, it is clear to everyone concerned that state censorship is a means of attempting to maintain elite control.

To a large extent in today's China, market ingredients govern media management and content. As a result, decisions are based largely on pecuniary interests, rather than on ideology. Elites have material interests in continuing these arrangements. Although views of the old guard are presented in China's media, media managers are aware that the public is bored with this view and that excessive attention to them would be financially ruinous. A return to complete government control of media suffused with propaganda that characterized Mao's time would entail enormous financial sacrifice in today's profit-driven society. With regards to Mao's era, China has long passed the point of no return.

Rapid economic development has allowed more independent thinking among previously dependent groups such as women, artists, farmers, and young people. As Zha Jianying says in *China Pop*, "The market reforms have created new opportunities, new dreams and to some extent a new atmosphere and new mind-sets. The old control system has grown weak in many arenas. There is a growing sense of increased space for personal freedom."[134] This new situation has manifested itself extensively in the arts, as more writers and artists have increasingly given up their government jobs to pursue an independent life. Here, as elsewhere in the new China, the market becomes a liberating force. The rise of a consumer society has transformed both media and audience. The media collectively has been described as an "omnipresent, organic, and independent [object] that flips the economic, social, and geopolitical framework all the time."[135] The attraction of commercial revenue and audience ratings have dictated media content to such an extent that the regime has little choice but attempt to maintain a semblance of historical continuity, justifying its rule as creator of modern China and heir to a tradition other than China's dynastic millenniums. The regime might otherwise become lost in a sea of modernity just at the time that China's long history is being decisively fractured, perhaps even more so than during the Cultural Revolution. The rapidity of change today is generated by markets, globalization, and myriad environmental and socials ills that litter the social landscape and foul its air beyond recognition.

In this context, the regime's frequent serial expression of familiar historical names linking the nineteenth and twentieth centuries to the twenty-first century is just such an effort at an evocation of history and, through this linkage, to claims of legitimacy. Thus, Marxism-Leninism, Mao Zedong thought, Deng's

Socialism with Chinese Characteristics, Jiang's Three Representatives and Hu-Wen's "harmonious society" serve just this purpose. Figures and ideologies are used as historical talismans, endowing the Chinese Communist Party's rule with a magical aura of legitimacy. What else could justify the contemporary rule of a Communist Party, when so many other Communist regimes have been swept aside, and socialism, the public ownership of the means of production and distribution, is repudiated daily? Of course, the evident fact that the extinction of socialism in China is gathering pace is the proverbial "elephant in the room." However disconnected with reality, the linguisitic symbols of the reigns of power must be grasped all the more firmly, the weaker and fewer they become. The government realizes it is in a precarious position, which is why it now arrests journalists for "divulging state secrets," when they cross the line.[136] In the past, the regime could have gotten away arresting journalists for ideological reasons, such as espousing "spiritual pollution," "counter-revolutionary," or "capitalist" rhetoric or for no reason at all. Today, however, such justification would be met with tremendous public resistance and, thus, is not an option. The media and the government's handling of its new censorship is a reflection of the imposing reality of the current state-society relationship.

This is "a new kind of revolution—a revolution in which rapidly commercializing media industries confront slow-changing power relations between political, social, and economic spheres."[137] Stephanie Hemelryk Donald and Michael Keane have given a name, "authoritarian liberalism," to this tension between an increasingly liberal society and continuing authoritarian state, which combines "the rational calculation demanded by the operation of the capitalist economy within the authoritarian shell of the state."[138] Under this model, Chinese people have fought to increase freedom to choose, to consume, and to be self-regulating, but once the consumer's freedom diverges from the party-state's interests, the state's strong hand will interfere to smother the freedom. However, the relatively liberal environment for expression has come with many years' struggle by Chinese who were tired of the party-state's control in their lives.

In our discussions, we have also demonstrated the effects of these informal and illegal activities on movements towards a more free press. A crucial dimension of this process has been trying to meet the demands of the consumers while trying to keep the government at bay. Pirated CD/DVDs, illegal satellite dishes, and the Internet become the best carriers of liberal ideas. An *International Herald Tribune* reporter, Howard W. French, is confident that people will win in this game: "In today's world, the effort to corral 1.3 billion Chinese and to sharply restrict their freedom of expression is a fool's game. The best that can be said about it is that it is an enormous waste of energy."[139] The link between piracy and liberalization in China is an organic one. In this chapter, we have shown that there are Chinese who have made use of informal channels to go around the state's media control to spread information. Not surprisingly, there are plenty of Chinese who have made use of piracy and other informal means who have some purely material interests at stake. But until the press in China becomes independent, the push to impose intellectual property rights from outside may give the Chinese government excuse to crack down on the informal channel that challenges their power, thus weakening the liberal voice in China.

John Perry Barlow's famous phrase "information wants to be free" captures the essence of the one of our central themes. At what point does one person's quest for free expression infringe on another's right to ownership? The discussion of rights in itself provides insight into what sort of movement has been occurring over the last three decades. We have attempted to explain the issue in its true complexity, rather than simply as a question of right or wrong. The creation of intellectual property rights in the West was intended to foster public disclosure and encourage the dissemination of new ideas. However, in China, violations of the rights were needed to jump-start this process or it never would have gotten off the ground. When the government controls all means of production and dissemination, there are few alternatives. More importantly, the indisputably positive dimension of this model of development is the emergence of a civil society, which has served as a catalyst for political, social, and economic transformation. As this society continues to develop, and further rights acquisition is sought by a greater percentage of the population, continued change is inevitable.

Notes

1. Guo Liang, Chinese Academy of Social Sciences, Beijing, in an interview with CPJ (Committee to Protect Journalists, USA).
2. Reporters without Borders, "The 2006 World Press Freedom Index," December 2006, http://www.rsf.org/rubrique.php3?id_rubrique=639.
3. The news is filled with stories of reporters being arrested for revealing state secrets, regarding everything from poor working conditions to land rights. Some sources include Gady A. Epstein, *Baltimore Sun* foreign staff, originally published March 13, 2005, http://www.baltimoresun.com/news/nationworld/bal-te.secrecy13mar13,1, 156684.story?coll=bal-nationworld-headlines&ctrack=1&cset=true.
4. Gao Hua, *How did the Sun Rise over Yan'an?* (Hong Kong: Chinese University of Hong Kong Press, 2000), p. 373-374.
5. Gao Song, "Differences between the Internal and the External News: Case Study of XHN Internal Reference Materials and the People's Daily from 1950 to 1960." M.A. Thesis, 2006.
6. Kenneth Lieberthal, *Governing China: From Revolution through Reform*, (New York: W.W. Norton & Co. Inc., 1995), p. 179. Lynn T. White III, *Policies of Chaos: The Organizational Causes of Violence in China's Cultural Revolution*, (Princeton, NJ: Princeton University Press, 1989).
7. He Qingliang, 2004, p. 44. "Media Control in China" (A Report by "Human Rights in China," part two,), *Modern China Studies*, Vol. 11, No. 4, (2004), pp. 44-78.
8. Kenneth Lieberthal, *Governing China: From Revolution through Reform.* (New York: W.W. Norton & Co. Inc., 1995), p. 171.
9. For a good discussion on the one party state control, see Hannah Arendt and Peter Baehr, eds., *The Portable Hannah Arendt*, (London: Penguin, 2000).

10. Charles F. Bahmueller, "Civil Society," 1999.
11. Harrison, Mark, "Information and Command," *The Warwick Economics Research Paper Series* (TWERPS), (2002), p. 635.
12. An excellent study on famine in this period and the rural basis for grassroots reform in China is found in Dali Yang, *Calamity and Reform in China*, 1996.
13. For more detail on propaganda's effect on the famine, see Jasper Becker, *Hungry Ghosts: Mao's Secret Famine Owl Books*, Reprint edition (1998).
14. Mark Selden, *Political Economy of Chinese Development*, (Armonk, NY: M. E. Sharpe, 1993).
15. Perry Link, Richard P. Madsen, and Paul G. Pickowicz, *Popular China: Unofficial Culture in a Globalizing Society*, (Rowman & Littlefield Publishers, Inc., 2001). Paul G. Pickowicz, Richard Madsen, and Perry Link, *Unofficial China: Popular Culture and Thought in the People's Republic*, (Boulder, CO: Westview Press, 1989).
16. Ba Jin, *Shuixiang Lu (Random Thoughts)*, (Beijing: Writers' Press [*zhuojia chu-banshe*], 2005).
17. Ba Jin, 2005, p. 219.
18. Deborah S. Davis, Richard Kraus, Barry Naughton, and Elizabeth Perry, eds., *Urban Spaces in Contemporary China: The Potential for Autonomy and Community in Post-Mao China*, (Cambridge University Press, 1995), p. 11-12.
19. Haraszti, 1989, #566.
20. Personal Interview with Xiao Yuan, July 7, 2002, Beijing, China.
21. Wang Xizhe, "For a Return to Genuine Marxism in China," *New Left Review* I/121, May-June 1980, http://www.newleftreview.org/?view=1517.
22. See a good discussion on the underground literature in Perry Link, "Hand-Copied Entertainment Fiction from the Cultural Revolution," (1989), pp. 17-36.
23. James Scott, *Domination and the Arts of Resistance: Hidden Transcripts*, (New Haven: Yale University Press, 1990), p. 4.
24. Personal interview with Ms. Jin San, January 2, 1995, in Guangzhou.
25. Perry Link, "Hand-Copied Entertainment Fiction from the Cultural Revolution," (1989), pp. 17-36. For more on official monitoring system in urban China, see Lynn T. White III, *Policies of Chaos: The Organizational Causes of Violence in China's Cultural Revolution*, (Princeton, NJ: Princeton University Press, 1989).
26. Kenneth Lieberthal, Governing *China: From Revolution through Reform*, (New York: W.W. Norton & Co. Inc., 1995), p. 172.
27. Zhao, 1998.
28. Participatory observation in house churches in Wuhan, Beijing, Shenzhen, Liji-ang, Hunan, and Shandong in 2000 to 2007. See more on Xiaoming and Jianan Shixuan (Songs from Canaan) in http://www.nimenqu.com/siten/modules...cat. php?cid=32.
29. Congressional-Executive Commission on China, Criminal Law of the People's Republic of China, http://www.cecc.gov/pages/newLaws/criminalLawENG. php?PHPSESSID=75cce7028e31869cb0e56e07a34acc25.
30. www.ChinaAid.org, personal communication with Bob Fu, who once worked with Cai in Beijing via email, "Renowned Beijing Church Leader Cai Zhuohua Released after Three Years Imprisonment for distributing Bibles; Forced Labor for Olympics Products Imposed," September 14, 2007.
31. www.ChinaAid.org, personal communication with Bob Fu who used to work with Cai in Beijing via email, "Renowned Beijing Church Leader Cai Zhuohua Released after Three Years Imprisonment for distributing Bibles; Forced Labor for Olympics Products Imposed," September 14, 2007.

32. Stephanie Hemelryk Donald, Michael Keane, Yin Hong, and Yin Hong, *Media in China: Consumption, Content and Crisis,* (London: RoutledgeCurzon, 2002).
33. For a good discussion on urban China, Deborah S. Davis, Richard Kraus, Barry Naughton, and Elizabeth Perry, eds., *Urban Space in Contemporary China: The Potential for Autonomy and Community in Post-Mao China.*
34. Personal conversation with Mr. Liu 1986 in Wuhan. Liu's experience was very common among teenagers at that time.
35. Personal interview with Lu in Shanghai, on July 18, 2007.
36. Bill Savadove, "Illicit books reveal lurid 'facts' of Shanghai sacking," *SCMP* Tuesday, January 2, 2007.
37. Susan V. Lawrence, "The Life of the Party," *Far East Economic Review*, October 18, 2001. Internet version.
38. The Chinese pinyin goes, *"baitian lao Deng de tianxia, wanshang shi xiao Deng de Tianxia."*
39. Two local police came to my house to search for Deng's tape. I was upset and threw the tapes at them. The police threatened to take me away when my father, a professor of English in Chinese University of Geosciences, who was sent to labor camps during the Cultural Revolution stepped in by apologizing on my behalf.
40. Personal interviews with Wu Meng, young college student in Wuhan China, on July 31, 1996.
41. Personal interview with Chen Ping, in Wuhan, August 1, 1996.
42. Personal interview with Vivian Xu in Shanghai, on July 16, 2001.
43. This is very similar to the Soviet model, see Abram Bergson, *The Real National Income of Soviet Russia Since 1928,* (Cambridge, MA: Harvard University Press, 1961). Bergson introduces the term "planners' preferences"—the notion that the Soviet administrative-command economy was ultimately directed by the top leadership of the Communist Party, unlike market economies, which are ultimately directed by consumer sovereignty.
44. Xinhua News Agency, "China to Inspect Newspaper Circulation Data," *Xinhua* (Beijing), September 5, 2006.
45. Li Ling, "On the Ecological Environment and Structural innovations of Press Groups in Chengdu," 2001, Chinese Communication Association Annual Meeting proceedings, http://ccs.nccu.edu.tw/history_paper_content.php?P_ID=642&P_YEAR=2001.
46. Li Ling, 2001, p. 8.
47. Yin Liangen and Wang Haiyan, "Profiting from the Media Industry: Common Practice of Reporters and Editors in China," *Modern China Studies,* Vol. 14, No. 2, (2007), p. 123.
48. Personal interview with Wu Litang, on November 20, 2005 in Wuhan.
49. Hamburg-Shanghai Network, "Looking at Chinese Media Industries," *Newsletter* No. 9, 2006 (online).
50. Li Ling.
51. Richard Baum, "Political Implications of China's Information Revolution:The Media, Its Minders, and Their Message," From Cheng Li, ed., *Changes in China's Political Landscape: Beyond the 17th Party Congress,* (Washington, DC: The Brookings Institution, 2007).
52. "The freedom of Chinese Press in my life (*Wo qingli de xinwen chuban siyou*)," www.epochtimes.com/gb/3/9/6/n371179.hum.
53. *The Chinese Newspapers Baoye Zhongguo,* (Beijing: *sanxia chubanshe*, 2002).
54. Speech for Xinhua News Agency English Service, Sept. 2, 2004, http://news.xinhuanet.com/newsmedia/2004-09/23/content_20011870).

55. *The History of Press in the People's Republic of China* (2nd Ed.), (Beijing: The Economic Daily Publishing House, 1996).
56. Li Dongsheng and Dun Yusheng, "*Xinwen buguo de xinwen* (The news behind the news)," (Beijing: Central Chinese Translation and Editing Press (*zhongyuan bianyi chuban she*), University of Illinois Press, 1998).
57. Yin Liangen and Wang Haiyan, "Profiting from the Media Industry: Common Practice of Reporters and Editors in China," *Modern China Studies*, Vol. 14, No. 2, (2007), pp. 123-33.
58. Lyric Hughes (2002), publisher and CEO of China Online Inc., a U.S.-based media company, "China's Cable TV Shake Up," 2001.
59. These data came from Chengju Huang, "Negotiating with the global: China's response to post-WTO foreign media penetration," 15th Biennial Conference of the Asian Studies Association of Australia in Canberra June 29-July 2, 2004. "Advertising expenditure," (2004).
60. Ni Ming, "*Zhongguo Qingnian*," *China Youth*, Nov. 5, 1998. He Qingliang, "Media Control in China" (A report by "Human Rights in China," part two.) *Modern China Studies*, Vol. 11, No. 4, (2004), pp. 44-78.
61. Susan V. Lawrence, "The Life of the Party*," Far East Economic Review*, October 18, 2001. Internet version.
62. He Qingliang, "Media Control in China" (A report by "Human Rights in China," part two.) *Modern China Studies*, Vol. 11, No. 4, (2004), pp. 44-78.
63. Ibid.
64. See more on *tiao/kuai* politics in Andrew C. Mertha, "China's 'Soft' Centralization: Shifting Tiao/Kuai Authority Relations," *The China Quarterly* (2005), 184, pp. 791-810.
65. Radio Free Asia, "*shengyuan beijianji jizhe ri* (Support The Day for Imprisoned Journalists)," 2006, 11, 20, http://www.rfa.org/mandarin/shenrubaodao/2006/11/20/jizhe/
66. Irene Wang, "Newspaper staff strike over reshuffle," December 30, 2005.
67. Personal interviews with Liao and Zhang, August 5, 2006, in Beijing. The other time was May in 1989 when thousands of journalists participated in anti-government demonstrations.
68. Personal interviews with Feng, July 21, 2007, Zouping, Shandong.
69. Vivian Wu, "Bai Xing's former editor stands by bold approach," *SCMP,* January 22, 2007.
70. Zhongguo Qingnian, *Chinese Youth*, No. 9, 1997, p. 5.
71. Personal interviews with Li Fei, the president of Chinese Prose Association, September 1998.
72. He Qingliang, "Media Control in China (A Report by 'Human Rights in China,' part two.)," *Modern China Studies*, Vol. 11, No. 4, (2004), pp. 44-78.
73. Tong Bao, "*Zhongxuanbu tongbao biping zhuanmei shida wenti* (The Centrol Propaganda Ministry circulated a national notice on ten problems of media)," Mingpao, Feburary 23, 2002.
74. Edward Cody, "Blackmailing by Journalists in China Seen as 'Frequent,'" *Washington Post* Foreign Service, January 25, 2007, http://www.washingtonpost.com/wp-srv/world/countries/china.html?nav=el.
75. Personal interview with Wu Qing on July 1, 2006, in Wuhan.
76. Edward Cody, "Blackmailing By Journalists In China Seen As 'Frequent,'" *Washington Post* Foreign Service, January 25, 2007.
77. Zhu Boru, "Microsoft mulls cheaper OS version in China," *China Business Weekly*, July 8, 2004, http://www.chinadaily.com.cn/english/doc/2004-07/08/content_3467 16.htm.

78. Information Office of the State Council of the People's Republic of China, "New Progress in China's Protection of Intellectual Property Rights," April 25, 2005, http://www.china-un.ch/eng/bjzl/t193102.htm.

79. Institute, 1997, #465, pp. 1385-91. (A Chinese source).

80. "China called To Pirate of Software," *International Herald Tribune*, (Oct. 21, 1993), p. 16.

81. "Games firm sues rival for a record 120m yuan," *SCMP*, May 9, 2006.

82. Institute, 1997, #465, pp. 1465-67.

83. Institute, 1997, #465, pp. 1465-67.

84. Personal interview with Professor Liao at Qinghua University, Beijing, June 24, 2001.

85. "White Paper on IPR Protection," *China Daily*, April 21, 2005. Copyright Law of the People's Republic of China, Regulations on the Protection of Computer Software, Regulations on the Protection of Layout Designs of Integrated Circuits, Regulations on the Collective Management of Copyright, Regulations on the Management of Audio-Video Products, Regulations on the Protection of New Varieties of Plants, Regulations on the Protection of Intellectual Property Rights by the Customs, Regulations on the Protection of Special Signs, and Regulations on the Protection of Olympic Logos, http://www.chinadaily.com.cn/english/doc/2005-04/21/content_436276.htm.

86. Carl Menger, *Problems of Economics and Sociology*, trans. Francis J. Nook, ed. Louis Schneider, (Urbana: University of Illinois Press, 1963).

87. Bai Fan, "Growing Pains of China's Media," Radio Free Asia, 10/02/08, http://www.expertclick.com/NewsReleaseWire/default.cfm?Action=ReleaseDetail&ID=23375&NRWid=5187.

88. Ibid.

89. Ibid.

90. Ibid.

91. Cynthia Wan, "Government pays 'hardship assistance' to mother of June 4 victim," Associated Press, Monday, May 1, 2006.

92. Charter 08, Translated from the Chinese by Perry Link, New York Review of Books, http://www.nybooks.com/articles/22210.

93. In 2006, there were 480 million mobile phones in China.

94. Rupert Murdoch, "The Consumer is in the Saddle, Driving the Telecommunications Industry," *The Times*, September 2, 1993.

95. C. C. Lee *Chinese media, global contexts*, (London & New York: Routledge Curzon, 2003a).

96. Richard Baum, "Political Implications of China's Information Revolution: The Media, Its Minders, and Their Message," From Cheng Li, ed., *Changes in China's Political Landscape: Beyond the 17th Party Congress*, (Washington, DC: The Brookings Institution, 2007).

97. Personal interviews with Wang Qinghong in May, 2002, Honolulu, HI.

98. Personal interview with Deng Zhixin on June 24, 2006, Honolulu, HI.

99. Personal interview with Gong Xiao, a local freelance reporter in Changhsa, July 22, 2007.

100. "China: China freezes licenses to publish foreign magazines," *Straits Times*, April 8, 2006, http://www.asiamedia.ucla.edu/article.asp?parentid=42506.

101. D. L. Li "Marriage between capital and Chinese media in vogue," (April 20, 2001), www.ultrachina.com, http://www.ultrachina.com/english/doc.cfm?OID=833&MIDtoc=0&CIDtoc=62.

102. "China Restricts Foreign Investment on Magazine Publications," *East Asian Economic Review*, April 10, 2006, http://www.e-economic.com/info/6440-1.htm.

103. Barrett McCormick and Qing Liu, "Globalization and the Chinese Media: Technologies, Content, Commerce and the Prospects for the Public Sphere" in Chin-chuan Lee, ed., *Chinese Media, Global Contexts*, (New York: Routledge, 2003).
104. Rupert Murdoch, "The Consumer is in the Saddle, Driving the Telecommunications Industry," *The Times*, September 2, 1993.
105. AGB Nielsen Market Research (Guanghzou) Co., Ltd., http://www.agbnielsen.net/whereweare/dynPage.asp?lang=english&country=China&id=303.
106. AGB Nielsen Market Research, "China Introduction," http://www.agbnielsen.net/whereweare/dynPage.asp?lang=english&country=China&id=303.
107. Chengju Huang, "Negotiating with the global: China's response to post-WTO foreign media penetration," 15th Biennial Conference of the Asian Studies Association of Australia in Canberra, June 29-July 2, 2004.
108. China Business Information Center, "Media moves towards privatization," February 12, 2004. ChinaBiz, http://www.cbiz.cn/NEWS/showarticle.asp?id=2034.
109. Personal interview with Wu in 2006.
110. "China: China cracks down on evils of 'foreign culture' on TV," *Taipei Times*, August 5, 2005, http://www.asiamedia.ucla.edu/article.asp?parentid=27735.
111. Geoffrey A. Fowler, "Chinese Bloggers Really Are Edgy," *The Wall Street Journal*, June 14, 2008, http://blogs.wsj.com/chinajournal/2008/06/14/chinese-bloggers-really-are-edgy/.
112. Telephone interviews with Qian Guoqian, Wuhan February 7, 2008, and with Wang You Xiang in Tianmen on February 10, 2008.
113. The Birth Guerrilla leader website, http://lwwxm1.blog.163.com/prevUser.do?hostId=12862194.
114. Gao Song, *"Wenchuan dizheng*: The Sign of Chinese Image Transformation," 汶川地震：中国形象的嬗变信号, *Financial Times* in Chinese, May 13, 2008.
115. Howard W. French "Earthquake Opens Gap in Controls on Media," May 18, 2008, *New York Times*, http://topics.nytimes.com/top/news/science/topics/earthquakes/sichuan_province_china/index.html?inline=nyt-classifier.
116. Personal communication with Hu, Xingdou, May 14, 2008.
117. Maureen Fan, "Chinese Media Take Firm Stand on Openness about Earthquake," *Washington Post* Foreign Service, Sunday, May 18, 2008; A18.
118. Cara Anna, "China allows bloggers, others to spread quake news," AP News, May 18, 2008.
119. World Public Opinion, "International Public Opinion Says Government Should Not Limit Internet Access," April 30, 2008, http://www.worldpublicopinion.org/pipa/articles/home_page/477.php?lb=hmpg1&pnt=477&nid=&id.
120. World Public Opinion, "International Public Opinion Says Government Should Not Limit Internet Access," April 30, 2008, http://www.worldpublicopinion.org/pipa/articles/home_page/477.php?lb=hmpg1&pnt=477&nid=&id.
121. Telephone interview with four Chinese reporters, May 13, 14, and 17.
122. *WSJ*, "Chinese children in Ethnic costume come from Han majority," August 14, 2008.
123. Rebecca Blumenstein and Mei Fong, "Big Sponsors Are Upset Over Visibility at Olympics," *Wall Street Journal*, August 13, 2008.
124. http://blog.sina.com.cn/s/blog_55c219d10100a9fg.htm.
125. http://blog.sina.com.cn/s/blog_5101a6250100a7cb.html.
126. https://www.cmule.com/redirect.php?tid=157754&goto=lastpost.
127. Yang Binbin, "A 'Double-pipe' Show about Two Girls," http://mxxom.spaces.live.com/blog/cns!C47E2EBC41761FD5!287.entry.
Translated by *China Digital Times*, http://chinadigitaltimes.net/2008/08/another-

olympic-secret-who-was-actually-singing-as-the-national-flag-entered-the-stadium/.

128. http://blogtd.org/2008/08/13/gjly/.

129. There are three.

130. Political campaigns such as the Great Leap Forward, Cultural Revolution, or a host of lesser known annual exercises in mobilization such as "anti-pornography campaigns" and "strike hard."

131. This does not imply that government is not still trying as in the case of Yahoo in China. See "Obeying Orders," *Washington Post*, September 9, 2005, http://www.washingtonpost.com/wpdyn/content/article/2005/09/17/AR2005091701135.html.

132. Howard W. French, "A warning on 'fakes' that doesn't add up," *IHT* Friday, November 16, 2007, p.

133. Zha Jianying, *China Pop.: How Soap Operas, Tabloids and Bestsellers Are Transforming a Culture,* (New Press, 1996).

134. Stephanie Hemelryk Donald, et al., *Media in China*, (Routledge Curzon, 2002).

135. See more on Chinese prosecution of journalists in Reporters without Borders, http://www.rsf.org/article.php3?id_article=17349.

136. Stephanie Hemelryk Donald, et al., *Media in China*, (Routledge Curzon, 2002).

137. Stephanie Hemelryk Donald, et al., *Media in China*, (Routledge Curzon, 2002).

138. Howard W. French, "Letter from China: Big Brother is playing a game he can't win," *International Herald Tribune*, January 12, 2006.

6

Sexual Revolution in China

Chinese people are experiencing a sexual revolution. Sex issues such as one night stands, extramarital affairs, prostitution, cohabitation, contraception and abortion have already become part of Chinese people's life.[1]
—Li Yinhe, China's first female sociologist, Keynote address to the 2005 Guangzhou Annual Sex Festival

The power which resides in [every individual man] is new in nature, and none but he knows what that is which he can do, nor does he know until he has tried.
— Ralph Waldo Emerson, The Essential Writings

This chapter examines how the discourse on sexual relations helps to establish and maintain the relatively liberal social environment in urban contemporary China. What roles did globalized images of sexual relations play in undermining Chinese Communism's puritanical domination of society? What is the relationship between a market economy and the emergence of gay identity in China? What is the role of global trade and media, cultural exchange, and global consumerism in the rise of cultural tolerance? What role has the global identity played in reducing both state control over personal life and the state-imposed nationalism in China? This chapter discusses how sexual revolution in China contributes to the construction of an ideology of modernity that undermines party ideology. By deconstructing seemingly monolithic anti-globalization discourses on gender analysis, this chapter details the complex linkage between global and local issues, portraying marginal groups (women and gays) as agents producing, modifying, and challenging the globalization discourse on citizenship and social change. This chapter addresses question of gender, sexuality, consumerism, global linkages, and the shift in tides of recent years.

In order to give a human face to China's social transformation, we show how many Chinese, especially the youth, make the best use of consumer society, modern technology, and global linkages to express individual identities that are independent of the party-state. At the same time, young people, better educated than their parents and earning much higher salaries, are rejecting the traditional path to marriage—and, in the case of women, motherhood—preferring to spend their money on luxury goods and travel. Some of these elements of urban China's new "decadence" have depoliticized Chinese society and sown seeds of individual liberty. Through this sexual revolution, we can see two kinds of changes occurring; one is a change from command to market economy, the other from agriculturally-based to industrialized society. We argue that there has risen in China a "creative decadence," or hedonism, which has in turn become a defining element of China's growing cosmopolitanism. This development has made the Communist state's ideology irrelevant in daily lives as most Chinese live a life that is neither puritanical nor Communist.

Market development in housing, non-state jobs, global media and information, and international trade provides the material foundation for this new cosmopolitanism with its cultural diversity, tolerance, openness, and (limited) freedom of expression. We can say without hesitation that without elements of capitalism, there will be no progress for individual liberty. Adam Smith's description of a free market system as a "system of natural liberty" is verified by the rise of personal liberty in China. The sexual revolution illustrates the Chinese people's natural desire for liberty. They have achieved their liberties through energy and perseverance, despite the state's continuing authoritarianism.

Background for Change

These rapid changes constitute a radical departure from the past. We must understand the past to appreciate how truly revolutionary these changes are. For almost forty years, the Chinese state attempted to regulate everything, including sexual desire. A well-known Chinese journalist, Gao Hua, argues, "The party's purpose was to build a pure society with new order and structure."[2] Controlling sexual desires was another purgative mechanism enabling the state to control the whole society.

For the most part, throughout the PRC's history, constrained heterosexual relationships became the state code for acceptable sexual identities. Forbidden sexual acts were labeled *liuman xinwei* (hooligan acts) while French kissing, extramarital affairs, premarital sexual acts, flirting, and masturbation were petty bourgeois acts, symbols of selfishness. Homosexual acts were considered worse than these that were considered "hooligan," while homosexual men labeled as "*jijian fan*" (rooster rapists) were sent to labor camps for three years hard labor if caught by the police. Police were sent to check in the public parks to watch out for "unhealthy, abnormal, and illegal sexual activities." Homosexuals suffered from both formal and informal discrimination (family and friends), and most were forced into loveless marriages.

Under the PRC, sexual life was discouraged and controlled. In practice, it was up to the party, operating through the work unit (*danwei*), to approve marriage, assign housing, and other welfare provisions to everyone. Extramarital affairs were a serious offense, while homosexual acts in public were a criminal offence.

Through civil marriage registration and other control mechanisms (*hukou, danan*, mass campaign, and police), marriage and lovemaking were state affairs.[3] Whenever leaders were punished, their sexual immorality was often publicized. In China, sex was the capital crime of all crimes, (in Chinese terms, 万恶淫 为首) or *zuiwo houshou* "罪魁祸首." Sexual desire was suppressed by the government. The party's puritanism demanded that everyone, including government officials, suppress sexual desire and resist sexual temptation. During the Cultural Revolution period (1966 to 1976), Chinese movies, art, and printed matter excluded any mention of sexuality.

Fang Zheng (not his real name), a student in Beijing Geology College, fell in love with a classmate from a landlord family background. To punish himself for having sexual fantasies about this beautiful woman, he married an educated rural woman from a poor family.[4] Another male government official, Du Mao (not his real name), recalled that in 1970, "as a married man and a party leader in the government, I felt anguish that I was constantly attracted to women younger than my wife. I felt very ashamed of myself and deliberately injured my *jingjing* [penis] every time a forbidden thought came to mind. I even wanted to castrate myself. In Mao's era, 'sex' was a forbidden word."[5] But today's China has changed.

Private Enterprises, Politics of Hedonism and Homosexual Emergence

In the past thirty years, the rapid development of non-state economic entities (private, "collective," and global), aided by the death of the Communist ideology of a great utopian future where all would be equal to enjoy the abundance of material and spiritual goods provides an economic foundation for personal space. Chinese people have become materialistic with a vengeance. This "decadent" secular materialism creates a social trend and meta-social value dominating not only the souls but also the bodies of most Chinese people. This cosmopolitan community has evolved despite the Communist one-party state. This chapter focuses on the challenge this cosmopolitanism poses to China's one party domination and the traditional values that have choked personal liberty for those who embrace it.

We will inquire how it is that the Chinese today have increasingly come to accept homosexuals, although social norms still make it difficult for gays to come out of the closet. According to a report by the Ministry of Health, between 2 and 4 percent of Chinese men are homosexually active, making the Chinese gay male population reaching either 5 million or 10 million.[6] But a 2004 government released survey put the number to 5 million, but gay people report double the official data.[7] Although this percentage is small, it affects many people, gay and non-gay alike, because it is linked to other aspects of personal liberty that contemporary Chinese are trying to expand, despite attempted control by the party-state.

To a great extent, limited but growing sexual liberties, and homosexuality in particular, have reemerged in China as a result of private sector housing development, the Internet, global trade and travel, the information revolution, and commercial markets. Thus, there is a direct link between sexual freedom and commercialized leisure businesses. As Communist ideology has lost its hold on people, many Chinese are trying hard to make up for a generation of opportunities lost under Maoist imposition of puritanism. To a great extent, hedonistic consumption negates the Chinese puritanical state, "To hell with the future of Communism," they seem to say. The new trend is to enjoy one's life to the fullest. To some extent, the hedonistic consumers help the Chinese to reconstruct themselves as autonomous individuals, as yesteryear's "blue ants" who wore Mao style blue color clothes and followed every whim of the state's dictation. In this way, China is following a pattern not unlike eighteenth-century Britain.[8]

The rise of individuals as rulers of themselves, not only as subjects of the state, is directly linked with the rise of a consumer society. Sexual freedom is expressed in clothing styles. The days when Chinese people dressed in baggy, unisex, and uncolored Mao suits, or were submerged in a sea of "blue ant" clothing, are gone. Gone also are the days when Chinese teenage girls bound their breasts with thick clothing for fearing of exposing sexual differences. Today's China has become the world's largest producer and consumer of lingerie. Many women spend thousands of Yuan to enlarge their breasts and alter their eyelids to appear more "Western."

The rise of private restaurants and private housing provided the material conditions for the possibility of a distinct and independent gay existence in China. On the busily thoroughfares of the new Chinese conurbations (Shanghai, Beijing, Shenzhen, Guangzhou, Tienjin, and Wuhan), on university campuses, in the new development centers where gay couples have settled, and in hundreds of gay websites, gay Chinese have become more visible. In order to survive fierce competition, business people have catered to the needs of this untapped market. This is especially true for most service industries in major cities like public baths (*yu chi*), high-end department stores, night bars, restaurants, and condominiums. Today, it is quite common for homosexual couples to spend time in gourmet shops, bars, groceries, café houses, and public baths. Both the police and ordinary people pay little heed. The gradual social acceptance of urban gays has reduced social stigmatization although social discrimination still exists.

A private gay bar provides an environment with colored lights and modern furniture for gay to meet, to chat, and to feel relaxed. The most well-known gay bar districts are the bar Sanlitun District and Houhai bar zone with "its atmosphere, a mix of chic and cozy, contemporary and edgy, its customers a fairly even mix of foreigners and Chinese."[9]

In the night bar districts of Shanghai (the Karaoke Bar District) and Beijing (San Lidun and Huohai districts), it is quite common to find two men or two women gazing at each other while onlookers are amused, indifferent, or offended. As one Western correspondent reported:

> From a plush Arabian-style restaurant with hookahs and divans in the centre of the city to discreet club-style bars in the backstreets of the old French quarter, from corners of certain parks to bathhouses, venues for gay encounters are quite openly advertised and tolerated.[10]

In Shanghai's Karaoke Bar District, one can meet a dozen gay men, most of them professionals, hanging around looking for partners. It is very common to see gay hosts in tight jeans and singlet-tops chat with customers in a gay bar. "It is cool to find a lover in the KM bar," remarked Jun Jun, a salesman of cell phones in Shanghai. "It was terrible in my hometown [a small city in Hubei] that we had to 'date' in the very dirty public bathroom. I love professional men from Shanghai because they are gentle and feminine."[11] Most professionals in Shanghai either rent a nice apartment or own one. It is also common for partners to take their chosen partners to spend night at their own apartments. When asked why the local police would not bother the gays, Huan Huan (not his formal name but a nickname among friends), a gay man in Shanghai replied, "They have better things to do than capturing lovers. Thieves, criminals, and other bad people cause social problems for Shanghai people. We harm no one. They mostly leave us alone."[12]

The spread of private ownership of bars and other service businesses provides social space for gay people. In Shenzhen, gays often go to Jiqing Jiuba (Exciting Bar), to socialize. Even in the hinterland, in cities like Wuhan, gay bars have appeared. Meet for example, Wei Wei (not his real name), a gay owner of a bar[13]: "My little place is to provide a communication space for comrades.... In Wuhan and neighboring cities, although there are a few places for gays to meet, they are hidden from the public with the usual shame and embarrassment attached. I do not think this is good. This is why I set up the bar to declare ourselves as 'comrades.'"[14]

Interviewing other gay bar owners in Beijing and Shanghai, we found that gay bars have costs beyond those of traditional bars. In addition to a high tax for private businesses, most private service businesses, including gay bars, must pay "*renqing fei*" (human feelings debt or bribes to government officials). Ordinary businesses often pay a smaller proportion of revenue in formal taxes than they do for bribery. But some gay bar owners, fearing punishment, often pay a higher percentage of taxes to avoid government accusations that might close them down. "Government officials change every four years," remarked one gay bar owner in Beijing. "With each newcomer, a new set of extortion games develops. Thus I have decided to forego a lot of profits to stay clean in term of taxes. Boy, it really hurts our bottom line."[15]

With lesbians drinking hard liquor, smoking, and dancing, many heterosexual girls (almost all from one-child families) envy this kind of rebellious lifestyle.[16] Thus, among the teenagers and college-age girls, to be "la la" (lesbian) is very cool—as fashionable as new gadgets. As June, an openly lesbian woman in Chongchi told a reporter: "Love between female students has become fashionable. What girl could reject a fashion? Without sex, 'la la' is not real. Sometimes, we have group sex with our closest friends."[17]

In 2007, Shanghai's Wenhui Bao released a survey of female students from universities around Shanghai, 31.5 percent identified themselves as part male and part female in temperament. Compared to a similar study of women born in the seventies that was conducted in 1998, about twice as many of the eighties generation were designated androgynous.[18]

Sometimes, to drum up business, bar owners will call or send text messages to gays to inform them of an ongoing party. Although some non-gay bar owners still feel somewhat uneasy about owning a gay bar, concern for their bottom line and close relationships has made them friends and strong supporters of gay Chinese. One Chongqi gay bar owner, a heterosexual man, was amazed by the large group of lesbians in his bar: "'La La' is playing like mad but free. Whenever they meet a 'la la' they like, they would invite them to drink and then start an intimate chat on the sofa. At first, I thought they were just good friends but later realized that they were "la la." I still feel a bit uneasy... How could so many teenagers become lesbians? They must be just having fun and not serious."[19] Young urbanites are setting trends in both fashion and socially correct behavior that would previously been frowned upon. For example, to play "hooky" from school is now considered "cool," as is sex before marriage. Being gay is also considered "cool," and the traditional ideas of marriage and children are considered much less desirable. These new ideas becoming popular among youth appear to spell an end to puritanical Communist ideology. Of course, those young people change their ideas as frequently as they change their fashion trends. But one thing is clear: the Communist ideology is dead in China. China has become a nation drowning the dream of money, as a popular saying goes, "Out of 1.3 billion Chinese, one billion are entrepreneurs." This passion absorbs the remaining leisure time at *majiang* tables, a national obsession with gambling. Leisure time is a new thing in China: previously the state occupied most of people's time, day and night.

Western images of consumerism have stimulated Chinese teens to emulate their Western counterparts in style, attitude, and manners. In a globalized world, modern products and name brands are found in diverse cultures, leading to a modern hedonism that weakens previously strong strains of traditional values and nationalist feelings. "Anti-imperialism and anti-Western nationalism disappeared and were replaced by Chinese pride."[20] Nationalism still exists in China as witnessed by the anti-Japanese demonstration in 2004 and anti-American demonstrations following the 1999 US bombing of the Chinese Embassy in Belgrade, the 2001 EP-3 collision incident, and the nationalist furor over Tibet's protest against Chinese rule in March 2008.

Another sign of what has been termed China's "moral decadence" is the increase in use of drugs. Like American youth, Chinese youth have increasingly begun to experiment with drugs of all kinds, including cocaine and opium, and the current drug of choice—ecstasy. A desire to improve one's sex life is one of the most important reasons for young Chinese to experiment with drugs. Some bars provide drug-laced drinks. In *baofang* (private rooms), one can take drugs and perform erotic acts among close friends, while the beautifully dressed waitresses constantly replenishing drinks and snacks. Urban Chinese enter into the stage of hedonism simultaneously with growing cosmopolitanism. The government is still trying to affect the daily lives of people. But today many Chinese, especially those with money, can live a life that gratifies most of their material desires. Compared with the West, China still lacks gay-oriented businesses despite the rapid growth.

The Private Housing Boom and the Rise of Privacy

Both Chinese men and women, and especially young urbanites, are enjoying relative sexual freedom, experimenting, and discovering themselves. Of course, the cosmopolitan lifestyle consists of more than eating, drinking, and social enjoyment. Another important commercial development directly contributes to more respect for privacy: the rise of private housing. Cities cater to the people's desire to have more private housing ownership. Earlier we discussed how the farmers in proximity to cities rent rooms to migrant workers and rural entrepreneurs.[21] Farmers in major urban suburbs have also built shant towns and matchbox buildings to provide low-rent housing for newcomers. For example, in Shenzhen, towns like Shanzui, Shuiwei, and Shangsha provide cheap housing for those with no Shenzhen *hukou* (urban household registration) or for those wishing to keep their identities secret. This private provision of cheap housing is crucial for rural women trying to escape the state's coercive one-child family policy, forced abortions, and forced sterilization. A 1999 interview with a Mr. Dongxia Wang from rural Hunan in Shenzhen revealed that she was living with five other mothers who fled to new shantytowns: "All six of us came from rural Hunan because we could not afford the heavy fine for violating the family planning policy. We had no money and had to squeeze in these two rooms for ten adults and ten kids. Our landlady is a kind grandmother and shows sympathy. We take turns working and taking care of our children. We learned about

Shangsha back home because four other women informed us that we could be safe here."[22] Shangsha, Shanzui, and Shuiwei have become so popular among rural women that people refer to them as battlegrounds for *Chaosheng Youjidui* (Extra-Quota Birth Guerrillas).[23] Without the private provision of housing, these women could not have survived in Shenzhen, where the rent is normally very high. This concern for privacy has begun a new housing culture. Even some private companies have begun protecting married couples' privacy rights by providing housing. For example, our interview in 2004 found that an increasing number of private businesses in Jiangsu and Zhejiang have recently been providing "*fuqi fang*" (couples apartments) for migrant workers. For many years, both the government and private businesses paid no attention to the migrant workers, as if they were subhuman, disposable tools. Due to labor shortage, as well as migrant workers' frequent practice of voting with their feet against living conditions, private businesses began catering to the privacy needs of such workers. Workers welcomed such initiatives. One Jiangxi migrant worker remarked: "My wife and I both worked in this factory for five years. But the factory only provided unisex dorms for migrant workers. We had to arrange our meeting once a week through our roommates, very inconvenient. One summer night, I missed my wife so much that I climbed [to the third floor] through the window to her dorm at night. When we made love, the bed shook so much that all her roommates [five other women] woke up. My wife was so embarrassed and asked me not to do such a thing again. So we had to use the mosquito net and only touched each other [without having intercourse]. It was so frustrating. Now we have our own small place, a sweet little home."[24]

Local private business people will not say they are facing a labor shortage. Their concern is more for their businesses than for migrant workers, but nevertheless, the result benefited the migrants. Like any other kind of non-governmental development and social change, the local people tried to tie this with the government discourse of "*hexie shehui*" (harmonious society) proposed by Hu Jingtao, the new Party boss in Beijing.

Private Space and Gay Life

Before 1980, gay people were one of the groups most discriminated against in state housing assignments. In the 1990s, the real-estate boom helped to liberate gay people because, for the first time, gays could live a life apart from their families and from the watchful eyes of the workplace (*danwei*). The rise of consumer culture and private housing created a relatively safer environment for gay people in China, compared to thirty years earlier when the Chinese urban economy was mostly state planned and controlled. With the rise of private sector development, especially in service sectors, Chinese have increasingly begun to accept alternative lifestyles in such rapidly growing cosmopolitan cities as Shanghai, Shenzhen, Beijing, Tianjin, and Guangzhou. What is more, the private housing market has made it possible for gay men and women to live together openly and legally.

For many gays, living in state-controlled housing arrangements meant that they had either to get married like heterosexuals or be forever consigned to single dorms (crowded with six to eight people). It was quite normal for a small group of single men and women to be assigned to poor, overcrowded housing dorms or to live with parents who controlled their sexual behavior. For many gay people, under pressure from parents and from scarcity of housing, the only choice was entering unhappy marriages. "My mother forced me into a loveless marriage when I turned 30, in 1981. She threatened to throw me out of her apartment if I remained single," recalled Wang Sheng, an art teacher in Wuhan. "As the only son in the family, I felt the pressure to produce a child for the family. My *danwei* (work unit) would not assign an apartment for an unmarried man like me. I married my wife and had a little girl. After the birth of my daughter, I never touched my wife. I felt sorry for my wife. We were *tongchuan yimeng* (sleeping in the same bed but having different dreams). I felt very guilty when I secretly dated my friend in the park and in the office at night."[25]

For many gay people, private housing is the first step in gaining privacy and choice in sexual partners. "My biggest happiness came in 1998, when my partner and I got a small two bedroom apartment," remarked Wei Wei, a lesbian in Wuhan.[26] Qing Qing, a gay man in Beijing, also stressed the importance of private housing in his life: "In the past, we had to arrange our meetings once a week either in our parents' homes or in a hotel. We had to live a double life, which was very painful. It is so great to have a home we can call our own. Our new apartment is far away from my workplace. I used to live in the apartment assigned by my work unit (*danwei*). Every time, my partner came for a visit, my neighbor became very curious. Many evenings, someone from the neighborhood committee even tried to get into my home to check us out. Now we do not know our neighbors. Sometimes in the summer, we go about naked in our home. We feel very safe there."[27]

The changing attitude towards gay people is a microcosm of what is happening across China. The Chinese case shows that there is a linkage between private enterprise (private housing markets and commerce) and the advent of gay life—if there was no private space, there would be little or no gay life.[28]

The Entertainment Industry, Gay Presence, and Cultural Renaissance

For many years, the state dominated Chinese culture. For more than a decade, 1965 to 1976, Chinese people were allowed to witness only eight specific modern dramas. But the rise of consumer society also includes cultural consumption. Today, China is experiencing a cultural renaissance despite the Communist state's attempt to control it. Global capitalism plays a key role in establishing cultural commodity markets. Just like other countries, the corresponding incentive structures of market mechanisms in China (*xiang qian kai*, or looking forward for money) are linked to artistic innovation and cultural vitality. But in China, cultural consumption has another powerful consequence: undermining the Communist state and the traditional culture. For example, rock and punk music has provided formally marginalized groups (women, minority, and gay people) an opportunity "to achieve a new public voice that is often independent of the state."[29]

The rise of the entertainment industry and the social obsession with celebrities has also played a role in the gradual social acceptance of gay people. Among two dozen urban, middle-class persons interviewed about their first acceptance of a gay life style, five identified a TV drama called "Tang Dai Gong Mi," (The Love Legends of Dang Dynasty). Li, the son of the emperor, has died of a broken heart after being forced to marry a woman, and Li's lover, a servant, has asked Li's parents' permission to die as well. "I was very touched by this moving cry of the servant," explains Mr. Lei Tao, a businessman in Shenzhen. "There is little true love in this world. I am moved by this gay couple's true love. No one should be so heartless as to destroy true love."[30]

To some extent, most people gain knowledge about gay life styles from high profile movie and sports stars. Icons such as Michael Jackson, Elton John, and various professional soccer players have created a new trend in China, especially among college students. To be gay has become "cool." The death of the Hong Kong gay movie star, Leslie Cheung (Zhang Guorong in Chinese), won the sympathy of Chinese people for gays. Leslie Cheung was openly gay and played flamboyantly gay characters. He starred in the 1993 Oscar-nominated film *Farewell My Concubine*, one of the first few PRC films to address themes of homosexuality. Cheung liked to challenge audiences' perceptions of sexual norms. During his 1999 Passion Tour, Cheung grew his hair to waist length and performed in eight outfits designed by Jean-Paul Gaultier, including a skirt and high heels. It was about this time that Cheung become more open regarding his sexual orientation, acknowledging his twelve-year relationship with banker Daffy Tong Hok-Tak in concert and at awards shows.[31] With superior acting in many good dramas dealing with gay people, Cheung won the hearts of many fans that might otherwise hardly be tolerant of homosexuality. "Zhang was my favorite movie star even though he was a gay man," remarked Liu Chuner, a businesswoman in Wuhan. "I was very shocked to know that he committed suicide because he was afraid that people might know that he was gay and had AIDS. I blamed Chinese traditional culture for killing him."[32]

There is a social tendency to identify most unmarried movie stars as "gay-suspects," further reducing the social stigma of being gay among urban, middle-class Chinese. In China, many gay rumors about the sexuality of American movie stars like Jodie Foster and Tom Cruise have deepened the social tolerance for gay people because gay identity is linked to the global fame cachet.

The news that Fennie Yuan, a Hong Kong female movie star, is a lesbian has increased her popularity among college girls. According to Pan Ling, an investigate reporter for a Chinese online news, one college student told her that, like Fennie Yuan, she was also "La La," because she regarded her lesbian tomboy lover as "clean, gentler, and handsome."[33] Another high-profile artist was pop singer Mao Ning, whose songs, "The Wave Still as Past" (*Tao Sheng Yi Jiu*), "Annie in Heart," and "Wait for You in Familiar Places" became popular in mid-1990s. His lyrics speak of love, life, and friendship with no political overtones. The young Mao Ning became a household name among Chinese youth, even better known than the old Mao—Chairman Mao. In 2002, Mao Ning was attacked by a male sex worker exposing his sexual preference. The scandal broke many young girls' hearts but not the homosexual act itself.

Chinese filmmakers add to the social tolerance of homosexuals in China by producing a number of films portraying male homosexuality. Prominent examples are the cross-dressing opera queen in *Farewell My Concubine*, the dilemma of a gay policeman whose job is to interrogate gay men in *Donggong, Xigong* (East Palace and West Palace), a millionaire's pursuit for a young boy in *Lanyu*, the queer oeuvre of *Tsai Ming-liang*, and *Mr. Butterfly*. *Jingnian Xietian* (This Summer) is a true love story between two women, one of few lesbian films played by lesbian actors. These films have introduced the Chinese public to representations of marginalized sexualities.[34] What is unique about these avant-garde films is that most are made through unofficial channels. The new "Sixth Generation" of Chinese filmmakers has become a loose network of independent producers. One of the PRC films on this topic was *Donggong, Xigong* (East Palace and West Palace) directed by Zhang Yuan, the avant-garde director in China. The movie educated Chinese viewers about gay peoples' sad lives.

Because of the wide spread of movie piracy, Chinese can watch the latest Hollywood movies sooner even than audiences in Los Angeles. Piracy and Internet have also helped to create a network for the pornography industry in China. Pornography has become widespread, despite being illegal. It has become another phenomenon of public defiance of the government. With so many consumers of pornography, it is impossible for the government to uniformly arrest and prosecute the offenders (in Chinese, it is called *fa bu zi zong*, 法不责众) although the government occasionally convicts one or two cases to set an example (killing the rooster to scare the monkeys). For example, in the fall of 2006, the Chinese government gave a long-term sentence to a pornography producer.

The New Sex Culture and the Awareness of Individual Personal Rights

One of the most important indicators of personal liberty is sexual liberty. The pursuit of sexual liberty is directly linked to the pursuit of individual rights, the most important of which is the right to privacy.

For many Chinese people, the problem of masturbation is directly linked to the notion of privacy. Although privacy is a natural human desire, physical conditions often constrain it. In rural China, where most people live with many family members in close quarters and among animals (roosters, hens, pigs, water-buffaloes, dogs, and ducks), masturbation for men is socially discouraged and physically difficult. Since traditional Chinese sexual culture precludes satisfaction of women's sex desires, for many years masturbation referred strictly to male behavior. The rise of private housing, the increase of living space, urbanization, and the "One-Child" policy have made it physically possible for both men and women to have the privacy required for masturbation. Although social culture norms and the state still discourage it, the practice is increasing.[35]

Although rich men and women can find the means to gratify their sexual desires, lower income Chinese, especially migrant workers, are more sexually spontaneous, as expressed by a popular song, "*Ge zhi ganjie zou*," (Following Your Feeling).[36] The new sexual culture is linked to the most basic rights that most Chinese people desire. For example, should ordinary people form their own groups either for sex or for other purposes? Should the police have the power to enter ordinary people's homes without a warrant to catch prostitutes, pornography viewers, enemies of the state, or religious worshipers? The author witnessed random police raids in 1967 and I 1968 in Wuhan city. Most nights, local police, the neighborhood committee leaders, and militia organized a *hukou* inspection team to go to specifically targeted families.[37] Often the capture of "sexual offenders" (pre-marital sex, extramarital affairs, male homosexual acts, and pedophiles) would signify successful raids. These random acts of state violence against people not only silenced political dissent but also nontraditional sexual behavior, and even sex itself. Chinese people were sexually oppressed. The brother of the author was detained in 1968 when he made his girlfriend of five years pregnant without marriage:

> I wanted to marry her but was not allowed because I was just 20 years old and she was 21 (although according to Chinese marriage law at that time, it was legal for a 20 year old to get married). We tried to hide from people until she was seven months along. She wanted to keep the baby but the government and the whole society, including her family, would not allow this illegal child to be born. But no hospital would take her in without a marriage certificate or a government letter of permission. Finally, her family turned us in. I was captured and she was taken to the hospital to have an abortion. She never recovered from this terrible experience. We were not allowed to see each other since.[38]

Sex Toys, Pornography, and the Right to Buy Happiness

Linking with other rights, the sexual revolution also reveals China's lack of legal protection for the right to purchase products that will not harm anyone, but may still be "immoral." The rise of the sex toy industry confronts this issue. Like many other grassroots reform initiatives, sex toy use challenges state regulations by flooding society with many sought-after goods. With so many users and producers of sex toys, the state lacks the personnel to confront the problem. At the same time, in private, officials also enjoy using them. The failure to prevent the use of sex toys shows how the commodity society has drowned the state. One reporter describes the popularity of sex toys in China this way: "What's the fastest-growing industry in China? Mobile phones? Computer components? Toys? The last wouldn't be too far off, but not in the sense that the word toy is conventionally understood. Call them playthings."[39]

Although money drives the sex toy industry, at the heart of the issues of sex toys, pornography, and other sex-related services is the question of whether or not Chinese should be allowed to buy these "sin products" for their private use. The official answer is no. But the demand is high for Chinese deprived of sexual satisfaction. Chinese began to consume sex-related products and services with enormous gusto. As some Chinese explain, "Chinese hunger for sex and food is like that of newly released prisoners."[40] The result is that unofficial China has triumphed over edicts. In 2005, more than 50,000 people rushed to Guangzhou to attend the "Third Annual Sex Culture Festival" to procure the "very latest in adult toys—70% of which are now manufactured in China. One of the most popular [is] the 'erotic butterfly,' specially designed for women."[41] The fact that women have become major consumers of sex toys shows that women have become more assertive of their sexual needs, sweeping away traditional taboos.

Linked with the sex toy industry is the rise of pornography of all kinds. Viewers of pornography DVDs (called *xiao dianying*) have become a favorite part of foreplay for many married couples and a favorite activity for many young single men. As Ms. Qian Guoqian, a manager in a windmill factory in Wuhan city said: "After 30 years of marriage, my husband and I lost sexual interest in each other. In 1995, a friend lent us some DVDs to watch. Now we cannot live without it. After all, we are partially animals. I am very grateful because it is good for our health and our relationship."[42]

In some cases, pornography can be a form of adult sex education. Accounts from medical practitioners of couples married for many years who, due to their sexual ignorance, never engaged in sexual intercourse. For example, in Wuhan, a couple sought medical help when, after several years of marriage, the wife had failed to become pregnant. Asked how often they had sex, the wife replied, "everyday." Upon examination, however, the doctor discovered that the woman was still a virgin and that the couple was simply unaware of the mechanics of intercourse.[43] In such cases, pornography provides basic sex education.

The rise of the pornography industry and the sex toy industry shows that in order for many changes to occur in China, there are several important variables: (1) Social demand or social need; (2) commercial value to be used by corrupt officials for personal gain; (3) global capital and manufacturing, leading to knowledge and technology; and (4) official tacit acceptance of the government.

Women's Liberation, Divorce, and Sexual Liberty

The rise of individual rights among women is another reason for the sexual revolution in China. To some extent, women are the revolutionary pioneers. It is young women who display affection (sometimes in public), wear sexy clothes, demand foreplay (including kissing) before sex, and define love as romance.[44] From promiscuous girls to *kuaidapang* (on the arm of tycoons), young Chinese women have transformed both traditional sex and sexual relationships under Communism.[45] Love and romance have been tainted with money (*jinqian*), sexual satisfaction (*chuanshang gongfu*), and material conditions (*wuzhi tiaojian*).[46] Interviews with a dozen such *kuaidapang* reveal the structured, business-like arrangements in dating and sexual relationships that have emerged in recent years in Beijing, Shanghai, Guangzhou, and Wuhan. A "pre-dating" agreement is often signed between a *kuaidapan* and a rich man, clearly specifying compensation. "This agreement is good for both of us because it avoids future legal battles if things turn sour," explained Tian Tian, a young woman in her late twenties with a graduate degree. "My boyfriend also needs such protection."[47] Detailed another young woman in her mid-twenties in Shanghai: "The *guanxi hetong* (relationship contract) was simple. If *Lao Xiao* (male partner) wants to end the relationship, the compensation package will be ten thousand yuan (approximately $1266 at the time) for the first year, with each additional year adding an additional ten thousand yuan. If we stay together for five years, the luxury condo belongs to me. If I want to end the relationship, I will get nothing from him."[48] Some tycoons even post pre-dating contracts on the Internet to attract potential female companions.

For many years, women were expected to suppress their sexual desires. Now, however, women increasingly express these desires. With the easy availability of birth control and abortion, sexual puritanism declined, and "more and more men and women in China these days are having sex before marriage, creating a new youth sex culture based on romance, leisure, and free choice."[49] Women who are virgins when they marry have become a minority. According to one report, in the 1990s, 86 percent of Chinese had premarital sex (before 2000, the government forced marriage applicants to have physical examinations).[50] The number will be even higher today as Chinese have increasingly adopted "'liberal' or 'worldly' views of passionate love, sexual desire, marriage for love (rather than arranged marriages), romantic and sexual diversity."[51] As women become more interested in their feelings and emotions, rather than personal honor and familial reputation, virginity as a value has diminished. Material condition is still important in dating and mate selection, but women now tend to place more emphasis on the personal characteristics of potential mates than on their family background. Although the Chinese saying *"men tang hu tui,"* the two families (joined in marriage) are to possess the same social status, still bears some weight, both men and women are increasingly more concerned with compatibility. Romantic love and loveless sex have become commonplace in China.

Li Li (pen name is Mu Zimei), "China's Madonna" and editor of one of the country's fashionable new magazines, has become the embodiment of carefree individualism in China. Posting a detailed account of sexual acts with fifty-two men on the Internet, her site is one of the most frequently visited sites in the country. She also published a book, *Old Love Letters*, a detailed diary of her lovemaking with fifty-two men in one year.[52] At the age of twenty-six, Mu Zimei has become "a new Chinese woman," whose goal is to revoke traditions including the Communist traditions. Mu Zimei, a graduate from Zhongshang University, represents daring new Chinese women—or as she puts it, "Lady now and China now," living for the moment. More than 50,000 people simultaneously tried to download the 25-minute podcast, crashing the host server. Despite government attempts to censor it, the sex diary became so popular that Mu Zimei is the most searched keyword on China's top search engine. "I express my freedom through sex," says Li unapologetically. "It's my life, and I can do what I want."[53]

Internet technology (podcasts, online chats, instant messages, cell phones, and digital cameras) certainly helps to spread her message, especially among youth. A group of young, female sex-fiction writers have used the traditional printing media to popularize the sexual revolution in China. By celebrating the hedonism of modern Chinese urban cities, such writers helped to destroy Chinese Communist moralist political culture. Urban women have become not only comfortable discussing taboo topics like sex, but also dare to imagine the unthinkable, a great leap forward from the days when many Chinese dared not to dream under Mao. When Ms. Wei Hui (Way Hway), a twenty-five-year-old Shanghainese woman published her first novel, *Shanghai Baby* (a work of sexual fantasies) through unofficial channels, it became a sensation and a national bestseller. With such demand, she began writing more in earnest. Such demand for such work stimulated others to write in a similar genre, such as *Beijing Baby, Guangzhou Baby*, and *Shenzhen Baby*. The state was alarmed and worked hard to ban these books, which only further boosted sales. Some Chinese wonder if Ms. Wei Hui had political connections (who cooperated by banning the book).

Since sexual fantasies express the suppressed longing of Chinese people, these writers in fact speak out on behalf of the amoral hedonistic Chinese national soul. With limited liberty, love, touching, and kissing are routine behaviors of the young. Sometimes, the lovers will go to stay at a lover's hotel. "I watched a movie where the man and woman kiss so passionate before they make love," recalled Ding Ding, a middle school teacher in Beijing. "I demanded my husband to do the same but he pushed me away saying that 'only with xiaojie (prostitutes)' want to do that. I felt hurt and refused to make love to him. I started having this great love affair with a friend. It is his fault that I betrayed him."[54]

This new sex genre plants destructive seeds in the Communist puritanical culture. Thus, we can call these sexual revolutionaries "cultural destroyers." Schumpeter characterized capitalism with the famous phrase "creative destruction," a process when the old ways of doing things are endogenously destroyed and replaced by the new. This new Chinese sex genre, trash by any literary standard, nevertheless serves a positive function in illustrating Schumpeter's concept of capitalism's "creative destruction": it destroys Communist political culture and replaces it with narcissism. This process might be described as the democratization of narcissism, since under Mao Communist political culture was largely the narcissistic expression of one person, while the new culture accommodates the narcissism of millions.[55]

Although the "cultural destroyers" are concentrated in the cities, rural villages are catching up. Erotic dancers and other sex-related entertainment have also invaded Chinese villages. With DVDs and pornography often readily available, watching pornography has become a pastime in many rural towns and villages. With local officials skimming the profits and enjoying the shows, the local police only make inspection when officers lose at their *majiang* and cards tables, to make up for the loss.[56]

With so many women and men challenging the state it creates problems for the Communist regime. With several thousand Internet police, the regime still does not have enough personnel to control sex offenders (although it does arrest pornography producers and in 2006 even sentenced one producer to life in prison). Since pornography carries so many Chinese characters, and many party politically correct words have also been appropriated in sex talks, the Internet police would have to eliminate most Chinese words in order to ban the pornography sites altogether. For example, the word *tongzhi* (comrades), which is used for greetings among party members, now also refers to gay people. Thus, the regime has to selectively ban politically sensitive words like *fa lungong*, June 4th, and names of political dissidents. It is in this aspect we say that China has become more liberal and cosmopolitan. Even before the Communist Party took over China, sex was a taboo subject. Mr. Zhang Jishen, one of the leading scholars who studies in France, was arrested twice and kicked out by Peking University because of his book, *The History of Sexuality,* in 1921 and 1926. Zhang was starved to death under Mao's regime in 1970.

The increasing commercialization of media in a way reduces the state's control over information. The very fact that one of China's most conservative organizations, The Women's Federation, publishes a tabloid loosely directed at female readers, shows the power of money in the information war. In an attempt to make money, government censors may blur the lines between different sectors of the media and what sorts of ownership are formally allowed and informally tolerated. Sex news stories are one of the "overlooked" expressions.

All these sexual temptations have taken a toll on marriage, with the divorce rate skyrocketing: 1.6 million Chinese couples divorced in 2004, a 21 percent rise from the previous year according to the Ministry of Civil Affairs. "Before in society, we had a sense of right and wrong," says the China Sexology Association's Hu. "Now, we can do whatever we want. But do we have any moral standards left?"[57] The rise of divorce shows that Chinese women in the cities have changed their values. As pointed out by James Farrer, "a quiet revolution" is evolving in Chinese society in gender-differentiated attitudes regarding women's virginity and the morality of premarital sex.[58]

Gay Websites and Virtual Gay Community

The widespread use of the Internet has provided gay "comrades" and their supporters an important vehicle to defend gays, in that the Internet provides a public space for gay people to meet and discuss issues. The Internet enables gay Chinese to create a virtual community to communicate both among themselves and, to gain social acceptance, with the public. There are hundreds of Mainland online organizations, such as Don't Cry, Friend, Light Blue Net, Boy Sky, Guangzhou Tongzhi, and Aibai. These gay online websites provide services for gay news, culture, health, literature, psychological consultation, dating, and other issues important to gay people.

One pioneer of gay websites, Ah Qian of Guangzhou, was among the first to establish a new gay Website:

I had started using the internet in 2000, and at the time of the Mao Ning incident, my biggest job for the week was to debate the issue with anti-gay posts on Sina.com. I remember that at that time, Sina.com set up a special column to debate the issue, where most writers were gay-bashers who cursed gay people as weird human trash. Many of the "comrades" were demoralized but very quickly, supporters of gay rights asked other gay chat room "comrades" to post their opinions, creating one of the most heated unofficial debates of the time. Six years have now passed, during which I have undergone a major transformation—from someone who refused to face his own gay identity and was willing to marry a woman, to someone who would marry only a man. As an openly gay man, I have been giving lectures and communicating with the media to improve reporting on gay issues. Such a rapid transformation startled even me.[59]

According to Ah Qiang, knowledge about gay culture through heavy use of the Internet has had the effect of reducing the social stigma of homosexuality and attendant oppression, particularly in urban centers. Gays no longer experience what was formerly known as the "dark period." This is partly because many detailed stories of persecution against gays were exposed through the Internet, and partly due to social change in general. Gone is the official media's ban on reporting about homosexual issues. The way to public understanding of homosexuality is open. Social understanding makes it easier for gays to come out. Ah Qiang also thinks that today's self-confidence among gays bodes well for the future of the gay movement in China, and that gays now realize that their rights must be fought for and, to borrow a phrase from Mao Zedong, that they "don't just drop out of the sky."[60] He contends that, "Instead of complaining and worrying, they act, using their sunny dispositions to diffuse the stubborn prejudice of the public. As pioneers, they claim new territories for future generations. Who knows what will happen six years hence? Legalization of gay marriage? Or an anti-discrimination law? Or movement towards a harmonious society without discrimination and prejudice? With so many of us struggling, all is possible because 'nothing is undoable if it can be thought.'"[61] His words constitute, in fact, a gay Chinese manifesto.

The Internet helps gay people to find love and identity. For example, Ruo Zhe, the founder of the first gay website www.gztz.org, attributed the Internet to his devotion to gay rights. The Internet opened up a new world for Ruo Zhe, "By visiting foreign websites, I realized that I was not the only gay man in the world." [62] The Internet provided a safe place for Ruo to put his personal ads in both English and Chinese. In order to provide a platform for other gay people to meet one another, in 1998, Ruo started the first Chinese gay website that "offers news, health tips, entertainment listings and overviews of gay and lesbian communities in other countries."[63] By 2008, Ruo has 220,000 registered members. This online group has played an important role in advocating freedom of association in China as a whole.

The Rise of Singles and Non-Marital Living Arrangements

With the rise of individualism, Chinese women and men have increasingly opted out of traditional marriage. This social reality, in addition to the "One-Child" policy generation (among which many children are spoiled) has led to China's radical individualism. The rise of significant numbers of singles and childless couples is a case in point.

As Chinese increasingly begin to make individual choices in daily life, including their sexual life, the rise in number of people choosing single life became inevitable. Some want to be alone to avoid responsibility. Others remain single because they do not want their lives arranged by their parents or the state. In this way, the private provision of housing facilitates the choice to remain single. Previously, under the planned economy, it was the state or workplace (*danwei*) that assigned housing. Only married couples were assigned private housing; singles had to share rooms with others. Now, however, singles can rent accommodation and purchase apartments solely for themselves. Given the fact that the centrality of family was at the heart of Chinese traditional culture,[64] remaining single today is still a difficult struggle both socially and psychologically.

Traditionally, a single woman assumed the title of "old maid" (*lao shunu* or "old virgin"). Today, singles do have sexual partners and sometimes they even live with them. Li Wei Wei, a single woman in her forties, complained that her family was her biggest enemy: "My parents never gave up trying to introduce some man to me every month. I was so sick of having my life arranged by my family and by suffocating social norms. I really enjoy my life as a single. I feel sorry for those mothers who have no life of their own but only their children. They look old and worried. I want none of it. At the age of 30, I declared to my family that I would be single all my life and moved out of my parents' apartment. It is really great to have my own life. I go to visit my family once a week."[65] With the advent of impersonal high-rise apartment buildings, and consequently most interaction taking place with non-family members, newly emancipated singles are less likely to feel guilty over liaisons with unmarried partners. Such newly emancipated urbanites have neither the time nor the patience to negotiate the social and moral rules of appropriate behavior.

There are, of course, intrinsic consequences of this newfound freedom for singles. Hannah Beech, a *Time* journalist, reported on a survey done by Shanghai medical researcher Yan Fengting. Yan's findings suggest that nearly two-thirds of urban women who had abortions in 2004 were single, compared with just one-quarter in 1999. "Rates of sexually transmitted diseases are skyrocketing too, with HIV infections growing most quickly among Chinese 15 to 24 years old,"[66] Beech reported. This finding is similar to Farrell's description of Shanghai in the 1930s: "[Y]oung men and women in Shanghai balance pragmatism with romance, lust with love, and seriousness with play, collectively constructing and individually coping with a new culture based on market principles."[67] Such sexual liberty has spread throughout most urban China today.

Sex and the Cash Nexus: The Rise of Prostitution

The growth of prostitution is also part of contemporary China's story. In fact, the sex industry is the fastest growing sector in the country, with numbers ranging from 10 million to 20 million sex workers, accounting for "fully 6 percent of the country's gross domestic product."[68] The rise of the sex industry is one of the best exemplars of unofficial China eclipsing official China. While official China criminalizes prostitution, unofficial China embraces it. The rise of the sex industry is the return of the old China and marks the decay of Maoist moral puritanism introduced after 1949. For many years, not only were prostitutes not allowed to sell their bodies but no one had the right to sell their labor. The state banned prostitution under the first 1950 marriage law. In the words of Howard French, "The existence of millions of prostitutes makes a mockery of China's legal code, whose formal banning of a deeply entrenched activity forces women into the hands of organized crime and furthers their vulnerability and marginalization."[69]

But with the rise of today's commercial society in the past twenty years, "the world oldest profession" has burgeoned. While more Chinese men than ever seek forbidden sexual pleasures, sex is pervasively available day and night, in hotels, bathhouses, barbershops, nightclubs, and beauty salons. Today, male travelers in hotels in major Chinese cities frequently receive sexual propositions by telephone, lasting from around midnight until they either accept the offer or unplug their phones. The pastor of First Presbyterian Church, Dan Chun, related that once while sleeping in a hotel in Beijing he was awakened by a call from an unknown but friendly voice: "The caller seemed to inform me that there was a message for me. I said fine. Get me the message. A few minutes later, someone knocked at the door. When I opened the door, in came a woman with skimpy clothes. When she noticed that my son was sleeping, she asked if the boy also needed the service. Then I finally understood that she wanted to give me a massage. It took hard work to push her away."[70] To gain such a direct access to hotel guests, prostitutes must pay off both hotel staff and the police. The Chinese government has responded by enforcing anti-prostitution legislation. Convicted prostitutes are heavily fined or sent for two-years of hard labor in "reeducation" camps (*lao gai*).

Nightclubs for the well-heeled, whether Chinese or foreign, are also heavily frequented by prostitutes. For about $10, one can arrange a young lover for the night. In beauty salons and spas (sauna bath-houses) a complete body massage costs $12-20. What differentiates today's Chinese prostitutes from the previous model is that the new Chinese prostitutes are more aggressive and entrepreneurial. They sometimes accost men in public, grabbing them physically. Gone are submissive oriental "girls." When Tim Conkling, an evangelical pastor from the US, arrived in China in 2006, he was shocked by the enthusiastic and entrepreneurial Chinese people he encountered: "I have already had to fend off 7 peddlers, at least 20 illegal taxi drivers, some of whom tried to grab my luggage and coerce me into their car, and about a dozen prostitutes, by either pretending that I don't speak English and speaking to them in a Taiwanese dialect which none of them understand, or temporarily blinding them with my personal security device when they wont let go of my arm."[71]

Sex-related business is linked to material desire and comfort. This is why many prostitutes often work in massage parlors, beauty salons, and barbershops. Bathhouses, foot-washing establishments, and Karaoke bars (KTV) have set up close relations with government officials. Feminists within and without China have labeled such businesses exploitative "commoditization" of women. But women are sometimes behind their own so-called commoditization and exploitation of the sex trade.

Courtesans have become the "middlemen" between officials and businesses. In the Chinese Communist puritanical state, extramarital and commercial sex are cardinal sins. Mutual trust between businessmen and officials for major business deals requires courtesans. These courtesans live a life of luxury.

Women or sex workers play important roles in smoothing the new *qian zhuang* business (money and power exchange). Sex entertainment establishments are especially lucrative. Business partners in such businesses need to share trust. "The best way to win high trust is to expose one's secrets, especially secret love affairs," remarked Yang Dalun, the vice president of Ganghua Bank in Shenzhen. "With each man learning the dirty laundry of the other, trust is built."[72] Courtesans have become middle people dealing with money transfers.

Business meetings would be impossible without frequenting bars and Karaoke establishments. Sex plays an increasingly important role in business transactions. This was also the pattern in Japan during its rapid development in the 1970s and 1980s.

In many Chinese saunas and massage parlors, male and female workers are paid between 20 and 30 percent of the client's bill. But an increasing number of new Chinese prostitutes have become more assertive by paying commissions to procurers, keeping most of the profits for themselves. They even use the word *ticheng* (meaning a deduction of a percentage from the total). Usually, it is the pimp and madams who use this term to give the prostitutes a percentage. Now the tables have turned. The pimps and madams receive an agreed percentage of their take. While sex workers are sometimes used by others to blackmail, they also have become blackmailers themselves.

If customers want extra services after-hours, male and female sex workers also conduct negotiations. For example, a Ms. Cui, a young sauna Kunming attendant, migrated from rural Sichuan. When asked if it is wrong and dangerous to sell her body in the era of AIDS, she replied matter of factly: "What is wrong with selling my young body? Everyone is selling and buying everyday. At home, my sister was sold for 20,000 Yuan to a farmer deep in the mountains. She will be his family's slave for life and will never have the opportunity to see the outside world. I could make that much money in a year. Sometimes, if I am lucky, I get that much in a single business deal. I am careful and carry a condom in my underwear. I have ten more years to make good money. Then I want to buy an apartment and set up a foot washing business of my own. I will get my sister out to work for me."[73] For many poor regions today, people are more inclined to look down upon poverty than they are upon prostitution.[74] This could be interpreted as indicating a decline in social morality among Chinese.

By the mid-1990s, the widespread growth of prostitution alarmed the state, which attempted to suppress it with legal penalties. The state responded by launching annual *sao huang* (anti-yellow, as the color of yellow represents obscene), anti-prostitution, and anti-pornography campaigns. In late November 2006, the Shenzhen government organized a parade of more than one hundred offenders including pimps, madams, prostitutes, and their customers through the cities' busy streets in an attempt to use traditional "public humiliation" (*xianchou*) to stem the growth of prostitution. Dressed in government-issued yellow shirts and black pants, this procession of unfortunates relived the shame of millions who suffered the same fate during the Great Proletarian Cultural Revolution.

The government campaign backfired, however, because today the Chinese are increasingly concerned about *yin si* (privacy), as many among them, including top government officials, were violated during the Cultural Revolution. Remembering the decimation of privacy, people now support some restriction of state interference and denounced this act by the state to humiliate the offenders. According to one online opinion survey, "70 percent of respondents condemned the Shenzhen police for violating the suspects' privacy and dignity. Legal experts say the public shaming of suspects is illegal."[75] According to Mark Magnier, a reporter from the *Los Angeles Times*, "within a week, more than 100,000 people had weighed in on the Internet, the closest thing to voting in China's one-party state, with opinions on the Sina Web portal running 7 to 3 against the police."[76] To make their websites competitive, several provincial government newspapers also condemned the move as a violation of privacy. This is the first time that Chinese took a case to protect the rights of "bad elements," of the society. Having experienced public humiliation, increasing urban Chinese can no longer tolerate the intrusion of the state into private life even the intention is to serve the public good. "The police may have had good intentions, but what they did was illegal," said Song Yixin, an attorney with the Shanghai Newhope law firm, citing a regulatory change in the 1980s that banned public humiliation of suspects. "This is reminiscent of China 20 years ago. And to have it happen in as developed a place like Shenzhen is shocking."[77] This incident shows that many Chinese are more concerned about privacy than about social morality. It also shows that the Chinese are beginning to develop a "rights consciousness."

In recent years, the state has repeatedly violated the laws it set in order to meet urgent social problems. For example, in 1983, Deng Xiaoping launched a "strike against crime campaign" (*yanda*) during which all pretense of respecting legal norms was cast aside.[78] This violation of law was supported by the majority of urbanites, unconcerned with the waste of innocent lives in the state's prisons and labor camps (*laogai*). After gaining a degree of privacy, private living space, and economic independence from the state, Chinese have begun to defend the rights of prostitutes and their clients. In telephone interviews of twenty Shenzhen residents, only two women supported the parade because they resented the prostitutes that their husbands frequently visit. The remainder of those interviewed felt that the government was backward and uncivilized. One male government official stated: "Police often get free sex services from prostitutes. I hope that some prostitutes could give them a lesson in sexual exploitation by kicking them in the balls. Those police are such hypocrites. Our government's real fear is 'social instability'. Prostitutes and thieves are just easy prey. Chinese society has lost morality. These is no shame in becoming a prostitute. Why do they use the old way [public humiliation]? This reminds me of the Cultural Revolution when we publicly humiliated teachers, officials and parents. China can not afford that anymore."[79]

In Shenzhen, the so-called capitalist window of China, there are red-light districts for high- and low-end prostitution. Four and five star hotels such as Fuyuan and Yangguang, high-class night bars, massage salons, and spas provide sex and sex-related services for Chinese and foreign business people and government officials. Migrants and workers frequent the low-end Karaoka bars, hair salons, foot-massage parlors, sex hotels, and private apartments. Some districts like Shanzui, Shuiwei, and Shangsha have become the city's de facto red-light districts.[80]

Another aspect of this sexual revolution is the phenomenon of middle-class women paying for sex. Although most prostitutes are women, male prostitutes for both gay men and heterosexual women have also emerged in major cities such as Shenzhen, Guangzhou, Shanghai, and Beijing. These consorts are known as "men eating soft rice" (吃软饭的男人 or *chi ruan fan de nanren*). From the late 1990s onward, bars and clubs catering to well-to-do women have appeared to meet the demands of women in the five categories: wealthy singles; wives seeking revenge on rich and powerful husbands with multiple mistresses; wives with impotent husbands; mistresses of absent lovers; and sexually and emotionally deprived wives. Entering such women-only clubs, one sees notices such as the following: "Leisure heaven for successful women; sorry, no male clients." Male sex workers in such clubs must pass a rigorous selection process, including a strict health examination and suitability assessment, and pay a sizeable fee for manners training, cultural enrichment, and basic business skills.

A more popular avenue for urban women to pursue sexual adventure is the Internet.[81] A typical exchange might be the following post from NetFriend:

I am a rich lady (*a fupo* 富婆)....Where can I find a (鸭子 *yazi*) duck? I am single and beautiful but my desire is not satisfied. I like to find some excitement, even if it's only a one night stand, but I do not know how. Who can help me?

A reply such as the following might soon appear:

My elder sister: I am 178 cm tall [5'8"]. Can I be your partner? My instant message address is [...] and my cell number is [...]

Such an exchange may seem unexceptional in North America. But it is revolutionary in China.

The increase in sex workers for both men and women has led to a corresponding rise in arrests for sex crimes, including prostitution. In 1984, there were 12,281 such arrests and in 1989, more than 100,000. By 1998, the number was 2.37 million and rising. Given the fact that prostitutes pay heavy fines, arresting them has become a lucrative means for police to supplement their meager salaries.[82] In Chinese, the term, 以娼养警 (*yi chang yangjin*, "prostitutes enrich police") describes this financial relationship. So long as money is the motivation for both prostitutes and police, the spread of prostitution will continue, since the police are mostly unlikely to allow a de facto decriminalization of prostitution. Thus, sex workers in China are set upon by four groups: law enforcement, pimps, family and friends, and violent and mean customers, some of whom carry disease.

The *Erna* (Mistress) Issue

The Chinese sexual revolution also includes restoration of an ancient Chinese tradition, according to which elite men may have more than one wife. A Chinese emperor might have more than three thousand wives. Traditionally, the degree of a man's power was reflected in the number of his wives. Although since 1950 Chinese law has banned polygamy, the practice has returned in a new form. Its name is now *erna* (second wife). As in old China, second wives (and their children) have lower social status than first wives. But unlike traditional China, new second wives and their children, on the account of their illegal status, live apart from first wives. This illegitimacy has, paradoxically, given *erna* a certain amount of bargaining power. Most *erna* we interviewed have either elaborate informal agreements or formal contracts with their married lovers. Ah Lan (not her real name), a woman in her early thirties, for example, became a mistress after she met an official in Shenzen in 1997:

> Lao Mao [not his real name] and his friends came to our restaurant frequently and booked the special room for Karaoke. I was the head waitress of that room. When he got drunk, I was the one who took care of him. He revealed many secrets while under the influence. I felt sorry for him and gradually came to like him. After a year, I was pregnant and had to ask him for support. He tried his best to get me to abort the baby, but I refused because I wanted the child and I wanted him to support the baby and me because he had the power and money to do so. We made an agreement saying that I would never reveal this affair but he would pay my rent and 3000 Yuan a month. Since the baby was illegitimate, we had to buy a fake state birth permission card (*zhui shengzheng*) in the street. After I gave birth to a boy, he changed his attitude towards me. He loves our son and comes to visit us more often than he does his wife and daughter.[83]

It is clear that many young women, especially rural women, prefer the *erna* status to becoming prostitutes or working in factories, since *erna* attached to well-to-do men have long-term financial security. In coastal areas, an increasing number of young women have become *erna* for wealthy Chinese, Taiwanese, and Hong Kongnese men. In major cities, "mistress villages" (*erna cun*) have been built to meet this social trend. "In one hamlet southwest of Huizhou [Guangdong Province, near Hong Kong], there are now so many triad [organized crime]-controlled prostitutes serving Hong Kong tycoons—above-board and underworld alike—that locals refer to it as 'Mistress Village.'"[84]

Ah Chun, a former restaurant worker in Shenzhen, met Ah San (not their real names), a Hong Kong businessman, in mid-1997. A man in his late forties, Ah San has a wife and three children. After the first years of their affair, Ah San asked Ah Chun to become his full-time *erna*. Ah Chun seemed to accept this hidden *hei hun* (black marriage):

> My husband is a kind and responsible man who works hard to provide for two families. He bought this two-bedroom apartment for me and in my name. Every month,

he gives me more than 3000-Yuan spending money. After the birth of our baby girl, we set up a savings account so that she can go to a good school in the future. The only sad part of my life is when he has to go back to Hong Kong once a month to be with his family there. We argue every time he comes back because I feel jealous. I know I should not feel this way but I can't help it because I always want more. I am so lucky. I know several friends who were abandoned by their husbands without housing and compensation.[85]

Although there are *erna* for foreign businessmen, especially overseas Chinese, most *erna* have relationships with Chinese businessmen and government officials. In today's China, *erna* are also called "*xiaomi*" (little sweetie). For many public officials it has become fashionable to keep several mistresses as a status symbol. One of the most famous, recent cases was Cheng Kejie, vice-chairman of the National People's Congress. "Cheng Kejie, the most senior mainland official to be executed for corruption, was born poor and had not owned a pair of shoes before going to school…The former vice-chairman of the National People's Congress later amassed an enormous fortune through his public position, siphoning off 41 million Yuan (about $5.3 million)."[86] His fall was directly linked with his *erna*, Li Ping, who acted as his "bag man" collecting bribes.[87] To please his *erna,* Cheng went on spending spree, buying a number of luxury condos in Hong Kong, one for her to live in and the others for their future retirement. Upon his deathbed, Cheng confessed that he loved both the Communist Party and Ms. Li. The party gave him all his power, while Li gave him love.

Commentary on this case too frequently focuses on Cheng and not his *erna*. Interviews in Guangxi in March 2004 established that his *erna,* Li Ping, was in fact the mastermind behind Cheng's corrupt behavior.[88] She was the one who actually demanded bribery. Women like Ms. Li realize that their position is precarious since other women may soon deprive them of their partners (whose wandering eyes are proverbial) and, thus, their livelihood. *Erna*, therefore, must attempt to accumulate what assets (including blackmail material) they can, while they can. Such women, therefore, cultivate the arts of social entrepreneur through sex appeal and well-executed stratagems. Such women learn to establish their own peculiar forms of social insurance by accumulating assets while the affection is still strong.

The prevalent practice of acquiring *erna* among government officials gives the central government a ready means to bring down anyone falling into disfavor. The 2006 arrest of Shanghai party leader Chen Liangyu illustrates this practice. Chen had kept several *erna*. A friend of his in Beijing, chief of the national statistics bureau, Qiu Xiaohua, was also found with thousands of cash and a mistress and illegitimate daughter in Shanghai. According to various Chinese news sources, to make his mistress happy, Beijing vice-mayor Liu Zhihua, who oversaw the city's Olympic construction projects, took bribes worth several millions of Yuan and helped his mistress seek huge profits in construction projects.[89] Most Chinese know that the falls of Liu, Qiu, and Chen were for political reasons, and not on the account of corruption, while many others in the new leadership circle continue their *erna* practices unchecked. Chinese love such gossip and constantly spread it through cell phones, text massages, Internet, and daily conversations. Even newspapers owned and controlled by the state boost sales by publishing such gossip. Gossip about *erna* is ubiquitous in China. In these circumstances, officials find themselves on the horns of a dilemma: on the one hand, they need *erna* as testimony of their power; but on the other hand, they fear exposure and downfall with so many eyes watching.

From the perspective of the center, it is vital to protect the public image of the puritanical basis upon which the Communist Chinese state was originally founded. But any attempt at fundamental reform would be suicidal, given the omnipresence of the power-sex-money triangulation. There is, thus, a tacit agreement between officials and the central government: so long as subordinates remain politically loyal to the top elite at the center, the center would give leeway for corrupt practices but also keep profiling those officials. For the Chinese government's elite officials, the profiling of those officals' *erna* can keep them in line; if anyone tries to disobey the center, he or she will end up like the three men discussed above. The result is a Chinese party-state that is feudal in character, based on interconnected loyalties. Lower officials can have discretionary power. In this feudal system, law and legality act only as window dressings.

In such a political and social climate, officials have developed strategies to keep *erna* while avoiding exposure. For example, they attempt to buy off the first wives through money, housing, and maintenance of domestic tranquility. In China, popular sayings describe such a phenomena: "The red flag [the legal wife] still flies, while pink flags [*erna* and speculation, etc.] also wave;"[90] and "after paying the state grain tax [having prescribed amount of sex with the first wives], the rest [of the sperm] is ours to do with as we please."[91] Since the party is officially still puritanical and discourages divorce, maintaining a marriage has become a requirement for promotion. When situations get out of hand, the party may choose to intervene. For example, *New York Times* correspondent Howard French reported, "the head of the Jiangsu Province Construction Bureau, Xu Qiyao, was found to have had relations with over 100 women, including a mother and her daughter. Lin Longfei, the former Communist Party secretary of Zhouning County, in Fujian Province, reportedly kept 22 mistresses simultaneously and held a banquet for them all in May 2002."[92]

Both scholars and public discussion about *erna* affairs too frequently emphasize the image of men as predators capturing helpless women. While such cases certainly exist, it is important to note that some *erna* are independent and may manipulate men into paying them. In some cases, an *erna* position is a better job option than the long hours and low pay of factory work. Such women in fact exercise an amazing degree of autonomy and control over their lives. This is especially so for *erna* of overseas Chinese (Taiwan and Hong Kong). A

Ms. Liao Xiaoping (not her real name), an *erna* for a Taiwanese businessman in Dongguan, described: "My husband returns to Taiwan three times a year. I enjoy his absence because I have more freedom…My only concern about being his 'black' wife is the future of our little girl. I always ask my husband for money for our daughter to study in the US or UK since she will not be looked upon by others [as illegitimate] at school. That is the reason I have my own *xiao jinggui* [little treasure box]. When business is good, he does not mind giving me more. But when it's not good, he loses temper and screams at me, calling me a whore."[93]

Interviews with nearly fifty *erna* in Shenzhen, Shanghai, Guangzhou, and Beijing revealed that such women pursue rational life strategies. Most stated that personal feelings and financial security are the two most important considerations. Some become *erna* for financial security, while others do so primarily for personal feelings or romantic attachment. Those who became *erna* for money have an easier life than those who become *erna* through personal attachment. It is the latter who often suffer, both financially and emotionally.

Those whose involvements are primarily for financial gain can be manipulative. At *majiang* tables, *erna* teach each other how they got their men to buy apartments for them, how they use defective condoms to get pregnant, how to frighten officials into giving money by talking to some lawyers, how to make men drunk so that they are unable to perform sexually, when and how to call the first wife, and how to make a man sign a marital agreement that can be used as legal proof of threatened or actual legal proceedings.[94] Sometimes, *erna* can make the life of their men so troublesome that they regret having *erna* relationships. One party official admitted: "Love existed between us for the first two years. But everything changed after the birth of our daughter. She became mad, demanding money for the girl's future. Now money alone links us together. I have become her money machine. I do not like it, but I have no way out. My best friend now is my real wife who delivers the money to the whore every month. With the baby girl as witness against me, I could lose my post in the party and have nothing. So we have to be nice to her. She has become our party secretary, although I am supposed to be the party secretary in my work-unit. I regret the whole thing."[95]

In 2006, Pang Jiayu, the deputy head of the provincial political advisory committee and the party secretary of Baoji city in the northwestern province of Shaanxi, was brought down by his eleven mistresses. Pang used his power to help his mistresses make money by assigning them or their husbands huge government or other financial projects. When one mistress's husband was sentenced to death for her involvement in a water-diversion project in which water pipes exploded and collapsed only half a year after completion, she persuaded the other ten mistresses to denounce Pang to the party. The central party sent a team to investigate Pang's case and arrested Pang in July 2007.[96]

The practice of having an *erna* is so common among government officials and businessmen that *erna* are "blamed for driving men to seek money through bribes or other abuses of power."[97] Sometimes, an *erna*'s demand can drive the officials to the extreme. In September 2007, Duan Yihe, former party chief of Jinan city, the capital of Shandong Province, was executed for killing his demanding *erna*. Duan had a relative in the police bureau plant a bomb in his *erna*'s car. This man's problems reflect the contradiction of coexistence of party's puritanical pretenses and the sex attraction and new sexual opportunities. One counter strategy for a man is to confine his *erna* to an outside location, away from his home with his first wife. But such strategies are not fool-proof.

Everyday, in Chinese blogs and Internet forums, people can get to know the details of public officials and their *erna*. According to state media, "95 percent of Chinese officials investigated or punished for corruption were also found to have mistresses, many of whom were pampered with public funds."[98] More and more Chinese people tend to sympathize with those *erna* who are abandoned by their men and with those men who are responsible for the women they love. This common knowledge plays a role in public cynicism about the system as a whole. A degree of transparency has been achieved through Internet publicity. *Erna* are part of civil society and in fact check the power of the state.

Walking a fine line between the anti-polygamy law and social tolerance for de facto polygamy, *erna* have established a new reproductive code (men can have more than one child, a violation of "One-Child" policy.) One perk for official men is to be able to have more than one child. The rise of prostitution and *erna* show that women are pioneers in creating an amoral society, which is undermining the basic structures of the Communist regime while redefining the discourse of emerging Chinese modernity. To some extent, the new modern China is defined by a diversified and complex world of individuals' sex lives that defy both tradition and the Communist state.

Open Marriage, Childless Groups, and the Right to Non-Government Organization

As the Chinese people begin to lead lives less dominated by the state and by tradition, alternative lifestyle groups have appeared. Open marriage (wife swapping) clubs, childless groups, and other non-traditional sex groups (polygamy groups, gay and lesbian organizations, and teenage naked dance clubs) have challenged the state's restrictions for non-state organizations in China. The very existence of such groups poses a question to urbanites of whether such marginal groups and individuals have the right to organize without fear of penalty. This development is directly linked to a modern urban life that is increasingly individualistic and free of direct state control. The marginal groups are the vanguard of this individualism and have been fighting for their right to exist.

Before 1997, the Chinese state used hooligan law (*liumang zui*) to punish group sex offenders and sexy dance groups. As we see over and over again, this is another incident where the state lags behind social developments that demand liberty to pursue desires and interests in the private realm. This is part of grassroots anti-totalitarism, but the difference between Mao's era and now is profound.

One of the principal open-marriage movement leaders is Sun, who opened China's first wife-swapping club for married adults. Her club, called *fuqibar* (Couple's Bar) on its website, functions both as a bar where couples can meet and as an online network, which in 2006 numbered more than 50,000 members. The twenty-nine-year-old Sun is not shy and has posted her own open marriage experience on line: "Switching partners is one possible choice for couples to improve their love life. But it is not the only way, a required way, or the final goal."[99] She is not trying to confront the state, but she casts her organization as a social experiment that scholars could study. By presenting the activities of her sex group as material for scientific research, Sun wins not only the interest of scholars but also journalists and government officials. As a result, her website is still open today.

Global Linkage

Global linkage has also been crucial for the rise of increasing personal liberty. International forces have acted as unwitting or witting accomplices in the creation of a more cosmopolitan China. The most important contribution in this regard has been a reduction of the fear of participating in politically heterodox but individually beneficial activities. Though Communist ideology is dead and people generally desire change, free-rider problems attendant to collective action inevitably arise. Most people would gain by collective action that contributes to a more liberal society, but individuals acting to serve that goal may face possibly severe punishment, making any organized resistance difficult, if not impossible. This is the typical collective action problem identified by Olson.[100] But in China, linkage with the outside world has enabled increasing numbers of dissenting Chinese to undertake defiant actions that in the closed China of the past would have landed them in prison. The glare of world publicity has emboldened numerous Chinese to set out in previously forbidden directions. Global linkages including global media, global trade, global travel, international non-governmental organizations, international personal contacts, and global businesses are playing a key role in opening China, making China a relatively more liberal place in many aspects of people's lives.

Most studies of globalization focus on economic and technological impact. This is true for both opponents (pessimists) and supporters (optimists) of globalization. For example, Samuel Huntington argues, "People define their identity by what they are not. As advanced communications, trade, and travel multiply the interactions among civilizations, people will increasingly accord greater relevance to identity based on their own civilization."[101] In China, global linkage leads to a new Chinese identity in which links to wider global cultures and values are essential components. This new, more cosmopolitan identity is limited in scale and in degree.

Figure 6.1
Spouse Exchange, *fuqibar* **(Couple's Bar) Internet Founder, Ms. Sun in 2006.**

Supporters of globalization such as Thomas Friedman, Milton Friedman, Jagdish Bhagwati, Nayan Chanda, and Thomas Barnett focus on the power of information technology and global trade. As Chanda states, "The most powerful force for transmitting the idea of democracy and liberty across borders is information technology."[102] Both pessimists and optimists for globalization fail to notice the power of activists borrowing elements of imported soft power like moral ideas that inform liberal freedoms (such as freedom of press, freedom of association, freed of religion, private property, privacy) to transform their societies. The struggle for personal liberty among Chinese in the past twenty years is a multifaceted and complex web of interrelated processes, such as sexual liberation, the appearance of private housing, global trade, contact with foreigners, international NGOs, migration, and sharing beliefs (such as gender equality, religious freedom, and gay rights). In China, global linkage has brought about reduction of state's control over people's lives, expansion of personal liberty, and unorganized and spontaneous acts of defiance against the party state.

With the flow of capital, goods, services, people, and ideas, existing state institutions cannot maintain their regime of popular control as before. Using recently established networks of association and communication, globalized Chinese share resources and information about ideas, social trends, artifacts, and images from all around the world increasing their social capital in the face of a resistant Communist state.

Global linkage empowers marginalized Chinese. For example, the first success of openly gay vocalist Coco Zhao Ke, a Hunan native, came when his first jazz album, "Heart Strings," became a hit in South Korea. Chinese tend to accept and follow internationally acclaimed artists because they do not accept the state's promoted artists. Coco Zhao sings nightly at Pu-J's in Shanghai's Grand Hyatt and after hours at the JZ Club.[103] It is often packed with people. Interviews of young Chinese suggest that such Chinese fans become more interested in artists who can claim overseas success.[104] Because of this social trend, even Chinese traditional performance groups such as "Twelve Girls Band" aim first at an international audience.[105]

The development of capitalism is accompanied by growing tolerance of the gay way of life. Some of Shanghai and Beijing's high-end clubs are gay friendly. With venues such as Club Deep, Max Club, Frangipani, and Pink Home; in Shanghai, the gay scene is moving from parks and dive bars to upscale clubs and what might be described as international yuppie culture. Kenneth Tan, a twenty-nine-year-old Singaporean expatriate and owner of the men's underwear store Manifesto, believes that ultimately the gay service industry must transcend the party and bar scene. "Flip through any gay magazine," Tan remarked, "and you will see gay financial services and gay weddings as well as big international brands with gay icons endorsing them. I don't see anything on the horizon in China that is not bar- or party-related."[106] Seizing on the "hardware/software" analogy, Zhao Dan, an openly gay lawyer in Shanghai, informed reporter, Pei-jin Chen of *Newsweek Select*, that hardware is what money can buy, such as bars. But if Shanghai aspires to be a global city, which of course it does, one thing it needs is "software," which Zhao defines as a culture of tolerance. "The degree of any society's development or civilization is measured by its level of tolerance," Zhao argues. If Zhao's thinking—that it is intangibles such as tolerance, rather than visible evidence such as buildings, that demonstrate widening social acceptance—is correct, then progress may also be witnessed on that front.[107]

What is more, interaction brought about by global businesspeople, professionals, and foreign workers removes ignorance and fear of the unknown. Women, gays, and other marginalized groups, together with private businesspeople and global media (MTV), have played an important role in the rise of global identities in China. Part of the global linkages is consuming foreign products: wine, cigarettes, clothes, styles, cosmetics, food, sex, even the English language.

The use of English has come to signify a high social status among the young. Many openly gay people use English names to show their global identity. For example, on April 11, 2007, a new video podcast claiming to be China's first gay online talk show, *Tongzhi Yi Fanren* (common translation, "Queer as Folk") was launched. Two of the hosts use only English names, Steven and Helen. This new alternative media is composed of people from four different countries: China, Germany, Britain, and the US. The first episode features "man in the street" interviews conducted by a foreigner who asks various people in Ritan Park what they think of homosexuality.[108]

The global influence on China's gay movement is illustrated by the new words, derived mostly from English, used by movement members. Examples include "straight" (*zhiren*) and "faghags" (women who like to spend time with gay men). This word has the same meaning in Chinese and is frequently used by urban girls.

In the 1990s, the hierarchy of marriage in Beijing, Shanghai, and Shenzhen can be best captured by a well-known popular saying:

The first rank beauty marries an American soldier [man];
The second rank beauty marries a Japanese soldier;
The third rank beauty marries a nationalist (a Taiwanese) solider;
The forth rank beauty marries a communist solider.

The word "solider" here means men. This saying suggests that Chinese women prefer to marry outsiders. The use of the word "soldier" is important because it is perceived as a new invasion by outsiders. This time it is in the arena of love.

Figure 6.2
Two Bold Young Men Kiss during a Contest Held by a Beijing Department
Store on the Valentine's Day in 2006.

Source: X e Fan, "Pride and prejudice," China Daily, 01/14/08, 07, p. 26, Photo by Li Fangyu.

The hierarchy of desirable marriage partners is based on perception of wealth and not exclusively of a hierarchy of nations.

Many urban Chinese women pay large amounts of money to post personal ads in search of Western men, who are considered as having more respect for women than Chinese men have. Thus, online matchmaking businesses are booming. Young professional women, who work up to twelve hours a day, spend scarce time and hard-earned money to visit expensive night bars in the pursuit of foreign men. Desperate to succeed, such young women can be aggressive in this pursuit, leading them to engage in risky behavior. Problems inevitably arise when these women are deceived or abandoned. "I am sick of Chinese men because of their nasty habit of having extramarital affairs. Most Chinese men do not respect women," remarked Ms. Yawen Yuan, vice manager of Shenzhen Opera Theater. "This is why I met a man through an online dating company in Shenzhen in 2001. I even traveled to the United States to meet him and got married." Forced to return to China by American immigration regulations, she soon found that her marriage had lapsed.[109] "When I got sick, he stopped communicating with me. I didn't know that American men could be so irresponsible." Stories like Yuan's frequently appear in Chinese news media but they do not deter Chinese women from continuing their search.

The globalization of dating and romance creates both a new competition between Chinese and foreign men, as well as new choices for Chinese women, forcing behavior change in both sexes. One long-term effect of the "One-Child" policy is a scarcity of women, due to the traditional preference for boys and consequential frequency of abortions of female babies. Among the most desirable women, this scarcity is compounded by the fact that rich and powerful men so often have multiple partners simultaneously, and the increasing reality of Chinese women's preference for foreign men.

In the new, more open China, it is impossible for the government to effectively regulate the new institution of international marriage. In 1980, the state's interference in a French diplomat's romance and marriage to a Chinese dissident artist, Li Shuang, created a diplomatic collision between the two countries. Li was sentenced to two-years in a labor camp for *liumang zui* (hooliganism) when she was caught living unmarried with the Frenchman. In 1980 Professor Elizabeth A. Wichmann-Walczak of University of Hawaii had to cry in front of a Nanjing government office to gain permission for her Chinese husband, an artist, to marry her. When in 1978 Ran Ying, a Chinese student, attempted to marry American Professor Edgar Porter in Xingyang, Henan Province, Deng Xiaoping had to give his approval.[110] In sum, the large number of Chinese women pursuing foreign men makes it impossible for the state to retain the control it once exercised.

Globalization has also played a role in the emergence of homosexual identity in China. Globalization has created a more accepting environment for gays to carve out a private sphere in which they can live their lives unmolested. But

Figure 6.3a and Figure 6.3b

homosexuality is not an import from the West, having existed in China for thousands of years. Indeed, traditionally bisexual behavior was tolerated among the elite class. The Taoist concept of *yin* and *yang* (female and male) included the idea that each person contains elements of both sexes. But, in the past, most gay people married and had children because it was considered a normal progression in the stages of life. For example, Harisu, a transsexual model, actress, and singer from Korea, was one of the most popular singers. Her record, *Fox*, broke all previous sales records when released on June 26, 2005 in China.[111] Many, especially young, people display her sexy photos on the wall or at their desk. In today's China, Mao portraits and political slogans have no place.

While homosexuality was not traditionally accepted among ordinary people, it must be borne in mind that Chinese tradition does not include elements analogous to biblical injunctions as found in *Leviticus*, the third book of Hebrew Bible, nor does it entertain the Christian idea of sin. Thus, less cultural baggage was in place to inhibit the acceptance of homosexuality. Through the Internet, defenders of homosexuality cite examples of famous minds, such as philosophers Socrates, Plato, and Nietzsche, and literary figures such as Europeans Marcel Proust and Oscar Wilde and Americans Truman Capote, Walt Whitman, and Tennessee Williams, among others, to show that their complex sexuality is part of high culture, accepted by international society and professionals in the most advanced countries.[112]

In addition, defenders of homosexuality use varieties of Western thought to support the argument that homosexuality is a part of human nature, citing writings from Plato's *Symposium* to contemporary "queer theory." Much important work on homosexuality has been translated. Gay-friendly researchers like Li Yinhe and others who trained in the West emphasize the social benefits of a tolerant society. Li has managed to work this benign concept into an endorsement of toleration for homosexuality. Li, who appears frequently in the media, was invited to meet and discuss traditionally forbidden topics with top provincial government officials.[113]

As the Internet, films, and other media continue to inform people about gay issues, homosexuality has become less of a stigma. The gay issue is just another new phenomenon for the Chinese. Some have become more tolerant of gays, while others have not. According to a recent web survey by Hong Kong's Phoenix TV, "83% of respondents express understanding towards or identification with the gay community, out of which 16.8% have come into contact with homosexuals or have had gay friends. Only 5.2% of those surveyed think that 'homosexuality is an abnormal state.'"[114]

To a lesser extent, foreign NGOs' pro-gay agenda has also created interest among Chinese who seek to get funding for gay-rights projects from such organizations. The mushrooming HIV/AIDS organizations across China have also facilitated an open discussion of gay life. Many local NGOs confront both the puritanism of the state and many older Chinese traditionals. Both the state and these traditionals tend to resent what they see as the import of the gay issue from the West. Gays and their allies, especially the educated young people, see the lifting of silence on the gay issue as a progressive Western influence. The new public consciousness of gay phenomenon is being regarded as Western imports like McDonalds and Pizza Hut.

Threatened by public emergence of homosexuality, the state attempted to use the fear of AIDS as means to limit the growth of gay related activities by linking AIDS with homosexual behavior. By labeling gay men as the primary vehicle of AIDS, the Chinese state in fact tried to create a social fear among the public. The state-controlled media have also portrayed the gay lifestyle as similar to drug addition in that both spread HIV/AIDS.

On the other hand, new HIV/AIDS centers require accurate data on homosexual behavior to conduct research and to report to world health organizations. Knowledge of AIDS and other sexual transmitted diseases "has led authorities, however reluctantly at first, to enlist the help of homosexual activists, while the Internet has provided a medium of advice, confession and contact...Chinese gays moved into a legal and social environment often described as the 'three no's'—'no approval, no disapproval, and no promotion.'"[115] The demand from international health organizations for AIDS data also pushed government officials and professions to deal with gay issues as a health issue. Without the cooperation of gay people, they could not get the data they needed. In this way, China's participation as a member of key international organizations plays another important role in the state's tolerance of gay people.

Thus, the state unintentionally created gay-friendly institutions. Although some Chinese may still believe the government's propaganda, still more have become informed about homosexuality in China. This knowledge is important in bringing about public discussions of sexuality, something the state had not envisioned. Every authoritarian state controls sexuality since sexuality infuses social life. That is why Mao and the party tried to control people's sexuality.

Due to increasing global trade and travel, and the worldwide reach of Internet, films, and television, the consciousness of homosexuality has become a complex phenomenon, both locally and globally. Chinese gay people themselves welcome global influence and often use global linkages for various purposes to defend themselves. But the state attempts to label this gay awakening movement as a manifestation of Western "cultural imperialism," an idea shared by certain Chinese and Western academics.[116] Clearly, there has been an influence from the West in terms of homosexual public awareness, but whether or not it is "imperialism" is another matter. It seems condescending to identify them as victims of "cultural imperialism." But in fact, these people are courageous and reject such claim. Why should anyone denigrate the attempts of self-help by a historically oppressed group?

Just like the left, the right does not seem to be interested in needs and interests of the historically oppressed group. Gay liberation in China is part of the progressive destruction of Chinese Communism. The whole idea of suppressing gay people without stressing the state is ill founded. While the left-leaning gay activists refuse to see the linkage between capitalism and liberty, certain conservatives fail to see that the pursuit of an alternative lifestyle in China is inseparable from a larger force of liberalization. The new, emerging gay population is another segment of liberalizing forces in Chinese society that challenge both state and traditional controls over sexual desire. By linking gay issues with emerging modernity, the new Chinese gay identity taps into the power of globalization to confront a declining puritanism of the Chinese state and weakening traditional sexual controls.

Both liberals and conservatives are driven by a narrow vision of their own politics, missing the ways in which globalization enables the Chinese people's pursuit for liberty. Nowhere is this more evident than in the post-modern and post-colonial studies. Many critics of China's new capitalism follow the Western post-colonial and Marxist orthodox notions of alienation and exploitation. On the account of life-changing benefits that globalization has brought for China, attacks on globalization by the state propagandists, academic post-modernists, the new left, and "post-colonialism" have been perceived by the Chinese public as "backward" (*zhuangtong*, or traditional) and, thus, "*bu wenming*" (uncivilized and contrary to most progressive forces of world civilizations). By focusing on the political economy of liberty, we hope to create new analytical tools for mapping out the diverse and intertwined trajectories of Chinese modernity, regime transformation, and globalization.

Gay People Fight for Their Rights

Gay Chinese lack the organizational power of gay groups in the United States, but nevertheless they are still pursuing their rights with great tenacity. This pursuit is directly linked to the grassroots struggle for freedom of movement. Thus, in migrant-dominated cities, gay people have more visible presence than in small cities and rural areas where migrants are scarce. In Shenzhen, Shanghai, Guangzhou, and Beijing many gay people flood the cities looking for both sexual and economic opportunities. The development of the Internet has aggregating power for gay people: to meet one other literally and in cyber space; to discuss ranges of issues; and to organize collective action. For example, in 2005, more than one hundred gay men paraded holding a rainbow banner at a Shenzhen seashore resort.[117]

An increasing number of gay people come out to confront the state and traditional domination of personal life. Remarked Li Li, a lesbian in Guangzhou:

"I am very tired of what other people tell me to do with my sex life,". "I agree with Wang Wenhua who separates men into three types: the 'fliers' (*cangying*, 蒼蠅) who control women and will not leave them alone; the 'sharks' (*sanyu*, 鯊魚) who eat up women sexually; and 'wolves' (*lang*, 狼) who conquer women through nice manners, fancy cars, fame and by spending time with them (*youce, youmin, you shijian*, 有車、有名、有時間). My mother was hurt by my father who was a shark. I don't want to follow in her example, living in tears for twenty years of my life. It is very tiresome to fight with my mom and my relatives who are afraid that no one will take care of me when I am old. So I may adopt a baby girl when I reach 40 years of age. I read on the Internet that in the United States, lesbians can have children of their own like the T.V. host, Rosie O'Donnell. I am waiting for the Chinese Rosie (O'Donnell) to appear before I try it. I am still young at 32."[118]

Gay People's Dilemma

Despite the formal and social relaxation, gay people in China are still waging an uphill battle. A number of difficulties confront gay people in China, especially family acceptance. Many are forced to marry and start a family before they venture into gay life style. "China is a land covered by the ice of bureaucracy and traditional ethics," remarked Tong Ge, a leading gay writer, in his interview with *Los Angeles Times*. "We comrades can only try to melt the frozen land with our body warmth."[119] This image is taken from one of the most commonly read stories in Chinese classics, in which a stepson melted a frozen lake to obtain fish for his sick stepfather. Here the stepfather is the state and society.[120]

There is no doubt that Chinese mainstream society is still traditional. In addition, the awareness of homosexuality creates problems for gays who do not want to come out of the closet. As a gay man in his fifties remarked, "In the past, few Chinese knew the term, *'Tongxin nian'* (homosexuality). No one dared to come out because social and political punishment was severe. But society didn't care if two men were holding their hands or putting their arms around each other. Now, many will not do such things for fear that people would identify them as gay, although political and social punishment does not exist."[121] As Chinese people become concerned about privacy, the previously frequent practice of "sleeping over" among most Chinese young urbanites has declined, although it is still quite common for young women to hold hands in public.

The new concern with privacy empowers individuals, including gays. A sense of self has appeared where previously individuality was folded into the masses. At the height of the Cultural Revolution, everyone was coerced into attacking any sense of self. Thus, the ubiquitous slogan "struggle hard against the moment when the word, 'self' comes to mind" (*hedou cisi yi sannian*) was constantly repeated through loud speakers, in struggle meetings, personal conversations, family chats, signs on walls, schools, the workplace, self-criticism reports, and the printed word.[122] Today privacy, and the new sense of self that has accompanied it, has facilitated creation of a separate gay identity. Businesspeople created gay bars catering to gay people. Public bathrooms (*gonggong cesou*) are not nearly as central for gay meeting places as they once were. There are increasing numbers of gay-friendly places in major cities.

Yet, at the same time, gays who want to remain closeted cannot express their affection for their lovers without being noticed. Gays are less afraid to touch as people have more knowledge about the gay culture. Twenty years ago, some gay Americans considered China a "gay heaven" because it was socially acceptable for the same sex to hold hands. There was no separate gay identity, although homosexuality was taboo and punishable by imprisonment for males. No one would bat an eye when two men crossed the street holding hands, or if two women put their arms around each other.

Gay people in China do not have freedom to organize as in the US because the state is vigilant against any organized activities that are not state approved. The violent crackdown at Tiananmen in 1989 and the persecution of Fa Lungong beginning in 2001 made gays shy away from organized self-assertion. As Er Yan from the Chinese Society for the Study of Sexual Minorities (CSSSM) explains when asked why Chinese gay people are not as loud as American gays, "If they were louder, it may be the case that they would not be heard...A gay rights movement? You say the word 'movement' and you associate it immediately with the Cultural Revolution. For many gays and lesbians, they don't want a movement—they want a boyfriend or girlfriend."[123]

The lack of formal organization, as with other liberal leaderless and unorganized grassroots movements we are discussing in these pages, does not mean members of gays and other sexual minorities cannot make a substantial impact on society. They are aware of the consequences of grassroots resistance. For example, in November 2006, a transsexual person spoke of their problems on the liberal Internet radio station, Vodone (the government took down the site). The renowned Professor Li Yinhe accompanied the transsexual person and showed support for the transsexual community by giving a sympathetic professional analysis. In major cities, there is a transsexual hospital.

The Role of Progressive Professionals

While China's economic revolution has provided economic basis for the rise of cosmopolitan society, the communication revolution (the Internet, television, phones, cell phones, and MP3 players) has formed the basis for a new cosmopolitan culture. The explosion of media contact (especially the Internet) cannot help but undermine Chinese Communism because it creates alternative media voices that challenge the ability of the party-state to dominate society. In a certain sense, it is civil society in the making.

Progressive professionals have played a key role in undermining the party-state ideology and in intellectually constructing a new discourse of modernity in China. Since many professionals work within the state's institutions, their progressive work creates competition as well as problems for the old institution of state control. A good illustration is the problem of the Harbin police when the city's AIDS prevention institute had a training class for *xiaojie* (prostitutes) and their bosses in October of 2006. The justification for holding the training was that the prostitutes were most at risk for the spread of HIV/AIDS. Public health requires those women to be educated, they argued. While the police would normally seek to arrest those *xiaojie* and their bosses, they refrained from doing so under the circumstances because such an act would constitute an attack from one part of the state on another and "tarnish the credibility of a government department"—the AIDS Prevention Institute.[124] This situation occasioned a public debate in the local newspaper. The health professionals triumphed in the end because the public cares more about public health than about morality. It is on account of such situations that in today's China, discussion about legalizing prostitution has become a normal part of life.

Legal reform in 1997 removed the all-purpose crime of "hooliganism," often applied to gay men arrested while looking for sex in public toilets and parks, along with the crime of sodomy—effectively decriminalizing homosexuality. In 2001, the Chinese state removed homosexuality from the list of mental pathologies. The Chinese psychiatric profession enlisted help from the American Psychiatric Association, which "urged the Chinese group to change its stance. The APA struck homosexuality from its own list of mental diseases in 1973, in a landmark step in the fight against discrimination against gays and lesbians in the U.S." The action of the APA lent legitimacy and acted as international precedents for the Chinese decision. "The Chinese crafted guidelines similar to the APA's 1973 decision, which included a caveat about homosexuality as a psychological 'disturbance' for people unhappy with their orientation. People should be given 'behavioral therapy' to change their feelings if they seek it."[125]

The Chinese state always lags behind social change. Chinese professionals and global communities have played an active role in declassifying homosexuality as a mental disease. Western, and especially American, professional standards are often used to make judgment and to make recommendations. "Chinese elite would not feel threatened if they are just 30 years behind the US," suggested one medical student in Beijing Medical School, "Chinese professionals respect American medical profession. We follow their model."[126] Both the political and cultural elite, including professionals, take it for granted that the United States is the richest and most powerful nation in the world. They, therefore, believe that China must learn from the United States and believe that the political elite can be persuaded to relax certain social control if such a relaxation can be justified as a twenty-first-century modernization. Many books on homosexuality have been translated from English, and an increasing number of Chinese read English themselves.

Dr. Li Yinhe has pioneered the study of homosexuality in China. Armed with a Ph.D. in sociology from an American university, she was the first to defend the rights of homosexuals for privacy.[127] She is now the first Chinese non-gay scholar to advocate gay marriage: "Homosexual people should be entitled to the same rights as any citizen of the People's Republic of China to freely choose their sexual partner and to get married [gays] instead of being deprived and discriminated against, and should receive [the state's] protection. I believe that the successful presentation of a homosexuality festival will help promote public awareness of homosexuality as well as self-understanding among the homosexual people themselves, and flourish development of homosexuality as a sub-culture in China."[128] Using American gay rights discourse, Li was able to win support from educated urbanites and the Chinese medical profession. The medical and legal professionals now use a new discourse that speaks of "leaping forward" towards the advanced West. By using the medical profession and linking China to the First World (*yu shijie jie gui*), the Chinese professionals helped to rid of the official discriminations against gay people.

The availability of private housing, foreign travel to culturally liberal locations (such as San Francisco, New York, Amsterdam, Berlin, and Paris), private businesses opening gay-friendly establishments, pirated pornographies and Hollywood movies (for the lower classes), and the growth of global trade have created a cultural tolerance for gay and other alternative life styles, formerly considered the bourgeois moral corruption. A tipping point appears to have been reached among professionals and urbanites of all ages across China.

In many instances, government officials take advantage of new liberal cultural norms to create their own vision of sexual revolution. Increasingly and publicly, a new culture of freewheeling hedonism has sunk in. It is increasingly considered acceptable for married men to have mistresses and extra marital affairs. Knowledge of rampant sexual amorality among public officials and the sympathetic portrayal of homosexuality in news media and scholarly journals are further reasons why tolerance of gays has increased. "My past job was to catch gay men who committed sexual acts in public bathrooms. I had strong distain for them and regarded them as 'social dirt,'" recalled a retired policeman in Wuhan. "But I changed my anti-gay stance in 1997 when I read an article by Li Yihe about the sad life of gay people. Those people just want to have their life and do no harm to others. Why is my business to impose my sexual preferences? What's more, cadres [public officials] are hypocrites, womanizing everyday and everywhere. They are much worse and dirtier than gay people. Now we do not arrest gays any more."[129]

The Chinese Communist Party is no longer the puritanical party of egalitarian justice that it attempted to be (in her new Mao book, Jung Chang portrayed Mao as a sexist and misogynist).[130] The monthly publication *Modern Civilization Pictorial* (*xiandai wenming huabao*) published an edition in 2002 full of semi-nude men (mostly by themselves and occasionally embracing others), showing the extent of the newfound tolerance of gay culture in China. Since the magazine could not be independently published, the developer had to ask a legal government institution (*popo*, or mother-in-law), the Chinese Academy of Social Sciences (CASS), the most important state think tank. This magazine, edited by both gay and straight editors, tested the limits of the state's toleration by portraying marginalized gay and lesbian communities, bringing them out of the shadows and onto the newsstands of China. It is important to notice the magazine's title, *Modern Civilization*. Using this language, the magazine seeks to portray gay culture as high culture, looking to reduce social discrimination against homosexuality and legitimate the gay lifestyle. It is also important to notice that the journal is published in English, which may partially explain how it escaped the censorship.

The magazine was intended to increase social tolerance for gays. "I'm a traditional guy," admits You Jie, the deputy editor-in-chief. "I used to look at homosexuals as strange people. Not bad, but definitely strange…Now, I've reached an understanding that the difference between homosexuals and heterosexuals is like the difference between left-handed and right-handed people…The majority is right-handed, but there is a minority who are left-handed."[131]

Chinese intellectuals are the main force behind the struggle for limited rights for homosexuals and other marginalized groups in China. Universities provide a safe heaven for gay men and lesbians. This is especially true of universities focusing on foreign studies, fine arts, music, liberal arts, and film. Illustrative institutes include: Shanghai Foreign Studies University, Zhongshang University, Beijing Foreign Studies University, Beijing Film Academy, Beijing Modern Dancing Academy, and Chinese Art Academy. In all major cities, gay people are increasingly visible. In 2006, Fudan University began offering a full credit course on Homosexual Studies for undergraduates. Other universities have begun to follow suit. "Gay people have the discourse of an avant-garde culture as if they are pioneers of high culture," complained one male student in Lu Xun Art Academy in Shengyang, Liaoning Province. "They don't know that it's a tiny minority population even in the US. Why must they wave their sexuality in our faces. I never wave my heterosexuality in their faces. I do not like this trend."[132] This sentiment still exists, but gays and their supporters have had a degree of success in reducing public fear of their lifestyle.

Touliang huanzhu (Steal the Beams and Pillars and Replace them with Rotten Timber)

Chinese intellectuals have made headway in co-opting the use of official discourse to expand public discussion on taboo subjects. The term "*tongzhi*" (or comrade) first appeared in the 1980s among gays and has become a common term for gays in China. Until recently, "comrade" was the imposed common greeting term for all Chinese to use, especially for Chinese Communist Party members. By adopting this term, Chinese gays sent a subversive political message as gay activities are contrary to the official puritanism of the Chinese Communist Party. Now in China, only the official media use the term, while the public has dropped it due to its present association with being gay. This is another leaderless and unorganized movement, as no one knows who first used the term even among the gays themselves. Although it appeared apolitical, this adoption of the word "comrade" was in fact a political act.

Gays often cite Deng Xiaoping's words "Unless China opens up, it has no future" to assert a new image of China as a world leader. For Chinese gays, opening up and globalizing means gay tolerance. When then-Party Secretary Jiang Zemin announced his theory of "three represents" (the party represents the advanced productive forces, the advanced Chinese culture and the basic interests of the majority of Chinese people), the elite identified gay culture as "advanced culture" as a tactic to promote acts of toleration. Gay rights activists and other marginalized rights activists adopted the same strategy, linking their action to Jiang's "advanced culture" admonition. Likewise, President Hu Jingtao's "harmonious society" slogan has been freely cited in defense of gay rights. Through such tactics, gay people and non-gay liberal intellectuals have

Figure 6.4
A Phoenix TV Ad Below Shows a Beautiful Girl Saying, "Hello, Comrade,"
with the Caption Saying, "Holding Hands with Sexual Marginalized Groups"
(Character Reading, 性情解码).

achieved a degree of tolerance in a culture that combines tradition with Communist puritanism.

Non-gay liberals such as Prof. Li Yinhe pay a price in defending marginalized groups. While her investigative report of the hidden life of gay men won public sympathy for gay Chinese, she and other defenders of gay rights risk accusation of helping the "disease of society" and spreading "bourgeois life style." At the same time, their friends and family members may become suspicious of their sexual orientation. For example, "When I tried to ask my boss to publish Li Yinhe's article on gay life," recalled one editor in Shanghai, "the chief editor immediately remarked 'I did not realize that you were one of them, too.'"[133]

Interviews with professionals in law, publishing, education, journalism, and government show that most favor China's move in a more liberal direction. In their daily resistance to the overreaching state, these professionals calculate how to advance personal liberty without jeopardizing their freedom. A critical mass of liberal professionals has pushed the envelope through pushing greater press candor and through legal maneuvering. Liberal-minded government officials and civil servants pull the levers of government to move toward greater transparency and accountability. Some liberals may lose their jobs, face workplace discrimination, lose opportunities, and endure family misunderstandings, and social ostracism. But their example encourages others to continue down the same road. This is the exact case with respect to gay social tolerance.

Testing the Limits of the State: The Art of *Da cai bian qiou* (Literally, "Landing the Ping Pong Ball Right at the Edge of the Table)

Given the heavy hand of government, today's Chinese in their daily lives must be careful in treading on thin ice. In Chinese, it is called *da cai bian qiou* (landing the ping pong ball right at the edge of the table). The long-term interaction between the powerful and powerless has evolved a tit-for-tat strategy. Those entering the list of liberal activism test the limits of state toleration by attempting to expand rights step by step, while the state, confronted with a multitude of challenges, is forced to choose which fight to fight. In these circumstances, alternative sexual lifestyle issues such as gay issues may seem to government officials as the lesser of many evils.[134]

Progressive liberals have become commonplace throughout urban China, with its complex social networks and political structures. Such individuals eat and drink regularly in gay bars and frequent gay hangouts. Some lawyers represent gay activists without fees. In many cities some police give "warning calls" to gay bar owners before raids of *saohuang jingcha* (sex police),[135] although many times those police are paid to do so. In urban cities, liberty is for sale with individuals willing to buy it. To some extent, the collective madness of the Cultural Revolution still haunts the soul of urban China. Chinese increasingly realize the importance of private sphere inured from arbitrary state interference. Gay Chinese activists and their supporters try to link the protection of privacy for gays to privacy of the greater public.[136] By focusing on privacy, gay Chinese educate the public on the importance of being left alone.

Professionals such as doctors and lawyers adopting global standards are important for the following reasons. First, such individuals represent China's most prestigious knowledge class, including the scientist community and other members of intelligentsia. By linking gay issues to elements of modern social norms, journalists, lawyers, and independent writers including some government officials use access to the Chinese education system, the media, the global networks, the Internet, their offices, and personal networks inside and outside the party-state machine to advance a progressive agenda. Given the fact that Chinese youth spend more of their free time "reading books, newspapers, and magazines than teens elsewhere," according to a McKinsey report,[137] the agenda of the educated class can be expected to have considerable impact on the minds of the young; further liberalization of contemporary youth, especially among urban one-child family princes and princesses, can be confidently predicted.

Secondly, progressive professionals label traditional sexual controls and the punishment of gays as "*luohuo*" (backward). Images in the media of the Taliban stoning supposedly "sexually immoral" people to death shocked people in China. The threat of being labeled "*yeman*" (uncivilized) may lead some police and public officials to hesitate before punishing gays and prostitutes for illicit behavior. But police in particular do want to keep illegality intact in order to assert power and to maintain the pool of people they might be able to extort in the future.

Third, progressive liberals are sufficiently pragmatic and seek incremental changes rather than wholesale reform. Although changes resulting from the progressive professional agenda are small and apolitical in appearance, they are significant and meaningful to the lives of those affected. As professionals increasingly join the liberalizing agenda, ordinary people will be willing to take risks in initiating change. The ripple effect of those changed will move China in a liberalizing direction. As the state relaxes the taboo of gay lifestyle, society at large, including the progressive liberals, will be benefiting from this more tolerant environment. As Ms. Li posts in her blog:

> Why should I speak for the rights of the minority? Because their rights are linked to the welfare of the majority of the people....I think there are two reasons to pay attend to minority rights: the first is to protect the rights of marginalized people because they are often discriminated against by society and do not enjoy the protection of basic civil rights. The second reason is to promote the interest of majority and to promote "harmonious society" [here again she is borrowing the term "harmonious society" from president and party head Hu Jingtao and premier Wen Jiaobao]...If a society cannot provide enough space and respect for the minority, society will not be harmonious. The Sixteenth Party's Congress raised the issue of "harmonious society". Respecting minority rights should be part of it. Many are worried that what I did for minority people would hurt the values of the majority. But protecting the interests of the minority does not harm the interests of the majority but promotes the interest of the majority and promotes social harmony...It is time they learned to be civilized people who know how to respect people who are different from themselves.[138]

Li's repeated uses of the words "harmonious society" protects her from political attack and simultaneously the fact that members of the political elite who are anti-gay are not following the new social harmony scriptures from the center.

Fourth, their experience plays an important role for those pushing a new liberal agenda. Having been brought up on party propaganda, a new generation of Chinese opinion adopts party propaganda tactics to enlarge the network of likeminded people to shape public opinion.[139] Professionals use the connection between a "modern, civilized" society and gay tolerance as a tactic to set up new trend that government officials have to follow.

After many years' struggle, in October 2006, the first gay national organization was established in Guangzhou. Like any other non-governmental organization, this national organization has an affiliated government organization (*popo*), Zhongshang University. This is an important victory for gay people and the protection of gay rights.

Undermining Party-State Domination

The sexual revolution discussed is the process of shrinking the state's control over life, or in other words the creation of a private sphere that is outside of the state's business. Therefore, the sexual revolution aims at de-communalization of the essential part of human existence in which millions of individuals gain previously unknown personal autonomy. The vitality, diversity, and depth of the sexual revolution in China contradicts relativists' arguments within China, which claim that sexual freedoms enjoyed by Western cultures have little bearing on the Chinese. It also runs counter to Western relativists who have made similar claims.

Since its inception, Chinese Communism has prided the party's virtue and morality as one of its founding traditions. Enforcing such puritanism involved constant vigilance in monitoring and restricting the sexual lives of hundreds of millions of human beings. The state's *dangan* (secret files) system, according to which secret files were kept at one's workplace (*danwei*) in the cities, attempted to control every aspect of life. For thirty years after its establishment, the PRC required every urban worker to seek permission from his or her workplace regarding whom to marry, where, and when. Thus, the *danwei* dictated when and under what circumstance sexual desires could be fulfilled. The heavy-handed regulation of outlets for sexual desire led to a wholesale suppression of desires that would otherwise have found some outlet amongst the details of daily life. The most notorious policy was *lian di feng ju* (husband and wife living in different locales). This involuntary separation was imposed by state the *hukou* system, *the danwei* system, and state regulations on holidays. Each couple was allowed to live together fifteen days a year—during Chinese New Year Holiday. Homosexual acts were criminalized, and hundreds of thousands of male homosexuals were convicted to three years of hard labor. Many were forced to marry.

For both the people and the regime, the elimination of prostitution from 1950 to 1980 symbolized a clean and healthy socialist China. But surges of prostitution, extramarital affairs, homosexuality, and other sexual activities have refined the formal role of the state from puritanical dictator to regulatory agency. This formal, rigid system, with its all-encompassing mechanism, its distrust of individuality, and its abhorrence of self-expression came to an end when the development of market society provided private space for millions of Chinese including ordinary women and men, prostitutes, professionals, foreigners, and gays.

The emergence of gay identity was one important factor in undermining the party-state's ideology. The most ironic occurrence is the new use of the word "*tongzhi*" (literally meaning "comrade"). *Tongzhi* was originally used to refer to the Communist fighters during the struggle against the Japanese and the civil war against the Nationalists (1937 to 1949). After 1949, the term was commonly used to refer to all Chinese who were assumed to share with the state the goal of working towards Communism. The term, borrowed from the formal Soviet Union, was akin to "Sir," "Mr.," and "Mrs." in English. But with the expansion of the Chinese gay identity, this formally unisex and Communist term has now acquired a different meaning: "Type it into an Internet search engine now especially in a Chinese-language version," Hamish McDonald, the *International Herald* reporter writes, "and today's China emerges in a whole new light—pink rather than revolutionary red. In one of the more delightful linguistic subversions of this fast-changing country, the term has been appropriated by China's male homosexuals to refer to themselves and has spread widely into the general community with the same meaning."[140]

No one knows how this term became synonymous with homosexuals. Today, only the very old still use the term to refer to fellow Communists. The party newspapers still use the term occasionally, the butt of many jokes among ordinary Chinese. For example, *People's Daily* refers to Jiang Zimin, the former party secretary, as "comrade Jiang Zemin" (*Jiang Zemin Tongzhi*). A gay man used this to inform his parents of his gay identity: "Mom, you see even our great leader is also a comrade. Why could not your son become one, too?"[141]

The movement subverting Communism and its controlling mechanism is also linked to the Chinese industrial revolution. Gay identity can only be possible when people migrate from rural to urban areas and from narrow cultural identities to cosmopolitanism and anonymity. Radical lifestyles and a decline in previous moral norms are now the defining features of the Chinese middle class. Limited sexual liberty in China is having a provocative and far-reaching impact on Chinese politics. The state's continuation based extensively on its crumbling and perfunctory ideology creates three Chinas: first, official China, where pristine, morally pure Communism exists only in officially controlled media and official directives and documents; second, the hedonistic China, in which the government officials, the middle class, and foreigners live today; third, the frustrated China, composed of untold millions, denied entrance to the hedonistic China by lack of resources.

Who could have imaged thirty years ago that an annual sex festival would be held in China? The new emancipated sexual culture has become so popular that since 2003 an annual "Sexual Culture Festival" (广州性文化节) is held in Guangzhou, a city that has become libertarian to the point of libertine. In 2005, more than fifty thousand participated in the sexual culture festival and increased to more than sixty thousand in 2006. Although consumer products are part of the festivity, theoretical discussions by leading Chinese sociologists such as Li Yinhe are an important part of the festival. "Chinese people are experiencing a sexual revolution," Li Yinhe remarked in her keynote speech for the festival in 2005. "Sex issues such as one night stands, extramarital affairs, prostitution, cohabitation, contraception and abortion have already become part of Chinese people's life."[142]

This cultural sea change has also influenced the political elite, who do, after all, breathe the same cultural air as everyone else. Government officials who are supposed to be the guardians of Communist morality have become infected by the same hedonism that has spread across China. Government officials are wrong in thinking that pleasure-loving people will be bought off by hedonism or that a more cosmopolitan society exists in opposition with party-state domination and fundamentally incompatible with dictatorship of any kind. The rise of actual gender equality, of consumer society, of individualism and the "me" generation, of tolerant anti-discriminatory and cosmopolitan culture, global trade and international media, and international pressure have forced the Chinese state "to respond fluidly and opportunistically to changing political-economic conditions."[143]

Between contrived charades and decadence, visitors to college campuses in China may encounter both defenders and ardent critics of this transformed cultural landscape. Chinese increasingly decry the opulence of official expenditure in the face of poverty of laid-off state workers. Bans on public criticism of the spending habits of government officials, who are, after all, active participants in the new hedonism, stir resentment on the part of vast numbers of Chinese who are not part of the game. What is more, traffic jams, urban noise, scarcity of water and electricity, anarchic sex, widespread availability of drugs, the fleshpots of the Internet, and ubiquitous protests in cities and towns fundamentally challenge the regime that wishes, ideally, to control every aspect of life. The Chinese desire for diversity, tolerance, free expression, and openness, and their curiosity for all things foreign is matched by their distain for the one party-state's domination for intolerance, suppression of personal freedom, and boredom resulting the routinization of life. In this context, the Chinese sexual revolution in all its manifestation constitutes the opening of a new Pandora's Box.

Theoretical Implications

The sexual revolution in China does not feel like a revolution. It feels more like a series of small but critical steps in an inexorable evolution toward the end of Communist culture and extinction of a Chinese Communist ideology characterized by frugality and puritanism. From the rise of consumerism, private housing, a sphere of personal privacy, to the emergence of gay culture and a steady transformation of sexual mores and behavior, China is experiencing grassroots transformation—revolution from below.

The Chinese case will shed light on theories of globalization. Our research on sexual liberty underlines globalization's complexity. The Chinese people's desire for freedom provides an essential precondition, and the global forces mentioned above (capital, trade, media, technology, and professional network) provide the material conditions to enable the sexual revolution. The material self-interest of Chinese officials and consumers allowed the emergence of a cosmopolitan culture that has mounted a frontal assault on the regime's puritanical ideology. The main driving forces that create the new cosmopolitan society are not the government officials or state policies but professionals, consumers, gay rights activists, and entrepreneurs as well as technology (Internet) and global linkages. Gays and the state acted under pressure from local forces, and a vigilant international community reacted.

Post-colonial studies focus on global capitalism's power to destroy indigenous culture and create oppressive new class structures. Post-modern and post-colonial theorists are critical of the achievements of modernity because indicators are material and physical, not spiritual and moral. For them, there is little or no progress in morality and spirituality in a consumer or cosmopolitan society. Such commentary suggests a distant but distinct echo of Rousseau's famous, impassioned, negative reply to the question posed by the Dijon Prize essay, "Has the Progress of the Sciences and the Arts Contributed to the Purification of Morals?" Rousseau, of course, went on to become a thoroughgoing opponent of cosmopolitanism and economic development, both of which he declared to be the enemies of moral goodness.[144] Chinese post-colonial studies likewise focus on the corruption of culture as a result of market development and global linkages.

Global capitalism as it affects China is also associated with reducing party-state domination of all aspects of life. Elements of global capitalist development, such as private housing, global trade, the Internet, private businesses, global technology, and global media, have provided the material basis for the rise of a cosmopolitan society, including social tolerance. Adam Smith in *The Wealth of Nations* explained how the free market system provides the foundation for greater liberties. In the wake of revolution resulting from private property, modern technology, and global trade, millions of Chinese have pushed the state out of their bedrooms.

The Chinese case shows that cosmopolitan values are linked to the effects of capitalist globalization because global trade provides a material basis for personal liberty.

The Chinese sexual revolution in all of its manifestations indicates the influence of global connectedness as clearly as the mushrooming of McDonalds and Starbucks across China. This liberty did not result from directives by the state but was seized from below in many cases against its will and without its permission.

Chinese gay awakening has been a complex process combining the human desire for freedom with local and global resources. The availability of private sector housing resulting from China's growing wealth, private commercial services, mobility achieved by ignoring law, and globalization's provision of employment has laid the foundations for the emergence of gay culture. Migration (job mobility), commerce, and private housing are necessary conditions in developing countries for gay culture to emerge. In China, at least, no capitalism means no gay culture.

Rapid cultural change from communist puritanism to cosmopolitanism suggests that David Harvey's pessimistic view about cultural change may require revision.[145] This cultural change has not escaped the notice of government officials who realize the party's loss and worry about the linkage between commercial development and the precipitous decline of the state's ideological hold on the population. In a 2004 issue of *Chinese News Weekly*, Zhou Xiaozhen, a high-ranking government official, described China's current nihilism as follows: stupidity, incompetence, emotionlessness, disloyalty, immorality, shamelessness, and rascality. Zhou traced the root problem of China's moral decline to the end of 1987 when the Shenzhen government, acting under the advice of Milton Friedman's protégé Steven Cheung, sold the communal land to private individuals.[146] He may be partially right because various aspects of sexual revolution are due to the growth of the private economy and the emergence of a private sphere, neither of which existed under the previous command economy. This finding is in line with the theory of social systems proposed by the late Marion Levy, one of the founding fathers of the modernization theory. Levy foresaw that new social systems are shaped by economic processes, in such a fashion that development engenders a degree of convergence of social values (Levy 1966, 1986).[147] Others have also found that there is a close fit between market growth and "sexualized modernity."[148] This sexualized modernity arrives freighted with a variety of vices and evils, such as trafficking of sex workers and rising rates of sexually transmitted diseases. A recent study by medical researchers from China's National Centre for STD Control in Nanjing and from the University of North Carolina School of Medicine shows that sexually transmitted disease rates have risen from 0.2 cases per 100,000 in 1993 to 5.7 cases per 100,000 in 2005.[149]

What concerns us is not a moral assessment of this sexual revolution, but rather its social and political impact. Thus is the regime fundamentally altered? The new sexual revolution is both anti-traditional and anti-Communist. Chinese people's preference for control over their own sex lives is another indicator of social rights awakenings in China. Sexual liberty is among the most basic human liberties. In the words of Qiu Feng, a liberal journalist and commentator: "This is an era of ignorance but also of wisdom; a time of suspicion and nihilism but also of faith; a season of darkness but also of a new dawn of enlightenment."[150]

Notes

1. *China Daily,* "'Sexual revolution in place," 11/08/05, 11, p. 47.
    http://www.chinadaily.com.cn/english/doc/2005-11/08/content_492507.htm.
2. Gao Hua, *Gap between the Positions and Backgrounds: the Political Levels of Chinese Society During 1949-1965*, (Hong Kong: Institute of Asia-Pacific Studies, Chinese University of Hong Kong, 2004).
3. Neil Diamant, "Making Love 'Legible' in China: Politics and Society during the Enforcement of Civil Marriage Registration, 1950-66," *Politics and Society,* 29, (September 2001), p. 3: 447-480; Lynn T. White, Policies of Chaos (Princeton: Princeton University Press, 1990).
4. Personal communication in 1980, in Wuhan.
5. Personal communication Oct. 12, 2005, Beijing.
6. *China Daily,* "Growing tolerance towards homosexuals in China," Updated: 12/10/04, 11, p.27. For the gay report, in Xu Lifan, "Gay Life in China," *Huaxia News*, December 02, 2004, http://news.tom.com.

7. Cheng Qingsong, *"Wode aiqing busanhuang"* (I Do not Lie about My Love), March 6, 2007, 15, p. 09, http://18x.phoenixtv.com/18x/gay/200703/0306_92_84463. shtml.

8. Roberta Sassatelli, "Consuming Ambivalence," *Journal of Material Culture*, Vol. 2, No. 3, (1997), pp. 339-60.

9. Jill Drew, "Chinese Officials Give Club District A Brusque Cleanup," *Washington Post Foreign Service*, (July 30, 2008), p. A01.

10. Hamish McDonald, "Gay revolution puts red China in the pink," *International Herald Tribune*, August 27, 2005.

11. Personal interview with Jun Jun on June 29 in Shanghai, China.

12. There are a number of varieties of Chinese police: national police, security police, local police, hygiene police, armed police, paramilitary police, and household registration police (*hujing*). From faculty of Chinese Police Academy in Muxudi, Beijing on June 25, 2001. The quote is from a personal interview with Huan, June 30, 2006, Shanghai.

13. The name Comrade Bar itself carries a subversive political message because gay activities are contrary to the official puritanism of the Chinese Communist Party. Until recently, "comrade" was the standard term of address among Chinese party members. However, also recently, the term has been discontinued in some contexts because of its present association with being gay.

14. Personal interview with Wei Wei and three other gay men in Wuhan on July 3, 2006.

15. Personal interviews with four gay bar owners in Guangzhou and Shenzhen, June 26-30, 2005.

16. According to government data, the percentage of families that have one child in the urban centers has more than 95 percent.

17. Pan Lin, "*Jieluo tongxinglian juhui neimu*" (Exposed the Lesbian Gathering: Female College Students Regard Lesbianism as fad, September 22, 2005, http://www. beelink.com/20050922/1938609.shtml.

18. *Wenhui Daily*, *"You tiaocha xianshi bashiguo nudaxuesheng shuangxin chizhi xianzhu"* (Survey Shows that the Post Eighties Generation Carry Androgynous Traits), October 31, 2007, http://news.xinhuanet.com/edu/2007-10/31/content_6976578. htm.

19. Pan Lin, 2005.

20. Personal interviews with four gay men at G 3 Shanghai, July 1, 2006. The English word, "cool," has been incorporated into the hip Chinese urban patois, especially among urban youth.

21. Kate Zhou, 1996.

22. Migrant interviews, August 6-10, 1996, Guangzhou and Shenzhen.

23. Interviews with female migrants in the mid-1980s and late 1990s showed regional differences between the North and South in their conscious coping with the term *Chaosheng Youjidui* (Extra-Quota Birth Guerrillas). While women in the North compared themselves to the grassroots anti-Japanese resistance movement, those in the South referred to Mao's guerrilla war against the nationalist army in the late 1940s. This difference may be due to the fact that most migrants interviewed were indigenous to Hunan (Mao's home province) and Hubei Province (contiguous to Hunan). For most Chinese, *Youjidui* (guerrillas) refers to the anti-Japanese grassroots resistance. For more on grassroots resistance movements against the state's "One Child" policy, see Kate Zhou, 1996.

24. Personal interview with "Lao Biao 1," in Huaxi Village, Jiangsu, in July 9, 2004.

25. Personal interview with Wang in Wuhan, on July 3, 2001.

26. Personal interview with Wei Wei, in Wuhan, on July 2, 2001.
27. Personal interview with Qing Qing at Beijing University, June 29, 2001. Qing Qing works for the central government in Beijing, while his partner works for a joint venture. This demonstrates the very fact that someone so close to the heart of the Communist Party is living in defiance of the party's puritanism.
28. Private space refers here to private housing and private ownership.
29. Nimrod Baranovitch, *China 's New Voices: Popular Music, Ethnicity, Gender, and Politics, 1978-1997*, (Berkeley, CA: University of Berkeley Press, 2003). This book gives a fascinating look at the relationship between popular music and broad cultural, social, and political changes that are taking place in China.
30. Personal interview with Lei Tao in Shenzhen on August 12, 2000.
31. Stephen Kelly, "Why Does It Have to Be Like This?: Leslie Cheung, 1956-2003," http://www.morphizm.com/recommends/film/leslie_cheung.html.
32. Personal interview with Liu Chuner on July 4, 2006 in Wuhan.
33. Pan Ling, 2005.
34. Song Hwee Lim, *Celluloid Comrades: Representations of Male Homosexuality in Contemporary Chinese Cinema*, (Honolulu, HI: University of Hawaii Press, 2007).
35. In the early 1980s, the author set up an informal group of working married women to discuss their sexual problems. It was through the group that women learned the term "masturbation." Most Chinese women in the past were aware of penetration as the only sexual act. But now, after exposure to imported and locally produced pornography, most Chinese are acquainted with other forms of sexual expression. Today, when asked, "Have you tried *ziwei* (masturbation)?" of more than fifty professionals with whom the author is acquainted, all but two answered in the affirmative. Familiarity with the practice is especially prevalent among professional women who are either divorced or whose husbands have mistresses. One has this to say about her experience: "I tried *ziwei* when I read a novel about it. I felt great and loved it better than sexual intercourse." (Interview with Ping in Wuhan on July 4, 2005). Another one said: "When I get frustrated with my work and my family, I masturbate. But I have to hide this from my husband who will be very upset with me. This is why I take long showers." (Individual showers were not possible for most Chinese before 1985. Interview of Hu in Beijing University, August 4, 2006.). Still another angrily stated, "Masturbation is the wife's revenge against those womanizing, unfaithful husbands." (Interview of Luo Dongxia in Shenzhen, June 28, 2005). The informal interviews were conducted during the summer months of 1994 to 2006. Previously banned books on sex including information about masturbation can be found everywhere in China today.
36. This song became popular in 1990 after the Tiananmen Square incident. During Mao's years, Chinese people were forced to sing the song, "Follow Chairman Mao and the Party." Now the Chinese are singing this new song to replace the old one—a revolutionary change.
37. For a good discussion on targeted people in China, see Fengling Wang, 2005.
38. Personal interview with Tao on December 26, 1994, in Shenzhen.
39. Howard W. French, "Letter from China: The sex industry is everywhere but no-where," *International Herald Tribune*, December 14, 2006.
40. This common expression originated in the 1980s and became popular in the 1990s.
41. Hannah Beech, "Sex, Please—We're Young and Chinese," *Time*, Jan. 15, 2006.
42. Interview with Ms. Qian, Wuhan, July 25, 2002.

43. The story was told in early 1980s by Dr. Wu Duan Xiu in Wuhan and Qian Simao (a nurse) in Wuchange. (The writer did not remember the exact dates for both accounts. But I heard the same accounts in Shanghai, Beijing, Liaoning, and Hunan.)

44. In most East Asian countries, kissing, especially "French kissing," even during sex, is not a usual practice. At one time, I organized a small, informal group of twenty-two factory women in Wuhan (1978-83) and, at another, lived two years in Tongxi village, Hubei. Through repeated intimate talks, I discovered that kissing was not usually considered part of lovemaking. Throughout the 1990s and 2000s, however, the writer has observed marked changes taking place. Nowadays, women demand kissing. In informal interviews with one hundred women during summers of 2004, 2005, and 2006, I found that among women over forty, kissing is considered something for the young. But among college and even high school students, kissing often takes place. In many cases, women initiate kissing. Interviewing more than fifty men since 1995, I discovered that men who have young mistresses do kiss their young lovers. When I asked Bosss Chen from Liaon, "Do you kiss your wife?" he replied with a big smile, "No. After kissing other young and beautiful girls outside, I have no interest in kissing her. We are a old couple (*laofu laoqi*)." Hollywood movies have played an important role in kissing becoming something to be desired, especially for the young. In some cases, government officials have attempted to keep their wives from learning about such new ideas. In 1983, wives of government officials complained that their husbands would not allow them to watch the movie *Anna Karenina,* which depicted kissing, when it was shown on Wuhan TV, because it was said to contain "dangerous" ideas (divorce and extramarital affairs). This account was also confirmed in Beijing in 1983 by wives of government officials when the writer became a graduate student in Beijing in 1984. In five visits to Japan in 1996, 1997, 1999, 2003, and 2005, informal interviews with Japanese women over fifty revealed that kissing is not considered part of lovemaking. I lived with a Japanese family for one week in 1999. Even in urban Japan, Japanese couples of an older generation do not express such intimacy at home. At Waseda University on June 22 and 23, 2005, a group of ten students related that they had never seen their parents kissing.

45. James Farrer, *Opening Up: Youth Sex Culture and Market Reform in Shanghai*, (Chicago: University of Chicago Press, 2002).

46. Chinese originals are here.

47. Personal interview with five students at Beijing University, July 28, 2005.

48. Personal interview with four Shanghai residents in Shanghai, July 1, 2006.

49. Farrer, 2002.

50. Li Yinhe Blog, Dec. 27, 2005, http://blog.sina.com.cn/u/1195201334#feeds_FEEDS_1195201334.

51. Elaine Hatfield, Richard L. Rapson, and Lise D. Martel, "Passionate Love," in S. Kitayama and D. Cohen, eds., *Handbook of Cultural Psychology,* (New York: Guilford Press, 2005).

52. http://www.zzhot.com/.

53. Beech, 2006.

54. Interview with Ding Ding, July 2, 2001, Wuhan, China.

55. Joseph Schumpeter, *Capitalism, Socialism and Democracy*, (New York: Allen & Unwin, 5th ed., 1976).

56. Large numbers of Chinese are *majiang* players, gambling from a few dollars to several thousands. It is common knowledge across China that local police and government officials undertake random neighborhood inspections to uncover such illegal gambling. Much of this inspection, however, is done by officials attempting

to cover their own gambling debts (especially at *majiang*) by shaking down other players.

57. Beech, 2006.
58. Farrer, (2002), p. 226.
59. Ah Qiang's Blog, "*Fufu shenghuo*" (The Life of Man and Man), http://blog.sina.com.cn/s/blog_482404000100071b.html
60. Ibid. American gay people's influence is also important see it in the later part.
61. Ah Qiang's Blog, "*Fufu shenghuo*" (The Life of Man and Man), http://blog.sina.com.cn/m/aqiang.
62. Xie Fan, "Pride and prejudice," *China Daily*, 01/1408, 07, p. 26, Photo by Li Fangyu, http://www.chinadaily.com.cn/china/2008-01/14/content_6390950.htm.
63. Xie Fan, "Pride and prejudice," *China Daily*, Updated: 01/14/08, http://www.chinadaily.com.cn/china/2008-01/14/content_6390950.htm.
64. Marion J. Levy, Jr., *The Family Revolution in Modern China*, (Cambridge, MA: Harvard University Press, 1949).
65. Personal interview with Li, July 1, 2001 in Wuhan.
66. Beech, 2006.
67. Farrer, 2002.
68. Wu Qiang,"A Feminist Prospective: Legalization or Decriminalization of Prostitution?" *Shimin Zaizhi*, (*Journal of Urbanites*), October 2006, http://www.worldofchinese.com/bbs/archiver/?tid-3196.html.
69. Howard W. French, "Letter from China: The sex industry is everywhere but nowhere," *The International Herald Tribune*, December 15, 2006.
70. Dan Chun, sermon at the First Presbyterian Church in Honolulu, HI, April 2005.
71. Tim Conkling, personal communication by email, December 15, 2006.
72. Interviews with several Shenzhen bankers in the summer of 1997, 1998, 2001. We discovered that prostitutes somehow are linked to savings. When anti-prostitutes campaigns were launched, each banker would discover that 10 to 12 percent of their money would suddenly disappear.
73. Interview with Ms. Cui, July 28, 2006, at Kunmin Railway Station.
74. In Chinese, this attitude is called *xiaoping bu xiaocang* "笑贫不笑娼."
75. Anthony Kuhn, "China Debates Morality, Exploitation of Women," National Public Radio, January 20, 2007, http://www.npr.org/templates/story/story.php?storyId=4458700.
76. Mark Magnier, "Campaign of shame falls flat in China," *Los Angeles Times*, December 18, 2006.
77. Mark Magnier, "Campaign of shame falls flat in China," *Los Angeles Times*, December 18, 2006.
78. One of the best incidents of resistance was from a student from Wuhan University.
79. Phone interviews with White, November 30, 2006.
80. Interview with Yuan Yawen, August 16-18, 2006 in Shengzhen.
81. Suitability assessment includes height (at least 175 cm, or 5ft 9in), looks, age (below 35), and size of their sexual organ. In some places, training involves voice.
82. Wu Qiang, "A Feminist Prospective: Legalization or Decriminalization of Prostitution?" *Shimin Zaizhi*, (Journal of Urbanites), October 2006, http://www.worldofchinese.com/bbs/archiver/?tid-3196.html.
83. Interviews with five *Erna,* Shenzhen, Dongguan, and Guangzhou, June 24-30, 2005.
84. Frank Viviano, "Hong Kong Triads' New Frontier South China is fertile ground for crime gangs, corruption," *San Francisco Chronicle*, May 28, 1997, http://www.sfgate.com/cgi-bin/article.cgi?file=/chronicle/archive/1997/05/28/MN25477.DTL.

85. Personal interview with Ah Chun, August 30, 2000, Shenzhen.

86. Personal interview with five Guilin residents on March 25, Guiling, Guangxi, 2004.

87. *South China Morning Post*, ""Clemency for Top Officials Rejected," December 14, 2006, http://china.scmp.com/map/shanghai.html.

88. Personal interview with five Guilin residents on March 24 and 25, 2004.

89. *SCMP*, "Party expels Olympics works chief over graft," Wednesday, December 13, 2006, http://china.scmp.com/map/shanghai.html.

90. In China, red is often related to politically correct behavior, while pink is linked to sexual immorality.

91. The popular saying is putting words into officials' mouths.

92. Howard W. French, "Letter from China: The sex industry is everywhere but nowhere," *International Herald Tribune*, December 14, 2006, http://www.iht.com/articles/2006/12/14/news/letter.php?page=2.

93. Interview with Ah Hua, Dongguang, summer 2001.

94. Personal observation in Shenzhen, speaking with these women.

95. Interview with Yao Shuji, September 2, 2000, Wuhan, China.

96. *Renmin wang* (People Web), "*Qingfu tuandui gaodao tanguang faying le naxie xianxiang*" (What has the Mistress Group's Winning the Case against the Corrupted Official Reflected on our Current System?), http://news.xinhuanet.com/newmedia/2007-09/11/content_6702593.htm.

97. Reuters, "Corrupt China official felled by 11 mistresses," September 7, 2007, http://news.yahoo.com/s/nm/20070907/od_uk_nm/oukoe_uk_china_mistresses.

98. Anthony Kuhn, "China Debates Morality, Exploitation of Women," National Public Radio, January 20, 2007.

99. The picture was taken from the website by Ms. Sun's website, *Guanzong laixin* (Letters from viewers), 10/23/06, October 23, 2006. http://18x.phoenixtv.com/18x/qg/200610/1018_91_21384.shtml.

100. Mancur Olson, *The Logic of Collective Action*, (Cambridge, MA: Harvard University Press, 1965).

101. Samuel P Huntington, "The Many Faces of the Future," *The Utne Reader* (May-June 1997), pp. 75-77.

102. Nayan Chanda, "Managing Globalization," *Far East Economic Review*, December 26, 2002-January 2, 2003. Jagdish Bhagwati, *In Defense of Globalization*; Thomas Barnett, *The Pentagon's New Map*, (Putnam Adult, 2004).

103. http://www.shjazz.com/artists.html.

104. Personal interviews with forty college students and fifty high school students in Shanghai, Shenzhen, Hunan, and Hubei during the summers of 1996, 2000, 2001, and 2002.

105. After success in Japan, Twelve Girls Band became one of China's most popular ensembles. Personal communication with Professor Fred Lau at the East-West Center, University of Hawaii, October 2006.

106. Peijin Chen, with editing by Megan Shank, "They're here, they're queer, they're Chinese," *Newsweek Select*, March 2007.

107. Peijin Chen, with editing by Megan Shank, "They're here, they're queer, they're Chinese," *Newsweek Select*, March 2007.

108. Jeremy Goldkorn, "Gay Internet Talk Show," April 12, 2007, 09:56 AM, http://www.danwei.org/.

109. Jeremy Goldkorn, "Gay Internet Talk Show," April 12, 2007, 09:56 AM, http://www.danwei.org/.

110. Personal interview with Yuan, August 16, 2006.

111. Personal communications with Wichmann-Walczak and Porter over the years as colleagues at University of Hawaii.

112. Jeremy Goldkorn, "Mainland China release for Korean transsexual's hit record," Posted by June 3, 2005, http://www.danwei.org/newspapers/mainland_china_release_for_kor.php.

113. http://www.gayboy.cn/.

114. *China Daily*, "'Sexual Revolution' in Place," 11/08/05, 11, p. 47, http://www.chinadaily.com.cn/english/doc/2005-11/08/content_492507.htm.

115. Joel Martinsen, "Gay Chat Show on Phoenix Online,"
Posted, March 14, 2007, http://www.danwei.org/tv/gay_chat_show_on_phoenix_tv.php.

116. Hamish McDonald, "Gay Revolution puts Red China in the Pink," *Herald* correspondent in Shanghai, August 27, 2005. http://www.smh.com.au/news/world/gay-revolution-puts-red-china-in-the-pink/2005/08/26/1124563027268.html.

117. He Qun, "*meiguo shehua—renqin wenhua diguo zhuyi de zhimeimu*" (The American Myth—See Through the True Face of Its Cultural Imperialism), *zhonguo dushu bao* (Chinese Reading News), 03/31/05. He blames Hollywood for introducing gay culture to China. Kuang Xingnian, "*Taitanike de shengli*" (The Victory of Titanic), No. 3, 1998; Yao Wenfang, "*Wenhua gong ye: dangda shenmei pipan*" (Cultural Industry: Cultural Critical of Contemporary Aesthetics), *Journal of Society and Science*, Vol. 2, 1999. Ian Ang, *Watching "Dallas": Soap opera and the melodramatic imagination*, (London: Methuen, 1985). J.O. Boyd-Barrett, "Media imperialism: Towards an international framework for an analysis of media systems," (1977), in J. Curran, M. Gurevitch and J. Woollacott, eds., *Mass communication and society*, (London: Edward Arnold), p. 116-35). D. Laing, "The music industry and the 'cultural imperialism' thesis," *Media, Culture and Society*, 8, (1986), pp. 331-41. E. W. Said, *Culture and Imperialism*, (New York: A.A. Knopf, 1993). H. Schiller, "Not yet the post-imperialist era," *Critical Studies in Mass Communication*, 8, (1991), pp. 13-28. J. Tomlinson, *Cultural Imperialism: A Critical Introduction*, (Baltimore, MD: John Hopkins University Press, 1991). W. Ware and M. Dupagne, "Effects of U.S. television programs on foreign audiences: A meta-analysis," *Journalism Quarterly*, 71, (1994), pp. 947-59. "TV & Media Imperialism" by Catherine Woods, *M Theory*, Vol 2, http://www.mala.bc.ca/~soules/mtheory/vol2/woods3.htm); Ashis Nandy, *Traditions, Tyranny, and Utopias: Essays in the Politics of Awareness*, (1987). Kenneth Raposa, "Down with Cultural Imperialism," *Foreign Policy*, No. 108 (Autumn 1997), p. 183; see a counter argument in David Rothkopf, "In Praise of Cultural Imperialism?" *Foreign Policy*, No. 107, (Summer 1997), pp. 38-53. "From Cultural Imperialism to Transnational Commercialization: Shifting Paradigms in International Media Studies," Michael Griffin, http://lass.calumet.purdue.edu/cca/gmj/SubmittedDocuments/archivedpapers/Fall2002/Griffin.htm; Livingston A. White, "Reconsidering Cultural Imperialism Theory," *Transnational Broadcasting Studies*, http://www.tbsjournal.com/Archives/Spring01/whiteref.html.

118. Personal interview with two Shenzhen government officials, August 15, 2006 in Shenzhen.

119. Wang Wenhua, *The Protein Girl*, (Taiwan: Time Press, 2000). Wang is a well-known writer on urban life in Taiwan and Shanghai.

120. Hamish McDonald, "China's gay comrades take first step," August 27, 2005. http://www.theage.com.au/news/world/chinas-gay-comrades-take-first-step/2005/08/26/1124563029550.html.

121. Filial stories cited here. There are twenty-four classic Chinese stories which existed for several hundreds of years.

122. Personal interview with Tong Xige (not his real name) on July 4 in Wuhan.
123. For slogans from the Cultural Revolution sites, see the analysis on party's political slogans and their impact on Chinese in Xing Lu, *Rhetoric of the Chinese Cultural Revolution: Impact on Chinese Thought, Culture, and Communication*, (Columbia: University of Southern Carolina Press, 2004).
124. Jo Lusby, "Coming out of the closet," *City Weekend,* January 24-February 2, 2002, cover story. *City Weekend* is an English-language magazine published in China.
125. Liu Shinan "AIDS fight needs a wider perspective," *China Daily,* October 18, 2006, http://www.chinadaily.com.cn/opinion/2006-10/18/content_710595.htm.
126. Personal interview with Dr. Zhou Qiang, Tongqi Medical School, July 2, 2006 in Wuhan.
127. Interview with Beijing medical school graduate student on June 26, 2004, Beijing.
128. Li Yinhe Blog, http://www1.tianyablog.com/blogger/view_blog.asp?BlogName=liyinhe.
129. Translation from http://en.thinkexist.com/quotes/li_yinhe/.
130. Personal interview with Jinghong Li, July 2, 2005 in Wuhan.
131. Jung Chang and Jon Halliday, *Mao: The Unknown Story*, (New York: Knopf, 2005).
132. Jo Lusby, "Coming out of the closet," *City Weekend,* January 24-February 2, 2002, cover story. *City Weekend* is an English-language magazine published in China.
133. Personal interview with Sheng 1, July 12, 2004, Beijing.
134. Personal interview with Li Zong (not his real name) July 28, 2005 in Shanghai.
135. Wang Shang, *The Third Eye to View China.*
136. *saohuang jingcha* (anti-pornography police).
137. Li Yinhe Blog, http://blog.sina.com.cn/liyinhe.
138. McKinsey & Company, Inc., "Understanding China's teen consumers," http://www.mckinseyquarterly.com/article_page.aspx?ar=1798&L2=7&L3=10.
139. Li Yinhe, November 11, 2006, http://blog.sina.com.cn/u/1195201334#feeds_FEEDS_1195201334.
140. Pan Lin, 2005, http://www.beelink.com/20050922/1938609.shtml.
141. Hamish McDonald, "Gay Revolution puts Red China in the Pink," August 27, 2005. http://www.smh.com.au/news/world/gay-revolution-puts-red-china-in-the-pink/2005/08/26/1124563027268.html.
142. Personal interview with G8 July 25, 2002, in Wuhan.
143. *China Daily*, "Sexual revolution' in place," 11/08/05, 11, p. 47, http://www.china-daily.com.cn/english/doc/2005.
144. Aihwa Ong, *Flexible Citizenship: The Cultural Logics of Transnationality*, (Duke University Press, 1998).
145. Jared Diamond, *Guns, Germs, and Steel: The Fates of Human Societies.* (W.W. Norton & Company, 1998).
146. David Harvey, *The Condition of Postmodernity,* (Wiley-Blackwell, 1991).
147. Zhou Xiaozhen, *"Zhongguo de yumei"* (Chinese Stupidity), *Chinese News Weekly,* July 2004.
148. Marion Levy, *Modernization and the Structure of Societies: A Setting for International Affairs*, (Princeton, NJ: Princeton University Press, 1966); Marion Levy, "Modernization Exhumed," *Journal of Developing Societies*, 2, (1986), pp. 3-11.
149. James Farrer, *Opening Up: Youth Sex Culture and Market Reform in Shanghai*, (Chicago: University of Chicago Press, 2002), p. 5.
150. Jill McGivering, "Syphilis rates 'soaring in China'" *BBC News*, January 12, 2007, http://news.bbc.co.uk/go/pr/fr/-/2/hi/asia-pacific/6253807.stm.

151. Qiu Feng, "*Chongjian zhongguo jingsheng*," (Reconstruct Chinese Spirituality), *China Newsweek*, October, 8, 2004, http://www.chinanewsweek.com.cn/2004-10-24/1/4472.html.

7

Global Trade, Foreign Influence, and the Effects of Globalization

Trade is more than about economic efficiency. It promotes the values at the heart of this protracted struggle (the war on terrorism).[1]
—Ambassador Robert Zoellick

Tashan zhishi, keyi gong yu (The stone of the other mountain may be jade in our mountain).
—Old Chinese Proverb

Getting the U.S.-China relationship right, which includes China implementing the reforms it has committed to, and doing so on a timeline consistent with its place in the global economy, is absolutely essential to China's future economic growth and stability. And China's growth and stability is a vital issue for the global economy.
—Secretary Henry M. Paulson, Jr.[2]

Introduction

In previous chapters, we have demonstrated how grassroots liberal movements in China have translated into social and economic changes to which the government has had to respond. As such, the transformation currently underway has been primarily grassroots-led, bottom-up reform, rather than government initiated reform. This chapter breaks from that pattern, as we accept that initial major movements in the globalization process—specifically, the evolution of an open door policy—have been government led. However, because of its tremendous impact on all facets of the reform period, including the rights acquisition movement on which we have focused, globalization is, in fact, integral to our analysis.

This chapter helps readers to understand how exactly China has achieved the status of a major global trading partner. The role of global trade is a primary facilitator of socio-economic and political reform in China. Government attitudes towards China's global linkage have vacillated between liberalization and suppression as it perceives the danger of losing political control through the dynamic of the globalization process. We focus on foreign influence affecting China in the political economy, legal and cultural spheres. Politics, economics, and culture are interconnected. China has benefited from the globalization of its economy and the rise of an interconnected world. This benefit, its WTO membership since 2001, and large foreign reserves gave the Chinese elite the incentives to reduce tariffs and other non-tariff related obstacles. China is the third largest trading nation and most likely soon to be the second.

It took China a long time to become a main stakeholder in global trade. In 1978, China's trade "accounted for less than one percent of the world economy, and its total foreign trade was worth $20.6 billion. China is now the third-largest trading nation in the world, accounting for 6 percent of the total global trading volume in 2006."[3] China's economy is more dependent on trade than that of Japan and South Korea, two strong American allies who have also benefited from American markets through international trade. As William Overholt explains, "China's trade was equal to 70% of its GDP, while Japan's was 24%; foreign direct investment in China was more than three times that of Japan, at $60.6 billion versus $20.1 billion, despite the fact that Japan has an economy four times the size."[4]

Compared with Japan and Germany, foreigners play a far more important role in China's trade. For example, in 2004, foreign-owned companies conducted 58 percent of China's imports and 57 percent of its exports.[5] In areas such as the technology sector, the percentage climbed to 80 percent.[6] By 2007, China surpassed Germany to become the world's third-largest trader, with its total foreign trade volume exceeding 2.1 trillion US dollars, and foreign-related production occupied one-third of China's industrial output.[7] Consequently, it is safe to say that the Chinese trade door has been opened.

How did China attain such a level so rapidly? Was it the result of structured policy designed to achieve an open economic society, or was it due to other factors operating both within and without the formal Chinese economic order? How has the globalization process affected the rights acquisition movement that was already in motion? To answer these larger questions, we focus our attention on the following specific inquiries: First, what was already transpiring in society prior to the initiation of legitimized trade? Second, how has society adapted to the manner in which the government initiated global trade? And finally, how much impact have sources outside of the Chinese government had on society and the rights acquisition movement?

Foreign ideas, culture, capital, technology, institutions (including international institutions), goods, and businesses, as well as foreigners themselves, have played a prodigious role in globalizing China and, therefore, in facilitating the various liberalization movements we have discussed in other chapters. The new China created by interaction with this vast foreign flow is increasingly challenging the decomposing authoritarian state's domination. Control over this interaction has proven unwieldy for a government previously unfamiliar with markets and more comfortable with a planned economy. The liberating/liberalizing effects of markets have been eroding party-state political control, creating an increasingly precarious situation for an authoritarian regime. The apprehension over this situation underlines the regime's new term for the Chinese economy, the Socialist Market Economy, officially given to the transitional economy in 1992.

The regime fears a competing power base in the form of strong economic units created outside of its direct control. Chinese entrepreneurs have created just such an economic unit that evades the complete control of the state through transnational networks. On the one hand, the basic instinct of the government is to control every facet of the dynamic society that is China today; but on the other hand, it is precisely the large degree of autonomy enjoyed by those engaged in global trade that has been the driving force of its stunning growth of the past thirty years. While the government keeps control over domestic operators, those engaged in global trade enjoy a much greater degree of autonomy. The government, therefore, cannot seriously consider substantial interference in this autonomy for fear that it will kill the goose that laid the golden egg.

Transnational forces (such as trade, ideas, culture, capital, technology, institutions, goods, businesses as well as foreigners themselves) have created a new source of power in China. Social scientists have for a long time distinguished between economic development that takes place through the efforts of entrepreneurs and a nascent middle class that promotes the general development of society, as opposed to the creation of wealth through possession of scarce commodities such as oil, precious metals, and diamonds. Oil has become a curse on a number of developing societies, leading to a Vladmir Putin or a Hugo Chavez. As espoused by John Powelson's political-economic theory, progress is more viable when there is a genuine diffusion of power among different groups within a society, which allows for the building of institutions such as property rights and the rule of law.[8] In China's case, this process, although not nearly complete, is manifesting itself through the collision of black markets, government policy, foreign influence, and the pursuit of rights.

Smugglers: The Original Traders

Before 1979, the Chinese government maintained strict control over international trade in keeping with Mao's policy of self-reliance. The Ministry of Foreign Trade and its provincial branches authorized trading companies with a limited range of commodities. Most of the trade was funneled through Hong Kong, through which China exported food and agricultural products, and imported items such as industrial machines for key state factories and medicines for high-ranking government officials. During Mao's reign, China's share of world trade dropped markedly, from 1.5 percent in 1953 to just 0.6 percent in 1977.[9]

Mass consumer goods were banned. Prior to 1990, when transnational corporations established a bridge between China and the global economy, the burden of providing consumer goods from the outside world fell primarily on a single group—smugglers. Initially, smuggling was an economic activity performed predominantly by commercial fisherman residing along coastlines, as well as entrepreneurs located along border areas. In coastal areas, trade on the open seas between Chinese fishermen and Taiwanese and Hong Kong merchants was a daily occurrence. This trade was limited, involving mostly cigarettes, TV sets, clothing, watches, and minor household conveniences. As a result, the absolute volume was small. Ironically, the move that would transform smuggling and take trade volume to a new level was the Chinese government's decision to ease open the economic door.

In 1980, the government created Special Economic Zones (SEZs) to allow limited foreign trade to be conducted. In addition to the well documented economic history that followed, this move also opened the floodgates to a new wave of foreign ideas, globalized culture, and rampant smuggling, which has affected the development of China ever since. The government immediately met one of its planned objectives, since the financial rewards were tremendous. The ability to contain the impact of this deal with the foreign devils, however, was far less successful in the sense that globalization was explosive result.

As with many policy initiatives in China, the secondary effects were not those foreseen by the government. The restrictive laws actually facilitated the development of backdoor trade channels that circumvented policy. In the years that followed, the smugglers stayed one step ahead of the government, helping to push trade to the next level by continuing to fill the voids left by inadequate markets. In this environment, cities such Shandou and Xiamen grew substantially, due, in part, to their functions as hubs for illegally traded merchandise.[10] Interviews in Shangdou, Shenzhen, and Panyu in the summer of 1999 showed that smuggling and legal trade were so intertwined that traders would not hesitate to refer to themselves as *zuocifan* (smugglers) by profession.[11] During this period (the early 1980s), inadequate market access, high tariffs, and institutionalized corruption conspired to hamper legitimate businesses, encouraging illegal activity to flourish.

During the initial experimentation with overseas commerce, only official foreign trade organizations were allowed to engage in international business. Non-state organizations and individuals resorted bribery to gain access to foreign markets. "I had to obtain five different state stamps in order to import Japanese-made washing machines," recalled one trader in Shenzhen. "Those in charge of foreign trade companies enriched themselves. For each import permit, I paid about 5000 Yuan. I, of course, also made some money."[12]

Those with connections to state trade organizations made tremendous profits selling permits to individuals and non-state organizations desiring market entry. Due to the influence of their parents, children of the elite prospered enormously under this system. The Kanghua Corporation owned by Deng Xiaoping's elder son, Deng Pufang, for example, opened an office in Shenzhen, the purpose of which was to sell export/import licenses. According to two former employees, each license cost 10,000 Yuan—a large sum in the early 1980s.[13] On the one hand, such corruption hampered legitimate growth and institutionalized irregularities that still exist in the marketplace today. On the other, such illicit activities by elite children had the effect of allowing smaller players to gain entry to global trade, leading to China's gradual opening.

The high tarrifs placed on foreign goods were another obstacle inhibiting legal foreign trade. As with the export/import license issue, high tariffs encouraged the creation of smuggling and black markets, which succeeded where formal markets, constrained by high tariffs, did not. Paradoxically, such tariffs, designed to protect inefficient Chinese enterprises, helped ensure the continuation of illegal trade. When more traders entered the market, smuggling became regarded as the quickest road to wealth since return on investment was in the thousands of percent. With smuggling networks in place, once the government decided to allow legal trade, given high tariffs in the 1980s, it was far easier to expand these networks than to initiate a new system altogether. By creating legal entry points in the SEZs, the government unintentionally facilitated this expansion. As a result of this growth, smuggling networks became wealthy and powerful enough to expand their influence into local government. Large bribes induced customs agents to look the other way. The practice become so prevalent that in Shenzhen, customs work became one of the more sought-after state jobs.

Some of the most powerful smuggling rings operated under the guise of the state, specifically the military. Since customs officials were not authorized to inspect military cargo ships, tons of "military equipment" were smuggled into China tariff-free. This method became especially prevalent in automotive, oil, and computer smuggling, generating millions of dollars in illicit profits. According to one trader, the standard fee charged by smugglers in the late 1990s to illegally import a Honda automobile was 35,000 Yuan, which could equal ten years of salary for a Shenzhen professional at the time.[14] Despite such costs, the practice continued on a scale rarely equaled outside of China. Given the scarcity of low-price consumer goods, many Chinese viewed smugglers favorably since they were the only viable source for what the people desired at prices they could afford.

At first, one of the first widely smuggled products was clothing. Fishermen and farmers in Wenzhou, Zhejiang Province and Shenzhen next to Hong Kong became leading smugglers. The most important source of capital for the Wenzhou industrial takeoff between 1978 and 1984 was the smuggling of Taiwan-made products such as household electronics and appliances.[15] "The first pile of gold for many Wenzhou people came from smuggling and illegal trading in the early 1980s," recalled Ye Wen, a Wenzhou government official.[16]

Zuo shuihuo (trading goods transferred at sea between Taiwanese and Chinese) was the quickest way to get rich. It was risky, but the reward was huge. That is why many took the risk and became smugglers. With so many people involved in smuggling, it was difficult for local government to control it. The activities of the smugglers, who bribed the local government officials to look the other way, contributed significantly to development of local market economies. Since so many were so poor, local government officials hesitated to choke off smuggling activities all together.

In the mid-1980s, several thousand South China vendors sold smuggled clothes throughout the country, creating a national market in the process. Not only were prices reasonable, which helped consumers, but also the demand for a variety of styles provided would-be Chinese entrepreneurs the motivation to enter the market. Within a year, the average urbanite stopped wearing Mao suits and began appearing in a combination of smuggled, knock-off, and "brand x" clothing. In Wuhan in the early 1980s, locals referred to the long distance clothing vendors as *san ke* (sun-tanned visitors) because they were constantly peddling their products on the street under the bright sun rather than in shops, which were closed to them. These motivated entrepreneurs, who came and went by bus and train daily, were at the forefront of the consumer revolution in the Chinese marketplace.

Hong Kong's proximity to Shenzhen ensured its resident smugglers' rise to prominence, since they were only a short train ride from Hong Kong and its rich array of goods. They worked closely with Hong Kongers, who came into Shenzhen under the auspices of *huixiang shenqin* (returnees visiting their relatives and hometowns) in the province. Those returnees traveled back and forth twice a week carrying as much merchandise as possible in oversize luggage. Since the bags were labeled "personal belongings," they often made it through customs without incident. Just in case, the travelers paid small "tips" to customs to ensure safe passage. As one such visitor remarked, "It was only too obvious that I had a lot of stuff in my bags since they were too heavy for me to carry. Often I had to ask porters to carry them for me. Since I paid off the officials, I was never stopped from carrying thousands of memory chips to Shenzhen three times a week."[17] Another electronics smuggler proudly stated: "I made about 20,000 Hong Kong Dollars a week. My partner in China made about 8,000 China Yuan."[18] Business boomed, and these were just two among thousands profiting from this underground system. One economist estimated that the value of smuggled goods in 1997 was probably greater than 1.5 percent of China's GDP.[19]

Those who had neither military connections nor merchandise small enough to fit in bags simply took advantage of the lack of enforcement agents to get their products into the mainland. This process was facilitated both by the container revolution and by the fact that the Chinese bureaucracy did not have the resources or the will to curb the problem. In many cases, it was as simple a process as improperly labeling a container to lessen the chance of it being inspected. For example, "containers filled with smuggled goods like Mercedes-Benz sedans were falsely declared to contain low-taxed items like wood pulp...Containers full of illicit goods were switched with legal ones that had already been approved by customs."[20] By method, "shipments were declared to be *entepôt* goods, meaning China was merely a transit port, so the containers were exempt from import duties."[21] The smugglers would then remove the contents of the containers and send them on their way. In addition to the inability of customs agents to verify the contents of all of these containers, in many cases the level of involvement in the smuggling rings was so high in the government bureaucracy that there was not even a remote chance of the products being stopped. Even when this was not the case, the potential financial upside was so great that many were still willing to take the risk, so the process continued.

By the late 1990s, smuggling was becoming so prevalent that the government was forced to increase its monitoring and alter its policy. "In 1997 and 1998, reports of high levels of oil product smuggling in coastal China emerged, leading both to a strong government crackdown and to the revamping of its oil policy, linking Chinese oil prices closer to the international market and favoring the processing of crude domestically over the import of products."[22] In another show of force, three high-ranking customs officials (located in Shanghai, Xiamen, Shenzhen) and another fourteen government officials were "put to death for their role in a multi-billion dollar smuggling racket in Fujian."[23] As a result of this increased effort from 1999 to 2004, customs agents and police officers were able to prosecute more than 90,000 smuggling cases involving goods worth 200 billion Yuan (US$ 24.2 billion).[24]

One of the most prominent and successful smugglers of the time was Lai Changxin, CEO of the Yuanhua Corporation. Lai was able to buy his way into the market and out of regulatory compliance. He claimed that the secret of his success was paying off all officials, from the small shrimp to the big sharks. Not long after creating his business empire, Lai had senior officials ranging from the Customs Bureau in Xiamen to the provincial government in Fujian on his payroll.

The smugglers responded to the demands of Chinese consumers unmet by domestic manufacturers and officially sanctioned importers. Even today, about thirty to forty thousand cars are smuggled every year.[25]

To an extent, these smugglers were crucial components of China's open door policy and entry into global trade, because they increased the scope of the market by increasing access to goods, while stimulating the creation of other businesses in the process. The volume of traffic was such that it demonstrated the government's inability to manage foreign trade or fill the holes in its policy. Today, a similar, but much smaller network of smugglers is helping to provide at least minimal commodities to North Korea.

Although the smugglers helped facilitate the rapid expansion of foreign trade beyond what the government dictated, their existence also created institutional problems for China as a whole. Because of the time, money, and effort they invested in their road to the top, the majority of the successful ones that we interviewed had become quite comfortable with the status quo. "I have spent so much money and time cultivating my relationship with the customs officials," grumbled one long-time smuggler. "I do not like more open policies. They allow newcomers to enter without having to do what we had to do to create the trade game in the first place."[26] Like many other successful businessmen, smugglers wanted to preserve their monopolistic share of the market because the smugglers had already created an environment of unfair competition hampering legitimate, tax-paying enterprises struggling to enter the market. Some of the enterprises most affected were those involving electronics, cigarettes, alcoholic drinks, gas, medical suppliers, and food products.

Not only did such an environment negatively affect legitimate business, it also created a situation in which it was in the interest of corrupt officials to maintain the status quo. This linkage between officials and smugglers has formed what Ting Gong called "collective corruption," which has been eroding steadily the Chinese state bureaucracy.[27] The erosion of government's legitimacy further motivated reform-minded people, because short-term smuggling institutionalized unnatural aspects of a transitional economy and would eventually serve as an impediment to growth. As result, by time the trade restrictions had eased, the scale of smuggling had declined.

Growth is Growth

Although the combination of an overly restrictive government and extraordinarily powerful smuggling rings made it difficult for new businesses to enter the market initially, the rapid growth needed to handle the products from both legal and illegal systems helped create the tremendous growth that China has witnessed over the last three decades. For example, smuggler-CEO Mr. Lai's Yuanhua Corporation, in smuggling goods estimated in the tens of billions of dollars, became Xiamen's economic backbone in the 1990s. His corporation not only employed thousands of workers, but also invested in transportation and other infrastructure projects. In Xiamen city, he promoted an image of philanthropy and was viewed as a friend of the poor. He owned the local soccer team, built a retirement home, a hospital, and a school for the disadvantaged.

Although such actions have endeared him to the people, the central government was less impressed, to say the least. In fact, the state government accused him of "having run a smuggling operation that racked up $6.4 billion in revenues from 1996 to 1999 alone—an amount almost equivalent to Xiamen's annual GDP. In that time, Beijing claims it lost $3.6 billion in unpaid tax revenues from Lai's activities, and China's state oil companies say they lost $360 million a year because of his smuggled oil. Lai was accused of sneaking everything from cigarettes to cooking oil, TVs to cars into Fujian province, with the direct complicity of hundreds of government officials."[28] Although his story is one of the more spectacular, it is not unusual. Smugglers were helping transform the new society in the absence of a comprehensive government strategic plan.

Equally as important as their role in the Special Economic Zones (SEZs), the smugglers' vast networks helped destroy the wall between the coastal areas and other regions in China. When the government prohibited the SEZ-based global companies from selling their products to China's other domestic markets, smugglers helped bridge the gap. In looking at the scope of their influence, one sees that they have successfully supplied goods not only to China's inland, but also to border areas of both China and its neighboring countries. One report suggests that the value of Chinese goods smuggled into the borderlands of the Russian Far East is worth $50 million per month.[29] Because of its scope, many Chinese feel that, despite its illegal nature, this trade could not have been accomplished without at least some involvement from government institutions. Similarly, at another border area, one report estimates that smuggling and informal trade between India and China accounted for one-third of all trade between the two countries.[30] By looking at these few areas, it becomes obvious that, even today, smuggling has established such a strong foothold in the global Chinese marketplace, that it will provide the government with problems for years to come.

The importance of providing this background on smuggling is twofold. First, it establishes a framework for explaining the intersection between government policy and the people's push for access to a better life. Similar to the migrants who disregarded governmental policy preventing them from accessing the booming coastal zones, smugglers did not accept limited access to global trade. The second reason is that this information helps accomplish our objective of explaining how China's transformation took place. An imprecise analogy can be made between Chinese smuggling and the piracy discussed previously: in the absence of choice, people resorted to the only means available to them. In the next section, we will discuss more of the globalization's effects on reinforcing the people's quest for rights, which falls more in line with the primary theme of this book.

Global Trade, Competitive Prices, and Consumer Society

Smuggling and trade liberalization have brought a wide array of choices to Chinese consumers. Global trade has provided a steady cadence of product competition while raising the expectations of Chinese consumers. Both the United States and Japan have played key roles in China's opening to trade, technology, loans, and direct investment. After the mid-1980s, Japanese companies started to invest heavily in China's industrial development. China has also gained from trade with the United States. According to American government statistics, its trade deficit in goods with China reached $232.5 billion in 2006, a 15.4 percent increase over the previous record of $201.5 billion in 2005.[31] The easy access to global products at world market prices not only gave Chinese more choices in commodities but also ended the state's distribution system for most goods (except oil). According to Nicholas Lardy, a leading economist on China, "Even in industries with few suppliers, for most buyers, there's always the alternative of importing. So the openness of the Chinese economy has [asserted] a discipline on domestic prices, most of which have converged toward international prices as a consequence of the high levels of imports."[32] The value of imports in 2005 was 30 percent of GDP—a very large proportion. "In Japan, for example, imports equal about 10 percent of GDP; for the U.S., it's something like 17 percent."[33]

As we have discussed in the previous chapters, "commercialization" and "consumption" led to a raising consciousness of public resistance to the state's monopolistic puritanical ideology. As other scholars have pointed out, the loss of state control over the production and distribution of commodities reduced its position to exert total economic control over the Chinese people.[34] This is the true effect of liberalization. Global products hence have become "important positional goods" to many Chinese, since these goods imply a new status.[35]

Even the party elite have discarded their Mao jackets to conform to the symbolically important new image of a globalizing China. Moreover, Chinese consumers do not buy products solely for their quality; they buy also for products' symbolic ethos. Tyler Cowen defines ethos as "a special feel or flavor of a culture."[36] Ethos is essential to a country, for it represents worldviews, cultural values, anesthetic traditions, and the societal confidence of its people. However, it is also possible for ethos "to be weakened or destroyed by external commercial influences."[37] In the Chinese case, the new consumer cultural revolution has weakened the strong state control over society. In other words, the capitalistic ethos is eroding the basis of China's socialist ethos. Arif Dirlik, who regards China's consumption revolution as a second Cultural Revolution, points out that, on account of society's embrace of capitalism, the tradition of "socialist frugality" has already disappeared. It is no longer possible to see everyone dressed in "sexless green and blue in the name of social equality."[38] Global brand names and widespread distribution have created a new culture of consumerism. In a consumer-driven economy, personal respect is now defined by money: French wine, global brand name clothes, and luxury cars (Mercedes Benz, BMW, Volkswagen, Ferrari Enzo, Porsche, Rolls-Royce Phantom.) Global firms like GM, Nestle, Samsung, Sony, and Microsoft have become household names.

Foreign Direct Investment (FDI)

Fundamental economic features such as market expansion and low labor costs are key elements, while FDI liberalization is another. Since the Chinese business environment was (from 1980 on) overly bureaucratic due to excessive government intervention, red tape, and poor business contract enforcement, foreign competition has the effect of opening China up, bringing export markets and price liberalization that reduce red tape. Economic fragmentation in China led to rapid inflow of and dependency on FDI. Labor-intensive and export-oriented industries are the most efficient form of FDI for foreign investors because they hedge against inefficiencies in Chinese economic policies and institutions.[39] Labor intensive and export orientated FDI brings business opportunities, export contracts, and broad benefits, such as financing and a superior legal status.

Chinese private entrepreneurs were left with no choice but to resort to the most expensive way of obtaining capital—conceding equality of control over their businesses to foreigners (Huang, 2008). FDI allowed them to have a degree of property rights security in a system where they were politically and legally disadvantaged. For some private companies, the entry of foreign companies helped them to escape considerable regulatory, legal and financial constraints through joint ventures and global trade. In this way, FDI helps the growth of the private sector in China. Since 2004, private enterprises, foreign-invested enterprises and, to a much smaller extent, collectively owned enterprises are responsible for China's growing net exports while the share of state-owned enterprises in total industrial output continues to fall and "their contribution to net exports is becoming increasingly negative."[40]

FDI rose in response to efficiency improving opportunities to ease credit constraints artificially inflicted on innately capable Chinese firms. Poor allocation decisions by the Chinese state created untapped opportunities for profit.

Foreign direct investment has helped China gain its current economic power. Japan's official development assistance and massive direct investment after the mid-1980s helped China's industrialization. Japan's presence was particularly important in 1990 since Western countries withdrew from China after the 1989 state crackdown against students and workers. Figure 7.1 below shows that since 1990, Japan has poured billions into developing the Chinese economy.[41]

The Beijing government allowed special economic zones to take in foreign investment. Realizing that trade liberalization has also brought benefits to Chinese governments at all levels through taxes, employment, and tariffs, local government officials try to attract foreign investment by tax and land preferential treatment. China is the world largest recipient of foreign direct investment. In dollar terms, annual FDI to China was less than $2 billion in 1985, but had ballooned to $61 billion in 2004, $72.4 billion in 2005, $69.5 billion in 2006, and $82.7 billion in 2007.

According to Yasheng Huang, foreign direct investment is the key to all of China's export growth since 1992.[42] The foreign technology and market know-how was the key to economic growth in China. "Foreign players improve the efficiency and productivity of a sector by bringing new capital, technology, and management skills, and forcing less efficient domestic companies to either improve their operations or exit."[43] Foreign competition motivates countries to create better-priced and more efficient products. Competition among countries in the process of globalizing enhances various aspects of the industry, which is another positive consequence of globalization for countries around the world,

Figure 7.1

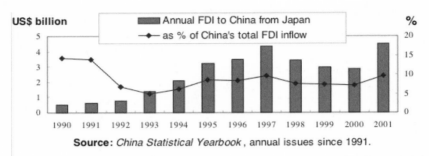

including China.

FDI and foreign trade have helped to transform China in several ways. First of all, foreign investment has helped China to gain entrepreneurship and technology. Second, Western standards of production are valuable for Chinese industry for their models of efficiency: Foreign Invested Enterprises (FIEs) employ only 24 million workers out of a total workforce of 752 million, while producing over 30 percent of China's industrial output.[44] According to political economist Yasheng Huang, China's economic fragmentation encourages inflow of and dependency on FDI. Labor-intensive and export-oriented industries are the most efficient form of FDI for foreign investors because they hedge against inefficiencies in Chinese economic policies and institutions. In 2006, labor productivity for FIEs was around nine times that of the workers in non-FIE companies.

Third, foreign-owned enterprises have become the driving force for China's economy, which account for over half of exports and 60 percent of imports. Huang argues that from a purely economic sense, China is better off owning a smaller portion of an economy flourishing with foreign direct investment instead of total ownership over a smaller isolated economy. The FIE sub-economy is currently growing at around 18 percent per year, while the non-FDI portion is growing at about 5 to 6 percent annually. This suggests that if FDI inflows level off, the sustainability of Chinese growth in the 7 to 10 percent range may be doubtful.[45]

It is important to point out that some Chinese money has also become part of this flood of foreign investment, as Chinese entrepreneurs try to take advantage of the preferential treatment foreign firms receive in tax and land policies. These entrepreneurs put money in Virgin Island accounts and then reinvest the money in China as, technically, a foreign direct investment. This is similar to those wealthy Americans who place their money in banks in the Bahamas, British Virgin Islands, and the Cook Islands to avoid heavy taxes.

Chinese Diaspora

One of important functions of the overseas Chinese is their role as a bridge between their country of residence and mainland China. In 1876, when China began to send students to Great Britain and, in the cases of Sun Yat-sen to Hong Kong and Hawaii, Deng Xiaoping, Huang Xi, and Chiang Kai-shek to Japan, students who have studied abroad and then returned have fundamentally transformed China.[46] The knowledge and experience of overseas Chinese studying and working in the West, especially in the US, has had a considerable impact in spreading liberal values to the mainland. Whether or not they remain in the US, such overseas Chinese establish the ties between cultures that transcend business transactions. According to 2007 Ministry of Education data, between 1978 and 2006, 275,000 of the more than one million Chinese overseas students returned to China.[47] One such returnee was Madame Xie Xide, who was educated at Smith College and MIT. Using US connections and financing, she was able to establish the Center for American Studies at Fudan University in 1980s. This center holds seminars and publishes books on American politics and Chinese economic reform. With the help of other American institutions such as Benchmarks, Inc., the Cato Institute, the Library of Congress, and the US Consulate in Shanghai, the center has created an English language website and a library housing thousands of books. This type of institute attracts students wishing to become policy makers, thus affecting both the present and the future of Chinese politics and foreign relations.

Although academic returnees at the university level have helped change the education system in China, the majority of successful returnees are those engaged in global trade. They have played a key role in China's globalization. These new global professionals speak fluent English and other foreign languages and travel back and forth between China and other countries, bringing international trade and business standards to China. For forty years, the Chinese *maibai* class (managers of foreign firms) was labeled as the running dogs of imperialists and capitalists. Today, matters are otherwise.

Members of today's *maiban* class work for multinational corporations or foreign-funded enterprises and are the envy of young Chinese for their higher salaries and opportunities to travel abroad. These people help international firms overcome red tape in linking Chinese markets and products to global networks. Michael Zhang, for example, is one of the most successful Chinese-Americans investing in China following business successes in America. Zhang set up a chain of Blue Hawaii stores in Shanghai, Beijing, and Guangzhou. "China is ready for my high end stores," says Zhang, explaining why he chose to invest in China in 2007, "because the Chinese middle class who demand brand names and good after-sale services has reached a critical mass."[48]

Many of the returnees also work in consulting, service industries, foreign culture, and media enterprises, foreign-funded enterprises or high technology parks.[49] Zhou Ke is a successful example. Zhou graduated from Tongji University in 1999 and went on to study urban planning at the University of Hawaii. After five years, Zhou received his Masters degree and gave up the pursuit of his PhD in architecture when he saw a good opportunity arise in Chongqi, China. "Chongqi is China's new West, providing me with a good opportunity. My training in the United States has enabled me to land a highly paid job with responsibility. My knowledge of advanced planning and my familiarity with modern design have changed the traditional design and planning work at my workplace. Although my company is state owned, our business model is based on the American design firm model. I am glad that I can put my knowledge to some practical use. I work day and night (close to 72 hours per week)."[50]

Many returnees received training in accounting and can easily find jobs in China. The global competition and requirement for transparency forced many Chinese firms to adopt global accounting standards. Many Chinese have worked hard in order to get a certificate as a Certified Public Accountant (CPA). For example, Zhang Jie, a holder of two Masters degrees—one in political science from the University of Hawaii and the other in accounting from University of Texas—worked for Deloitte for three years in New York and returned to Beijing to work for the Deloitte's China Branch in 2003. "I am so lucky to be able to use my knowledge to help Chinese firms to meet the global accounting standard," Zhang Jie remarked. "So far, big Chinese firms have used only international accounting firms to prepare their IPO and other matter legal matters. Global firms coming to China also use our service. I work hard and have a good financial package. Most of my classmates and friends envy me because I am paid an American salary but live in China. I make ten times more than my mother, who is the president of a major university in Beijing. I bought a nice high end apartment in Beijing, a dream for most young Chinese. I am achieving my American dream in China."[51] Zhang's salary and self-confidence have become a new Chinese dream.

The most important overseas Chinese are PRC-born and overseas educated IT entrepreneurs. One of the most important IT entrepreneurs is Edward Tian, who helped China understand Internet technology through his AsiaInfo Holdings, an Internet firm he founded in the early 1990s. In 1999, Tian, a self-made IT millionaire, was invited back to run China's Netcom Group to bring broadband to the People's Republic. It is entrepreneurs like Zhang and Tian who led China to a dot.com boom from the late 1990s until today. These individuals not only helped China economically but, more importantly, they brought with them new values and concepts that will have political implications.

Hong Kong and Taiwan Influence

The largest number of overseas Chinese reside in Hong Kong and Taiwan. Most were refugees who escaped from China for political and economic reasons in the past sixty years. A close look at Chinese foreign investment and trade shows the key role that Hong Kong and Taiwan have played in China's economic integration with the world economy, making the historical case that refugees shaped the economy of their former homeland.

China got its first lesson in global exchange from Hong Kong. Before the Communists took over China, the inhabitants of Guangzhou, capital of Guangdong (adjacent to Hong Kong), were considered city slickers, while Hong Kong was full of country bumpkins of low culture. But during the first thirty years of Communism, Hong Kong surged ahead of Guangzhou and the rest of China. Lack of freedom and economic opportunities drove several million Guangdongese to escape to Hong Kong. Under a British colonial regime that respected the rule of law, these refugees transformed Hong Kong into an economic miracle. By the late 1970s and early 1980s, the pendulum had swung: the former country bumpkins had become the city slickers, and vice versa. Friends and families lined up in long queues in Guangzhou to receive hand-me-down clothes from their Hong Kong friends and relatives. "It was such a humiliating thing to get the used clothes from our uneducated relatives from Hong Kong," Ouyang, a music professor of the Guangzhou Music Academy recalled, "but the style and design were so much better in Hong Kong than in China at that time. We had to swallow our pride. During the CR, families with overseas Chinese relatives became the targets of the government. But in the late 1970s and 1980s, people like us with many overseas relations became a new elite class. Young urban women wanted to marry men with overseas family relations. I was not able to find a wife until the late 1970s." [52]

The variety of consumer goods available from Hong Kong was eye-opening for mainland Chinese. When the government first set up Special Economic Zones in Shenzhen (near Hong Kong), Zhuhai (near Macau), Shantou (hometown of Hong Kong refugees), and Xiemen (near Taiwan) the Chinese had no idea how to run a modern economy. They borrowed all their new rules and regulations directly from Hong Kong. The Guangdong entrepreneurs copied the Hong Kong model of "Front Shop, Back Factory," while others set up joint factories together with Hong Kong small business owners. With family and cultural ties, Hong Kong cousins were able to overcome the bureaucratic red tape.

The Hong Kong economic elite also assisted in pushing China in a more liberal direction in matters of business and trade policies. Hong Kong business tycoon Gordon Wu (a Princeton graduate) built the first toll expressway linking Guangzhou to Hong Kong by promising to cede the highway to the Chinese government after fifteen years. Zhao Zhiyang, then China's premier, personally helped Wu gain land access from local governments for the expressway. The local elite's respect for Zhao and the no-cost freeway ensured that Wu had green lights throughout the planning and construction. This toll road became the model for expressways and highways across China in the 1990s.

In this way, Hong Kong business people provided both hard and soft infrastructure for China. Hong Kong, moreover, the largest container port center in

Asia, has facilitated the movement of goods between Southeast/East Asia and the world. Apart from Narita, Japan, Hong Kong has the largest international airport and harbor in Asia. Thus, Hong Kong is the premier parking space for Asian markets. It is through Hong Kong that many Chinese have ensured their goods reach global markets: "From 1997 to 2005, Hong Kong's re-exports of Chinese goods to overseas destinations amounted to one third of China's total reported exports. In 2005, the value of U.S. goods re-exported to China through Hong Kong was 14% of total reported U.S. exports to China."[53]

With more than 3,500 global companies based in Hong Kong, many international firms have used Hong Kong to launch their products or services or to build their brand names before entering the China market. Hundreds of Fortune 500 Companies, like Walmart and Pfizer, partnered with Hong Kong companies to open their businesses in China. During the same period, Hong Kong won more foreign direct investment than mainland China because foreign companies had more faith in Hong Kong's legal system and in its local services that play an essential role in supporting a successful business enterprise.

Still, despite an overwhelming interest in Hong Kong, this exposure to entrepreneurship, technical work, and Western standards of production is valuable to Chinese industry. Seventy of the one hundred largest banks worldwide have offices in Hong Kong. Capital flows through Hong Kong to China witnessed a significant rise each year between 1980 and 2006. Since most businesspeople did not trust Chinese currency, Hong Kong's financial services played a key role for international currency transfer. After China joined the World Trade Organization (WTO) in December 2001, Hong Kong's middleman position became less crucial. But economic interdependence between Hong Kong and the mainland has continued. Such interdependence has led to a strong mutual interest in keeping Hong Kong's rule of law-based capitalism intact, although Beijing has attempted to disrupt Hong Kong's political freedom through financial and political manipulation.

The Rise of *Dingdan* and Commodity-Driven Regime

A close look at Chinese foreign investment and trade shows how Hong Kong and Taiwan businesspeople have played a key role in transforming China's economy from a state-planned, isolated economy into a market-driven, trade-dependent nation. This transformation has great implications for the world commodity market. Hong Kong and Taiwanese traders developed a system of competitive bidding in which a firm would issue a product order form, or *dingdan,* which set forth specific instructions to Chinese factories competing to produce the product. The best quality and lowest price, therefore, tended to win, which in turn led to the rise of a low-cost manufacturing regime. Hong Kong and Taiwanese entrepreneurs are responsible for the rise of the global regime driven by *dingdan* manufacturing.[54] With experience in global business, product design, and sales networks, those entrepreneurs act as middlemen to help Chinese manufacturers overcome a hostile regulatory environment, state export promotion policies, strong competition in China, and the zero-sum game of regional trade barriers between provinces in China.

Dingdan was first used in Jingjiang County, Fujian Province, where there has been a tradition of overseas migration for the past two hundred years. In the early 1980s, when rural Jingjiang people first gained some limited control over their economic life, they invited their relatives and close friends who had become overseas businesspeople to return home and invest. These overseas Chinese brought *dingdan,* design, and information of global markets with them to Jingjiang. Thirty years, Jingjiang has become one of the world's main sites for shoe production. A former village township, Chenlu, has more than three thousand shoe manufacturers.[55]

Taiwan and Hong Kong businesspeople have helped Chinese companies not only in quality control but also in navigating the international global trade regulatory environment. This knowledge helps Chinese firms to continue to gain access to *dingdan.* For example, Taiwanese and Hong Kong business-people helped Chinese firms to gain FDA approval by obtaining patent license applications, labels, and environment-friendly raw materials. Thomas Moore found that the rise of international trade regulatory regimes parallels the rapid increase of global trade, attributing China's export market growth to its regulation regimes.[56] However, he ignores the role of the middlemen, the overseas Chinese, and the quick adaptability of Chinese firms. Parallel development does not mean causal development. Some international regulations are helping China in terms of forcing Chinese manufactures to pay attention to product safety and environmental concerns. But many international regulations are protectionist. China, as a main target of international regulations, will come out strong in

Figure 7.2

Source: Wu Ahlu, *"Ding Zhizong, xue chulai de xiewang"* (The Learned Shoe King), *South Weekend,* July 24, 2007.

the future because manufacturers will factor those concerns in their production design and cost, which will make it more difficult for new developing countries to compete against the Chinese manufacturing sector. In the long run Moore's thesis, which attributes China's acceptance of the international trading regime to its economic rise, may make sense.

Following the example of Hong Kong businesspeople, Taiwanese investors began to flow into China in the early 1990s to fill the void left by the departure of global firms after the 1989 massacre. These entrepreneurs crossed to the mainland despite the Taiwanese government's ban (President Lee Teng-hui had enacted strict regulations). The Taiwanese had to go through Hong Kong to establish businesses in China. Since the Chinese government regarded Lee as its number one enemy, it provided generous tax incentives for Taiwanese businesses. Some local governments, such as Kunshan in Jiangsu Province, also provided preferential land policies to Taiwanese businesses. Facing great global competition, many Taiwanese businessmen chose mainland China as their first choice to set up manufacturing bases. By 2004, Taiwanese investment in China comprised close to 3 percent of China's GDP.

When the Taiwanese started investing in China, other international investors became interested in Mainland investment, wondering why so many Taiwanese would go over to the enemy. Rather than directly investing in China, global companies often used Taiwanese as middlemen to subcontract in China. Hong Kong and Taiwanese middlemen are the key factors in explaining why international investors keep investing in China, despite the low world competitiveness marks given by international ratings agencies such as the World Economic Forum and International Institute for Management Development (IMD). Those middlemen built trust and secured contracts.

In this way, Hong Kong and Taiwanese business people helped Chinese businesses and workers to produce for the world market. Hong Kongers and Taiwanese have actively helped China to develop closer commercial and trade ties with Japan, the US, and Europe: they have improved competitiveness of China's industrial structure as well as assisted in promoting the privatization of China's once vast state-owned enterprises (SOE). For example, Hong Kong-nese businesses helped French companies to enter the water market, formally a state monopoly. A French company, Veolia, and a Franco-Belgian company, Suez, set up a joint venture (Sino-French Water Development) in Hong Kong helped to privatize water supply in China.[57] Taiwanese people we interviewed all asserted that they work only with private enterprises because "leaders in SOE change frequently. But our supply chain needs stability, responsibility, and accountability, which SOE cannot provide."[58]

Foreign global markets provide opportunities for Chinese private companies to expand. The state's lack of commitment to admitting private ownership as the driving force in goods production, however, is a structural weakness that creates uncertainty. What is more, China's business environment is overly bureaucratic due to excessive government intervention, red tape, and poor business contract enforcement. Chinese legal, financial, and ideological constraints placed on domestic private investors have limited development of a thriving private sector. Overseas Chinese, including Hong Kongers and Taiwanese, have helped China's private sector to link to global markets. China's global dominance in textile manufacturing illustrates the linkage between overseas Chinese and Chinese producers. The interplay of domestic and international business people led to the *dingdan* textile-buying regime, which affects both consumers and producers around the world.

It is important to note the new *dingdan*-driven textile regime is revolutionizing the industry by placing marketing management at the center of operations. There is no doubt that textile manufacturing in China has moved from being entirely state owned to nearly all private owned. After the entry of private and non-state textile factories in the 1980s, state textile factories fell because they could not compete. The *dingdan* revolution launched by Taiwanese entrepreneurs in the mid-1990s brought not only improved design and international consumer demand but also privatization of the textile industry.

Kenny Wang, CEO of Meridian Inc., a Taiwan global firm, is emphatic in his refusal to deal with state-owned manufacturers: "The government factories often change the head of the company, which creates uncertainty. Second, the state factories cannot give immediate answers of inquiry from foreign retailers who order products. Third, the work ethic among state employees is not good. In our business, the competition is fierce. Only the private owners will give 100 percent attention to the bottom line because any delay will increase costs."[59] Wang held clothes *dingdan* for several American garment retailers like Jones Apparel Group, Tommy Hilfiger, DKNY, Liz Claiborne, Eddie Bauer, JCPenny, and Walmart.

In addition, Hong Kong and Taiwan businesses have protected fragile and burgeoning private sectors by enlarging and complicating China's global supply chains so that government officials in China cannot trace back the products or distributors. The Hong Kong and Taiwanese network of middlemen obscure who actually produces goods, complicating efforts for government regulators to police the production process and reducing the political control over producers and distributors.[60] Most Chinese entrepreneurs have also strived hard to use the Taiwanese and Hong Kong businesses to reach for world markets to escape both cutthroat competition and the political control and economic exploitation of government officials. These circumstances are reminiscent of Schumpeter's remark that successful innovation is normally a source of temporary market power, eroding the profits and position of old firms, yet ultimately succumbing to the pressure of new inventions commercialized by competing entrants.[61]

The benefit of this revolution is twofold. On the one hand, Chinese textile manufacturing has been transformed from a monopolistic market to a competitive one. With *dingdan* in their hands, Taiwanese entrepreneurs like Kenney Wang can cut manufacturing costs by demanding that Chinese subcontractors lower production costs and increase quality of their products. That is why retail giants in the US and Europe have fallen in love with Chinese-made products. The developed market retailers may charge lower prices to customers, thereby drawing customers away from less efficient competitors who eventually close their doors or move into other product lines where they are able to find a cost advantage.

The *dingdan* revolution enabled Chinese firms to become competitive producers of low-cost and high quality textiles. The new *dingdan* regime has saved consumers (mostly middle- and low-income families) billions of dollars. On the other hand, the new regime has brought challenges to textile manufacturers through competition in both global and domestic markets. It presents serious structural problems for state-owned manufacturers in China: the *dingdan* revolution is, indeed, the straw that broke its back.

Technology Transfer and IT Global Chains

The *dingdan* revolution is not limited to traditional manufacturing sectors. Taiwanese IT entrepreneurs have played a key role in China's entry into the world market. Taiwanese IT people (both technicians and entrepreneurs) have formed loose high-tech *guanxi* networks around the world. For example, many firms and IT workers in California's Silicon Valley are from Taiwan. Jerry Yang, the cofounder of Yahoo, emigrated from Taiwan. With the cost of building a cutting-edge silicon foundry approaching $4 billion, electronics companies have a compelling reason to outsource chip fabrication to Taiwan, where entrepreneurs have the knowledge and experience of American IT businesses. For many years, Taiwan semiconductor has gotten order forms (*dingdan*) from such giants as Broadcom, Sony, and Texas Instruments, which focus on design. In the mid-1990s, Taiwan ran into bottleneck difficulties due to shortages of land and IT human capital, the high cost of the work force, and a limited market.[62]

During the late 1990s, Taiwanese IT entrepreneurs started to invest in China, which soon became the leading global computer chip fabricator. After the 1989 Tiananmen Square massacre, the US and Europe banned the sale of high-tech products to China. But Chinese demand for these products has been consistently high. With their knowledge in both IT and global marketing, Taiwanese high-tech business connections are much sought after by Chinese IT entrepreneurs and government officials. While American IT firms have avoided serious capital investment on the Mainland, in 2005 Taiwanese invested $2.6 billion. The stock market, in turn, has rewarded such Taiwanese firms investing in China, the world's most dynamic market.[63]

The Chinese government has also supported such investment by generous loans. This favorable IT investment environment attracted IT entrepreneurs to build semiconductor factories in China. For example, in 2000, Wang Wen-hsiang, son of the board chairman Wang Yung-ching of a Taiwan plastics company, set up Shanghai Hongli Semiconductor Manufacturing Company in the Shanghai Pudong Zhangjiang High-tech Park, investing US $1.63 billion. The Zhangjiang IT Park in Shanghai was created with public and private investment. The example of Hong Kong, Taiwan, and other overseas Chinese helped create a new middle class of Mainland traders. Buoyed by the upward mobility of *maiban* (middlemen) in the 1990s, a critical mass of young educated Chinese professionals made it into the middlemen network.

Drawing on interviews with thirty prominent Chinese middlemen to gauge the rise of a *dingdan*, we found that *dingdan* involves a network of Chinese political elites, businesspeople, professionals (lawyers and media), higher education, and global retailers. Hong Kong and Taiwanese middlemen are at the top of the *dingdan* hierarchy. It is important to note that these Taiwanese-led firms not only bring highly-valued manufacturing knowledge, organization skills, and global market access to China, but more importantly they are changing the way Chinese business is operating and the way the state exerts political control as well.

For example, the Taiwanese-American CEO of Xin, Mr. Zhang, insisted that the Chinese government allow freedom of religion for his Mainland employees. Zhang, himself a Christian, creates strong Christian worship networks in his factories. We visited a Christian meetinghouse where the company's missionaries hold weekly Bible study for new workers from Mainland China. While "house churches" are often attacked elsewhere in China, Xin's house churches are flourishing in Zhangjiang, Shanghai.[64]

In 2001, the handful of Taiwanese companies dominating the manufacture of laptop computers started moving production to China. By the end of the third-quarter of 2006, the last production line in Taiwan had closed. These Taiwanese companies account for 80 percent of global production of laptops. So today, 80 percent of global laptop output originates in China.

China is not simply the passive receiver of low value-added global manufacturing business. Rather, global entrepreneurs actively interrogate, negotiate, strategize, and adopt global forms and processes to meet global consumer needs. In the process, both the manufacturing base and international trade regime have transformed each other. The Chinese have learned the importance of intellectual property rights from foreign companies. Foreign firms and multinational corporations have received 80 percent of China's high-technology patents.[65]

Non-Economic Effects of Trade

The increasing economic integration between China and Taiwan creates shared interests. The greater the volume of trade and investment that takes place between the two countries, the greater is each side's interest in avoiding conflict and preserving peace.[66] Liberal optimists believe that bilateral economic exchange creates shared interests and good relations between states. The Chinese story supports the liberal trade theory that regards trade as a key element of the liberal path towards peace, starting with Adam Smith, and then the comparative advantage of David Ricardo.[67]

Apart from economic integration, Hong Kong and Taiwan have played and will continue to play an important role in China's further liberalization in non-economic areas. Hong Kong's rule of law and Taiwan's liberal democracy have become *de facto* political opposition to the undemocratic Mainland.[68] Hong Kong also stands as an example for China in terms of government transparency, the rule of law, and protection of civil liberties. Hong Kongers regard themselves as "modern Chinese" representing "freedom, openness, choice, equal opportunity, and international horizons."[69] They believe that in this regard, Hong Kong is China's future. The most attractive organization in Hong Kong for Mainland Chinese is the "Independent Committee of Anti-Corruption" (ICAC).[70] The Chinese translation of ICAC is "clean and just governance." After visiting the ICAC in Hong Kong in 2006, Jia Minzhong, deputy chair of the People's Consultancy in Jishou, remarked, "What China needs most is a Hong Kong-style ICAC. It is better to move that office to China." Jia hoped that an independent organization like ICAC is the first step for the government to deal with the widespread corruption.[71]

The Hong Kong people's brave protest against the Chinese state's attempt to hamper their liberty provided China with a potentially potent example. When the Chinese state attempted to export to Hong Kong its style of rule and social order by posting the Public Order Ordinance in 2000, more than one million Hong Kongers demonstrated in the streets, forcing the Chinese authorities to back down. The most important reason that Beijing capitulated on this issue was that it realized that its failure to keep its promise to practice "one country but two systems" in Hong Kong could end in Taiwanese resistance to unification and a movement for Taiwanese independence.

With elevated consciousness of civil rights, Hong Kongnese have taught the Chinese how to expand their autonomous space. Hong Kongers donated time and money during the 1989 student movement. After the June 4th crackdown, they set up an underground railroad to rescue China's most wanted student movement leaders. We might say that Beijing is now trapped in Hong Kong. It must either constrain or release Hong Kong's society. Beijing's dilemma is the following: If Hong Kong is further constrained, Beijing might be denounced internationally for maintaining Hong Kong's status as a global *entrepôt*. But if it is released from authoritarianism, it sets a powerful example for the Mainland—an example Beijing fears.

Taiwanese entrepreneurs rushed into China for profit, but their presence has also influenced the Chinese in a variety of ways. Most have informed their Chinese employees and business partners about political democratization and civil liberties. Some 4.1 million Taiwanese visit mainland China annually, bringing with them ideas of freedom and democracy, a kind of soft power for common people. No longer can Beijing cast democracy as a Western value when Chinese in Taiwan have freely chosen free markets and freedom of association, press, and religion, as well as democratic elections and the rule of law. Hopeful Chinese in both Taiwan and China have placed democracy as precondition for reunification, thus casting the undemocratic Chinese regime as a unification barrier.

This new unification discourse may become the catalyst for a democratic breakthrough. As pointed out by James C. F. Huang, Minister of Foreign Affairs of Republic of China (Taiwan), "We firmly believe that the ultimate cure to the cross-strait issue is a democratic China. Taiwan has the experience of being the first successful democracy in predominantly Chinese societies; it will and is willing to be the best partner to China on her way to democracy."[72] Taiwanese people are proud that Taiwan scores high in Freedom House's annual surveys on the state of political rights and civil liberties, placing it "in the ranks with the United States, Canada and Switzerland—the freest countries in the world."[73] Like many other Chinese liberal scholars, Liu Junning and Qiu Feng claim liberal democracy as unification's *dixian* (the most basic condition). The Taiwan card can be effective in increasing pressure within the party to push political reform.[74] Nationalism, in this instance, can be beneficial for China's democracy.

On the other hand, the economic dependence of Hong Kong and Taiwan business elites has made economic elite hesitate to push for democratization. The overseas Chinese understand that the government still has direct control over the economy, and they have worked closely with government elites. Some have even argued that Hong Kong businesspeople had formed an "unholy alliance" with Beijing elite.

Elite Learning Curve and Globalizing China

There is also a "push factor" within China eager to link the global economy and institutions. Traditionally, the Chinese central government pursued a policy of "atomization" aimed at isolating individual provinces from each other so that contact and direct trade between them would not develop. During the Imperial period, this was accomplished through vertical control, with authority running from the emperor down to the clan, and from there to the family. According to Liu, dynastic rulers always tried to discourage the development of provincial political identities. This is why Chinese provinces have typically been given place names, such as Hebei "north of the [Yellow] river.[75]

During the Mao era, the Chinese continued to pursue a policy of atomization, but through more modern policies, such as by restricting travel in the absence of specific permission or by allowing food ration coupons to be honored only in the holder's local area. These policies discouraged the development of "horizontal" identities and, during the Mao era, became stratagems for discouraging provincial power. Under Deng Xiaoping, this habit of provincial atomization was intensified when provincial governments played a zero-sum game, making horizontal trade difficult if not impossible. According to Breslin, "Whilst the preferential treatment of Special Economic Zones (SEZs) given to Guangdong in the early 1980's did give the provincial authorities considerable leeway in their relations with Beijing, this does not necessarily equate with strong provincial autarky. The extent to which the market and the foreign sectors penetrated the Guangdong economy made it difficult for even the provincial authorities to control the local economy."[76]

Now, however, Chinese merchants use global networks to forestall these traditional stratagems. What is more, new technologies such as the Internet and cell phones allow for easy intra-provincial contact, as well as contact with the highly integrated world outside China. Faced with an external world bursting with accelerating international trade, new interconnections, and rapidly increasing horizontal ties, the authoritarian party-state is finding it ever more challenging to maintain vertical control. In many ways, atomization could be seen as an antithesis of globalization. Foreign investment provided new business opportunities and practices that spurred "distributive consequences" from the highest levels of government to the common people in state-controlled Special Economic Zones.

In the beginning, political tension between those like Zhao Zhiyang, who pushed towards opening, and those like Bo Yibo, who pulled in the opposite direction, created a gridlock. According to Thoburn and Howell, political friction existed between those who viewed opening as an opportunity for personal gain and those who feared losing power. An open policy pushed political leaders into three groups—radical reformers, moderate reformers, and conservative reformers. The ideas of these respective groups range from hasty opening to measured and planned strides in opening, to criticism of the consequences of opening, and disdain for worldly values. This elite debate has slowed China's opening in terms of the state's policy, but the door was pushed open everywhere by grassroots and foreign forces.

The process of globalization has become a learning curve for government officials and ordinary Chinese who gradually gave up anti-imperialist nationalism for greater pragmatic players. In looking at China's government as the least flexible body of those undergoing restructuring during the reform period, it appears that Beijing is pressured from both below and above. By this we are referring to pressure not only from its citizens, but also from other countries and world organizations. Such pressure is not as effective when it is applied in the form of threats or demands as when it comes in the context of mutual adherence to a higher set of regulations such as those of the World Trade Organization (WTO) and International Labor Organization (ILO). When confronting an international set of norms, reform-minded leaders are able to harness the need for adherence to global requirements as an impetus for change.

In the absence of ideology, as the Communist Party is well aware, living standards become a measure of a government's success or failure. The statement of an old party official sums up the challenge they face. "The young generation is so ungrateful. When I told them that they should show some appreciation to us, older revolutionaries who fought so hard to liberate them. My granddaughter replied: 'if you had not defeated the nationalists, we could live a good life just like people in Taiwan today.'"[77]

An example of using international regulations to push for change can be witnessed in the actions of Zhu Rongji and others when trying to defend the reform agenda. They were able to use WTO membership requirements as motivation for achieving structural reforms that had previously failed because of strong resistance from more conservative party officials. Although Zhu had a difficult time reforming banks and other key institutions, he was able to push for the elimination of many institutional regulations that hampered China's opening. Under Zhu's leadership, the state abolished seventy-one administrative regulations, which were viewed as constraining China's global trade. In addition, China cut tariffs to 11.5 percent to meet World Trade Organization requirements.[78] The United States took a leading role to help Zhu and other reform minded officials meet WTO requirements. China has kept much of its WTO promise by lowering its tariffs on a wide range of goods from an average of 25 percent to an average of 7 percent and eliminating most import license requirements, which in turn boosted global trade. Non-tariff barriers have been harder to quantify, however. On this front as well there have been indications of progress, most importantly, in the areas of import licensing and quotas, and limits on trading rights.

China began implementing import licensing and quotas in the early 1980s. At their peak, 46 percent of all imports were subject to licensing requirements. Because of international pressure, however, the Chinese Ministry of Foreign Trade began reducing the level and scope of licensing restrictions in the 1990s.[79] Remarkably, by 1997 only about 8.45 percent of all imports were still subject to import licensing restrictions.[80] On this front, there have been indications of progress, the most important of which is in the areas of import licensing and quotas, or limits on trading rights. As we sit now, debate rages over further unpegging of the currency due to international pressure. What can be inferred from these actions is that the success of China's foreign trade has finally convinced an increasing number of China's elite that global engagement neither can be, nor should be, avoided.

Interdependence and Role Models

The Chinese story shows that greater international involvement has brought about healthier, faster, and sustainable progress in an ancient, sometimes backward, land. The shift of manufacturing activities to less-developed nations and the collapse of Soviet Communism have played an important role in China's rise. As this once-closed nation opens to the world, increased interdependence among markets has also helped to bring change.

Developed nations like the US, European states, and Japan have played key roles in setting up models for market development and free trade, generating opportunities for China: a model, a source of technology, and a market for low-wage products. As pointed out by Hayek: "The benefits of freedom are therefore not confined to the free....There can be no doubt that in history unfree majorities have benefited from the existence of free minorities and that today unfree societies benefit from what they obtain and learn from free societies."[81] Hayek's statement fits the dynamic economic relationship between China and liberal democracies like Japan and the US.[82] The developed nations continue to act as the leaders; late developers can benefit by learning from earlier experiences.[83]

This interdependence and the actions of Chinese global entrepreneurs have transformed the structure of China's economy from a closed to an open economy. By 2006, China's trade/GDP ratio reached 66 percent, making China the world's most open major economy, "compared to the corresponding ratio of 22 percent, 64 percent, and 28 percent for the United States, the European Union, and Japan respectively."[84] The sum of exports and investment reached about 80 percent of GDP by 2008. Thus, most Chinese aggregate demand depends on its ability to sustain an export-based economic growth.[85] Global interdependence has allowed Chinese entrepreneurs to escape red tape of bureaucracy as more and more have become productive and gained full membership in global community.

Trade dependence makes China more vulnerable to international downturns as it is happening in 2009. Accordingly, the US and others have advised the Chinese to develop their home markets.

China's economic future lies in integration with the global economy. This should bode well for the improvements that still need to be addressed under the current system. It does not imply, however, that the government will choose one direction over another. What it does mean is that in facing both deregulation pressure from foreign companies and liberalization pressure from private domestic companies and from the people, further change is inevitable. Local government officials have realized that global interdependence helps to increase employment rates and local government tax revenue. In some cases, local partnerships help foreign businesses "to cut through red tape."[86] The flow of foreign trade gave rise to incentives to build a strong infrastructure in order attract various businesses. A strong infrastructure in turn also encourages more foreign direct investment because transportation and communication networks facilitate the flow of goods and services. Roads, power supply, and container ports facilitate export-oriented foreign investments.[87] An increasing number of the Chinese elite are willing to study modern management and regulatory systems, innovation techniques, and other market friendly institutional solutions to its public and for-profit governance challenges. Their favorite country to visit is the United States.

Global travel and interaction with the outside led to more tolerate habits and attitudes that are new. For example, Chinese travel overseas are often fined at international airports for pirated DVDs and carrying fake brand names such as Louis Vuitton and Polo Ralph Lauren. Chinese global travelers have also learned some Western etiquette and do not seem offended when told many "don'ts": "Don't pick your teeth, touch your belt, pull at your pants or take off your shoes in public"; "Don't point fingers at people you're talking to and don't put your hands on others' shoulders." As a staggering number of Chinese travel aboard—nearly 40 million in 2006, 50 million by 2010, and 100 million by 2020—their familiarity with modern culture and customs can be expected to reduce the nation's inferiority complex and anti-Western cultural sentiment.[88]

Although numbers are useful in providing a statistical measure of growth, they do not effectively capture the impact of globalization on Chinese society. One of the more positive aspects of this new socio-economic existence has been interaction with foreign enterprises and exposure to their corporate culture. From the business perspective, the stagnating bureaucratic mindset had to be altered for continued economic growth to be realized. Thus, changes were needed in work culture and organizational structure. Such changes would not have been implemented by the government because it was more concerned with technology transfer and the ability to bring in much needed capital. Consequently, these changes played out more in the corporate sector as the result of personal interaction.

It should be noted that such interaction was feared, not facilitated, by the government. During the early days of the SEZ's, the state's fear of such interaction led to a policy that prohibited entry into Shenzhen by nonresidents and called for the use of military personnel, rather than contract laborers, to do much of the major construction. In the eyes of the state, foreign influence was a threat to the single party state and thus must be limited as much as possible.

Another impact of this fear was that, initially, private companies were not allowed to establish joint ventures with the foreign companies. However, despite continual government attempts to limit their influence, foreign companies played an ever-increasing role in the Chinese economy, and their resulting influence was harder to control than the government envisioned. As this corporate culture redefines what traits are considered valuable, individuality, innovation, and audacity will compete with both traditional values and Communist ideology for primacy in the new China. As such, in business culture, the pursuit of rights has been reinforced and has found an additional outlet for release. But over time, the expansion of China's global economic reach has drawn Chinese bureaucrats and party-state managers into a thickening web of ties with international institutions (regulatory agencies, WTO, customs, law enforcement, and government agencies). The frequent communication and contact will over time, gain greater mutual understanding while the economic benefit of trade on China's part will make Beijing leaders become more responsible players in promoting the stability and continuity of the existing global order.[89]

Labor Market and Labor Standard

In addition to companies looking for a new type of employee, in gaining experience through the market, workers began to expect more from the companies than during the socialist time period. Previously, most people were not given the opportunity to look for a job because of state control over mobility and work allocation. Thus, people's expectations were limited by the reality of the situation in which they found themselves. When foreign companies poured in, Chinese from around the country journeyed to Shenzhen (most illegally) to look for jobs in multinational companies. Thus, in great part due to the demand created by the global firms, many Chinese felt freer—and were freer—to move to seek new opportunities, regardless of the slow (or in some cases nonexistent) pace of reform in the Hukou system.

For those were trapped in dead-end situations, work migration was itself liberating. "I had no connections and had a poor relationship with my boss back home," recalled Luo Dongxia, a migrant woman from Hunan. "When I learned that some global firms were hiring, I gave up my secure but boring state job in Hunan and came to Shenzhen in the 1990's. Very quickly, I found a job working for a large firm from Hong Kong. I was initially very scared because I did not know anyone in Shenzhen and my mother-in-law threatened to disown me. Now, I am grateful to the company. As long as I do well in my job, the boss leaves me alone. The work is hard but rewarding."[90]

This story is not unique. The global factories opened opportunities for millions of young rural women who had been desperate to create a new existence for themselves outside of the family/village oriented one that they currently endured. Our findings on globalization's effect on women were thus in line with those of Blumberg, Rae Lesser, et al.[91] It was empowering, not repressive. The scale of female exodus from rural areas was tremendous. An estimated five million female workers from the countryside were able to find jobs in the factories established by global firms in the late 1980s and early 1990s. The numbers now are even more impressive.

The competition among these enterprises for workers has created an environment which encourages job mobility regardless of government regulation. If a distant company provides better benefits for doing the same work, why not move? Although some foreign companies are in situations that prevent them from disregarding *Hukou* regulations, many are willing to help their workers find means of getting around the restrictions whenever possible. Thus, at a minimum, economic growth has provided an impetus for the migrant flow to continue.

Interestingly, the residence dilemma was not merely a rural migrant issue, as graduates from Beijing's top schools often found themselves working for global firms without a Beijing *Hukou*. Amazingly, this did not seem to bother them. "I never have to worry that I do not have a Beijing *Hukou*," said Michael Chu, a business manager at the American company. "I have other important things to worry about."[92] When worrying about violating government regulations becomes a secondary consideration in China, things have definitely changed.

The multinational corporate presence has also opened up access to other forms of monetary and capital accumulation previously unavailable.[93] For example, the multinationals were the first ones in China to establish a means for financing home ownership. In the early 1990s, some firms used corporate-based financing programs to help their Chinese employees purchase their place of residence (the government did not encourage similar action until the late 1990s.) Although the multinational housing ownership primarily affected the urban employed, the long-term societal impact is permanent. With this ownership comes a more self-reliant individual—less dependent on, yet more demanding of, the government. To such individuals, the role of government is to protect what they have accumulated through their diligence.

The multinational corporate presence also brought in an international labor standard. Scholars like Anita Chan in Australia and international labor NGOs have followed the working conditions of those multinational corporations closely. Their criticism of poor working conditions for Chinese workers led to the development of Chinese local NGOs. Almost labor NGOs in Guangdong Province depend on international NGOs for their funding.[94]

Danwei Transformation

As part of this redefining of employees and employers, the workplace is undergoing a corresponding evolution. For most of those employed in urban areas, the workplace was previously one where cooperation was as important as productivity. Catering to the boss was a primary concern since it ensured continued security and protection of basic interests (housing, welfare, education, pension, and medical care). Thus, the culture of the workplace was not one of strong personality or innovation, but more one of a façade of social harmony designed to ensure the boss was content. Although state employment did provide life-long security for most workers, they had little in the way of individual rights or any form of recourse against their employer, since the government served an all-encompassing role. During this pre-reform era, workers were thus forced to exchange economic security for political loyalty, a theory well documented by Andrew Waldon.[95]

With the addition of foreign companies in the marketplace, workers in the city traded a secure existence for one with some freedom. The most important of these newly acquired freedoms was one of no longer existing under the watchful eye of the state, epitomized by the *dangan* (or secret personnel file). Foreign firms obviously do not keep a *dangan* on their workers and, thus, do not exert the same coercive power over their lives. Since no one knew what was written in these files and they are kept for life, people lived in constant fear, worried about committing transgressions that they did not know existed. Regardless of the many instances of poor working conditions in China today, which most certainly need be addressed, at least they are not institutionalized and universally enforced as the *dangan* was. In escaping this engine of personal control, the average citizen was allowed more freedom to pursue those things he deemed important, thus changing the context of his existence.

As part of the individual rights being attained by those employed in foreign firms, the right to strike and that of establishing contracts have been especially welcomed by the workforce. Although some of contracts have been shown to be exploitative, the very contract itself gave many of the workers a sense of empowerment. Thus empowered, however, some have learned harsh lessons about making their own choices. But if one examines the number of lawsuits brought against corporations by workers for failure to adhere to a contract, one comes to the conclusion that the level of consciousness of the average worker has increased tremendously. To many, the contract is the first step towards equality under, and protection by, the law. "I kept my work contract in the safe box in the bank," said Wu Jinghua, a rural migrant worker in Shenzhen. "If my boss fires me before the term ends, I can sue him."[96]

The bottom line is that as more Chinese gain the opportunity to choose with whom they work; businesses in China will be forced to pay attention to workers' rights or they will not keep good employees. For the workers, fighting to protect what is written in their work contract often translates into protecting what they view as their rights as workers. This is not something that then ceases to exist outside of the workplace. When firms violate worker rights as laid out by the Chinese government, workers expect the government to respond. The slippery slope for the government then comes in the form of two very real challenges. The first is how it can enforce worker rights as prescribed by law, but not enforce other rights as prescribed by the Chinese Constitution. The second dilemma is one of defining where worker rights end and human rights begin. What are the consequences when individuals receive far better treatment from their employers than from their government?

An additional influence of the international community on China has been an increased consciousness of the moral legitimacy of gender equality. Although Mao's China claimed to achieve gender equality by doctrine, the reality was that, in most cases, Chinese women still had few chances for upward mobility. Although China had limited affirmative action for females, few women held high government or advisory positions under Mao. When foreign businesses began establishing operations in China, women were hired at record levels. Because of their early entry, over time some have been able to achieve high levels of leadership.

Even though such a process takes time, the existence of female executives in many foreign firms helped not only to change the outlook of many males but also provided a system of mentorship and other assistance to young women seeking to excel. "I was only a taxi driver," recalls Ms. Zhang, a manager at Kamsky Associate in Beijing, "Gini [her boss] found me while taking my cab and then hired me to work for her. Previously, it would have been impossible for me to get a job without a college degree and no government connection. After working here, I realized that Gini had helped all of the women workers in our company."[97] Her boss, Virginal Kamsky, remarked, "In the very beginning, in the early 1980's, there were almost no women in the government posts that I had to interact with as an American executive. When I set up my own consulting firm, I made an effort to bring women into more upper management positions. Now, it just happens that all of my key people are women."[98] Such examples will continue to occur as more businesses operate in the new Chinese economic landscape. Foreign companies were the first in China to provide low-interest mortgages to their workers, which directly affected real estate development in China.

Benefits of World Trade Organization Membership

Besides the great amount of foreign investors and companies to expand its businesses in the country, in 2001, the Chinese state itself took a giant step toward playing a major role in the world of globalization by becoming a member of the World Trade Organization (WTO). WTO membership enticed China to become a responsible global trade partner by reducing both tariffs and non-tariffs barriers.[99] By 2006, foreign trade volume tripled, from US$474.3 billion in 2000 to US$1.422 trillion 2006, with exports jumping from US$249.2 billion to US$762 billion in the same period. WTO membership, robust trade growth, and strong inflows of foreign direct investment has allowed China overtake Japan as the world's wealthiest nation with respect to foreign reserves, which hit US$1.4 trillion in 2007. By 2007, China has surpassed Germany in terms of trade, which has great implications for other developing countries.

Compared with its big trading neighbor countries, such as Japan and South Korea, China is more open to foreign direct investment. China began to open some long-closed sectors such as telecommunications, banking, insurance, asset management, and distribution to foreign investment. According to economist Nicolas Lardy, China has attempted to "abide by all of the WTO rules—from the protection of foreign intellectual property to the elimination of local content requirements that China had imposed on many wholly foreign-owned and joint venture manufacturing companies."[100]

The membership of WTO increases the strength of Chinese comparative advantage in the international market (garment, electronics, fish, pork, and poultry). According to World Bank economists Elena Lanchovichina and Will Matin, entry into the WTO helps China to become the biggest beneficiary (US$31 billion a year from trade reforms in preparation for accession and additional gains of $10 billion a year from reforms after accession), followed by its major trading partners that also undertake liberalization, including the economies in North America, Western Europe, and Taiwan. Accession will boost manufacturing sectors in China, especially textiles and apparel, which will benefit directly from the removal of export quotas. Developing economies competing with China in third markets may suffer small losses.[101]

In short, WTO membership helped China to become a leading trade nation, ranking with Japan, US, and Germany. China has learned how to use the WTO's Dispute Settlement Body to resolve economic disputes rather than use the traditional anti-imperialist nationalist finger-pointing.[102] Since becoming a WTO member, China's trade soared, as overall trade surplus reached $177.5 billion in 2006 and its foreign currency reserves reached $1.4trillion by 2007.[103] The WTO is not just an international influence on trade and investment but also promotes other "Western" institutional building. Thus, China's admission into the WTO on December 11, 2001, became a great catalyst for development of the rule of law in China. Since each of the 151 members has a different legal system, the WTO has set regulations and standards (set up with liberal traditions) to govern this international economic forum.

WTO rules require member nations to have transparent trade laws and policies that directly link to political economy. The WTO itself provides an example of the rule of law since nations must comply with the policies set forth by the WTO or face sanctions. As China has benefited from freer global trade and global competition, this liberal system, encompassing a systematic of rule of law, provides a carrot for China to gain greater access to world markets and access to legal systems from which to learn and adapt policies. China's political and economic elite have increasingly realized that, without a rule of law system, foreign investors will lose confidence in trading with it, as is often the case with African countries. Based on this premise, in order to improve trade with other nations, many Chinese are aware that it behooves China economically to have a strong legal system.

The Chinese elite have tried to separate economic law from other law, delaying the institutionalization of the rule of law while accepting the necessity to deal with trade-related transparency issues. Soon, the regime will discover that such separation is not easy to do. WTO membership will force China to realize its stake in obeying international legal norms.

Non-Economic Cultural Influence: The Rise of New Ideas and Civil Society

Global trade and global capital increased China's openness despite the regime's attempt to keep the minds of Chinese people closed. Trade with the world at large also inspires alternative ideas, and influential ideas lead to societal change, while a closed economy stifles individual thought and increases the possibility of radical nationalism. More and more Chinese have realized that China's secretive internalization of its affairs not only tainted its public relations with other nations but also brought disaster to China (famine and the Great Proletarian Cultural Revolution are two prominent examples). Only an open China can optimally develop and modernize the country. For such a process to gather steam, especially in the face of the entrenched and hidebound Chinese bureaucracy, creativity is vital. It requires creative thought and action to give life to entrepreneurial ideas; innovative ideas and corresponding means are required to turn such ideas into tangible reality. Creativity is the agent that can lead China's individuals out of poverty and the political and social oppression that attends it.

To this point, we have focused on the socio-economic aspects of globalization. Without doubt, economic interaction with the world was needed to push the Chinese door to the external world from cracked to slightly ajar. The process of the door swinging from slightly ajar to completely open, however, has also been and will continue to be influenced by non-economic interactions ranging from elite dialogue to student/scholar exchanges, international conferences, and non-governmental organizations (NGOs). These non-economic cultural influences, plus foreign trade and foreign investment, "create a dependency on exports, imports, and foreign investment and other interaction with the outside world in China, which in turn strengthen relations with the Western world, create centers of power outside the Chinese Communist Party."[104] These non-CCP power sources are important for the world and for the Chinese people to stand up to or at least evade the authoritarian state.

Concern about trade has played a role in Beijing's decision to release political prisoners when international, especially American, pressure has focused on China's human rights record. Every time a Chinese head of state visits the US, or vice-versa, the regime releases some well-known dissident, who usually settles in America. For example, China released Jiang Weiping, a prominent dissident, in January 2006, ahead of President Hu Jintao's visit to the US. Jiang was detained in 2000 and sentenced in June 2001 after writing articles for a Hong Kong magazine in 1999 accusing the governor of the northeastern province of Liaoning of covering up corruption. Jiang was convicted under China's notoriously vague "state secrets" law, used recently against other journalists.[105] A court later cut his sentence from eight to six years.

Leaders of the 1989 Tiananmen student movement such as Wang Dan, Wangjuntao, Muslim activist Rebiya Kadeer, and the 1979 Democracy Wall activist Wei Jinsheng were released after an American president's constant pressure. Such elite pressure is important for the emboldening of other dissenting voices in China. Dissident activist Xiao Yuan, who was jailed for three years after helping leaders of the 1989 student movement escape capture, was grateful for American government pressure: "My living conditions changed for the better when my name was listed as one of the 1989 jailed dissidents in late 1990. Jailers allowed my family to visit, and I was able to buy food through guards, which had been impossible for most 'political criminals.' Starvation was part of the punishment in Chinese prisons at that time."[106]

Most early releases of Chinese dissidents have been leveraged by the San Francisco-based Dui Hua Foundation (*dui hua* means "dialogue" in Mandarin), dedicated to improving universal human rights by means of a well-informed dialogue between the United States and China. Through its partnerships, research, and publications, the Dui Hua Foundation has helped secure ""better treatment of Chinese detainees, particularly early releases and sentence reductions for non-violent political and religious prisoners."[107]

The number of NGOs currently operating in China is estimated in the tens of thousands. Although registration requirements and other bureaucratic impediments previously hampered their expansion, more recently the Internet and other channels have helped spur growth. As a non-governmental link to the rest of the world, NGOs have the ability in many cases to push for reform with the well-being of the people as their focus, unencumbered by political loyalties. For example, although the business community took the leading role in giving more Chinese women the opportunity to advance in the workplace and in other organizations, including the Ford Foundation's Chinese branch, NGOs have also played a role by providing scholarships to women graduates and holding conferences on gender equality.

One such event was the 1995 United Nations International Women's Conference. The conference provided Chinese women, especially female scholars, a chance to voice their displeasure with the current state policy regarding women. As a result of the conference, many universities, some with the help of international groups but many on their own, established departments of Women's Studies. The world attention focused on China during and after the conference also alleviated some of the harassment towards progressive thinkers such as Ai Xiaoming, a professor and leading Chinese feminist scholar. She is grateful to the international feminist support coming from within and outside of international non-government organizations. "After the United Nations Fourth World Conference on Women (FWCW) in Beijing in 1995, life became relatively easier for feminists like me. First of all, I was invited to give lectures in the United States, where I learned feminist theories, social movements, and the power of media and law. When I returned to China, I founded my own women's research center, focusing on exposing gender discrimination in government and society."[108] There is little doubt that international feminist networks are helping to promote a transnational feminist movement that now challenges not only traditional social patriarchy but also discriminatory state gender and family policies.

International NGO's have also played a key role in attempting to focus government attention on such issues as HIV/AIDS awareness and environmental destruction. One example of such an organization is the US-based Nature Conservancy, which established the Yunnan Great Rivers Project to protect an area about the size of West Virginia. As explained on the organization's website, "The Conservancy is now assisting with one of the most ambitious projects we have ever undertaken—a nationwide assessment of China's biodiversity that will result in a plan to protect the country's most important natural resources for future generations."[109]

Many Chinese citizens have been motivated by the fact that there are global communities also concerned for their environment. "I was very moved by people like Carole Fox who cares about China's natural beauty," remarked Wang Yongchen, an environmental journalist and advocate in China, "As a Chinese (citizen), I must do my part to educate our young people to take care of our beautiful land."[110] Wang followed through on this commitment by establishing Green Earth Volunteers together with friends and other journalists. In 2004, the organization helped prevent the government from building thirteen dams on the Nu River in Yunnan.[111]

As summarized by one author, the Chinese have become not only politically aware in embracing values such as gender equality, HIV/AIDS awareness and prevention, gay rights, and protection of the environment, but have also revealed newly acquired cosmopolitan taste.[112] The fact that such a cultural shift may also be representing itself in the form of individual expression, such as the clothes young people choose, also bodes well for China. As pointed out by Orville Schell and David Shambaugh, the new Chinese lifestyle, in imitating the West, may be a preview of revolutionary future change. It is our contention that this "revolution" is already well under way.[113]

Global interaction has worked both ways. In addition to increasing external influence on China, globalization has also raised world consciousness of Chinese culture. In doing so, it has helped reinforce pre-Communist cultural linkages, which had been struggling for survival in the pre-reform era. Xuan Ke, a Naxi Tibetan artist, who had been imprisoned for twenty-one years, for example, was nevertheless able to become an internationally renowned artist once linked to the global community. When the outside world recognized his role in reviving an ancient ritualistic form of Daoist music, traced to the thirteenth century reign of Kublai Khan, he was invited to perform in Europe and the United States. This newly acquired recognition not only made him popular but also encouraged young people to continue learning the art of traditional music. "Among the young musicians, most came to me because they wanted to have the chance to study and perform aboard, and to make money. But a small minority of young people came to me because they are really interested in continuing the traditional cultures. It does not matter [what brought them here, the result is that] global linkage has helped to strengthen local cultures."[114] In examining both economic and social trends, two recurring themes are choice and opportunity. The power of choice is that it implies a sort of independence of thought that was previously not available.

Chinese Global Reach

Although many claim that Chinese steal intellectual property, some accusations have concealed protectionist motivations. In 1998, for example, European Union cigarette lighter manufacturers proposed a draft law requiring safety locks for lighters worth less than two euros. This provision was aimed at

Chinese manufacturers of cheap lighters. EU lighter companies also accused their Chinese counterparts of dumping. Previously, the Chinese would have simply accepted the law and gone their quiet way. This time, however, the affected parties were private Wenzhou lighter manufacturers, whose market share reached 90 percent in Europe and 70 percent in the world as a whole. So many manufacturers' profits were on the line that they organized through their professional association and fought back. Huang Fajing, board chairman of Wenzhou-based Rifeng Lighter Co. Ltd., filed a lawsuit. Representing the Wenzhou Cigarette Manufacturers Association and fifteen other manufacturers, Huang used well-prepared and detailed evidence to show no damage had been done. The international court accepted Huang's argument and the EU side withdrew the proposed law.[115] "This was the first time for a non-government organization in China to win a lawsuit involving international trade barriers, and Huang played a leading role in achieving its successful settlement."[116]

Limits of China's Openness

Measured by FDI and trade, China is increasingly open. But due to one-party domination and widespread corruption, the rule of law, property (including intellectual property) rights protection, and other modern international norms are still lacking. The continuation of the one-party authoritarian regime with its secrecy in military, Chinese foreign investment (energy investment in Latin America and Africa, for example), and governmental budget data (although more open than previously) has given rise to the view that China's rise as an economic, technological, and military power poses a threat to liberal democracies such

Figure 7.3

Source: http://www.chinadaily.com.cn/en/doc/2004-01/08/content_296850.htm

as the United States. If China does not show its willingness to reduce such fear by adopting needed political and administrative reforms, liberal democracies such as the United States might be goaded to adopt protectionist policies or other measures that would hurt mutual interests.

China's global linkage has regional variation in assessing the extent and nature of domestic and external openness.[117] The lack of rule of law and government transparency has given rise to considerable difficulties for foreign businessmen and lawyers when doing business in China. Lack of protection of property rights means that political connections are crucial for the sustainability of successful businesses. Since political connection means dependence on certain party patrons, which come and go every few years, this creates uncertainty whether a contract can be honored and enforced in China.

China's global linkage has regional variation in assessing the extent and nature of domestic and external openness. Lacking favorable places for investment, global investors have rushed to China with little understanding of its political economy. The lack of openness, hostile regulatory environment, intellectual property rights protection, and rule of law have created uncertainty, which forced some global firms to withdraw from China. For example, Whirlpool Appliances, British retailer Marks & Spencer, Quaker Foods, Royal Ahold, and Australian brewery Fosters all pulled out of China in 1999. The government was so surprised by the rapid foreign take over of Chinese industries that in December 2006, the State Council listed seven strategic industries for absolute state control, including armaments, power, oil and petrochemicals, telecommunications, coal, civil aviation, and shipping.

"Beijing has rolled out a set of stricter takeover rules aimed at restricting foreign control of sectors deemed vital to the national interest. In August [2006], rules were set on mergers and acquisitions by foreign investors in the property market. In September, six ministries enacted regulations that gave the Ministry of Commerce expanded power to block foreign purchases of local companies. Also, an anti-monopoly law is being drafted."[118] This ruling will also limit the scale of foreign investment in China in a long run.

Problems of Global Linkage

This discussion has so far focused on aspects of foreign influence that reduce state control over production, marketing, and the lives of ordinary Chinese. But, in some cases, foreign influence has assisted government in its continuing attempts to control the population. First, the government can use foreign technology to control people. For example, Microsoft's decision to help shut down a Beijing blogger at the regime's request, Cisco Systems' technological enabling of Chinese Internet censors, and Yahoo's assistance in the government's Internet censorship by identifying senders are all instances of the regime's use of global technology to silence dissent. Thus, Yahoo helped the Chinese police arrest Shi Tao, accused of leaking state secrets, who received a ten-year prison term. Under pressure from the US Congress, in November 2007 Yahoo founder Jerry Yang bowed to Shi Tao's mother Gao Qin Sheng, prior to a congressional hearing and granted her an out-of-court cash settlement. Yang also established a foundation to help other Chinese to hire lawyers to sue the government.[119] Some Chinese Internet chat rooms discussed this development and guessed the settlement amount.

This knowledge will embolden other Chinese journalists to tell the truth. According Reporters Without Borders' 2005 Report, "at least 32 journalists and 62 cyber-dissidents are currently in prison in China."[120] These figures, the organization has stated, place China first among nations jailing journalists and Internet bloggers. Global businesses' willingness to cooperate in censorship and, "if need be, the occasional jailing of some dissident," is a negative aspect of the global technological revolution.[121] Jerry Yang from Taiwan may dislike the Chinese regime but surrendered due to business concerns because his competitors are in China. The failure of the Internet business elite such as Yang to stand up for principle will have serious consequences for liberty in China. Thus, Congressman Tom Lantos commented on the Yahoo settlement: "It took a tongue-lashing from Congress before these high-tech titans did the right thing and coughed up some concrete assistance for the family of a journalist whom Yahoo had helped send to jail…Today's settlement is long overdue…Yahoo and other U.S.-based Internet companies need to work harder to ensure that they resist any attempts by authoritarian regimes to make them complicit in cracking down on free speech."[122]

Figure 7.4

Note: CEO Jerry Yang (L) testifies. Gao Qin Sheng (C), mother of Chinese journalist Shi Tao, looks on.
Source: http://news.yahoo.com/s/afp/20071113/tc_afp/uschinainternetrightstrial companyyahoo_071113205715

Increasing inequality is another aspect of China's globalization. Trade liberalization and market development in the past thirty years have helped rural Chinese to escape absolute poverty (defined as insufficient food) from nearly 300 million in 1978 to less than 30 million in 2002.[123] "The incidence of rural poverty has fallen equally fast, plunging from 32.9 percent in 1978 to less than 3 percent in 2002."[124] Although global trade is a powerful leveling force to reduce the gap between China and the developed world in national GDP statistics, the process has also increased inequalities within China. Although globalization has reduced the urban-rural income inequality in those regions that experience a greater degree of openness in trade, the poor regions, the West and other inland regions in which the state did not allow foreign trade until late 1990s, have witnessed an increase of inequality. Scott Rozelle has found that since the mid-1980s, inequality had increased among regions, between urban and rural, and among households within the same location.[125] Since most foreign investment has been concentrated along the coast (Pearl River Delta and the Yangtze Delta), inland regions especially in West China witnessed a widening gap. By concentrating on already developed coastal cities, globalization intensified geographical inequalities, between city and countryside as well as between coastal and inland regions.

In China, the Gini co-efficiency (measurement of income disparities) has risen rapidly from 0.24 in 1978, 0.35 in 2000, 0.32 in 2001, to .45 in 2003 and close to 0.5 in 2007.[126] The effects of globalization as well as government policy have played significant roles in transforming China from one of the world's most egalitarian income distribution patterns to among the most skewed. Despite massive movements of labor from the countryside, where incomes are low, to the cities, where incomes are about three times higher, the government *Hukou* discrimination system underwrites systematic inequality by maintaining rural migrants at lower income ranks even while market competition has forced the regime to lay off large numbers of state workers. Global trade has created an urban middle class as well as a working class whose income has increased rapidly in the past ten years. Global firms' competition in hiring Chinese professionals has led to increasing income gaps in major cities such as Shanghai, Beijing, Guangzhou, Shenzhen, and Chongqing. The average incomes of the lowest fifth of Chinese urban workers are only about 5 percent of the top fifth.[127] The sale of urban and rural land, some of which became offices for foreign companies through lease or purchase, has resulted in the transfer of vast sums to the pockets of officials along with Chinese and international speculators at the expense of rural *Hukou* holders, who in theory owned the land. Global firms helped to reduce the importance of *danwei* (urban work-units), which was the main providers for urban social welfare system, increasing urban unemployment and reducing the social welfare benefits of many state workers.

Some scholars challenge this linkage between trade and inequality and find that there is negative association between openness and inequality: places that "experience a greater degree of openness in trade also tend to demonstrate a greater decline in urban-rural income inequality."[128] Others find the globalization linkage is much more complex. According to economists Jikun Huang, Zhigang Xu, Scott Rozelle Ninghui Li, the impact of trade liberalization is a complicated process while it "stimulates domestic production of sectors that are producing commodities in which the nation has a comparative advantage while dampening those in which producers do not have an advantage...While nearly all farmers in many provinces in the east and south will benefit from trade policy, liberalization will hurt producers in the west and north primarily because the region is the largest producer of maize, wheat, cotton, edible oil, sugar, and soybean, the sets of commodities that are most hurt by liberalization."[129]

The flow of international competitive products such as wheat, diary, maize, cotton, oil crops, sugar crops, soybean, and cotton helps Chinese consumers obtain lower prices and better products but hurts traditional grain farmers. This global competition will drive farmers either to give up farming or to focus on farming those commodities such as rice, vegetable, fruits, meat, and fish in "which China has comparative advantage in the international market."[130] Fred Pearce points out in 2004 that due to abandonment, the area of land that was devoted for agriculture declined by 15 percent, pushing grain production down by 0.2 percent.[131] Although this rural restructure through industrialization, services, and diversification of commodities can in the long-run benefit rural welfare, many, especially those in West and Northern China will suffer.

In the cities, moreover, jobs at foreign firms increase the growing gap between skilled (technology savvy) and unskilled workers. Although this income structure fits the Confucian ethic, which dictates that intellectually-minded people control those working with their hands, this radically restructured the Maoist urban wage structure where gap among state workers was small.

Concluding Thoughts

While economic freedom is a necessary condition for civil and political freedom, political freedom, desirable though it may be, is not a necessary condition for economic and civil freedom.[132]
—*Milton Friedman*

In this chapter, we have focused our attention on the role of smuggling and foreign influence in shaping globalization's effect on reform era China. This was not meant to minimize the role of the government, as much as it was to emphasize globalization's creation of a non-confrontational foundation for further reform. The government opened the door with the intent of minimizing secondary effects, but found that this was nearly impossible to accomplish. The explosion of smuggling along with the promulgation of a more globalized business culture led to changes far greater than those intended. Despite the government's attempt to limit access to the new market, the will of the people prevailed to the extent that even in the more rural areas, the impacts of globalization can be felt.

The reason that this is such an important part of the story that we are telling is that globalization provided an environment conducive to the continued pursuit of civil rights. The flood of foreign technology, the broadening reach of global media through legal and illegal means, the proliferation of transnational capital exchange, professional outsourcing and subcontracting, large-scale consumption, and mass migration have created a new China, struggling to find its new Chinese identity.

With the driving factors of this liberal movement being the push for greater self-sufficiency, more non-governmental space, and more control over the decisions that affect one's life, globalization provided the ideal backdrop as all three of these objectives were made more attainable by the establishment of global firms and the culture they brought with them. We are not attempting to portray a rose-colored image of life in a global factory, but simply contend that at least in this environment hope for these ideals is more possible than was the case under the closed society model. *Baochan daohu* marked a beginning of the people's push for rights, having the world globalizing and becoming smaller as it is, helped ensure that this movement was not ended prematurely before it had time to expand.

Globalization has helped most Chinese gain not only material comfort (consumption and trade) but also, to an important extent, the ability to exercise certain fundamental rights (freedom of religion, movement, choice, association, and speech), though not because the regime allows these rights, which it does not, but because the people have seized them. It is significant, too, that the rise of China's global economy has caused a shift from a debate for or against globalization to an effort to expand it to regions hitherto relatively untouched by the global economy.

Most Chinese foreign reserves came from exports, which were produced mostly by foreign firms or subcontracted through Hong Kong and Taiwan firms. China's dependence on trade shows that China needs the global market to sustain its growth. In 2005, China's per capita foreign-trade volume reached $1,000 but its "per capita GDP was $1,231 for 2005…Take away foreign trade, and Chinese per capita GDP would be $231, or 63 cents a day.[133]

As a result, the new Beijing consensus on trade liberalization must be in line with Washington's because China enjoys a trade surplus with the US. Gone are the days when most Chinese were obsessed with anti-imperialist sentiment. That is why today the Chinese are less nationalist in their attitudes towards the West, especially towards the United States. A 2006 *Global Times* poll found that fully two-thirds of the Chinese have "positive feelings" for Americans, and 70 percent were satisfied with Sino-US relations. Nearly half the respondents regard the United States as either a friendly country (10.4 percent), an example to emulate (11.7 percent), or a partner (25.6 percent). On the other hand, the US is still seen as a rival by about the same number (49.2 percent).[134]

This survey confirms a positive attitude towards toward trade liberalization. About half the respondents did not discriminate against American products and another 25 percent, who were positive about US-made products, said they believed trade benefits both countries. Such pro-America attitudes are relatively rare today, even among longtime American allies such as Japan, Germany, France, and Britain. To a great extent that pro-American attitude came about because China has enjoyed trade surplus vis-à-vis the US since 1990s, reaching $262 billion in 2007, which almost equaled most of China's total trade surplus. Since most Chinese are mercantilist, they are grateful to the United States. According to Stephen Green of Standard Chartered in Shanghai, China's trade surplus is roughly equivalent to 10.5 percent of GDP in 2007, making Chinese economy dependent upon the US.[135] Thus, pockets talk.

Pro-American attitudes among the Chinese have important policy implications for both countries. First, the West cannot punish the Chinese government through trade sanctions without hurting its own liberal values since the Chinese economy is connected with its global integration. Second, the United States has gained strategically through China's becoming a stakeholder in the liberal, rules-based global system through foreign direct investment (FDI), large-scale imports from China, its entry into the World Trade Organization (WTO), cultural exchange and tourism, and the operation of Western NGOs in China (to be discussed in another chapter). By choosing to join the global economic system, China as the largest developing and authoritarian state has "reinforced trends that favor the continued industrial and technological preeminence of the United States and other advanced industrialized democracies."[136]

On the other hand, the Chinese party-state's lack transparency in governance and hostility toward liberal values continues to generate fear abroad. Practices cited include its sly military spending policies that attempt to deceive the world about how much it spends; its recent use of a missile to destroy one of its satellites; its more recent combining space weaponization with its lunar landing program; its growing blue-water naval assets; its aggressive military modernization program; its pervasive spying in the United States attempting (and succeeding) to gain militarily sensitive technological and other information; its military buildup in the Taiwan Straits; and expressions of Maoist thinking in the military.

The rise of China, on the other hand, has led to concern and misgivings about China's international intentions. For many years, China has been supporting a string of crude despots, nuclear proliferators, and genocidal regimes. Using its UN veto power, China was able to protect them from international pressure and was thus viewed as reversing progress on human rights. China' irresponsible behavior and its military buildup led some like John Mearsheimer to propose that "the United States has a profound interest in seeing Chinese economic growth slow considerably in the years ahead."[137] Combined with increasing American protectionist tendencies reacting to the growing US trade deficit with China, this line of thinking worries the Beijing elite; the nation enjoyed the highest trade surplus of $250 billion in 2007 in US alone. It is easy for a bipartisan Congress united against China's "unfair trade" in order to appeal the special interest groups for both parties in 2008 election year and beyond.

There is also a native aspect to China's structural dependence on foreign trade. National dependence on the US market led to Deng Xiaoping's use of the classic advice, "*taoguang yanghui*" (conceal brilliance and lie low). While politically, China is radically different from the United States, economically, China and the United States have become interdependent. China must appear weak and backward to reduce the threat that a powerful, democratic United States might perceive. The undemocratic nature of the PRC ensures that the regime is not transparent in its true intentions.

Regardless of Deng's precise meaning, *taoguang yanghui* has already formed the perception that the PRC elite are intentionally concealing strategic aims, and waiting to avenge historical resentments over its treatment by the West over the past two centuries. When China's 2007 trade surplus reached a record $262 billion, such the perception of a China threat, combined with protection-ist forces, became real in the minds of many in the US and the West generally. When the West suffers from economic recession, the perception of threat from an undemocratic and secretive regime can be expected to become more wide-spread. According to a 2007 UPI/Zogby poll on American attitudes towards China, 75 percent said China is America's top economic rival, while Japan came in a distant second at 14 percent. Some 60 percent, moreover, said they view China as an economic threat to the US (in other words, not simply a rival) and 22 percent believe China to be a threat to US national security. Only 6 percent said they would describe China as an economic partner and an ally.[138]

Under the pressure from the US and China's trade dependence on the US market, Beijing was forced to make certain changes in its policies. For example, under pressure from the US, China has played a key role in forcing North Korea to show up at the Six-Party Talks, whose aim is to end Pyongyang's nuclear program. Together with the United States, China was responsible in "drafting a sweeping UN sanctions resolution against Pyongyang" in 2007.[139] Despite its concern for Iran's energy reserves, China was pressured to impose and then tighten sanctions on Iran in 2007 while also forcing the Sudanese government to accept the deployment of a UN/African Union force in the violent and troubled Darfur region.

What is more, China even condemned the Burmese government for its crackdown on peaceful demonstrators, a strange departure given its own record and its refusal to admit the mistakes of the June 4th crackdown. "There is no doubt that China did all of these for its own interests."[140] There is also no doubt that China's economic dependence on trade with the West, especially the US, is the main reason for China to appear more responsible while enjoying a free ride in the US-led security and trade regime.

Given the fact that China's authoritarian regime is powerful and undemo-cratic, China can play a role in opening up dictatorship states like Iran, North

Korea, and Cuba. China can act as a powerful counter to anti-globalization, fundamentalist backlashes, and it can help Africa, Latin America, and the Middle East build both nations and markets. According to one scholar, "Loaded with excess bodies willing to scour the world for economic opportunity, China is America's natural ally in extending globalization's reach and absorbing those off-grid regions where rogue regimes, failed states, and transnational terrorism thrive."[141] Although China has not played an important role in Afghanistan and Iraq, it is in China's long-term interest to work with the US to bring changes to rogue states. China, as a developing country, looks credible in the eye of developing countries with its growing wealth and military power.

The US and Japan are uncertain about what China wants. Global economic and cultural interdependence collides with Leninist, neo-imperial China and its system of political paternalism.[142]

The US government funded much of its recent current account imbalance by borrowing from Beijing the dollars (mostly through the sale of US Treasury Securities) the Chinese have earned selling consumer goods to America. By 2006, this borrowing reached $347 billion. If Beijing sells many of these highly liquid notes, US interest rates will rise up overnight. Much of China's surplus is a product of Chinese companies importing parts from Taiwan or elsewhere that are then assembled and exported to America. This role as the global-manu-facturing middleman enhances Beijing's influence throughout Asia. Thailand and Indonesia need China now more than previously.

Moreover, China's global market dependence means that a slowdown in large world market economies (especially the US economy) will slow China's growth. A sharp fall in exports and real investment will likely trigger a hard landing in China. "A hard landing in China will have severe effects on growth in emerging market economies in Asia, Africa and Latin America, as Chinese demand for raw materials and intermediate inputs has been a major source of economic growth for emerging markets and commodity exporters."[143] If the Chinese are not busy making consumer goods to sell to the world; if due to the 2008-2009 economic slowdown they lose their dependence on the American and Japanese markets, the old anti-imperialist nationalism will sure arise. The party-state will blame foreigners for the nation's economic and political problems.

The rest of world, especially liberal democracies, must deal with both the positive development of Chinese society and possible confrontational situations with its government in the future. The Chinese regime must realize that the Chinese people care not only about material improvement but also about human rights. The regime will continue to ignore widespread popular desire for greater freedom at its peril. It is important for liberal democracies (both peoples and governments) to communicate to the regime the message that the responsible world will not accept China as an equal partner if its top leaders care only for appearances (which it constantly attempts to manipulate), all the while demonstrating in practice cynical or blasé attitudes toward human life and human rights in general. If the Chinese state continues its traditional realist power politics game without redeeming graces and demonstrating a sense of decency as well as limits, China will be perceived as a threat. The world will continue to believe that desire for power on the world stage with benign appearances when it suits the moment, wealth dependent on a currency whose value is not determined by markets, and national glory, and these alone drive elite policy formation. The fear will increase protection sentiment against China, which has come a long way to become part of the global economy.

It is a difficult task for the world to find incentives to induce the Chinese elite to become responsible for its behavior with regard to transparency and accountability. Global linkage through trade, travel, and cultural and political change has transformed China. The country has benefited tremendously from this linkage, and, in turn, has pushed the globalization process forward. China, a latecomer to the process, has become a powerful force in globalization as well as in modernization. The United States, together with Japan and European countries, has helped China become a beacon of possibility for other developing countries in this age of globalization.

Notes

1. Ambassador Robert Zoellick, "The US Trade Representative Countering Terror with Trade," *Washington Post*, (September 20, 2001), p. A 35.
2. http://www.ustreas.gov/initiatives/us-china/.
3. Zheng Bijian, "China's "Peaceful Rise" to Great-Power Status," *Foreign Affairs*, September/October 2005.
4. William H. Overholt, "China and Globalization"; May 2005 testimony presented to the U.S.-China Economic and Security Review Commission on May 19, 2005, p. 7.
5. http://www.stats.gov.cn/tjgb/ndtjgb/qgndtjgb/t20050228_402231854.htm.
6. Ibid.
7. Xinhua News Agency, "China's total trade volume may exceed $2.1 tln this year," *China View*, 10/28/07, 20, 34, p. 59, www.chinaview.cn.
8. John P. Powelson, *Centuries of Economic Endeavor*, (University of Michigan Press, 1994).
9. Nicholas R. Lardy, *China in the World Economy*, (Washington D.C: Peterson Institute for International Economics Institute for International Economics, 1994), p. 1.
10. Interviews with twenty-five traders in Shandou, Shenzhen, Panyu in the summer of 1999, 2000, 2001 in Zhongshan, Shenzhen, and Guangzhou.
11. Interviews with traders in Shenzhen in 1998, Shangdou in 1998, and Panyu in 1998 and 2005.
12. Interview with trader on January 5, 1995.
13. Interview with Kanghua workers, January 4, 1995.
14. Phone Interviewed with trader, May of 2000.
15. Zhang, Xiaoxia, *Zhongguo gao ceng zhi nang: Ying xiang dang jin Zhongguo fa zhan jin cheng de shi yi ren, (shaaxi shifan daxue chubanshe,* [Shaaxi People's Press], 2000), p. 43.

16. Interview with Ye, in Wenzhou, July 2005.
17. Interview with Lao Cai, in summer of 1998, in Hong Kong.
18. Personal Interview with Kwok in Hong Kong, December 15, 1994.
19. Andy Xie Guozhong, "Viewpoint: How Good China's Data? With globalization, a need for fast policy adjustments," *Asian Week,* 2001, http://www.asiaweek.com/asiaweek/99/0528/feat8.html.
20. Interviews with customs officials in Shenzhen in July 1998. Also documented in Hannah Beech, "Smuggler's Blues: Is Lai Changxing China's public enemy no. 1 or a hero for his time?" *Time Magazine,* 10/10/02, http://www.time.com/time/asia/covers/1101021014/story.html.
21. Hannah Beech, "Smuggler's Blues: Is Lai Changxing China's public enemy no. 1 or a hero for his time?" *Time Magazine,* 10/10/02, http://www.time.com/time/asia/covers/1101021014/story.html.
22. Jonathan E. Sinton and David G. Fridley, "Comments on Recent Energy Statistics from China," Lawrence Berkeley National Laboratory, www.china.lbl.gov/publications/ sinton-fridley_sinosphere-oct03.pdf.
23. BBC News, "China sentences 14 officials to death," 11/08/00, http://news.bbc.co.uk/1/hi/world/asia-pacific/1012619.stm.
24. "China Steps up Efforts to Crack down on Smuggling," *Xinhua News Agency,* October 27, 2004.
25. *China Digital Times,* "90 percent of China's billionaires are children of senior officials," November 2, 2009, http://chinadigitaltimes.net/2006/11/90-percent-of-chinas-billionaires-are-children-of-senior-officials/.
26. Interview with a Shenzhen trader Zhao in Shenzhen, on Dec. 25, 2004.
27. Ting Gong, "Dangerous collusion: corruption as a collective venture in contemporary China," *Communist and Post-Communist Studies,* 35, (2002), pp. 85-103.
28. Hannah Beech, "Smuggler's Blues: Is Lai Changxing China's public enemy no. 1 or a hero for his time?" *Time,* 10/10/02, http://www.time.com/time/asia/covers/1101021014/story.html.
29. Sam Vaknin, "Trading from a Suitcase—The Case of Shuttle Trade," March 27, 2002 issue of East West Institute's "Russian Regional Report."
30. Nicholas R. Lard, "Permanent Normal Trade Relations for China," http://www.brookings.org/comm/policybriefs/pb058/pb58.htm.
31. Bureau of Economic Analysis of the US Department of Commerce (2007a) "Trade gap widens in 2006."
32. Nicholas R. Lardy, "China's Economy: Problems and Prospects," *Foreign Policy Research Institute,* Vol. 12, No. 4, February 2007.
33. Nicholas R. Lardy, "China's Economy: Problems and Prospects," *Foreign Policy Research Institute,* Vol. 12, No. 4, February 2007. http://www.fpri.org/footnotes/124.200702.lardy.chinaseconomy.html.
34. Deborah Davis, "Introduction: a revolution in consumption," In Deborah S. Davis, ed., *The Consumer Revolution in Urban China,* (California: University of California Press, 2000), pp. 1-25.
35. Michael Kane, "Creativity and complexity in post-WTO China." *Journal of Media and Cultural Studies,* 17 (3), (2003), pp. 291-301.
36. Tyler Cowen, *Creative Destruction: How Globalization is Changing the World's Culture,* (Princeton, NJ: Princeton University Press, 2002).
37. Cowen, 2002.
38. Arif Dirik, "Markets, culture, power-the making of the second cultural revolution in China," *Asian Studies Review,* 25, (2001), pp. 1-33.

39. Huang Yasheng, *Selling China: Foreign Direct Investment during the Reform Era*, (New York: Cambridge University Press, 2005).
40. Pieter Bottelier and Gail Fosler, "Can China's Growth Trajectory Be Sustained?" *China Economic Quarterly*, December 2007.
41. He Liping, "Sino-Japanese Economic Relations: A Chinese Perspective," *China & World Economy*, (Institute of World Economics And Politics at Chinese Academy of Social Sciences, 2003), 16 Dec. 2007, http://old.iwep.org.cn/wec/2003_9-10/heliping.pdf.
42. Yasheng Huang, *Selling China: FDI during the Reform Era*, 2005.
43. Diana Farrell, "The Case for Globalization," *The International Economy*, (2004), p. 53.
44. John Whalley and Xian Xin, "China's FDI and Non-FDI Economies and the Sustainability of Future High Chinese Growth," National Bureau of Economics, Working Paper No. 12249, May 2006. Matt Nesvisky, "Will Super-High Chinese Growth Continue?" *NBER Digest*, November 14, 2006.
45. Huang, 2005.
46. Cheng Li, *China's Leaders: The Next Generation*, (Rowman and Littlefield Publishers, 2001), p. 77.
47. Zhang Ming'ai, "Success and confusion: The lives of overseas returnees," China. org.cn, November 19, 2007, http://www.china.org.cn/english/China/232355.htm.
48. Personal interview with Zhang, November 14, 2007 in Maui, HI.
49. Zhang Ming'ai, "Success and confusion: The lives of overseas returnees," China. org.cn, November 19, 2007. http://www.china.org.cn/english/China/232355.htm.
50. Personal interview in Chengdu, July, 2005, China.
51. Personal Interview with Zhang Jia, Beijing, 2004.
52. Personal interview with Prof. Ouyang in Guangzhou, August 5, 1986.
53. US Treasury, www.treasury.gov/offices/international-affairs/economic-exchange-rates/pdf/2007_Appendix-2.pdf.
54. For more on Taiwan's role in China's global economic reach, see Suzanne Berger and Richard K. Lester, eds., *Global Taiwan: Building Competitive Strengths in a New International Economy*, (Armonk, NY.: M. E. Sharp, Inc., 2005).
55. Interview with overseas Taiwanese businessman, Ding, in 2005, Honolulu, HI.
56. *World Market*, (Cambridge and New York: Cambridge University Press, 2002), Chapter 2.
57. Hao Yuanchao, "Foreign investments get involved with Chinese water supplies: some reflections on the provision of water," *The China Commercial News*, November 4th 2007. Anonymous article, "Veolia 'gets into bed with local governments' and invests 2.5 billion dollars in China," *Diyicaijing*, November 9, 2007, Translation provided by China Analysis (*Les Nouvelles de Chine*), http://www.centreasia. org/en/6/articles-et-publications/7/china-analysis/.
58. Personal interview with Tainanese business association, 2005, Shanghai.
59. Interviews with Kenny Wong in Shanghai, 2005 and 2006.
60. See a good discussion on the complex supply chain in Nicholas Zamiska and David Kesmodel, "Growing Concern: Tainted Ginger's Long Trip From China to U.S. Stores—Supply Chains Make Finding Source Tough; Lots of Small Farms," The *Wall Street Journal*, (November 19, 2007), p. A1. Personal communication with Nicholas Zamiska in 2007 by email.
61. Joseph Schumpeter, *Capitalism, Socialism, and Democracy*. (Harper, New York, 1950), p. 83.
62. Hai Sun, "The Comparative Research between High-tech Industry, Investment Mode of Shanghai and that of Taiwan," China-USA Business Review, July 2004, Volume 3, No. 7, pp. 1537-1514.

63. http://www.wired.com/wired/archive/13.05/wired40.html?pg=4.

64. Personal interview with Liu in Shanghai, 2004.

65. Hu Xingdou, "Reform National Innovation system: Pushing China to become a Research Institute for the World," (改革国家创新体制，推动中国成为世界研究院), http://www.huxingdou.com.cn/.

66. We must not forget that the famous lecture before WWI arguing that, on account of economic interconnections, European countries could not possibly go to war.

67. For a detailed analysis of the relationship between free trade and peace, see George T. Crane and Abla Amawi, eds., *The Theoretical Evolution of International Political Economy: A Reader*, 2nd ed., (New York: Oxford University Press, 1997), pp. 6-8. Later analysis would indicate that trade was an important element to promote peace, but was less important than the integration of global financial markets. Erik Gartzke, "The Capitalist Peace," *American Journal of Political Science*, 51, no. 1, (2007), pp. 166-191.

68. Fei-Ling Wang, "Taiwan: A Key to China's Rise and Transformation," *Foreign Policy In Focus*, December 21, 2006.

69. Yuk-Lin Renita Wong, "*Going 'back' and staying 'out'*: Articulating the postcolonial Hong Kong subjects in the development of China," *Journal of Contemporary China* 11, pp. 141-160.

70. http://www.icac.org.hk/.

71. Personal interview with Jia Minzhong, July 13, 2007, in Jishou, Hunan, China.

72. James C. F. Huang, "Taiwan Is China's Best Partner to Democracy," Conference entitled "Democratization in Greater China: What Can We Learn from Taiwan's Past for China's Future?" at Stanford University on October 20, 2006.

73. James C. F. Huang, "Taiwan Is China's Best Partner to Democracy." Conference entitled "Democratization in Greater China: What Can We Learn from Taiwan's Past for China's Future?" at Stanford University on October 20, 2006.

74. Personal interviews with Liu Junning and Qiu Feng on July 20 and July 21 2007 in Zouping County, Shandoong Province.

75. Alan P.L. Liu, "Provincial Identities and Political Cultures: Modernism, Traditionalism, Parochialism and Separatism," *Chinese Political Culture 1989-2000*, edited by Shiping Hua, (Armonk, NY: M.E. Sharpe, 2001), p. 247.

76. Shaun Breslin, *China in the 1980's: Centre-Province Relations in a Reforming Socialist State*, (New York: St. Martin's, 1996.), p. 151.

77. Personal interview with Mr. Jiang, former party secretary of the Wuhan Technology University, June 1998, Wuhan, China.

78. Personal interview with Mr. Wu Zhengzhang, former chief economist at the Research Center of the State Council and Beijing Officer Director, Shenzhen Development Bank, Beijing, July 6, 2000.

79. Nicholas R. Lardy, *Integrating China into the Global Economy*, (Brookings Institution Press, 2002), p. 39.

80. Nicholas R. Lardy, *Integrating China into the Global Economy*, (Brookings Institution Press, 2002), p. 39.

81. Friedrich Hayek, *The Constitution of Liberty*, (Chicago: University of Chicago Press, 1960), p. 32.

82. Erich Weede, "Economic Freedom and the Advantages of Backwardness," *Economic Development Bulletin*, No. 9, January 31, 2007, http://www.cato.org/pub_display.php?pub_id=9300.

83. George Zhibin Gu, *China and the New World Order: How Entrepreneurship, Globalization, and Borderless Business Are Reshaping China and the World*, (Fultus Corporation, 2006).

84. Fred Hu, "The Role of the Renminbi in the World Economy," *Cato Journal*, Vol. 28, No. 2 (Spring/Summer 2008).
85. Nouriel Roubini, "Hard Landing In China?" Forbes.com, Nov. 6, 2008, http://www. forbes.com/2008/11/05/china-recession-roubini-oped-cx_nr_1106roubini.html.
86. Farrell, (2004), p. 55.
87. Farrell, (2004), p. 55.
88. Howard W. French, "Chinese tourists: The next big wave," *New York Times*, May 16, 2006.
89. Thomas P.M. Barnett, *The Pentagon's New Map: War and Peace in the Twenty-First Century*, (Putnam Adult, 2004).
90. Interview with Luo Dongxia, July 21, 2003.
91. Blumberg, Rae Lesser, et al., *Engendering Wealth and Well-being: Empowerment for Global Change.*
92. Interview with Chu, Beijing, July 5, 2002.
93. N. R. Lardy, "The Role of Foreign Trade and Investment in China's Economic Transition," *China Quarterly*, 144, (1995), pp. 1065-1082.
94. Huang Yan, "Self-Help Labor NGOs in the Era of Globalization," *Nanfeng Chuang* (South Wind Window), November 16, 2007. http://news.sina.com.cn/c/2007-11-15/122014311592.shtml.
95. Andrew Waldon, *Communist Neo-traditionalism: Work and Authority in Chinese Society*, (Berkeley: University of California Press, 1986).
96. Personal Interview with Wu, July 11, 1999, Shenzhen, China.
97. Personal interview with Ms. Zhang Yi, Beijing, July 2001.
98. Telephone interview with Ms. Kamsky May 15, 2000.
99. Nicolas R. Lardy, "China Enters The World Trade Organization," *Integrating China into the Global Economy*, (2002) p. 2.
100. Nicolas R. Lardy, "China Enters The World Trade Organization," *Integrating China into the Global Economy*, (2002).
101. E. Elena Ianchovichina and Will Martin, "Trade Impacts of China's World Trade Organization Accession," *Asian Economic Policy Review*, 1(1), (June 2006), p. 4565.
102. "International Studies Research Institute and Research Institute of Economic Diplomacy," *China's Economic Diplomacy 2006*, (Beijing: *renmin chubanshe* [People's Press], 2007).
103. Xinhua, "China to raise reserve requirement ratio," *China Ministry of Commerce*, 19, (09/06/07), p. 15, http://www.chinadaily.com.cn/china/2007-09/06/content_6086995.htm.
104. Thomas Lum and Dick K. Nanto, "China's Trade with the United States and the World," CRS Report for Congress, April 29, 2005, fpc.state.gov/documents/organization/48587.pdf.
105. Ming Wan, "Engaging China: The Political Economy and Geopolitical Approaches of the United States, Japan and the European Union," *Japan Focus Newsletter*, 2008, http://japanfocus.org/products/details/2576.
106. Personal Interview with Xiao Yuan, July 23, 2004 in Kunmin, China.
107. John Kamm, Dui Hua's founder and executive director, was an early advocate of corporate responsibility and has intervened on behalf of hundreds of Chinese detainees. A former businessman, Kamm has been the recipient of several awards for his human rights work, http://www.duihua.org/.
108. Personal Interview with Ms. Ai Xiaoming, telephone interviews in Kunmin, Yunnan, and China, July 24, 2004.
109. The Nature Conservancy China website, http://nature.org/wherewework/asiapacific/china/.

110. Interview with Wang Yongchen.
111. Interview with Zhang Zhi Jun, an editor of San Lian Presss in Beijing who went with her to Nu River and wrote a report on this event, July 8, 2004 in Beijing.
112. Gerald Segal, "Enlightening China?" In David S. G. Goodman and Gerald Segal, eds., *China Rising: Nationalism and Interdependence*, (New York: Routledge, 1997), pp. 172-191.
113. Orville Schell and David Shambaugh, eds., *The China Reader: The Reform Era*, (New York: Vintage Books, 1999), pp. 260-296.
114. Personal interview with Xuan Ke in February 2004, Honolulu, HI.
115. Personal interview with Ye, a Wenzhou government Official in Wenzhou, on July 8, 2004.
116. *China Business Weekly*, " Movers and shakers in China's economy," (01/08/04,) p. 22, http://www.chinadaily.com.cn/en/doc/2004-01/08/content_296850.htm.
117. S.G. Goodman, *How Open is Chinese Society?*, in Goodman and Segal, *China Rising: Nationalism and Interdependence,* (1997), pp. 27-52.
118. TING SHI, "State control spelled out for strategic industries," *SCMP*, December 19, 2006.
119. Associate Press, "Yahoo settles jailed Chinese journalists case: lawyer," November 13, 2007, http://news.yahoo.com/s/afp/20071113/tc_afp/uschinainternetrightstrial-companyyahoo_071113205715.
120. Reporters without Borders, http://canada.ifex.org/fr/content/view/full/70972.
121. Richard Cohen, "Business, and Repression, as Usual," *Washington Post*, (January 19, 2006), p. A 19. The Gini coefficient is a measure of equality, defined as a ratio with values between 0 and 1 with a low Gini coefficient indicating more equal income or wealth distribution, while a high Gini coefficient for more unequal distribution, http://en.wikipedia.org/wiki/Gini_coefficient.
122. Associate Press, "Yahoo settles jailed Chinese journalists case: lawyer," November 13, 2007, http://news.yahoo.com/s/afp/20071113/tc_afp/uschinainternetrightstrial-companyyahoo_071113205715.
123. NSBC (National Statistical Bureau of China), *China Rural Household Survey Yearbook, 2003b*, (Beijing: State Statistical Press).
124. Jikun Huang, Zhigang Xu Scott Rozelle Ninghui Li, "Impacts of Trade Lib-eralization on Agriculture and Poverty in China," FED Working Papers Series, No. FE20050018.
125. Rozelle Scott, "Stagnation Without Equity: Changing Patterns of Income and In-equality in China's Post-Reform Rural Economy," *The China Journal* 35 (January 1996), p. 63-96.
126. NSBC (National Statistical Bureau of China), *China Rural Household Survey Yearbook,* (Beijing: State Statistical Press, 2003). Robert Lawrence Kuhn, "What Will China Look Like in 2035?" *BusinessWeek*, October 16, 2007, http://www.businessweek.com/globalbiz/content/oct2007/gb20071016_143714.htm.
127. Stephen Roach, "Globalization's New Underclass: China, the US, Japan and the Changing Face of Inequality," *Japan Focus,* http://japanfocus.org/products/de-tails/1923.
128. Yi Wu Shang-Jin Wei, "Globalization and Inequality: Evidence from Within China," NBER Working Paper No. 8611, Issued in November 2001, http://www.nber.org/papers/w8611.
129. Jikun Huang, Zhigang Xu Scott Rozelle Ninghui Li, "Impacts of Trade Liberal-ization on Agriculture and Poverty in China," FED Working Papers Series, No. FE20050018.

130. Jikun Huang, Zhigang Xu Scott Rozelle Ninghui Li, "Impacts of Trade Liberalization on Agriculture and Poverty in China," FED Working Papers Series, No. FE20050018.

131. Fred Pearce, "Sowing the seeds of starvation," *The New Scientist*, 02624079, 9/18/04, Vol. 183, Issue 2465.

132. Milton Friedman, *Capitalism and Freedom* (Fortieth Anniversary Edition), (Chicago: University of Chicago Press, 2002), ix.

133. Henry C. K. Liu, "The US-China trade imbalance," *Asian Times*, April 1, 2006, http://www.atimes.com/atimes/China_Business/HD01Cb05.html.

134. *China Daily*, "Most Chinese like Americans: Poll," 03/20/06, p. 1, 10. The survey was conducted in Beijing, Shanghai, Guangzhou, Chongqing, and Wuhan by random house-to-house interviews in February 2006. It collected valid samples from 1,175 people.

135. Richard McGregor, "China 2007 trade surplus a record $262bn," The *Financial Times,* January 11, 2008, http://www.ft.com/cms/s/0/e83a2524-c013-11dc-b0b7-0000779fd2ac.html.

136. George J. Gilboy, "The Myth Behind China's Miracle," *Foreign Affairs*, July/August 2004, http://www.foreignaffairs.org/20040701faessay83405-p40/george-j-gilboy/the-myth-behind-china-s-miracle.html.

137. J.J. Mearsheimer "The future of the American pacifier," *Foreign Affairs* 80:5, pp. 46-61.

138. UPI/Zogby Poll, "75% say China top U.S. economic rival," May 23, 2007, http://www.zogby.com/news/ReadNews.cfm?ID=1314.

139. Stephanie Kleine-Ahlbrandt and Andrew Small, "Beijing's dictatorship diplomacy," *IHT*, December 20, 2007.

140. Willy Lam, "China flexes its new muscle," *IHT*, December 20, 2007.

141. Thomas P. M. Barnett, "Managing China's Ascent," Posted 7/29/07, http://www.usnews.com/usnews/news/articles/070729/6china.fear.htm.

142. Ross Terrill, "What does China *wang*?" *Wilson Quarterly*, (Autumn 2005), pp. 50-61.

143. Nouriel Roubini, "Hard Landing In China?" Forbes.com, Nov. 6, 2008, http://www.forbes.com/2008/11/05/china-recession-roubini-oped-cx_nr_1106roubini.html.

Conclusion

*The "only future" for China is "democracy, rule of
law, free press, religious freedom, free information.
China's future depends on these factors.*
—Dalai Lama, 2007[1]

*As China reforms its economy, its leaders are find-
ing that once the door to freedom is opened even a
crack, it cannot be closed. As the people of China
grow in prosperity, their demands for political
freedom will grow as well...The efforts of China's
people to improve their society should be welcomed
as part of China's development. By meeting the
legitimate demands of its citizens for freedom and
openness, China's leaders can help their country
grow into a modern, prosperous, and confident
nation.*
*—President George W. Bush, Speech in Kyoto,
November 21, 2005.[2]*

China is experiencing a social revolution towards a more liberal society.
How and why do societies liberalize? Is the world preconditioned to expect a
dramatic event such as a revolution or governmental collapse to set the whole
process in motion? What would a society look like if there was no such defining
event? Instead of collective action, what if individual efforts undertaken in a
spontaneous,[3] unorganized, leaderless, non-ideological, and apolitical pursuit of
limited rights began to erode the foundation of state-controlled existence? Would
such a movement be recognized? Throughout this book, we have examined just
such a process—a rights acquisition movement—which has been at the core of
the reform era transformation. This struggle, conducted by individuals rather
than groups, has led to an integrated socio-political-economic change that has
often been neglected by contemporary scholars.

Grassroots Modernization versus the China State

Most major changes in Chinese society emerged as a result of grassroots
movements and globalization: decollectivization, migration, private enterprise,
global trade, the information revolution, the sexual revolution, and the rise
of civil society. In this transformed world, the largest transformative process

(from socialist to state capitalism and from agricultural to industrial society), the Chinese government has responded to social change; it has not led.

Ordinary people affected initial grassroots change, often illegally in its beginning stages. When adopted by more people in more places, the demonstration effect spread, forcing the government to adopt reform policies.

Bao Tong, a leading Chinese reform official, attacked Deng Xiaoping for constantly changing policies in order to ensure party-state survival. One minute Deng urged reform, and the next he resolutely upheld the four basic principles of socialism: one minute he wanted to escape from some political dead end and the next he returned to it.[4] Thus, government policy swung like a pendulum.

The strength of a strong, authoritarian state and the revival of civil society are two Chinese cultural traditions.[5] The conflicts between them include questions regarding respect for private property, a culture that nurtures civil society and entrepreneurial enterprise. The Chinese miracle has involved a process of growing disenchantment with the officially sanctioned "big state" tradition. During this process, ordinary Chinese and officials alike have benefited from the new incentives created by the "small and weaker traditional culture of entrepreneurship and respect for private property." This interaction between the widespread practice of illegal activity of all kinds and gradual official acceptance has formed the basis of Chinese reform. The game demands on the interdependence.

There are many factors contributing to this movement which have been overlooked—the economic miracle, the peaceful rise of Chinese debate, and the lack of substantial government political reform being at the top of the list. However, even more important than these issues has been the fact that the movement's characteristics have made the movement itself difficult to recognize. The pursuit of rights has transpired in an apolitical, individualistic fashion, centered on those issues that each person has defined as most critical to their life, manifested in the form of non-confrontational subversion of policy. Although the desires of all of these individuals contain common themes, such as access to food, some control over where to live and where to work, and some level of freedom of information, the way in which the people have pursued these rights has neither been coordinated (the house churches, sexual freedom) nor methodologically consistent. As such, the early years of the movement were harder to recognize than one that continually manifests itself in more visible forms such as protests and speeches designed to rally the public.

Private Property and Entrepreneurship

Private control over production after the successful decollectivization movement was the basis upon which private property took root in Chinese society. The spontaneous drive to own housing and material products and for control over harvests was the engine that drove first rural society, then urban society toward the new China. The development of private enterprise also followed the same path, from illegality to informal toleration to formal recognization. In many places, private enterprise paid more taxes to the government than state factories. This private development was linked to market development, while competition from non-state sectors increasingly forced state enterprise to retreat.[6]

The Chinese story shows that entrepreneurs are key players for the latecomers to modernization to successfully undergo economic development. Individual incentive, not It is no surprise that with 40 million entrepreneurs China has excelled in entrepreneurship and economic growth, and there is every indication that it will continue to do so.

There is a very simple reason as to why the movement transpired the way it did: the less visible, non-confrontational nature made its existence possible. Had it started differently, it may have gone the way of the Democracy Wall Movement, or worse, 1989 Tiananmen Square and 2001 Falungong, as the government would not have tolerated open confrontation, especially during such a time of uncertainty. In addition, the initial success of *baochan daohu* validated the method. Rural citizens learned that they could positively affect their lives through the localized pursuit of basic necessities—in this case, control over subsistence. In fact, they actually brought local government officials into a status of unwitting compliance by paying them bribes and providing increased agricultural revenue. Because of this localized success and the central government's eventual acquiescence, the other lesson that was learned was that a possible result of non-confrontational direct action was government withdrawal from an area of which it previously controlled. The feeling of self-reliance gained from this experience was important as it helped to create a mindset that the government need not control all aspects of one's life.

As self-reliance and self-confidence again became phrases with positive connotations (in society at least), the time was right for further action. That the government did not have the capacity to deal with so many issues at once resulted in grassroots disobediences of so many kinds (gay culture, millions of counter government culture websites, tens of millions of migrants, several millions prostitutes/sex workers, tens of millions of text messages, millions of chat rooms and instant messaging) that it was forced to tolerate a certain type of action despite the fact that the people initiated it; consequently, life just became an issue of how far to push the limits. The entrepreneurs were some of the first who tested this water, as each market they attempted to create was either for a product or service that did not exist or one whose existence was previously restricted, or exclusively managed, by the government. As such, these individuals were not only working without the protection of the law, but were often in violation of existing regulations. As such, we reemphasize the fact that the initial entrepreneurs were not beneficiaries of economic liberalism, but they helped facilitate its development.

In addition to their role in creating markets, the businesses created by entrepreneurs, along with those newly established by global firms, helped set the conditions for the freedom of mobility movement. Had the government still been the only employer, those who left their villages in violation of established law, would have had even less opportunity for success. Although we contend that people moved for reasons in addition to those of pure economics, had there been no jobs at the other end, this process would have been complicated tremendously.

The growth of non-state enterprises also helped spur the development of the informal market, which we define as production and consumption existing outside of government regulation. As such, it provided another environment in which people could pursue rights. This desire manifested itself in the creation and dissemination of TIA (technology, information, and artistic expression). The importance of this merging of the rights movement with the informal market lies in the creation of a parallel society, outside of the government purview. This society increased the pace of liberalization and further facilitated the development of a civil society. It is due to these market linkages that we recognize economic liberalism as the primary facilitator of this movement.

Although this informal market, along with technology improvements, led to an increase in intellectual property rights violations, this was a necessary first step (not an end state), since given the economic status of the common man and the disposition of the government, there would have been no other way to spread information, ideas, and entertainment so rapidly. As we described previously, we are not advocating this as a replacement for intellectual property law as much as we are trying to explain the complexity with which China has evolved. Similar arguments can be made with respect to smuggling during the same time period; in the absence of choice, people resorted to the only means available to them.

Through this process of examination, we have seen how entrepreneurs, migrants, and other ordinary citizens are, as individuals, challenging the status quo by pursuing increased rights, creating a synergistic liberalization movement. This has led to a primarily bottom-up (government reacting to the movements and ideas of the people) movement, rather than top-down (government action being responded to by the individual).

Liberty as the Engine of Growth

A limited form of liberty has been at the heart of China's economic development. Migration of millions (150 to 250 million strong) not only freed China's labor market but also led its growing urbanization, despite the government's attempt to limit it. Migrants have brought with them their own folkways—religious beliefs, tendencies to self-government, even dietary habits—that have enriched urban life. This new decentralized urban culture has made for cultural pluralism. Rural migrants who were the children of the Great Leap Famine have adopted a healthy skepticism towards a socialist planned economy and helped China to embrace a new culture of independence and autonomy. This contrasts sharply to the closed China, divided into separate urban and rural worlds, of thirty years ago.

Technology as Empowerment: The Internet and Telecommunications

The Internet has provided a highly effective means for Chinese self-expression. As a current popular saying has it, in real life, people lie when they use their real names; but online, people use invented names to tell the truth.

Liberal grassroots movements have significantly benefited from telecommunication technology. Links between technology and the growth of civil society are apparent: cellular technology has increased from 10 million users in 1997 to over 600 million as of July 2008. Important market developments and technologies (instant messaging, digital cameras, phones, fax machines, websites, blogging, computers, and cellular telephones) also enable ordinary Chinese to establish civil society organizations despite government restrictions. Millions of social groups have been formed. Citizens can call on others with similar interests to rally around a common goal and reduce the fear of imprisonment because they are so numerous.

One of the most interesting civil society formations is the use of email and text messaging to spread information on the issues of the day and propose public action. Like the May 2007 Xiamen residents' and May 2008 Chengdu residents' successful protests against a local government development project (discussed previously) and the June 2007 Shanghai residents' *sanbu* (group walk) the very day that the government announced a revised "maglev" (magnetic levitation) route connecting the city's Pudong and Hongqiao airports. Text messages in Shanghai coordinated several hundred walkers, forcing the government to extend the time for the expression of public opinion on the matter. Since *sanbu* (literally an "after-dinner walk") is a common social practice of urban Chinese, it would be difficult for the regime to shut one down without causing a major social reaction.

Had they applied for a protest permit, walkers would have been denied for two reasons. First, June is a month that the Chinese state does not allow any organized protest because of fearing people commemorating the 1989 student movement of June 4th—a politically sensitive day. Second, the Shanghai government supported the new train rout because it was regarded good for the local economy.

All three cases show that local governments can no longer run business as usual, forcing some degree of accountability and transparency in large government projects.

These Chinese cases confirm Pierre Levy's concept of real democracy, as mobile technologies such as cellular telephones and personal computers inform huge swaths of connected communities. In essence, protest through cell phone coordination led to alternative voice transmission and thus, in a sense, enriched the concept of government by the people. Informal groups and underground groups depend on those new technologies to coordinate national and local activities.

The Internet age has allowed for the interaction of people and groups that previously were separated by geography or social constraint. This interaction has been beneficial in building social awareness around various issues, including the environment, democracy, and human rights. As a blogger informs the Chinese online public of his or her interests, concerns, ideas, projects, and products in a timely fashion, online users respond accordingly. As a result, clusters of similar interest groups emerge. Most clusters form around hobbies such as auto owners, stamp collectors, dancing and singing groups, film and TV viewers, and bibliophile groups—normal constituents of civil society.

Many of these apolitical groups also touch sensitive issues, however, and spontaneous response to them may trigger a national interest group collective action. It is on account of this potential challenge to its power that the Chinese government annually spends billions of Yuan on the Great Fire Wall and fields vast squads of Internet police and imprisons numerous political bloggers. In 2007, the Chinese state placed twenty-nine journalists and fifty-one cyberdissidents in prison, making China one of the least free nations in the world, according to Freedom House. But despite state oppression, millions continue to use the Internet and cell phones to coordinate, plan, and act.

The power of video and broadcasting are new tools for the Chinese people to hold government officials responsible for their actions. The 2007 beating to death of a Tiananmen man who videotaped the government trashing the community showed how government at all levels fears the broadcasting potential that lies in the palms of 600 million hands. If officials know their wrongdoings will be exposed, they may commit fewer of these transgressions.

The Internet provides an alternative voice about citizen rights and responsibilities. Such online civic education raises the "rights consciousness" of the Chinese people, since most users are educated. Once the public gains information, online responses will have the force of public opinion to apply pressure for some form of transparency and accountability in government. It is precisely for this reason that the Chinese premier traveled to the Sichuan earthquake epicenter in May 2008 and had his trip nationally televised.

The Global Environment

Global linkage has also played a role in China's rise. Without access to developed markets, latecomers like China and India could not have achieved economic success. A liberal, open international environment has helped China enter a new stage of industrialization and commercialization.

The influence of the global environment has been not only in the economic arena but in the cultural realm as well. Behind these changes, three new developmental lessons appear to have emerged from China's experience: new growth is based upon entrepreneurial force, not on government; development benefits from an open society; and substantial international involvement brings healthier, faster, and sustainable progress.[7]

As the world's largest developing nation, China's growing role in the global economy is changing the world because people in other developing nations share the same dream as the Chinese: a higher living standard, better education for their children, and more personal liberty. China's transformation plays a central role in setting the new order, a new mind set, and the map for other developing countries, especially in Asia and Africa. Gone are the days where the anti-imperialist sentiment filled the air of developing world.

How Critical Mass is Formed

The rise of sexual liberty and other social movements can also help us to understand how a critical mass of resistance to party-state domination can be formed in a Communist regime. This inquiry is more important when we study a Communist regime like China, where the state bans all forms of non-state collective action. In the eyes of public choice theory, the free rider problem would have inhibited the Chinese people from participating in any resistance movement. Any individual who attempted to defy the state to achieve personal liberty would be crushed by the state's powerful apparatus of oppression. In his classic 1965 work, *The Logic of Collective Action*, Macor Olson argued that people generally will not contribute to public goods because they believe that others will not contribute their fair share, or they can gain the benefit's other's action without paying the price themselves.[8] The latter circumstance is the classic "free rider problem." According to this argument, only small groups can induce members to make sacrifices necessarily to obtain public goods. They can do so because individual responsibility is visible to all members and internal pressures can produce conformity.

Clearly this is not case with the decollectivization movement, private sector development, migration movements, information revolution, and sexual revolution in China. Rise of cosmopolitan society and the decline of the party-state ideology confirm that the free rider problem can be overcome if people individually can simultaneously benefit from the "public good" in question. In China, a critical mass for the appearance of anti-state counter-culture was reached when public defiance became part of everyday life—what James Scott terms "everyday forms of resistance" and what Václav Havel has called "living in truth."[9] Like Havel's grocer, who decided no longer to co-operate with Communist authorities in spreading propaganda by stepping "outside the lie" and living in truth, millions of Chinese have also begun living in truth. Living in truth, Havel says, is like a contagion that spreads from individual to individual, making it possible for large number of people to change their lives.

Because of the Chinese Communist state's ban on organized opposition, anti-state political and social behavior is necessarily individualized or in small groups. It is as if some are losing the habit of obedience. But aggregating the actions of millions of individuals tending in the same direction appears as if it is coordinated by leaders or other agents of shaping conscious group intention. But in this case, however, there are few leaders or other formative agents. The aggregating mechanism of this leaderless movement is based at least in part on two factors acting synergistically: desire for freedom and greater prosperity and resentment of the government. The memory of Mao's famine and the state's attempt to control every aspect of life is still fresh in the minds of citizens, as expressed by Tong Ge, a writer and an independent gay researcher, "The more you try to oppress sex, the more resistance will rise up."[10]

Such an individually based social movement is enhanced by global linkage when the weaker forces of society can borrow power from external forces to strengthen themselves against the state. These external forces may be global capitalists, multinational corporations, foreign culture sources, global media, international professional networks, international NGOs, global travel, and visiting foreigners. Such borrowed power strengthens China's social capital in a political and general social setting (Putnam, 1993, 2000; Coleman, 1990).[11] This is especially true for formally marginalized groups like gays, entrepreneurs, women, and migrant workers.

One of the best examples for the formation of critical mass is the popularity of Christmas. In China, Christmas has become increasingly popular in recent years, especially among young people and merchants. In Shanghai, on Christmas Eve, young people are crowded into Nanjing Road until after midnight, when they make raucous celebration much like New York's Times Square on New Year's Eve. The government has not declared Christmas a national holiday because Communists are atheists. In the beginning, only some Chinese Christians and foreigners celebrated Christmas in China. Now on Christmas, Christian churches are packed with people, believers and non-believers alike, because going to church on Christmas is an act of defiance towards a domineering state while at the same time a fun and new thing to do. To capture this social trend, commerce, both domestic and international, stepped up and flooded shops with Christmas goods. Commercialization finalized the social trend. It is interesting to note that in America, saying "Merry Christmas" has become somewhat controversial, but in China, officially an atheist state, it is most urbane to send Christmas greetings to friends, colleagues, and family members. Asked why he buys a Christmas Tree, Li Jinghong, CEO of a technology firm in Shenzhen, had this to say: "Isn't this a custom in America? I think it is a great tradition to have family and friends gathered to open up gifts and presents around the tree. This is very much like Chinese tradition. We celebrate the holiday not because of religion but because of globalization. We want to be more like people in the USA."[12] The commercialization of Christmas in China, some Chinese Christian argue, reduces the true meaning of Christmas. Nevertheless, the unofficial holiday, Christmas, has become a de facto national holiday. On December 26 (the birthday of Mao), the Chinese state has always attacked the celebration of

Christmas as a symptom of China's creeping internationalization. But as with other areas we have discussed, the government is helpless to alter the actions of millions of people.

In sum, commercial development (capitalism) and a consumer society provide an economic platform for liberty; global linkage (trade, travel, media, and education) supplies empowering resources; intellectuals and marginalized groups (such as gays) have lent impetus to set a new social trend in motion; and rapid technology development (such the Internet and cell phones) plays an aggregating role in mobilizing the sentiments and energies of millions weary of state's controls and a steady drum beat of revelations of official malfeasance.

Combined with the growing wealth of industrial revolution, the migration of millions from villages to cities, the global financial revolution, an information explosion available to ordinary people, and vast and far-reaching international influences, the new sexual revolution, a potent indicator of personal liberty has fundamentally altered key elements of the moral content of the party-state regime, even if it has not changed its name. The puritanism, so fundamental a component of the new revolutionary regime installed in 1949, is now in the process of being swept away.[13] Although remaining a part of the regime's rhetorical facade, its demise is in fact well advanced.

Through our discussion, we have attempted to demonstrate that China is more than a socialist market economy being led by a continuous succession of evermore reform-minded leaders. China is also about people seeking liberty on a daily basis, the results of which has been phenomenal given the continuation of single party rule.[14] At no time has this discussion been more relevant than now, as it makes clear distinctions between the actions of the people and actions of the government, showing that true liberalization must come from the people, not imposed from above as a system.

Although a large percentage of the citizenry have been part of this process, farmers, entrepreneurs, migrants, gays, non-traditional sex pleasure seekers, and black-marketers are some of the ones who played a particularly important role in the beginning, while lawyers, scholars, journalists, and rights activists have jumped in more recently to ensure that it continues into the future. As such, social dissatisfaction with the government is no longer restricted to low whispers in the back rooms of houses. It is now published in various forms of the media (especially on the Internet), addressed in public forums, and deliberated in courtrooms. Some might even say it now has a voice in constitutional scholars and a growing segment of intellectuals devoted to rights improvement and continued liberalization.

In addition to the social transformation, there have also been structural changes, the most important of which has been the contemporary rise in prominence of the legal system. Although this process has a long way to go, further reliance on the courts, as dictated by entry into the global market place, will certainly change the dynamic of state-society confrontation. In addition, by pursuing a rights oriented culture, the Chinese people are creating a society that can accommodate the socio-political-economic conditions needed for a freer future.

Limits of the Grassroots Liberalization Movement

While many Chinese civil rights movement actions have led to changes in the government, the movement has its limitations as well. In the opening phase of China's struggle for freedom, corruption was the price that had to be paid. But today's systematic and rampant corruption is creating problems for China. First of all, today's widespread corruption makes it difficult for the regime to undertake major changes, because every office in the system has a "price tag": officials buy titles from their superiors. According to a government report from the Chinese Supreme Court, between 1998 and 2003, the Supreme Court in Beijing handled 99,306 cases of bribery charges and sentenced 83,308 officials. After five years, the bribery related corruption cased reached 120,000.[15]

Second, widespread corruption makes it difficult for China to become a society based on the rule of law. Bribery sustains the old habit of arbitrary rule. The Chinese have been successful in reducing the Communist regime's harm by using bribes to sidestep state rules and regulations. This engrained Chinese custom can create problems for China to institute the rule of law as it is practiced in Japan and Hong Kong.

A less dangerous, but equally difficult, concern is that of the institutionalized irregularities in the Chinese economic system. We contend that the homegrown approach to intellectual property rights has shown proof of success over the last ten years, due to increased awareness led by more local production. However, despite the relative reductions in piracy and increase in the number of people working within the system, the absolute volume of those not complying is still immeasurably large. Although economic gains have been made by hundreds of millions of Chinese citizens, there will be extremely poor people in China for the foreseeable future. Consequently, there will always be individuals existing in those situations, which we described previously as ideal for the existence of piracy and smuggling. As Chinese companies reach out for the global markets, the rise of institutionalized irregularities in the Chinese economic system will have a native impact in the world political economy.

Third, corruption leads to the rise of a Chinese-style kleptocracy (so-called "socialism with Chinese characteristics"). The government is confiscating massive amounts of capital (both personal savings through its banking monopoly and financial institutions like stocks and mutual funds) to fund its grandiose programs, such as Olympic buildings, state enterprises, sprawling bureaucracy, government office buildings, and ever-growing military power.

Fourth, the grassroots movement has not been able to eliminate the collective mindset of hyper-nationalism. The rise of popular cultural products (books, TV dramas, and films) has strengthened the worship of ruthless dictators (a Qin Shi Huang-Li Si style of legalism, Maoism).

Why One-Party Domination in China Caused the Lack of Rule of Law

First of all, party-state domination has led to individualized arbitrary power, centered around one or a few party officials, creating a network of personalized power. The main function of officials at all levels is protection of the interests of such human networks. Although the central government may throw a few officials into prison as token anticorruption showcases for public consumption, the positions of top officials themselves are also built upon the complex of the *guangxi* inference network. In this system, the party controls the judicial system to ensure its interests are protected from independent scrutiny.

Since the rule of law and a fair and independent judiciary are keystones of property ownership, free enterprise, and limited government; failure to establish a rule of law also limits the expansion of grassroots movements.

Another huge limitation on the grassroots movements is the difficulty of gaining formal government recognition. Freedom of association is the least developed among fundamental rights in modern China today. Although it does not have the organizational capacity to ban all social organizations and private clubs, the regime is effective in suppressing large organized groups like house churches and FanLunGong, because it worries that what people learn in organizing in civil society could quickly be turned to political goals. Grassroots movements cannot increase the CCP's tolerance of social organizations, although they may exhaust the state's bureaucratic machine attempting to control them.

Struggling Civil Rights Movements

Illustrative of the lack of freedom of association in China today is the government's strict control over nongovernmental organizations. Nevertheless, the grassroots movements we have discussed so far have led to a new kind of social movement—*xinmingquan yundong* (civil rights movements).[16] These new movements differ from the previously described grassroots movements in that the former avoid direct confrontation with the government, while the latter directly confronts the state despite the regime's attempts to crush them.

The grassroots movements described so far have had an impact on civil liberties (freedom of movement, free enterprise, private property rights, freedom of religion and freedom of contract, and free press). But unorganized and leaderless movements cannot bring elections, the rule of law, and a free press although the press has penetrated by a degree of liberty due to its commercialization. Chinese seek specific issues when confronting the government. Those issues often appear not to be politically motivated.

When an increasing number of ordinary people start to acquire the power to force change, the Chinese state reacts. A corruption-dependent state system has delegitimized the Communist moral basis to the degree that Beijing has found it necessary to adopt mechanisms to deal with conflicts by launching anticorruption campaigns and changing old methods of control. The passage of new laws on property rights and citizens' rights to access information are cases in point. When the Chinese state adapted to social change by passing certain laws and regulations, the Chinese people began to act upon them by making government institutions and officials accountable. But at other times state officials refused to adapt—for example, the crackdown on the Free Tibet movement.

Public attempts to establish certain rights have led to "rights consciousness" among ordinary Chinese. As Chinese have become aware of their rights, loosely formed independent organizations have begun to emerge.

According to the Chinese government's statistics, the number of registered nongovernmental organizations reached a total of 317,000 in 2006. These NGOs are dwarfed by unofficial grassroots NGOs, however, which have been estimated at as many as 3 million and remain a relatively under-studied segment of China's third sector.[17] The strategy of founding "house churches" to evade regime control led to the increase of countervailing regime policies attempting to adjust to the new reality and capabilities of emerging civil society. With the state's ideology gone, religions of all kinds fill the void. Since religion provides a firm moral code, spiritual reassurance, and comfort many Chinese, vexed by rapid social change and state oppression, find religion appealing.[18]

According to a recent survey by East China Normal University in Shanghai, "31.4 percent of Chinese 16 or older are religious, putting the number of believers at roughly 400 million."[19] According to Christian house church leaders, house churches occupy 70 percent while the so-called "Three Self-Churches" controlled by the state comprise 30 percent.[20] The number of Christian house churches in China has been growing exponentially in the past two decades, reaching between 80 and 100 million believers.[21] Although independent organizations have increasingly emerged, informal and unorganized defiance still dominates China today.

The most widespread politically motivated resistance against the national government was the 2008 Charter movement when several thousand of Chinese people signed a letter demanding the rule of law, a free press, an end to the one-party state, and democracy. Charter 08, finally, signified a turning point at which informal dissent became formal resistance. In this case, the movement may be a harbinger of a larger and more thoroughgoing democratization movement in China in the coming years. Unlike the Czechoslovak Charter 77 movement, which was the creature of intellectuals such as Vaclav Havel, the Chinese Charter 08 movement involved people from all walks of life, including reporters, teachers, students, entrepreneurs, social workers, lawyers, ordinary employees, farmers, and civil rights activists. Unlike the Solidarity movement in Poland, which began in the resistance of disgruntled Catholic workers, the Chinese constitutional movement already has a much boarder base, which includes angry rural people, middle-class critics, and pro-democracy advocates.

The story of China in 2008 shows that individual liberty (freedom of movement, free enterprise, private ownership, freedom of religion, freedom of association) is the base for civil society in an authoritarian regime. These elements are key measures for the grassroots political movements to sustain: individual liberty, global trade, and modern technology (cell phones and the Internet). Each depends and builds upon the other—namely, individual liberty (limited though it may be) as a prerequisite for economic growth and prosperity; free trade as a prerequisite for the spread of ideas; the Internet and the cell phone as prerequisites and platforms for informal organization and coordination. Events in the years that follow will show whether such grassroots movements can sustain themselves and bring fundamental change to China's dynamic social landscape.

Holding Government Accountable to the Laws it has Created

Liberal Chinese legal professionals have played a major role in the growth of constitutional liberalism at the grassroots level. The legal aspect of this grassroots movement to make the government officials and government accountable for the laws it has created itself. The strategy is called *jiaxi zheng chang* ("playing the fake drama"). Even though there are loopholes in many Chinese laws, numerous lawyers and ordinary people pretend that the laws are sound: governments and government officials should be held accountable to the law like everyone else. Thus, every month ordinary citizens bring about twenty thousand legal cases against government officials in an attempt to hold them accountable to their own laws.[22] Although only few succeeded, the few cases became precedents for future legal protection for the people. The more and more legal professional are joining the movement across China. The 2008 case which 35 Beijing lawyers called for the free election of the Beijing Bar Association illustrated the grassroots legal fight. On August 26, 2008, thirty-five lawyers posted an online petition entitled "Accord with the Tide of History, Directly Elect the Beijing Bar Association—Announcement to all Beijing Lawyers, Beijing Justice Bureau, and the Beijing Bar Association." Those lawyers also sent text messages to other lawyers, supporting them by calling for reduced Bar Association membership fees, a restructuring of the tax system, and pushing other lawyers for "Direct Elections to the Beijing Bar Association." The state-controlled Beijing Bar Association issued a serious statement in an attempt to stop the movement. But more and more lawyers joined the campaign. The government revoked the licenses of the leaders. But it cannot stop the movement, as the 2008 Charter movement followed soon after the government crackdown.

In short, issue-related rights pursuits have provided practical benefits for most Chinese and have helped build societal pressure for change. Building a modern China is the process of reducing despotic Chinese Communist feudalism and putting empowered individuals, often formally or informally associated with each other, in place of the state.

Four Possible Futures

Our examination has shown how China has developed over the last three decades. Unfortunately, this does not mean that this is how it will continue to develop into the future. As an overview, we feel that the focus on rights has created a base from which the people can prosper. However, there is too much that is beyond their control to ensure that this happens. As such, we identify four that will require more time and further study, as they will help define the future of this movement.

1. Fascism and Hyper-nationalism

The first future may be a radical nationalist China. Chinese nationalism has historically gone wild when the economy is thriving. Economic success has enhanced the expectation of Chinese people for their global importance to bring China back to the center of the world. The very word, China, means "middle kingdom of the world." After suffering a defeat, Chinese elite has tried to bring China back to its rightful place of dominance, especially in Asia. During the March 2008 anti-Chinese protest in Tibet, most Chinese, especially the young, strongly support their government's crackdown.

There are negative possibilities for the rise of Chinese fascism if the economy goes south. Since the Chinese economy is so much linked to the global economy, anti-foreign sentiment will be high. The PRC education system has indoctrinated a whole generation of Chinese who regarded the past China as a victim of foreign powers. Although the information revolution helps Chinese gain different perspectives, the pride of the past thirty years and the one-child family make it difficult for Chinese to listen to any kind of criticism. There is new term in China called *fenqing* (the angry and nationalist youth). Despite diversity of *fenqing*, these Chinese youth are nationalistic, political, and anti-foreign. They played a large role for the 2005 anti-Japanese demonstrations and anti-Western media campaign in 2008 following the Tibetan rebellion. Thus, the online-educated Chinese may become tools to spread Chinese nationalism. The growth of China's economy gave rise to a new kind of nationalism, which is enhanced by the Internet. This is true for young Chinese who have not experienced the terror of Maoism and China's backward past. They do not accept criticism of China from the international community.[23] According to a 2008 PEW Global Attitudes survey, Chinese people frequently express negative attitudes toward other countries—69 percent have an unfavorable opinion of Japan, with 38 percent calling Japan an enemy. About one-in-three (34 percent) refer to the U.S. as an enemy.[24]

Social Darwinism, fascism, and military increases have become a sign of worry for everyone, including the Chinese, who wish for world peace and free markets. The recent collective madness over the Tibet issue in 2008 is a sign of trouble for social Darwinism, where Chinese felt sense of betrayal after helping to modernize Tibet.

The most popular book in China today is called (狼图腾) *Wolf Totem*, by Jiang Rong. The book attributes most of China's success and glory of Chinese civilization fundamentally to the wolf/predator spirit that was supposedly the spirit of Qin, Han, and Tang and the non-Han empires of the Mongols and the early Qing. The movie *Hero*, by Zhang Yimo, and several well-made TV history drama series of Qing emperors glorified the Chinese territorial expansion that arose from popular worship of strong state imperial power force/violence. This line of thinking will scare China's neighbors Japan, Korea, Vietnam, Laos, and Cambodia.

Chinese people have long suffered from such bloodthirsty policy and have paid dearly. One Chinese historian, Yu Jie, has coined the term "blood debt" as the pervasive and absolute power of a polity that has led to so much destruction, stagnation, and corruption. But Yu's voice is weak amidst an overwhelming nationalist sentiment.

China's fundamental flaw remains one of a self-serving bureaucracy and ubiquitous internal corruption due to unchanged political one party system, resulting in the lack of rule of law. Grassroots movements can change the nature of their regime but have done little to weaken the political party-state structure and to strengthen rule of law. Although the elite have come around in terms of developing some elements of state capitalism, the retention of monopoly power to redistribute economic benefits to the political elite causes troubles for the expansion of grassroots modernization movements.

Such radical nationalism will make the international community worried. The history of a frustrated German and Japanese power led to the terrible world war. It is in the interest of the world to give China incentives to reduce such nationalism.

2. The Status Quo or Internal Party Democratization?

The second possible future is a continuation of the status quo. Will the government continue to bend to the actions being pursued within the rights acquisition process without fully breaking its policies? Can various forms of rights movements eventually bring the institutionalized irregularities of the transitional economy into some sort of manageable modern state?

The first question is obviously more critical, and if major problems develop in this area, the second issue will become irrelevant. We have espoused that the success of the grassroots movements has been a direct result of its original non-confrontational nature. We also documented how the nature of this is changing to one of more direct confrontation. This is a positive reflection of how far the movement has progressed; however, it is also indication that society has moved closer to wider scale social unrest as well as encroached on that indefinable line that the government does not want crossed. Unfortunately, no one knows exactly where that line is, including the government leaders themselves. Given this, in light of the yearly rise we see in the number of violent confrontations, there may be an extremely dangerous undercurrent in state-society relations that will be exposed as this movement continues.

David Shambaugh and Li Cheng believe that intra-party democratization is happening in China to handle conflicts.[26] Others believe that the tension and conflicts between two societies will continue.[27]

Still others think the party-state's attempt to revive Confucianism will transform Chinese politics and society—the government has spent money in building Confucian schools all over the world.[28] Some Chinese scholars try to bring back Confucius, the sixth century BC philosopher, to deal with the complexities confronting a modernizing China.[29]

"[T]here is no reason to expect that China will—or should—have the same set of moral and political priorities when it engages with other countries," Daniel Bell writes. Echoing the Chinese state, Bell argues that Confucius dictates the state's obligation is to secure the people's basic subsistence and only afterward to address the individual's rights. But, until today, the government never admitted that the Great Leap Famine cost close to 40 million's lives. "The idea that certain rights can be sacrificed for the sake of enriching the people is not nearly so controversial in China," he argues. "If there's a conflict with liberal democratic theory, the problem may lie with liberal democratic theory." But the use of tradition to cover up for institutional corruption is refuted by the voices of Chinese people and by the grassroots rights movement inside China.

3. Chinese Federalism

A more optimistic future is Chinese federalism. An increasing number of Chinese scholars have explored opportunities to borrow elements of federalism as a way to help China's political reform. China has already achieved de facto federalism on two fronts. Economically, the decentralized nature of Chinese economies provides economic base for federalism.[30] Dramatic economic and technological changes—globalization, the Internet, the emergence of entire new industries—heighten the appeal of competitive federalism.

In the past, federalism as a political future for China was an esoteric topic of discussion among academics. Today, however, an increasing number of Chinese scholars have explored borrowing elements of federalism as a way forward in the process of Chinese political reform.

A future federalist China must be based on the idea of limited national government power, so that provinces as well as large cities (population of 1 million) can compete for ordinary people's assets, talents, and business. China, in fact, already has an informal federal system, which renders the real possibility for a federalism arrangement. First of all, the Taiwan and Tibet issues provide practical reasons for the Center to agree to such an arrangement. Second, economic decentralization at local levels has become a way of life. Federalism can formalize the distinction between national and local authority. Third, dramatic economic and technological changes—globalization, the Internet, the emergence of entire new industries—heighten the appeal of competitive federalism.

Some of these changes provide opportunities to promote political reform and to replace one-party domination with competitive, federalist approaches. Competition maps the structure and logic of the US Constitution, which arms rival institutions with the means and the motives to resist each other's ambitions and encroachments. The separation of powers and bicameralism reflect this orientation. But an equally most pristine and consequential structural principle is federalism—a federal government of limited, enumerated powers that leaves the local governments (state or cities) with considerable (if shrinking) autonomy.

Finally, federalism can help China to solve the Tibet and Xiangjiang issues peacefully. The situations of Hong Kong and Macau have already provided models for federalism, giving practical reasons for the center to agree to such an arrangement to solve Taiwan, Xingjiang, and Tibet issues.

4. Rule of Law

China has restored a true imperial power. But like all empires, the forces of disintegration eventually overwhelm the forces of integration. To continue its rule without major social instability, rule of law must be built. Wealth and corruption have inevitably rotted out the legitimacy of the one-party state that is not based on a strong rule of law. But when the masses become affluent and cannot adjudicate disputes on a personal basis through rents/bribes, they will demand the only alternative: the rule of law, which allows a process of adaptation and change.[31] The Chinese political elite want to follow this rule of law road without democratization. Can China follow the Singapore model with 1.3 billion people?

Final Thoughts

The central premise of this book argues that a grassroots social revolution through entrepreneurship, migration of millions from the countryside to cities, the explosion of information available to ordinary people (especially via the Internet), far-reaching international influences, and a multifaceted sexual revolution have fundamentally altered key elements of the moral and material content of China's party-state regime and society at large, even if it has not changed its name. This social revolution is moving China towards a more liberal society, even if the government remains in its current illiberal and grasping mode. An important finding of this book is that the Chinese government *reacts*, rather than *leads,* in this transformative process.

It is important that the international community stand behind grassroots modernization movements, while at the same time pressuring Beijing not to undo the progress its own people have made.

The pursuit of rights is a movement that transcends national boundaries. Although there is much written about the difference in cultures dictating whether or not certain forms of government are more or less compatible with certain societies, rights are universal. As such, when individuals in any country are fighting for their rights, they are not just fighting for themselves or their country, they are fighting for a better global society, and that makes it everyone's fight.

In the words of Martin Luther King, Jr., "Injustice anywhere is a threat to justice everywhere... Whatever affects one directly, affects all indirectly."

Notes

1.   Mary Kissel, "21st-Century Monk: Tibet's spiritual leader thanks America for its support," *Wall Street Journal*, September 22, 2007, http://www.opinionjournal.com/editorial/feature.html?id=110010638.
2.   Bush's Kyoto speech, *Asian Political News*, November 21, 2005, http://findarticles.com/p/articles/mi_m0WDQ/is_2005_Nov_21/ai_n15868319.
3.   Bao Tong, "Chinese 'Party Interests' 'Drive China,' Civil Rights Movement Holds Key," broadcast on RFA's Mandarin service. Directed by Jennifer Chou. Translated by Luisetta Mudie. Edited by Sarah Jackson-Han. January 6, 2009, http://newsblaze.com/story/20090106100021zzzz.nb/topstory.h08.
4.   Personal interview with Feng Xingyuan, August 5, 2007 in Beijing.
5.   Feng Xingyuan, et al., *Gaoxiao guojian de xixing* (Habits of Highly Effective Countries—Lessons for Chinese Experiences), (Beijing, 2008).
6.   Bao Tong, "Chinese ' Party Interests' 'Drive China, ' Civil Rights Movement Holds Key," broadcast culture, see Wu Si. Feng Xingyuan and Xia Yeliang, "*Zhongguo qiye ziben ziyou du yanjiu*" (Capital Liberalization of Chinese Enterprises, Hu on RFA's Mandarin service). Directed by Jennifer Chou. Translated by Luisetta Mudie. Edited by Sarah Jackson-Han. January 6, 2009, http://ne08.
7.   Vaclav Havel, *The Power of the Powerless: Citizens Against the State in Central-Eastern Europe*, (M. E. Sharpe, 1985), 5.
8.   Olson, 1965.
9.   Václav Havel, "Politics and Conscience," in *Open Letters: Selected Writings*, Paul Wilson, ed., (New York: Random House, 1985), pp. 249-71.; James C. Scott, *Weapons of the Weak: Everyday Forms of Peasant Resistance*, (New Haven, CT: Yale University Press, 1985).
10. Xie Fan, "Pride and prejudice," *China Daily*, updated 01/14/08, 07:26, Photo by Li Fangyu, http://www.chinadaily.com.cn/china/2008-01/14/content_6390950.htm.
11. Robert Putnam, Robert Leonardi, and Raffaella Y. Nanetti, *Making Democracy Work: Civic Traditions in Modern Italy*, (Princeton, NJ: Princeton University Press, 1993).
     Robert Putnam, *Bowling Alone: The Collapse and Revival of American Community*, (New York: Simon and Schuster, 2000). James S. Coleman, "Social Capital in the Creation of Human Capital," In *Social Capital: A Multifaceted Perspective*, ed., Partha Dasgupta and Ismail Serageldin, (Washington, DC: World Bank), p. 13-39.

12. Phone interview with Mr. Li Jing Hong, December 23, 2001.
13. The first law passed by the Mao regime government was the 1950 Marriage Law, which banned prostitution and polygamy.
14. David M. Lampton, *The Three Faces of Chinese Power: Might, Money, and Minds* (Berkeley: University of California Press, 2007).
15. *Wall Street Journal/Asia*, July 4, 2008. John Kamm is founder and executive director of the Dui Hua Foundation, http://online.wsj.com/article/SB121511904579427751.html?mod=todays_asia_opinion.
    By civil rights, we mean the individual right to form or join movements, the right to free religious worship, the right to occupational choice, private property rights, personal choice of varying kinds, and the right to justice.
16. *2006 Annual Report*,
17. Muthiah Alagappa, "Introduction," pp. 1-21; "Civil Society and Political Change: An Analytical Framework," (Stanford, CA: Stanford University Press), pp. 25-57.
18. Howard W. French, "Religious surge in China surprises leaders," *International Herald Tribune*, March 4, 2007.
19. Yu Jianrong, "Christianity and social stability in China" *Leadership*, April 2008, no. 21, http://www.chinese-thought.org/shll/005460.htm.
20. Yu Jianrong, "Christianity and social stability in China" *Leadership*, April 2008, no. 21,yhttp://www.chinese-thought.org/shll/005460.htm.
21. Interviews with Dr. Fan on July 9, 10, and 11, 2005 in both Beijing and Hunan.
22. Evan Osnos, "Angry Youth: The new generation's neocon nationalists," *The New Yorker*, July 28, 2008, http://www.newyorker.com/reporting/2008/07/28/014th Beijing and Hunan.
23. Evan Osnos, "Angry Youth: The new generation's neocon nationalists," *The New Yorker*, July 28, 2008, http://www.newyorker.com/reporting/2008/07/28/015.
24. Cheng Li, ed., *China's Changing Political Landscape, Prospects for Democracy*, (Brookings Institution Press, 2008).
25. David Shambaugh, *China's Communist Party: Atrophy and Adaptation*, (University of California Press, 2008).
26. David M. Lampton, *The Three Faces of Chinese Power: Might, Money, and Minds*, (Berkeley: University of California Press, 2007).
27. Daniel A. Bell, *China's New Confucianism, Politics and Everyday Life in a Changing Society*, (Princeton University Press).
28. Michael C. Davis, "The Case for Chinese Federalism," *Journal of Democracy*, Volume 10, Number 2, (April 1999), pp. 124-137. Zheng Yongnian, *DE FACTO FEDERALISM IN CHINA: Reforms and Dynamics of Central-Local Relations*, (Singapore: World Scientific Press, 2007), 80728fa_fact_osnos.
29. PEW Global Attitudes Project, "The Chinese Celebrate Roaring Economy As They Struggle with Its Costs," July 22, 2008, http://pewglobal.org/reports/display.php?ReportID=261
30. Daniel A. Bell, *China's New Confucianism: Politics and Everyday Life in a Changing Society*, (Princeton, NJ: Princeton University Press, 2008).

Bibliography

Hannah Arendt and Peter Baehr, eds., *The Portable Hannah Arendt*, (London: Penguin, 2000).

Ba Jin, *Shuixiang Lu* (Random Thoughts), (Beijing: Writers' Press [*zhuojia chubanshe*], 2005).

David Bachman, *Bureaucracy, Economy, and leadership in China: The Institutional Origins of the Great Leap Forward*, (Cambridge: Cambridge University Press, 1991).

Charles F. Bahmueller, "Civil Society Reconsidered," in Charles F. Bahmueller and John F. Patrick, eds., *Principles and Practices of Education for Democratic Citizenship: International Perspectives and Practices*, (Bloomington: IN, ERIC Clearinghouse for Social Studies/Social Science Education, 1999), pp. 101-121.

Judith Banister, "Urban-Rural Population Projections 1982-2000" *Medium Projection*, (Washington, DC: China Branch, Center for International Research, U.S. Bureau of the Census), CIR staff paper; no.15.

——.1991, *China's Changing Population*, Stanford University Press.

Nimrod Baranovitch, *China's New Voices: Popular Music, Ethnicity, Gender, and Politics, 1978-1997*, (Berkeley, CA: University of Berkeley Press, 2003).

Shuming Bao, Shuanglin Lin, Changwen Zhao, eds., *China's Economy After WTO Accession*, (Ashgate, 2006).

Bao Tong, "Chinese 'Party Interests' Drive China, 'Civil Rights Movement Holds Key," broadcast on RFA's Mandarin service. Director: Jennifer Chou. Translated by Luisetta Mudie. Edited by Sarah Jackson-Han. January 6, 2009, http://newsblaze.com/story/20090106100021zzzz.nb/topstory.h08.

Bao Tong, "A Pivotal Moment for China," broadcast on RFA's Mandarin service. Director: Jennifer Chou. Translated by Luisetta Mudie. Edited by Sarah Jackson-Han. December 12, 2008, http://newsblaze.com/story/20090106100021zzzz.nb/topstory.html.

Thomas P.M. Barnett, *The Pentagon's New Map: War and Peace in the Twenty-First Century*, (Putnam Adult, 2004).

Richard Baum, "Political Implications of China's Information Revolution: The Media, Its Minders, and Their Message," From Cheng Li, ed., *Changes in China's Political Landscape: Beyond the 17th Party Congress,* (Washington, DC: The Brookings Institution, 2007).

Benjamin Barber, *Jihad vs. McWorld*, (Times Books, 1995).

Robert H. Bates, *Markets and States in Tropical Africa,* (Berkeley, CA: University of California Press, 1981.

Jasper Becker, *Hungry Ghosts: Mao's Secret Famine*, (New York: Owl Books, 1998).

Hannah Beech, "Sex, Please—We're Young and Chinese," *Time*, Jan. 15, 2006.

——."Smuggler's Blues: Is Lai Changxing China's public enemy no. 1 or a hero for his time?" *Time*, Oct 10, 2002.

Daniel A. Bell, *China's New Confucianism: Politics and Everyday Life in a Changing Society,* (Princeton, NJ: Princeton University Press, 2008).

Thomas P. Bernstein and Xiaobo Lu, "Taxation without Representations: Peasants, the Central and the Local States in Reform China." *The China Quarterly*, 163, (2000), pp. 111-32.

Jagdish Bhagwati, *In Defense of Globalization.* (New York: Oxford University Press, 2004).

Yanjie Bian, "Chinese Social Stratification and Social Mobility," *Annual Review of Sociology* 28, (2002), pp. 91-116.

Yanjie Bian, "Bringing Strong Ties Back In: Indirect Connection, Bridges, and Job Search in China." *American Sociological Review,* 62:2, (1997), pp. 66-85.

Rae Lesser Blumberg, et al., *Engendering Wealth and Well-being: Empowerment for Global Change.*

Pieter Bottelier and Gail Fosler, "Can China's Growth Trajectory Be Sustained?" *China Economic Quarterly,* December 2007.

David Bray, *Social Space and Governabhhnce in Urban China: The Danwei System From Origins to Urban Reform*, (Stanford, CA: Stanford University Press, 2005).

George W. Bush, "Kyoto Speech," Asian Political News, November 21, 2005, http://findarticles.com/p/articles/mi_m0WDQ/is_2005_Nov_21/ai_n15868319.

William A. Byrd and Qingsong Lin, "China's Rural Industry: An Introduction." in *China's Rural Industry, Structure, Development and Reform,* ed. by William Byrd and Qingsong Lin. (Oxford: Oxford University Press, 1990).

Cai Cai, Zhongguo, *liudong renkou wenti* (The Problem of Chinese Migrants), (*henan renmin chubanshe* [Henan People's Press], 2000).

Cao Haidong and Zhang Peng, "The Ambazing Poer of Wenzhou Business Association," (*Wenzhou shanghui de jingren liliang jiemi*), September 14, *The Economics,* http://www.cat898.com.

Kam Wing Chan and Li Zhang, "The Hukou System and Rural-Urban Migration in China: Process and Changes," *The China Quarterly*, 160, (1999), pp. 818-855.

Kyung-Sup Chang, "Economic Privatism and New Patterns of Inequality in Post-Mao China," *Development and Society*, Vol. 29, (2000), pp. 23-54.

Nayan Chanda, "Managing Globalization," *Far East Economic Review*, December 26, 2002 - January 2, 2003.

Jung Chang and Jon Halliday, *Mao: The Unknown Story*, (New York: Knopf, 2005).

Jie Chen and Bruce J. Dickson, "Allies of the State: Democratic Support and Regime Support among China's Private Entrepreneurs," *The China Quarterly*, 196, December 2008, pp. 1-25.

Peijin Chen, ed. by Megan Shank, "They're here, they're queer, they're Chinese," *Newsweek Select*, March 2007.

Tiejun Cheng and Mark Selden, "The Origins and Social Consequences of China's Hukou System." *The China Quarterly*, 139, (1994), pp. 644-668.

Cheng Qingsong, "Wode aiqing busanhuang" (I Do not Lie about My Love), March 6, 2007, 15:09, http://18x.phoenixtv.com/18x/gay/200703/0306_92_84463.shtml.

Charter 08, Translated from the Chinese by Perry Link, *New York Review of Books,* http://www.nybooks.com/articles/2a2210.

Chen Jianyuan, *Zhongguo shehui: yuanxing yu yanhua* (Chinese Society: Original Pattern and Transformation) (Shenyan: Liaoning renmin chuban she [Liaoning People's Press], 1988).

Chen Yun. *Chen Yun wensuan (1949-1956)* (Selected writings of Chen Yun, 1949-1956), (Beijing: renmin chubanshe, 1984).

Tiejun Cheng and Mark Selden, "The Origins and Social Consequences of China's Hukou System," *The China Quarterly*, 1994.

Peter T.Y. Cheung, Jae Ho Chung, and Zhimin Lin's eds., *Provincial Strategies of Economic Reform in Post-Mao China: Leadership, Politics, and Implementation.*

Eun Kyong Choi and Kate Zhou, "Entrepreneurs and Politics in the Chinese Transitional Economy: Political Connections and Rent-seeking," *The China Review*, Vol.1, No. 1, (Fall 2001), pp.111-135.

Ronald H. Coase, "The Problem of Social Cost," *Journal of Law and Economics* 3, (1960), pp. 1-44.

Tyler Cowen, *Creative Destruction: How Globalization is Changing the World's Culture*, (Princeton, NJ: Princeton University Press, 2002).

George T. Crane and Abla Amawi, eds., *The Theoretical Evolution of International Political Economy: A Reader,* 2nd ed., (New York: Oxford University Press, 1997).

Michael C. Davis, "The Case for Chinese Federalism," *Journal of Democracy* Vol. 10, Number 2, (April 1999), pp. 124-137.

Delia Davin, *Internal Migration in Contemporary China*, (New York: Palgrave, 1999).

Deborah S. Davis ed., *The Consumer Revolution in Urban China,* (California: University of California Press, 2000) pp. 1-25.

Deborah S. Davis, Richard Kraus, Barry Naughton, and Elizabeth Perry, eds., *Urban Spaces in Contemporary China: The Potential for Autonomy and Community in Post-Mao China*, (Cambridge University Press, 1995).

Hernando De Soto, *The Other Path: The Economic Answer to Terrorism*, (Perseus Books Group, 2002).

Deng Xiaoping, *Selected Works of Deng Xiaoping, 1974-1982* (邓小平文选, 1974-1982), (Beijing: *renminchubanshe*).

Diao Xinshen, "Shichang Xing Cheng Zhong di Gaige Renwu" (Task of the Reform in Market Forming), *Jingji Yanjiu* (Economic Research) 8, (1986), pp. 43-48.

Jared Diamond, *Guns, Germs, and Steel: The Fates of Human Societies*, (W.W. Norton & Company, 1998).

Neil Diamant, "Making Love 'Legible' in China: Politics and Society during the Enforcement of Civil Marriage Registration, 1950-66," *Politics and Society* 29, 3 (September 2001), pp. 447-480.

Bruce Dickson, *Wealth into Power: The Communist Party's Embrace of China's Private Sector*, (New York: Cambridge University Press, 2008)

—— *Red Capitalists in China: The Party, Private Entrepreneurs, and Prospects for Political Change*, (Cambridge: Cambridge University Press, 2003).

Stephanie Hemelryk Donald, Michael Keane, Yin Hong, and Yin Hong, *Media in China: Consumption, Content and Crisis*, (London: RoutledgeCurzon, 2002).

Jill Drew, "Chinese Officials Give Club District A Brusque Cleanup," *Washington Post Foreign Service*, (July 30, 2008), p. A01.

Jane Duckett, *The Entrepreneurial State in China*, (London: Rutledge, 1998).

Jie Fan, Thomas Herberer, and Wolfgang Taubmann, *Rural China: Economic and Social Change in the Late Twentieth Century*, (Armonk, NY: ME Sharpe, 2006).

Diana Farrell, "The Case for Globalization," *The International Economy*, 2004.

James Farrer, *Opening Up: Youth Sex Culture and Market Reform in Shanghai*, (Chicago: University of Chicago Press, 2002).

Fei Xiaotong, *Xingxing chong xingxing* (Travel and Discorvery), (Yingchuan: *ningxia renmin chubanshe* [Ningxia People's Press],1992).

Feng Kaiwen, *Hezuo zhidun bianqian yu chuangxin yanjiu* (The Research on Transformation and Innovation of Cooperative System), (Beijing: *zhongguo nongye chubanshe*, 2003).

Feng Xianzhi, *Mao Zedong he tade mishu Tian Jiaying* (Mao Zedong and His Secreatry, Tian Jiaying), (Beijing: *zhongyang dangxiao chubanshe*, 1989).

Feng Xingyuan, et al., *Gaoxiao guojian de xixing* (Habits of Highly Effective Countries—Lessons for Chinese Experiences), (Beijing, 2008).

Adam Ferguson, *An Essay on the History of Civil Society*, 5th ed. (London: T. Cadell, 1782).

Edward Friedman, Paul Pickowicz, and Mark Selden, *Chinese Village, Socialist State*, (New Haven: Yale University, 1991).

Joseph Fewsmith, *Dilemmas of Reform in China: Political Conflict and Economic Debate*, (Armonk M. E. Sharpe, 1994).

Ted Fishman, *China, Inc.: How the Rise of the Next Superpower Challenges America and the World*, (Scribner, 2006).

Howard W. French, "Letter from China: The sex industry is everywhere but nowhere," *The International Herald Tribune*, December 15, 2006.

——. "Chinese tourists: The next big wave," *The New York Times,* May 16, 2006.

Milton Friedman, *Capitalism and Freedom* (Fortieth Anniversary Edition), (Chicago: University of Chicago Press, 2002).

Thomas Friedman, *The Lexus and the Olive Tree*, (Anchor Books, 2000).

Gao Hua, *Gap between the Positions and Backgrounds: the Political Levels of Chinese Society During 1949-1965,* (Hong Kong: Institute of Asia-Pacific Studies, Chinese University of Hong Kong, 2004).

How did the sun rise over Yan'an? (Hong Kong: Chinese University of Hong Kong Press: 2000).

Gao Song, "Differences between the Internal and the External News: Case Study of XHN Internal Reference Materials and the People's Daily from 1950 to 1960," M.A. Thesis, 2006.

Gao Song, "*Wenchuan dizheng*: Wenchuan Earthquak," *Financial Times* in Chinese, May 13, 2008.

Gao Yang, *Hu Xueyan, the Businessman with A Red Hat* (*Hongding shangren Hu Xueyan*, 红顶商人胡雪岩), (Beijing: Sanlian Press, 2001).

Hans Heinrich Gerth and C. Wright Mills, *From Max Weber: Esjsays in Sociology*, (New York: Oxford University Press, 1958).

Erik Gartzke, "The Capitalist Peace," *American Journal of Political Science* 51, no. 1 (2007), pp. 166-91.

Anthony Giddens and David Held*, Classes, Power, and Conflict: Classical and Contemporary Debates*, (Berkeley: University of California Press, 1982).

Malcolm Gladwell, *The Tipping Point: How Little Things Can Make a Big Difference*, (Abacus, 2002).

Jeremy Goldkorn, "Gay Internet talk show," April 12, 2007, 09:56 AM, http://www.danwei.org/.

Jeremy Goldkorn, "Mainland China release for Korean transsexual's hit record," Posted by June 3, 2005, http://www.danwei.org/newspapers/mainland_china_release_for_kor.php.

Ting Gong, "Dangerous collusion: corruption as a collective venture in contemporary China," *Communist and Post-Communist Studies*, 35, (2002), pp. 85-103.

S. G. Goodman, "How Open is Chinese Society?" in Goodman and Segal, *China Rising: Nationalism and Interdependence,* (1997).

Michael Greenwood, "Internal Migration in Developed Countries." In *Handbook of Population and Family Economics*, edited by Mark R, Rosenzweig and Oded Stark, (Amsterdam, Lausanne, New York, Oxford, Shannon, Tokyo: Elsevier, 1997), pp. 640-720.

Jonathan Gruber, *Public Finance and Public Policy*, (NY: Worth Publishers, 2005).

George Zhibin Gu, *China and the New World Order: How Entrepreneurship, Globalization, and Borderless Business Are Reshaping China and the World*, (Grand Rapids, MI: Fultus Corporation, 2006).

Harold Demsetz, *Ownership, Control and the Firm*, (Oxford: Blackwell, 1988).

Oliver Hart, *Firms, Contracts and Financial Structure*, (New York: Oxford University Press, 1995).

Mark Harrison, "Information and Command," *The Warwick Economics Research Paper Series* (TWERPS, 2002), p. 635.

Václav Havel, *The Power of the Powerless: Citizens Against the State in Central-Eastern Europe*, (M. E. Sharpe, 1985).

——. "Politics and Conscience," in *Open Letters: Selected Writings*, selected and ed. Paul Wilson, (New York: Random House, 1985), pp. 249-71.

David Harvey, *The Condition of Postmodernity*, (Wiley-Blackwell, 1991).

Elaine Hatfield, Richard L. Rapson, and Lise D. Martel, "Passionate Love," In S. Kitayama and D. Cohen, eds., *Handbook of Cultural Psychology* (New York: Guilford Press, 2005).

F. A. Hayek, "The Fatal Conceit: The Errors of Socialism," in *The Collected Works of F. A. Hayek*, (Chicago: University Of Chicago Press, 1991).

——. "The Use of Knowledge in Society," *The American Economic Review*, XXXV, No. 4, (September 1945), pp. 519-30.

——. *The Road to Serfdom,* (Chicago: University of Chicago Press, 1994).

——. *Law, Legislation and Liberty, Volume 1: Rules and Order*, (Chicago, University of Chicago Press, 1978),

——. *The Constitution of Liberty*, (Chicago, University Of Chicago Press, 1978).

——. "The Fatal Conceit: The Errors of Socialism," in *The Collected Works of F. A. Hayek*, (Chicago: Reprint edition, 1991).

He Qinglian, *Zhongguo de xianjing* (China's Pitfall), (Hong Kong: Mingjing chubanshe, 1998).

——. "Media Control in China," a report by "Human Rights in China," part two, *Modern China Studies*, Vol. 11, No. 4, (2004), pp.44-78.

Caohui Hong, "*Zhongguo xiangzhen qiye chanquan gaige yu zhongyang - difang quanli de hudong*" (China's Rural Industrial Ownership Reform and Its Interaction with the Central State and Local Government), *Modern China Studies*, No.46. Vol. 2. 1995.

Huang Yan, "Self-Help Labor NGOs in the Era of Globalization," *Nanfeng Chuang* (South Wind Window), November 16, 2007, http://news.sina.com. cn/c/2007-11-15/122014311592.shtml.

Jia Yunyong and Jiang Yingshuang, "Shazhi Nian Guangjiu" (The Idiot Niang Guangjiu), *South Metropolis News*, March 24, 2008, http://www.sina.com. cn.

Liping Jie, et al., *Zhejiang Siying Jingji Yanjiu* (Economic Studies on Private Enterprises in Zhejing), (Hongzhou: *zhejiang renmin chubanshe* [Zhejiang People's Press]).

Jin Shaoce, "Qingbeida di jiedai shengyi" (The Loan Business of The Money Middle Men), May 02, 2007, http://jinshaoce.blshe.com/post/495/44909.

Ellen R. Judd, *Gender and Power in Rural North China,* (Stanford, CA: Stanford University Press, 1994).

Michael Kane, "Creativity and complexity in post-WTO China," *Journal of Media and Cultural Studies,* 17 (3), (2003), pp. 291-301.

Stephen Kelly, "Why Does It Have to Be Like This?: Leslie Cheung, 1956-2003," http://www.morphizm.com/recommends/film/leslie_cheung.html.

Kellee S. Tsai, *Capitalism without Democracy: The Private Sector in Contemporary China,* (Ithaca, NY: Cornell University Press, 2007).

——. *Back-Alley Banking: Private Entrepreneurs in China*, (Ithaca, NY: Cornell University Press, 2002).

Israel M. Kirzner, *Competition and Entrepreneurship*, (Chicago: The University of Chicago Press, 1973).

Janos Kornai, *The Socialist System: the Political Economy of Communism*, (Princeton, NJ: Princeton University Press, 1992).

Anthony Kuhn, "China Debates Morality, Exploitation of Women," National Public Radio, January 20, 2007, http://www.npr.org/templates/story/story. php?storyId=4458700.

Václav Havel, "Politics and Conscience," in *Open Letters: Selected Writings*, selected and ed. Paul Wilson (New York: Random House, 1985), pp. 249-71.

——. *The Power of the Powerless: Citizens Against the State in Central-Eastern Europe* (Armonk, NY: M. E. Sharpe, 1985).

He Qun, "*meiguo shehua—renqin wenhua diguo zhuyi de zhimeimu*" (The American Myth—See Through the True Face of Its Cultural Imperialism), (zhonguo dushu bao, [Chinese Reading News], 2005).

Shenjing He, Zhigang Li, Fulong Wu, "Transformation of the Chinese City, 1995-2005: Geographical Perspectives and Geographers' Contributions," *China Information*, Vol. 20, No. 3, (2006), pp. 429-56.

He Liping, "Sino-Japanese Economic Relations: A Chinese Perspective," in *China & World Economy*, (Institute of World Economics and Politics at Chinese Academy of Social Sciences, 2007), http://old.iwep.org.cn/wec/2003_9-10/heliping.pdf.

Hong Tao, "Woguo xiao shangpin pifa shichang mianlin de tiaozhan he fazhan qvshi" (Challenges and Development Trends of Our Country's Small Commodity Retail Market), *Journal of China Commodity Circulation Economy* (zhongguo liutong jingji), December 2005.

Caohui Hong, "*Zhongguo xiangzhen qiye chanquan gaige yu zhongyang - difang quanli de hudong*" (China's Rural Industrial Ownership Reform and Its Interaction with the Central State and Local Government), *Modern China Studies*, No. 46. Vol. 2. 1995.

Fred Hu, "The Role of the Renminbi in the World Economy," *Cato Journal*, Vol. 28, No. 2, Spring/Summer 2008.

Hu Jingbei, "China's Economic System Patterns after the Reforms: From Ideal to Scientific," *Journal of Shanghai University of Finance and Economics*, Shanghai, No. 2, (2000), pp. 3-11.

Hu Xingdou, "Reform National Innovation system: Pushing China to Become A Research Institute for the World," (改革国家创新体制，推动中国成为世界研究院), http://www.huxingdou.com.cn/.

Chengju Huang, "Negotiating with the global: China's response to post-WTO foreign media penetration," 15th Biennial Conference of the Asian Studies Association of Australia in Canberra, June 29 - July 2, 2004.

James C. F. Huang, "Taiwan Is China's Best Partner to Democracy," Conference on Democratization in Greater China: What Can We Learn from Taiwan's Past for China's Future? Stanford University, October 20, 2006.

Huang Jiajin, *"Wenzhou de guahu jingying jiqi wanshan wenti"* (Improvement of Wenzhou's Guahu Management System), *zhejiang xuekan* (Zhejiang Academic Journal), Vol. 5, 1986.

Jikun Huang, Zhigang Xu, Scott Rozelle, Ninghui Li, "Impacts of Trade Liberalization on Agriculture and Poverty in China," FED Working Papers Series, No. FE20050018.

Yasheng Huang, *Capitalism with Chinese Characteristics: Entrepreneurship and the State*, (Cambridge University Press, 2008).

———. *Selling China: Foreign Direct Investment During the Reform Era*, (New York: Cambridge University Press, 2005).

Zheng Huang, *Wang Guomei fangtanlu* (The Interview of Wang Guomei [Liu Shiaoqi's Wife]), (Beijing: *zhongyan wenxian chubanshe*, 2006).

Ronald Inglehart, *Modernization and Postmodernization*, (Princeton, NJ: Princeton University Press, 1997).

International Studies Research Institute and Research Institute of Economic Diplomacy, *China's Economic Diplomacy*, (Beijing: *renmin chubanshe* [People's Press], 2007).

Samuel P. Huntington, "The Many faces of the Future," *The Utne Reader*, May-June 1997.

Daniel Kelliher, *Peasant Power in China: the Era of Rural Reform 1979-88,* (New Haven: Yale University Press, 1992), p.103.

Azizur Rahman Khan and Carl Riskin, "China's Household Income and Its Distribution, 1995 and 2002," *China Quarterly*, 182, (2005), pp. 338-55.

Mary Kissel, "21st-Century Monk: Tibet's spiritual leader thanks America for its support," *Wall Street Journal*, September 22, 2007, http://www.opinion-journal.com/editorial/feature.html?id=110010638.

Anthony Kuhn, "China Debates Morality, Exploitation of Women," National Public Radio, January 20, 2007.

Nicholas R. Lardy, "China's Economy: Problems and Prospects," *Foreign Policy Research Institute*, Vol. 12, No. 4, February 2007.

———. *Integrating China into the Global Economy*, (Brookings Institution Press, 2002).

———. *China in the World Economy*, (Washington, DC: Peterson Institute for International Economics Institute for International Economics, 1994).

———. "State Intervention and Peasant opportunities," in William Parish, ed., *Chinese Rural Development: The Great Transformation*, (Armonk, NY: M. E. Sharpe, 1985), pp. 33-56.

C. C. Lee, *Chinese media, global contexts*, (London and New York: Routledge Curzon, 2003).

Keun Lee, *Chinese Firms and the State in Transition: Property Rights and Agency Problems in the Reform Era*, (Armonk, NY: M.E. Sharpe, Inc., 1991).

Margaret Levi, *Of Rule and Revenue*, (University of California Press, 1988).

Marion J. Levy, Jr., *The Family Revolution in Modern China,* (New York: Atheneum, 1948).

———. "Contrasting Factors in Modernization of China and Japan," In Sunion Kuznets, Wilbert Moore, and Joseph J. Spengler, *Economic Growth: Brazil, India and Japan,* (Durham, NC: Duke University Press, 1955).

——. *Modernization and the Structure of Society,* (Princeton, NJ: Princeton University Press, 1966).

Cheng Li, *China's Leaders: The New Generation*, (New York: Rowman & Littlefield Publishing, 2001).

David Daokui Li, Junxin Feng, and Hongping Jiang, "Institutional Entrepreneurs," *American Economic Review*, Vol. 96, 2, (May 2006), pp. 358-62.

Li Dongsheng and Dun Yusheng, "*Xinwen buguo de xinwen*" (The news behind the news), (Beijing, Central Chinese Translation and Editing Press [*zhongyuan bianyi chuban she*] University of Illinois Press, 1998).

Li Ling, "On the Ecological Environment and Structural innovations of Press Groups in Chengdu," 2001, Chinese Communication Association Annual meeting proceedings, http://ccs.nccu.edu.tw/history_paper_content. php?P_ID=642&P_YEAR=2001.

Li Mengbai and Hu Xin, *Liudong renkou dui dachengshi fazhan di yingxiang ji duice* (Impact of Migrants on Big City Development and Policy Implications), (Beijing: *jingji ribao chubanshe*, 1991).

Peiling Li, ed., *Nonminggong* (Migrant Workers) (Beijing: *shehui kexue wenxian* Press, 2003).

Qian Li, *Nongmingong yu zhongguo shehui fengcheng* (Migrant Workers and China's Social Stratification), (Beijing: *shehui kexue wenxian chubanshe* [Social Science Document Press], 2004).

Li Yining, "Chinese Economy Will not Fall After the Olympics," *Beijing Daily*, February 5, 2007.

Kenneth Lieberthal, *Governing China: From Revolution through Reform*, (New York: W.W. Norton & Co. Inc., 1995).

Song Hwee Lim, *Celluloid Comrades: Representations of Male Homosexuality in Contemporary Chinese Cinema*, (Honolulu, HI: University of Hawaii Press, April 30, 2007).

Nan Lin, "Local Market Socialism: Local Corporatism in Action in Rural China," *Theory and Society* 24, (1995), pp. 301-54.

Perry Link, Richard P. Madsen, and Paul G. Pickowicz, *Popular China: Unofficial Culture in a Globalizing Society*, (Rowman & Littlefield Publishers, Inc., 2001).

Liu Jixin, "*Woguo feigong youzhi qiye jin qunti jiben xianzhuang*" (An Analysis of None-state Entrepreneurs and Their Basic Conditions), *Shehui Xue Yanjiu* (Sociological Research) 6, (1992), p. 3-20.

Liu Shinan, "AIDS fight needs a wider perspective," *China Daily,* October 18, 2006, http://www.chinadaily.com.cn/opinion/2006-10/18/content_710595. htm.

Yia-Ling Liu, "Reform From Below: The Private Economy and Local Politics in the Rural Industrialization of Wenzhou," *The China Quarterly*, 130, (1991), pp. 293-316.

Lou Xiaopeng, "Ownership and Status Stratification," in Lin and Byrd, ed., *China's Rural Industry,* (1990), pp. 147-62.

Lu Xueyi, ed., *Dangdai zhongguo shehui jieceng yanjiu bao* (Study of Social Stratification in Contemporary China), (Beijing: *shehui kexue wenxian chubanshe*, 2002).

Lu Xueyi and Li Peilin, *Zhongguo Shehui Fazhan Baogao* (A Developmental Report on Chinese Society), (Shengyang: *liaoning renmin chubanshe*, 1991).

Robert E. Lucas, Jr., "Life Earnings and Rural-Urban Migration," *Journal of Political Economy*, 112, 1, (2004), pp. S29-S59.

Thomas Lum and Dick K. Nanto, "China's Trade with the United States and the World," CRS Report for Congress, April 29, 2005, fpc.state.gov/documents/organization/48587.pdf.

Luo Weidong, *Zhidu bianqian yu jingji fazhan: wenzhou moshi yanjiu* (Institutional Transformation and Economic Development: A Study of Wenzhou Model), (Hangzhou: *zhejiang daxue chubanshe* [Zhejiang University Press], 2002).

Mark Magnier, "Campaign of shame falls flat in China," *Los Angeles Times*, December 18, 2006.

Mao Zedong, *jianguo yilai Mao Zedong wengao* (The selected Works of Mao Zedong since the Foundation of the PRC), vol. 5, (Beijing: *zhongguo wenxian chubanshe*, 1991).

Mao Zedong wenji (Selected Works of Mao Tsetung), vol. 6, (Beijing: *renmin chubanshe*, 1999).

Roderick MacFarquhar, *The Origins of the Cultural Revolution*, Vol. 3, (Columbia University Press, 1999).

Karl Marx and Friedrich Engels, *Communist Manifesto*, (New York: Penguin Group, 2002).

Barrett McCormick and Qing Liu, "Globalization and the Chinese Media: Technologies, Content, Commerce and the Prospects for the Public Sphere" in Chin-chuan Lee ed., *Chinese Media, Global Contexts*, (New York: Routledge, 2003).

Hamish McDonald, "Gay revolution puts red China in the pink," *International Herald Tribune*, August 27, 2005, http://www.smh.com.au/news/world/gay-revolution-puts-red-china-in-the-pink/2005/08/26/1124563027268.html.

James McGregor, *One Billion Customers: Lessons from the Front Lines of Doing Business,* (Free Press, 2007).

J. J. Mearsheimer, "The future of the American pacifier," *Foreign Affairs* 80, 5, pp. 46-61.

Andrew C. Mertha, "China's 'Soft' Centralization: Shifting Tiao/Kuai Authority Relations," *The China Quarterly* 184, (2005), pp. 791-810.

Lizhi Ming and Zhang Houyi, eds., *1999 Zhongguo siying qiye fazhan baogao* (1999 Report of the Development of Private Enterprises in China), (Beijing: Social Science Press, 1999).

Mo Yan, *Life and Death Are Wearing Me Out*. Translated by Howard Goldblatt, (Arcade Publishing, 2008).

Barry Naughton, *Growth out of the Plan: Chinese Economic Reform, 1978-1993,* (Cambridge University Press, 1996).

Victor Nee and David Stark, eds., *Remaking the Economic Institutions of Socialism: China and Eastern Europe*, (Stanford University Press, 1989).

——. Victor Nee and Yang Cao, "Path Dependent Social Transformation: Stratification in Hybrid Mixed Economies," *Theory and Society* 28, pp. 799-834.

Douglas North, *Institutions, Institutional Change, and Economic Performance*, (Cambridge University Press, 1990).

Jean C. Oi, *Rural China Takes Off: Institutional Foundations of Economic Reform*. (Berkeley: University of California Press, 1999).

Mancur Olson, *The Logic of Collective Action*, (Cambridge, MA: Harvard University Press, 1965).

Aihwa Ong, *Flexible Citizenship: The Cultural Logics of Transnationality*, (Duke University Press, 1998).

William H. Overholt, "China and Globalization," testimony presented to the U.S.-China Economic and Security Review Commission on May 19, 2005.

Pan Lin, "*Jieluo tongxinglian juhui neimu*" (Exposed the Lesbian Gathering: Female College Students Regard Lesbianism as fad), September 22, 2005, http://www.beelink.com/20050922/1938609.shtml.

Kristen Parris, "Local Initiative and National Reform: The Wenzhou Model of Development," *The China Quarterly*, No. 134 (June 1993), pp. 242-263.

Fred Pearce, "Sowing the seeds of starvation," *The New Scientist*, 9/18/2004, Vol. 183, Issue 2465.

Margaret M. Pearson, *China's New Business Elite: The Political Consequences of Economic Reform*, (California University Press, 1997).

Paul G. Pickowicz, Richard Madsen, and Perry Link, *Unofficial China: Popular Culture and Thought in the People's Republic*, (Bouder, CO: Westview Press, 1989).

Frances Fox Piven and Richard Cloward, *Poor People's Movements: Why They Succeed, How They Fail*, (New York: Vintage Books, 1979).

Sulamith Heins Potter and Jack M. Potter, *China's Peasants: the Anthropology of a Revolution*, (New York: Cambridge University Press, 1990).

John P. Powelson, *Centuries of Economic Endeavor*, (University of Michigan Press, 1994).

Wenbao Qian, *Rural-Urban Migration and its Impact on Economic Development in China*, (Aldershot: Avebury, 1996).

Qiu Feng, "Chongjian zhongguo jingsheng" (Reconstruct Chinese Spirituality), *China Newsweek*, October 8, 2004, http://www.chinanewsweek.com.cn/2004-10-24/1/4472.html.

Thomas Rawski, ed., *How to Study China's Economy Today*, (Hongkong: Chinese University Press, 1991).

Richard Price, "Transnational Civil Society and Advocacy in World Politics," *World Politics 55*, (2003), p. 580.

James C. Scott, *Weapons of the Weak: Everyday Forms of Peasant Resistance*, (New Haven: Yale University Press, 1985).

Research Office of the State Council, *Guowuyuan yanjiushi ketizu* (The Investigative Survey of Chinese Rural Migrant Workers), (Beijing: *zhonggguo yanshi chubanshe* [Chinese Yanshi Press], 2006).

A. Rona-Tas, "The First Shall Be Last? Enterpreneurship and Communist Cadres in the Transition from Socialism," *American Journal of Sociology*, 100, (1993), pp. 40-69.

Nouriel Roubini, "Hard Landing In China?" Forbes.com, Nov. 6, 2008, http://www.forbes.com/2008/11/05/china-recession-roubini-oped-cx_nr_1106roubini.html.

Roberta Sassatelli, "Consuming Ambivalence," *Journal of Material Culture*, Vol. 2, No. 3, (1997), pp. 339-60.

Rozelle Scott, "Stagnation without Equity: Changing Patterns of Income and Inequality in China's Post-Reform Rural Economy," *The China Journal* 35, (January 1996), pp. 63-96.

R.J. Rummel, *China's Bloody Century*, (New Brunswick, NJ: Transaction Publishers, 1991).

Orville Schell and David Shambaugh, eds., *The China Reader: The Reform Era*, (New York: Vintage Books, 1999).

Joseph Schumpeter, *Capitalism, Socialism and Democracy,* (New York: Allen & Unwin, 1976).

James C. Scott, *Domination and the Arts of Resistance: Hidden Transcripts*, (New Haven, CT: Yale University Press, 1990).

——. *Weapons of the Weak: Everyday Forms of Peasant Resistance*, (New Haven, CT: Yale University Press, 1985).

Gerald Segal, "Enlightening China?" In David S. G. Goodman and Gerald Segal, eds., *China Rising: Nationalism and Interdependence*, (New York: Routledge, 1997), pp. 172-91.

Mark Selden, *Political Economy of Chinese Development*, (Armonk, NY: M. E. Sharpe, 1993).

David L. Shambaugh, *The Making of a Premier: Zhao Ziyang's Provincial Career*, (Boulder, CO: Westview, 1984).

Raphael Shen*, China's Economic Reform: An Experiment in Pragmatic Socialism*, (Westport, CT: Praeger Publishers, 2000), p. 18.

Anqing Shi and Shuming Bao, "Migration, Education and Rural Development: Evidence from China 2000 Population Census Data." *Journal of Chinese Economic and Business Studies*, Vol.5, (2), (2007), pp. 163-77.

Susan Shirk, *Competitive Comrades: Career Incentives and Student Strategies in China,* (University of California Press, 1982).

David Stark, "Recombinant Property in East European Capitalism" *American Journal of Sociology,* 101, (1996), pp. 993-1027.

Helen F. Siu, *Agents and Victims in South China: Accomplices in Rural Revolution*, (New Haven, CT and London: Yale University Press, 1989).

——. "Socialist Peddlers and Princes in a Chinese Market Town," *American Ethnologist*, Vol. 16, No. 2 (May, 1989), pp. 195-212.

——. *Agents and Victims in South China: Accomplices and Victims in Rural Revolution,* (New Haven: Yale University Press, 1989).

Adam Smith, *The Wealth of Nations.* (New York: Bantam Dell, 2003).

Dorothy J. Solinger, *Contesting Citizenship in Urban China: Peasant Migrants, the State, and the Logic of the Market*, (Berkeley, CA: University of California Press, 1999).

Sidney Tarrow, *Power in Movement: Social Movements and Cotentious Politics*, 2nd ed. (Cambridge: Cambridge University Press, 1998).

Ross Terrill, *Mao: A Biography,* (Stanford, CA: Stanford University Press, 1999).

Ross Terrill, "What does China *wang?*" *Wilson Quarterly*, (Autumn 2005), pp. 50-61.

J. Tomlinson, *Cultural Imperialism: A Critical Introduction*, (Baltimore: John Hopkins University Press, 1991).

David Rothkopf, "In Praise of Cultural Imperialism?" *Foreign Policy*, Number 107, (Summer 1997), pp. 38-53.

Sam Vaknin, "Trading from a Suitcase—The Case of Shuttle Trade," March 27, 2002 issue of East West Institute's "Russian Regional Report."

Frank Viviano, "Hong Kong Triads' New Frontier South China is fertile ground for crime gangs, corruption," *San Francisco Chronicle*, May 28, 1997, ,http://www.sfgate.com/cgi-bin/article.cgi?file=/chronicle/archive/1997/05/28/MN25477.DTL.

Andrew Walder, "Local Governments as Industrial Firms," *American Journal of Sociology,* 101, (1995), pp. 263-301.

——. *Communist Neo-traditionalism: Work and Authority in Chinese Society*, (Berkeley: University of California Press, 1986).

Fei-Ling Wang, *Organizing Through Division and Exclusion, China's Hukou System*, (Stanford: Stanford University Press, 2005).

——. *From Family to Market: Labor Allocation in Contemporary China*, (Rowman & Littlefield Publishers, 1998).

Genjin Wang and Zhang Xuansan, *Woguo nongye xiandaihua yu jilei wenti yanjiu* (A Study on Agricultural Modernization and Capital Accumulation in China), (Tanyuan: *shanxi jingji chubashe*, 1993).

Wang Kesi, *Zhongguo jieduan siying qiye tansuo* (The Exploration to Current Chinese Private Enterprises), (Shanghai: *Fudan daxue chubanshe* [Fudan University Press], 1988).

James Wang, *Contemporary Chinese Politics: An Introduction*, 6th ed. (Upper Saddle River, NJ: Prentice Hall, 1999).

Wang Xizhe, "For a Return to Genuine Marxism in China," *New Left Review* I/121, May-June 1980, http://www.newleftreview.org/?view=1517.

Wang Wenhua, *The Protein Girl*, (Taiwan: Time Press, 2000).

Wei Li and Dennis Tao Yang, "The Great Leap Forward: Anatomy of a Central Planning Disaster," *Journal of Political Economy*, vol. 113, (2005), pp 840-77.

Yuk-Lin Renita Wong, "Going 'back' and staying 'out': Articulating the postcolonial Hong Kong subjects in the development of China." *Journal of Contemporary China*, 11, pp. 141-160.

John Whalley and Xian Xin, "China's FDI and Non-FDI Economies and the Sustainability of Future High Chinese Growth," National Bureau of Economics, Working Paper No. 12249, May 2006.

Lynn White, *Policies of Chaos: The Organizational Causes of Violence in China's Cultural Revolution*, (Princeton, NJ: Princeton University Press, 1990).

H X. Wu, "Rural to urban migration in the People's Republic of China," *China Quarterly* 139 (Sept. 1994), pp. 669-698.

Wu Jinglian, "*shichanghua congnanlai? Daonanqu?*" (Whither the Reform of Market?), Septmber 12, 2008.

Wu Xiaopo, *Jidang sanshi nian* (The Surging Thirty Years), (Beijing: Caijing Press, 2006).

Wu Qiang, "A Feminist Prospective: Legalization or Decriminalization of Prostitution?" *Shimin Zaizhi* (Journal of Urbanites), October 2006, http://www.worldofchinese.com/bbs/archiver/?tid-3196.html.

Biao Xiang, *A Village beyond Borders*, (Chinese by Sanlian Press, 2000; English by Brill Academic Publishers, 2007).

Hai Sun, "The Comparative Research between High-tech Industry, Investment Mode of Shanghai and that of Taiwan," *China-USA Business Review*, Vol. 3, No. 7, (July 2004), pp.1537-14.

Xu Lifan, "Gay Life in China," *Huaxia News*, December 02, 2004, http://news.tom.com.

Yan Sun, "Reform, State and Corruption: Is Corruption Less Destructive in China than in Russia?" *Comparative Politics*, 32, 1, (1994), pp. 1-20.

Dali Yang, *Calamity and Reform in China: State, Rural Society, and Institutional Change Since the Great Leap Famine*, (Stanford: Stanford University Press, 1996).

Keming Yang, "Double entrepreneurship in China's economic reform: An analytical framewor," *Journal of Political and Military Sociology*, Summer 2002.

Xun Yang and Liu Jiarui, *The Road to Chinese Rural Reform* (zhongguo nongcun de gaige daolu), (Beijing: Beijing University Press, 1987).

Minchuan Yang, "Reshaping Peasant Culture and Community: Rural Industrialization in a Chinese Village." *Modern China*, 20(2), (1994), pp. 157-79.

Yang Xueye, "*Jueqi de zhongguo siying jingji*" (The Rise of China's Private Economy), *Modern China Studies*, No. 63, Vol. 4, (1998), http://www.chinayj.net.

Yao Wenfang, "Wenhua gong ye: dangda shenmei pipan," (Cultural Industry: Cultural Critical of Contemporary Aesthetics), *Journal of Society and Science*, Vol. 2, 1999.

Zha Jianying, *China Pop: How Soap Operas, Tabloids and Bestsellers Are Transforming a Culture,* (New Press, 1996).

Zhang Renshou and Li Hong, *Wenzhou moshi yanjiu (Study of Wenzhou Model)*, (Beijng: *zhongguo shehui kexue chubanshe* [Chinese Academy of Social Sciences], 1990).

Yang Yaqin and Shi Zhangzhong, "*Shanghai minying kejiqiye fazhan zhong de wenti jiqi zhiyue yinsu*" (The Development of Private High-Technology Firms in Shanghai: Problems and Measures), *Shehui kexue* (Social Sciences), No. 8, 1999.

Yin Liangen and Wang Haiyan, "Profiting from the Media Industry: Common Practice of Reporters and Editors in China," *Modern China Studies*, Vol. 14, No. 2, 2007.

Li Zhang, Simon X. B. Zhao, J. P. Tian, "Self-help in housing and chengzhongcun in China's urbanization," *International Journal of Urban and Regional Research* 27 (4), (2003), pp. 912-37.

Zhang Jun, "*Feigongyoushi jingji falu diwei de bianlian jiqi qishi*," (Transformation and Lessons of Private Economic Sector's Legal Status), *Xinhua wenzhai* (Xinhua Readers' Digest), No. 395, Vol. 23, pp. 18-21.

Li Zhang, *Strangers in the City*, (Stanford University Press, 2001).

YaoHui Zhao, "Leaving the Countryside: Rural-to-Urban Migration Decision in China," *American Economic Review*, 89(2), (1999), pp. 281-6.

Wei Zhao, "The Life of Zhao Ziyang," (1989), p. 112-3.

Zheng Bijian, "China's 'Peaceful Rise' to Great-Power Status," *Foreign Affairs*, September/October 2005.

Zheng Yongnian, *De Facto Federalism in China: Reforms and Dynamics of Central-Local Relations*, (Singapore: World Scientific Press, 2007).

Zhongguo tongji nianjian (China statistical yearbook), Various Years. (Beijing: *zhongguo tongji chubanshe*).

Yang Zhong, *Governmental and Party Organizations at County and Township/Town Levels, Local Government and Politics in China*, (Armonk: M.E. Sharp), pp. 47-93.

Kate Zhou, *How the Peasants Changed China, Power of the People*, (Boulder, CO: Westview Press, 1996).

———. *How the Farmers Changed China: Power of the People*, (Boulder, CO: Westview Press, 1996).

Mingzheng Zhou, "*Jiedu zhejiang mingying jingji*" (The Analysis of Zhejiang Private Economy), *Zhongguo Gaige* (China Reform), no. 8, pp. 4-10.

Zhou Qiren, "What Did Deng Xiaoping do Right?" *China Economist Forum*, 10,09 (July 28, 2008), http://chinaeconomist.org/archives/236.html.

Zhou Xiaozhen, "*Zhongguo de yumei*" (Chinese Stupidity), *Chinese News Weekly,* July, 2004.

Xueguang Zhou, "Rethinking Property Rights as a Relational Concept: Explorations in China's Transitional Economy," International Economic Association Round Table on Market and Socialism in the Light of the Experiences of China and Vietnam, January 14-15, 2005.

———. Wei Zhao, Qiang Li, and He Cai, "Embeddedness and Contractual Relationships in China's Transitional Economy," *American Sociological Review* 68, (2003), pp. 75-102.

Zhu Xueqing, Jidang, *sanshi nian* (Thirty Year Surging: The Truth of Reform and Openness).

Robert Zoellick, "The US Trade Representative Countering Terror with Trade," *The Washington Post*, (September 20, 2001), p. A 35.

Zweig, David, *Freeing China's Peasants Rural Restructuring in Reform Era*, (Armonk: ME. Sharpe, 1993).

Centennial Group Holdings for Asian Development Bank, "The Development of Private Enterprise in the People's Republic of China," Asian Development Bank, 2003, http://www.adb.org/Documents/Reports/TAR3543/default.asp.

Index